IRFAN

BLACK & WHITE VERSION

A SEEKER'S GUIDE TO SCIENCE OF OBSERVATION

By

Faqeer Noor Muhammad

Sarwari Qadri

Vol 1

ISBN 978-1-961227-49-1 (paperback)
ISBN 978-1-961227-50-7 (hardcover)
ISBN 978-1-961227-51-4 (digital)

Noor (The Light)
Faqeer Haroon Ahmed Sarwari Qadri,
2nd spiritual successor, Noori Darbar
Kulachi, Pakistan
PH: 92-302 5797919

Printed in the United States of America

هُوَ

FOREWORD

At the time of writing this introduction to *Irfan*, I strongly feel that I shall not be able to discharge my duty adequately. However, since it is essential to explain to readers the importance of this book, in spite of my incapacity, I will try my level best to express my thoughts in words, and the honor that shall accrue to me in the course of introducing this rare book to the public I will consider sufficient for my success and good fortune.

Irfan, as its name indicates, is a valuable compendium and unique record of religion, spiritualism, and the secrets of Sufiism. I kept the dictates of the times and the satisfaction of modern minds fully in view at the time of its composition. Its study completely exposes the object of spiritualism.

Intentionally or otherwise, the world today is engulfed in a strange intellectual strife and insoluble mental enigma. No sooner do we step into the world of religion than we are overtaken by a sort of estrangement. It has been transformed into a complete query. Every object of *that* world seems to us a thing unseen, an object unknown, and we resemble the fresh schoolboy who determines to fly away at the very sight of the strange surroundings of the school. At present, our knowledge of religion is extremely flimsy. The Occidental deluge of heresy and materialism has engulfed us in a whirlpool. We can neither think correctly about religion nor see it properly.

The modern educated class is perplexed about religion and spiritualism and the legacies of the two to humanity. Their minds are frequently confronted with the questions: Why do we need religion? In the absence of religion, would the world's access to the essential goals of life be an impossibility? In the course of evolution, what help are God and religion to the world? How far is the religious aspect of life founded on truth? For the pacification of their hearts, they cast searching glances in all directions—but in vain. No one can explain to them the meaning and object of religion and spiritualism.

Upon hearing the words *religion* and *spiritualism*, some people—especially the Westernized science-ridden fellows—because of their extreme shortsightedness and pitiable error—pretend to know everything and to not need further learning and knowledge. While pretending perfect comprehension, they know nothing, and with all their knowledge, they are perfectly ignorant. Their vision, in this connection, has always been superficial, and their discoveries invariably summaries. They are absolutely unaware of the world's internal secrets. A superficial observation of a thing is insufficient to fully understand its nature and reality. From the commencement of creation, we have been observing the wonders of existence in every atom of the universe, but none could probe its depth and point out its source or end. For thousands of centuries, humanity has been constantly watching the disc of the sun glittering, but so far, none can discern its substance or whence it derives such boundless light and heat. To unveil the secrets preceding the beginning of life and following death has always been beyond the reach of human knowledge, and in this respect, humanity has ever remained in need of heavenly leadership and invisible guidance.

For all time, religion has always existed in some form or other. In the face of its universal popularity and generality, one cannot overlook its importance. The orbit of religion and spiritualism is not confined to words and letters or the hypocritical performance of a few set laws and regulations. Contrarily, religion encircles the entirety of human life and dominates all of its details.

Religion directly invites man toward the Holy Essence, who sustains and illuminates every particle of the universe, who is the source of this amazing chain of creation and the beginner of this majestic and munificent universe, and who is the nucleus and fountainhead of the unlimited power and endless light, boundless heat, and imperishable life on earth and in heaven and holds in His grip the astounding system of annihilation, eternity, life, and death. Religion guides us on the path lying in the depth of esoteric existence, concealed from exoteric vision, and like the true dawn, it extends the invitation of certainty to the esoteric eye at the farthest extremity of the stage of life, which our spirits and real selves are treading involuntarily. Religion is an amazing and universal secret and a profitable track whereby man can master both the spiritual and corporeal worlds and make union with that mine of power and life that in religious phraseology and parlance is termed "God."

A review of the oldest history of man combines the origin of religion with man and his comprehension. Prior to the origin of man, the world was wholly devoid of reason and understanding. The foundations of the history of that period have to be laid on philosophic theories and scientific conjectures. So far, we possess no knowledge of reliable facts about the advent of man in this world. In this connection, the theory of evolution is at a loss to lead us to complete guidance, and modern scientific theories are no more reasonable than the old religious ones. Both sorts of theories, in the end, leave us empty-headed. The theory of the creation of man might not have resulted in affirming his existence, if his presence had not kept us from denying it. Human intellect cannot precisely visualize the scene when, on attaining physical perfection, man had the first look at the limitless expanse of heaven and earth, the thoughts that might have struck his mind, the word and language in which he might have expressed his astonishment, and that to which he might have imputed his own helplessness. Undoubtedly, he must have thought of a superior existence alongside his own. On discerning the articles of the universe to be outside the pale of his domain, he must have contemplated its creation. The alternation of the day and night and the solar system must have astonished and compelled him to ponder their manager. This is the beginning of religion. Hence, for the history of religion, we stand in no need of the materialistic philosophy of history. Religion begins and ends in man. Man has imported the idea of religion into the world along with his own advent. This is what is called religion—irrespective of the variety and nature of that idea at the commencement. In other words, religion is the mutual relation between the Creator and the created. In Islamic canons, no difficulty is experienced in this respect. Here, this relationship has been acknowledged from the Day of Eternity— prior to the time of the creation of man.

Anyhow, there is no difficulty in believing that ever since man became conscious of his own existence and was endowed with the light of intellect, he imbibed the idea of his Creator and Master. This is the start of religion! The subsequent stages through which religion has passed and the various forms that it has assumed at different times is a lengthy discussion. But with all those differences, the idea of a superior Existence has been constant. Diversities came into play later when men devised different regulations, laws, and methods of worshipping their Creator. Some of them gave currency to the methods that led them to apostasy. They diverted from the real object of religion, and then the idea of God was molded on entirely fallacious lines. Eventually, the foundations of true religion were laid, and its authentic history commenced when His guidance was sent to man through prophets and apostles by the Creator Himself. So that the revealed books, namely the Psalms, the Pentateuch, the Bible, and the Quran are solid historical realities of this chain. As you would say, religion has always been twinkling on the forehead of the fable of life in the form of a picturesque frontispiece and directing human intellect toward the deep and pleasant subject of life. The past and future of the world are aglow thereby. It was the same religion that began with a rudimentary conception of the Creator and touched the boundary of the miracles, captivating the world by astonishing it. It was this religion and spiritualism that culminated in the unfathomable spiritual attainments of the prophets, which the world is still unable to interpret and explain. Intellectual conjectures and scientific theories always roam within the limits of possibilities and fail to accompany nature outside the circle of possibilities because human science and intellect lose their particular nature there. In their race with nature, science and intellect have always suffered defeat. The pursuit of nature is beyond their means. Finding the impossible becoming possible so very often, humanity has been obliged to admit the possibility of all the impossibilities of nature. A deep study of the universe confronts us with more impossibilities than possibilities. Under these circumstances, if we accept the precepts of religion and spiritualism, our truthfulness cannot be challenged even in an impartial atmosphere, and if we begin to believe in miracles, we cannot be accused of superstitiousness even outside the pale of the world of religion. The practicability of a single Pentateuch, the Bible, and the Quran is a solid historical reality of this chain.

The practicability of a single impossibility is sufficient to fringe open to us the doors of all the impossibilities of nature.

We are so placed today that in spite of leading a religious life, we are far removed from the real import of religion and are entertaining false conceptions of God despite laying claim to His gnosis. Otherwise, how can a man resist turning to complete astonishment at achieving a true conception of the wonderful existence of God or going mad out of extreme perplexion at discerning the truth about religion and spiritualism? Undoubtedly, we have not understood God. Else, we could not help falling prostrate before Him, having admitted His grandeur. We have certainly failed to comprehend the holy object of religion; otherwise, how could we afford to avert our faces from Him and attend to other worldly pursuits. We are absolutely devoid of these delicate spiritual sensations that make possible the true conception of God. We are lacking in the wisdom and knowledge that can point toward the reality of religion. In the present age too, we can discern some mad lovers of the beauty of nature extreme joy, they swing about unconsciously, looking at the evening star or morning sun; the scene of flowered valleys, the sea, the moon, the Milky Way, the horizon, and the clouds make them unconscious. Why then shouldn't we be affected by a true conception of God, who is the Creator and quickening soul of all these objects? In the absence of a true conception, it is impossible to attain one's object, both in individual and social life. Erroneous conceptions cause clashes. Success is the result of true and correct knowledge and propriety, and failure is the second name of ignorance and error. Today, we have to take practical steps toward creating a true conception of God in the minds of the people and to impress on their memories the necessity of religion, in order to enable religion and spiritualism to attain once more the eminence that they previously enjoyed. There is a dire need for the renaissance of religion and its utilization for the exoteric and esoteric progress and welfare of man, just as the sciences and arts have been revived, taken to the zenith of eminence, and used for the service and progress of man. The Muslims, especially, should try to obtain this neglected legacy and missing treasure of theirs and pioneer the way to orthodoxy and salvation by inviting the entire world hitherward because religion is the legacy of the Muslims. *Irfan* is the first successful step in this direction and the foremost golden ring of this chain. It gives a real insight into religion and spiritualism and presents Islam in its true colors. If Muslims attend this way and are successful in devising an individualistic and personal program for the purification of their souls, they will be able to chalk out a universal program for the reformation of the whole world and cultivate in themselves the virtue of proudly announcing Islam and spiritualism to the world. But this object cannot be achieved through mere verbal talk. No! It necessitates an immense practical strife for which we have to create practical and standard men who can once again make this mission universally successful. We have to set up an extensive system of publications and broadcasting that can change the defective conceptions of the peoples and create in their minds true notions of God. Through *Irfan*, the author has set up the first example of the preceding, and his labors deserve merit.

Many people avoid religious books and spiritual subjects, taking them for the aggregate of lengthy, dry, and complicated propositions. To a certain extent, they are right! It is generally so! However, the world today does not tarry where it stood centuries ago. Human knowledge has thrashed the space of the world, and entering the cavities of microscopic atoms, man has divulged the incomprehensible secrets and clandestine mysteries. In the absence of exhaustive proof and explanation, the present world would not accept anything.

In *Irfan*, however, this subject (of religion and spiritualism) has been rendered so interesting and pleasing through astonishing and perplexing observations, unique and rare experiments, and strange, curious, true, and modern information that one does not feel bored by its study. While reading the book, one often feels as if someone is removing the veils of darkness from one's mind and one is studying spiritualism from very close quarters. A study of the book itself, and not this brief introduction, can furnish details of the contents of *Irfan*. But this much can safely be said that hithersofar such an interesting and informative book has not been written on the subject. In India and Pakistan, this honor is reserved to the author of *Irfan* for which he deserves congratulations. By writing such a standard work in the English language, he has not obliged the English-knowing public alone, but by making such a valuable contribution to English literature, he has shown much favor to that language as well. The more he is thanked for it the lesser it is.

The sciences of concentration and invocation have been specially and conspicuously dealt with in *Irfan*, and these two sciences alone form the real subject-matter of the book.

Concentration consists of acquiring willpower and spiritual powers through the centralization and accumulation of human thoughts and hidden spiritual talents on one point (the name Allah). Invocation is the wonderful science of bidding the spirits.

The world today is madly roaming after a science whereby it would be practicable to invoke spirits and master solid spiritual power. Thousands of people have unsuccessfully spent their lives acquiring such sciences. The author of *Irfan* has acted most graciously in giving the world details of these wondrous sciences and valuable secrets. There are very few people in this world who, on achieving a valuable secret, would allow others to share it.

The science of concentration might appear novel to some people. But as far as the historical position of the word is concerned, it has been prevalent in different forms from olden times and expressed through different terminology. Various methods of acquiring willpower through fixing the gaze and concentrating the thoughts on a thing placed before one are in vogue today as they were before. Some people practice gazing at the sun. It is said about Rasputin that he could gaze at the sun from morning until evening. Some would place an effigy in front of them and gaze on it. The Hindus of yore exaggerated it to the extent of carving and concentrating on the idols of gods, leaders, and rulers. This method of theirs later on degenerated into absolute infidelity and idolatry, yet it finds its foundations in concentration. Some have practiced it on mere imaginary dots, so that mesmerism is based on concentrating on hypothetical dots. But the concentration dealt with in *Irfan* differs from all these. Herein, instead of hypothetical dots and effigies, the name Allah alone is concentrated upon. Since God the Most High is incorporeal, possessing no particular shape or form, it is hypothetical and wrong to carve and frame His imaginary effigies and forms and worship them. Commemoration of and concentration on His true name الله alone are permissible. In this system, in the beginning, the name الله is fixed in concentration either by being placed in front of one or without that. It is then transferred, through the faculty of concentration, to the heart, brain, and requisite limbs. Since the name is deeply connected with the Named, along with the transference of the name, the personal and attributive illuminations and lights of the Named also get transferred, which causes the appearance of spiritual life, light, and sensation in the aforementioned limbs.

Concentration is God's wonderful gift to man. Words and conversation are the expression of concentration and imagination.

Primarily, reflection and a portrait of a thing appear in concentration and are subsequently expressed in words and conversation. One can contemplate in two ways: (1) through concentration and (2) through the agency of the faculty of speech. First of all, the contemplation or portrait of a memorable object appears in concentration and is then expressed by the faculty of speech. Not until a thing has come into concentration can it come to the tongue. Hence, real recollection is effected through concentration. Words and speech are not as vast as concentration, which can hold a universe. What concentration can grasp, the tongue cannot. For this reason, the author of *Irfan* has given preference to concentration over the other methods of commemoration. He considers the name as synonymous with the Named. Though he has picked up this expression from the compositions of Hazrat Sultan Bahu (R.A), the honor of presenting it to the world in detail goes to him.

The science of invocation, as already stated, is the science and system of bidding the spirits and meeting them. Some people will view this expression with astonishment, because the science of invoking the spirits of the dead has never been expressed by this term, so far. But they need not wonder. The bosom of the universe still holds many a dormant secret. Some of these are being unsealed now, and the world is astonished and dazed to behold them.

The tumult caused by the new science of spiritualism has brought about a revolution in the intellectual world of the Occidentals. For centuries, this science remained concealed from their eyes. Having come to know of it now, they are beginning to confirm the existence of spirits and derive benefit from them. Likewise concentration and invocation remain unexplored secrets so far. Compared to Occidental spiritualism, Islamic spirit invocation is a far superior and a perfect science. By presenting concentration and invocation in a scientific manner, the author has rendered valuable service to religion and spiritualism alike.

The Occidentals are trying hard to promulgate the science of spiritualism. They have written thousands of books on the subject and formed hundreds of societies. But we could not produce a single individual who could answer them by presenting solid realities. If this state of affairs is allowed to go on, the Occidentals will supersede us in spiritualism as in the other sciences. It will be highly regrettable should the science of spiritualism revert to us from the Occident, whose irreligiousness and heresy has been proclaimed to the whole world by us. If we stick to our lassitude, the day is not far off when the West shall lead and direct us in this respect too, and we shall be obliged to accept their theories and to follow them. God forbid, should such a state appear, it will be difficult to cope with it. It will be a deluge that shall wash away the religious convictions and spiritual theories of the Musalmans. Our spiritual life will be totally expunged, and we will be obliged to solicit the Occident for a fresh spiritual lead. It is high time to save the Musalmans from such a spiritual extermination and religious annihilation and to show them such a bright path of Islamic spiritualism that they should begin to regard Occidental spiritualism as a mere dust of the path. Kindred considerations prompted Faqir Sahib to write this splendid book, *Irfan*, in which he has successfully attempted to redirect the Muslims toward Islam and its spiritualism. *Irfan* is the highest achievement of his life and the greatest masterpiece of the time. He is the pioneer Muslim writer on Occidental spiritualism and has explained its reality, furnished argumentative and educational discussions, and recorded its full history. In Urdu literature, none had touched this interesting subject previously, and no one else has gathered so many true facts about spirits and spiritualism before. If his labors are appreciated by the Muslims, he will pay more attention to this side and will expand the chain of publications for the fulfillment of these noble intentions. The importance and value of some books is due to personalities. Those works are not so important. While some other books proclaim the personality of their authors, the personality of the author is not the cause of their popularity. Because of their excellence, the books are the means of their own popularity and the fame of their authors. *Irfan* can be classed among the books that indicate their authors' personality. Its perusal clearly reveals that the author's records are not confined to mere verbal talk. He has reduced to writing his practical experiments and ocular observations. He wrote what he saw and presented what he experimented.

The desire to gather information about the life history of the author naturally creeps up in the mind of many a reader either before or after reading a fine and pleasant book. Occasionally, this desire assumes the form of perplexion and madness. The importance and worth of *Irfan* demand that some information be furnished about the personality of its author. The author's personality is dripping from every letter of *Irfan*, and a great gap may ensue if a brief biography of the author is not recorded here and he is not briefly introduced to the reader.

The audience is all ears.

The storyteller's tale it hears.

Hazart Qabila Faqeer Noor Muhammad Sarwari Qadri R.A (Author)

BIOGRAPHY OF THE AUTHOR

In the last edition, partly because of a lack of space and partly because of my fear of their being interpreted as prodigious and laudatory, I had intentionally refrained from including some episodes in the biography of Faqir Sahib. Moreover, he himself disdains self-praise and self-advertisement.

This time, I felt the urge to record some further important memoirs lest they escape the memory and be forever lost.

In this brief sketch, I have tried to provide his followers and disciples with an ample glimpse of his life. Presently, as previously, this introduction has no accommodation for a detailed biography. That will be made available in a separate volume, God willing. May God endow me with that felicity!

Faqir Sahib himself intends to publish an account of his spiritual accomplishments under the title *Asrar-i-Sarwari andAsya-i-Sarwari* from which his followers will be able to derive full benefit. The study of these books will furnish further details of his biography. May God endow him with the grace of accomplishing that task! Amen!

Faqir Sahib's blessed name is Noor Mohammad. He adds to his name the word *Faqir*, because all his life has been spent in acquiring the science of Faqr and navigating its unfathomable sea. Faqr is his aim and object in life. The inscription of the words *Sarwari Qadiri* is on account of his spiritual path. Thus he signs his full name as Faqir Noor Mohammad Sarwari Qadiri.

He was born in Kulachi—a little-known village in the district of Dera Ismail Khan in the Khyber Pakhtun Khowa Province. He is a Pathan by tribe and Gandapur by caste. The Gandapurs trace their descent from the famous saint Sayyid Ahmad Gesudaraz, whose mausoleum in Hyderabad Deccan is a common, respectable shrine.

His father, Haji Gul Mohammad Sahib, was a very pious and God-fearing man. He had performed the pilgrimage to Makkah thrice and was well-versed in Arabic and Persian.

That Faqir Sahib would attain to be a man of spiritual perfection is a fact about which his father was confident from the earliest time—having also received premonitions to the same effect detailed as follows.

While Faqir Sahib was still an infant, his father used to take him to receive blessing from Hazrat Mada Khan—a divine saint of Kulachi—who was then alive and whose tomb now is visited by all. Mada Khan cherished a particular love for his father. The former, one day, told the latter, "I have dreamed an exquisite spiritual phenomenon. According to that, your son Noor Mohammad must grow into a saint. I visualized last night that I was esoterically voyaging in a sea-ship. The voice of a child screamed from the midst of a cradle in the ship, 'Stop the ship! My father is coming.' On approaching the cradle, I saw your son Noor Mohammad lying therein. Afterward, I saw you from a distance paddling the water and approaching the ship, which set off after you had boarded it."

Mada Khan said he greeted him, saying, "Haji Sahib! This child shall be the cause of your entering the realm of saints." On hearing this, his father was highly pleased and hopeful, and he often used to narrate this story. Mada Khan died during the infancy of Faqir Sahib. But even after his death, he used to be considerate toward Faqir Sahib and helped him esoterically, which Faqir Sahib acknowledges.

During his student life, Faqir Sahib once injured his knee while playing football. That very night, his father saw Mada Khan in a dream in his house asking him, "Haji Sahib, how is your son's knee? I have come to inquire after him."

Faqir Sahib narrates that early in the morning, his father came to him very jubilant and satisfied and said, "Noor Mohammad, I am highly astonished that after a very long time, tonight, I have seen Mada Khan come to my house and inquire after your health." This dream also subscribed to his father's expectations and hopeful thoughts about Faqir Sahib.

Faqir Sahib acquired his primary education at Kulachi. In the middle examination, he topped the whole province. He appeared at the matriculation examination from Dera Ismail Khan. From the start, he did not pay much heed to his studies. Yet he topped the list at every examination, and on account of his ability, he enjoyed a distinguished position in every class. He was a regular scholarship holder from the fifth to F.A. standard.

After matriculation, he took a fancy to higher education and joined Islamia College, Lahore. In those days, his father went to Baghdad for the second time, and there earnestly entreated Sayyid Mustafa Gilani, the chamberlain of the holy shrine of Mahbub-i-Subhani (may God sanctify his secret) to augur Istikhara for him. A similar request in the past had resulted in postponement. But on being pressed hard, he consented to do so this time. Having agreed in the night, he intimated in the morning, "I do not recollect but of what I saw about you, but after the augury. I saw that someone repeatedly whispered into my ear the words 'Lahore Noor.' I cannot make head or tail out of that. You may if you can. I have played my part, and this is all that I got out of it."

On hearing these words, his father immediately comprehended that they pertained to Noor Mohammad then studying at Lahore.

Highly interesting and educational are the mental states, pleasant and unpleasant physical conditions, and struggles that accosted Faqir Sahib from the time of his going from school to college, leaving the college, denouncing the world, and assuming faqr and darveshi.

From the time of his acquiring a bit of understanding, he was confronted by a curious mental state. Occasionally, he sensed within himself the wave of an innate, resplendent electricity that created a spiritual revolution in his heart and mind and strongly affected them. All terrestrial objects seemed submerged in the glories of an eternal beauty.

Natural beauty in its utmost nudity exhibited itself in every object. Totally absorbed in the observation, he lost himself and derived intense joy and ecstasy in that condition, which lasted for a long while. This often happened at the time of offering prayers, and to continue it incessantly, he repeatedly offered the supererogatory prayers. After continuing for some time, this condition began to intensify, and a sort of tenderness also accompanied it. Tears used to flow from his eyes involuntarily. Sometimes, when he studied and did his school tasks late in the night alone, this phenomenon set on voluntarily. Then it so increased that streams of tears used to flow from his eyes while he was sitting in the classroom. To conceal this, he used to hold a book before his eyes, lest someone got a hint of the secret. This condition intensified to the utmost degree at the time of his appearing at the matriculation examination at Dera Ismail Khan.

He became nervous about it—wondering what had happened to him. Such was the state of his esoteric attraction, on the one hand, and the desire of pursuing his studies and joining the college on the other. He was in a fix, unable to decide what to do and what to shrink, whether to join the college or forsake it. In his perplexity, he went to the tomb of Faqir Mohammad Aslam, in Dera Ismail Khan, one morning. Offering a twofold supererogation, he augured and lay down on a bed for a while, closed his eyes, and fell asleep. He dreamed himself standing at the door of the luminous grave of Hazrat Sultan Bahu Sahib, who came out of his shrine and said to Faqir Sahib, "Don't go to the college. English education won't suit you."

So saying, he entered the tomb, and Faqir Sahib's eyes opened. He entertained the craze for higher education and the aspirations of youth. His parents, relatives, and almost all the members of his family had centered in him high hopes of worldly promotion, as he was a very shining student.

All these things together pushed him toward college education, and he joined Islamia College, Lahore, saying, "Come what may; we've set our boat asail." But God willed otherwise.

In the college, the two contradictory esoteric and exoteric impulses clashed bitterly. The foretime state of weeping persisted there too—nay, it intensified!

He couldn't control himself in the classroom in the presence of the professor. His book was his last resort to serve as a curtain and hide his tears. When he found seclusion in the room of the hostel, he passed the night away in shedding tears. During his leisure hours in the day, the same state continued. In the night, his pillow got so drenched with tears that to dry it, he had to keep it in the sun every day. In severe summer days, it hardly dried from midday to evening. This was the daily routine.

Because of his abundant weeping, his eyes had assumed a queer look. Thereupon, Ahmad Khan, one of his classmates and a very intimate friend, used to ask him, "What has happened to your eyes?"

Faqir Sahib used to reply, "My eyes have become sore."

But he wouldn't accept that and said, "No, sore eyes are not like that."

God alone knows the thoughts and doubts that crept up in the mind of Ahmad Khan and prompted him to investigate the matter. When Faqir Sahib would lie down in his room, Ahmad Khan used to peep through the window glass panes stealthily. No one could tell how long he peeped or how far he succeeded in his object. But Faqir Sahib soon became aware of it and pasted thick brown paper on the inner side of all the panes in order that nothing should be visible from outside and none should discern his secret. (The present writer chanced to see these papers in 1935, after about thirty or thirty-five years.) It happened thus: In 1935, Faqir Sahib took me to Lahore to pick up calligraphy. We passed by Islamia College, Lahore, one day. Faqir Sahib recollected his college days. While walking, he narrated the story of sticking papers on the glass panes. I requested he enter the college and show me his room. This he did. Behold the glory of Allah, the papers were still there. The sight of the papers brought us both to tears. Someone had removed those papers when I joined Tibbiya College, Lahore, in 1943.

The more he tried to conceal himself, the more evident this phenomenon became, and the more he tried to suppress it, the more forcibly it sprang up. Yet he continued his studies. After some time, he fell seriously ill in the college hostel in Lahore.

He was confined to bed for a long time and got so lean and weak as to be unable to sit or move; simultaneously, the spiritual attraction was still there. The dream at Dera Ismail Khan was soaring in his eyes. Finally, he decided in his mind that if he recovered, he would quit the college. He resolved thus in the night and found himself quite healthy in the morning. He forthwith set off for the railway station. Some esoteric power and invisible hand seemed to drag him along. At the station, he felt neither weakness nor exhaustion. His spontaneous recovery astonished him.

He stayed at home for some days, reluctant to discontinue his studies and because he thought he would be able to find a job after some more study. Under this impression, he returned to the college and resumed his studies. The aforementioned condition continued vehemently. The tears were always there. He tried to control himself but in vain. It took further guts to combat these states. He had to leave the college.

So from Lahore, he went straight to the holy shrine of Hazrat Sultan-ul-Arifin via Shorkot. He renounced the college for good, leaving behind all his belongings and books.

During his stay at the august court, he cherished no fancy for anyone in the beginning. A curious estrangement overfilled his heart. His relatives and sympathizers were surprised at this news of his. They could hardly conceive that such an intelligent young man could possibly transform thus.

Everybody pitied his future. After relinquishing the college, home, and all worldly connections and assuming the order of dervishes, he had to pass through sundry ordeals. But he remained steadfast with the dervishes; he was having but half a meal of dry bread, sleeping on the bosom of the earth, and wearing a patched garment and a loincloth. In spite of all this, he had contentment in his heart, light in his eyes, and joy in his spirit. All his kinsmen and the inmates of his house wondered as to what had happened to this educated and intelligent youngster! In the faqir's habit, many people suspected him of insanity. Those who had seen him in the up-to-date collegian dress were surprised at his new state. But he did not care.

He had married at the beginning of his college career and had one child, whom he entrusted to God at his home. Commemoration and worship of God was his occupation day and night.

In those days, he came across a manuscript composition of Hazrat Sultan-ul-Arifin's. He studied it very carefully and felt like he had obtained an invaluable treasure of gnosis. He enjoyed its study so much that he spent years studying his works. Thereafter, he obtained many other manuscripts with which he quenched his spiritual thirst. He gathered about thirty or forty manuscripts, which he copied repeatedly and read hundreds of times each. But he couldn't be satisfied with them; nor is he now. Through writing these books with the pen for scores of years, his handwriting improved to the extent of his becoming a calligraphist.

He reckoned these books as his companion-teacher and acquired everything out of them. Later on, it so happened that through the esoteric concentration and lighted books of Hazrat Sultan-ul-Arifin whatever place, stage, and spiritual phenomena of the path he copied in the daytime, he crossed it in the night, and every written esoteric phenomenon became manifest to him. He said, "It appeared that the author had composed and bequeathed those books to me exclusively. Because, hithersofar, none had either comprehended or benefited out of them like myself." And it is a fact that the honor of acquainting the world with the real import of his holiness's books and the seekers of the right path with his faqr rests solely with him.

He became the pupil of Hazrat Salih Muhammad, a successor of Hazrat Sultan-ul-Arifin. At a tender age, his father took him to Darbar Sharif and presented him to his own guide and patron, Hazrat Salih Mohammad, with the request to accept him as his pupil, which the hazrat very affectionately did. Long after this, when he left the college and began to live at the Darbar Sharif as a dervish, Hazrat Salih Mohammad had passed away and Hazrat Noor Ahmad had succeeded him. The latter had a special liking for him and often sat in his company.

About the early days of his stay at the Darbar Sharif, when his desire was at its climax, Faqir Sahib says, "One night, I was asleep in the mosque of Darbar Sharif, along with my father. In a dream, I saw Hazrat Sultan-ul-Arifin sitting in the palace like a resplendent sun and watching me with a particularly favorable look. From his shining face up to my body, there emanated a beam of light. Its strong, brilliant rays pierced my brain, heart, and every particle of the body. The form of my father came out of that brilliant beam and conveyed the joyful tiding.

"'Noor Mohammad, Hazrat Sultan-ul-Arifin has declared orders of granting you the great esoteric alchemy and elixir of insight کیمیا اکسیر نظر.' On hearing this, tenderness overtook me, and I submitted I am not worthy of this.

"In short, when we both woke up in the morning, my father said to me, 'Last night, you were telling me in the dream, "Dear Father, I dreamed a very blessed dream last night." Did you see last night anything?'

"I answered in the affirmative but avoided furnishing details, as I was then very, very particular about hiding my secrets."

Faqir Sahib said, "From that very night, a regular flow of esoteric favors from Hazrat Sultan-ul-Arifin attached itself to me, which, thank God, is still there and would continue up to the Day of Eternity without an end. May God increase it and never decrease it!"

Faqir Sahib said كان فضل الله عليك عظيماً "I hear this voice from the beyond that God's great favor is on you. Through this divine favor, I have been toillessly gaining untold and invaluable wealth from every spiritual court and spirit of every dead or living soul from whom I intended to draw esoteric gain."

So much so that he was immediately granted audience at the court of Hazrat Pir Mehbub-i-Subhani at Baghdad (may his secret be guarded) when he visited it in 1912. He said, "Among other esoteric favors I saw, one night, having entered in audience, I witnessed all the great men and founders of the sajjadas سجادہ of the world sitting respectfully in the magnificent mosque of Hazrat Pir Sahib. Among others, I recognized Hazrat Noor Ahmed Sahib and Hazrat Amir Sultan Sahib (the successors of Hazrat Sultanul-Arifin), whom I approached and paid my respects.

"They very gently whispered in my ear, 'Noor Mohammad, this is the court of a very magnanimous ruler. Remain respectful here.' Taking my leave thence, I went to the gate of the shrine of Hazrat Pir Dastgir to gain audience.

"The watchman on the gate questioned me, 'Do you seek from this sublime court the rank of Abdal or Qutb?'

"To which, I replied, 'What is the value of these ranks to be asked from such a supreme court? I wish to obtain from here the unlimited wealth of faqr.'

"At this, the gatekeeper smiled joyfully and allowed me in. That which passed on my heart thereafter and the immense wealth of faqr eMuhammadi, which I received from the august court of Ghausiya majesty, is beyond the realm of description and shines daily on the esoteric horizon up to eternity as he has said."

The suns of the predecessors have set, but ours is eternally shining on the highest heaven; it won't set. Narrating another incident of Baghdad, Faqir Sahib said, "In the court of Hazrat Pir Mehbub-i-Subhani, in front of the parlor of the Afghans, there used to sit an attractive majzoob faqir named Abdur Rehman, who used to utter irrelevant and ununderstandable things. The Afghans used to serve him, feed him, and remove by their hands his filth, which used to be odorless. For about twelve years, he had not risen or shifted from his place.

"One day, when I was sitting in my parlor, he rose from his seat, entered my parlor, and standing in the door, he fixed his gaze and stared at me. After a few moments, he resumed his seat. On his unusual departure from his place, the Afghans came running to my parlor and began asking me as to why Abdur Rehman had come to my parlor and what he had talked about to me. I told them that undoubtedly he had come to my parlor but had returned after looking at me for a few minutes. The Afghans wondered much at his unusual movement.

"A little while after the Afghans had quitted my parlor, a strange awe overtook my heart ceaselessly and increased every moment. Though I had seen nothing, this spacious world appeared to me very narrow, and I began shivering out of fear. When I came out of the parlor, my legs staggered. I was greatly perplexed at the cause of that fear. At that moment, I recited and blew over myself the opening chapter فاتحه, that of the chair آیت الکرسی, the four Quls, and many other verses—but in vain. The fear went on increasing. Entering the blessed shrine of Hazrat Pir Dastgir and grasping the net, I requested he help me in the name of God—but to no avail. Coming out of it, I set out for the house that I had rented, intending to lie down and repose.

"But I felt suffocated through fear and further progress seemed difficult. Meanwhile, someone put this thought in myheart by way of spiritual inspiration: *Recite Risala-i-Ruhi* رساله روحی. While walking along, I began reciting that treatise of Hazrat Sultan-ul-Arifin, which I remembered by heart and which is an effective remedy against suchlike esoteric retrogressions. At its very commencement, that fear dampened and a wave of comfort shot through me. I recited it three or four times before reaching my home, where I wrapped myself in a quilt and continued repeating it until I fell asleep. In a dream, I saw myself standing at the gate of a magnificent fort and Abdur Rehman (surrounded by a herd of long-horned oxen and buffaloes) running toward me.I feared lest the herd should trample me. Standing in that state of apprehension, I saw Hazrat Sultan-ul-Arifin running toward me from a distance with the speed of electricity—so fast that his turban had slipped from his head and was hanging on his neck. Abdur Rehman and his dreadful herd had not yet approached me before his holiness intervened between him and myself, telling him something in Arabic and dismissing him. At that moment, my eyes opened. I found myself quite satisfied. Afterward, when I left that place and entered the court of Pir Dastgir, Abdur Rehman was astonished to see me. Then he began to laugh at his foolish act. I entered my parlor and resumed my work."

According to Faqir Sahib, the substance of all this phenomena is that the said majzub tried futilely to attract him with his suggestion and dye him in his own color, but he was saved from him through the favor of his spiritual leader.

Hafiz Musa, who ran an ideal school of commemorating the Holy Quran, was alive in the days when Faqir Sahib was staying at the court of Hazrat Sultan-ul-Arifin. Faqir Sahib said, "Hafiz Musa had constructed a thatch of rushes on which the students recited the Holy Quran at nighttime. One noon, I was sleeping on a bed under the thatch. An esoteric light overpowered and enfolded me. At that time, all the hair on my body was revolving and announcing, 'Allah Hu, Allah Hu هو الله.' Just then, my eyes opened. I saw Hafiz Musa sitting on a bed near me, watching me with astonishment and trying to give his heart the blows of Allah Hu, Allah Hu هو الله. I think that having sensed my Zikr-i-Sultan somehow, he was trying to imitate it."

Faqir Sahib also said, "During the days when the River Chenab was washing away the old Darbar, the blessed coffin of Hazrat Sultan-ul-Arifin was lying excavated. His spiritual reflection was usually more evident at the new Darbar than the old one. We had heard stories that the river will sweep away the shrine of Hazrat Sultan-ul-Arifin during Muharram. His coffin will be pulled out.

"He would come out of it and shout. At hearing that, all the people present there would turn into live-hearted saints. On seeing everything contrary to my expectations, I was lying very dejected and broken-hearted in the parlor of Hafiz Musa. In a dream, I saw myself walking in the populace of Sarang Khan Baloch, near Shorkot, where the parents of Hazrat Sultan-ul-Arifin used to reside when he was a child. Unintentionally, I chanced to enter that old house of his where he had been brought up. I saw his father sitting on a bed and mother sitting on the earth by the hearth, under a reed thatch. On seeing me enter the house, his mother, Hazrat Rasti Sahiba, had raised in her hands the little innocent figure of Hazrat Sultan-ul-Arifin and showing him to me said, 'Noor Mohammad! this is my child Bahu. I have brought him up in my hands like this.' When his lucid brilliant glance fell on me, I was attracted and opened my eyes saying, 'Haqq Bahu, Haqq Bahu.'"

After this pleasant and memorable time of Hazrat Noor Ahmed, there came the regime of his eldest son, Hazrat Amir Sultan, who also cherished a special affection for and made a distinguished companion of Faqir Sahib with whom he often used to discuss important worldly and spiritual matters. So much so that he appointed Faqir Sahib as a special tutor of his sons. The present successor and his three brothers remained his pupils for years. Faqir Sahib also enjoyed the honor of remaining the tutor of the daughters of Hazrat Pir Al-Sayyed Haider-al-Qadri-al-Gilani Baghdadi.

He has copiously traveled all over India in connection with the "Invitation of Graves دعوت القبور." He has recited the invitation on them and reaped spiritual gain from the holy graves of almost all the munificent saints and great magnates. He says the one night's invitation at the grave of a saint is more beneficial than hundreds of Quadragesimals and fasts, seclusion, and years of asceticism and austerities. If the enshrined soul cooperates, he can cause the inviter to traverse overnight all the stages traversed by him in his own lifetime.

Faqir Sahib is a high-ranked scholar, a noble Sufi, a granddervish, a far-sighted humble faqir, and an experienced saint. In his seventy-five years, he has witnessed innumerable worldly vicissitudes, untold secrets, and open revolutions. He has had occasion to meet and talk to people of different schools of thought and various ideas, including scholars, muftis, Sufis, pious spiritualists, leaders, statesmen, pious people, and so on. He takes a very wide and liberal view of Sufiism, faqr, and spiritualism and has spent all his life in researching this spiritual world. Theoretically and practically, he is fully cognizant of all the ups and downs and bends of faqr and

Sufiism. He has had the full experience of differentiating between the genuine and counterfeit, reality and imitation, truth and falsehood.

I have had copious occasions to travel with him, and each time, I had to acknowledge his minute observation in this field. I have often noticed that through his spiritual sight, he judged in a moment the esoteric capacity of every faqir, dervish, or Sufi who came to see him or whom he met. I have also seen repeatedly that he can gauge the spiritual power of the spiritualistic bygones.

Another strange thing that I have seen is that he can sense the tombs of saints without seeing them. Out of hundreds of such incidents, I will confine myself to the mention of only a few.

Faqir Sahib and I were passing through a lane in Lahore in 1935. He said, "I feel the presence of the tomb of some saint here. It must be somewhere close by." I inquired from some shopkeepers near about, but they expressed their ignorance. I informed him that no tomb was traceable there.

"It is there. I feel it outright. Make further inquiries," he said.

I interrogated some more people. At last, one older man said, "Yes, there is a saint (buried) in this street." Guiding us through winding lanes, he took us to the tomb of a Faqir. We read the opening chapter سورة فاتحه and returned.

Later on, I inquired from Faqir Sahib how he came to knowabout it. He replied, "Wherever there is the grave of some saint, the hearts of the insightful living feel its spiritual waves inaccordance with its spiritual power. The more powerful the saint, the more forcibly and distantly his waves strike the heart and his spiritualism is felt. The orbit of the waves of the saintly dead with ordinary power is limited according to their power."

Hakim Ghulam Sarwar, elder brother of the writer, also narrates a similar occurrence. He narrates, "Traveling with theFaqir Sahib, once, we passed near the tomb of a Faqir in Mianwali, which the Faqir Sahib sensed. We retired thither. The Faqir Sahib remarked, 'This dead Faqir has great spiritual power and though not very popular now, he will become very famous someday. We sojourned there for the night. Late in the night, he went to recite the invitation and retired to sleep. In a dream, I saw an oldman with a white beard come out of the grave and reenter it after shaking hands with me. When my eyes opened, I saw the Faqir Sahib still busy in reciting the invitation. On his return, I narrated to him my dream, to which, he replied, 'This was the very saint.'"

Faqir Sahib said, "In the course of composing the book, *Makhzan-ul-Asrar* مخزن الاسرار, out of my excessive love for the family of the Holy Prophet and extreme reverence to Hazrat Ali (may God bless him), I once intended to include therein some passage denoting the supremacy of Hazrat Ali over the other three companions with the antecedent danger of derogating their position. I was therefore indecisive whether to include it in the book or not. In the night, in a dream, I saw Hazrat Umar (may God be pleased with him) showing me a mirror-like tablet which he was holding in his hand and in which I could see all his achievements in the service of Islam. At that moment, I felt sorry for intending to include that passage in the book, and addressing him forthwith, I submitted, 'O Great Farooq فاروق اعظمDistinguisher, you have certainly rendered great services to Islam and the Islamic world is highly indebted to you.' I then abstained from including the passage in the book."

He said, "Once in a dream, I saw the following inscription written in bold, brilliant letters in beautiful Arabic script on the sky: 'Noor Muhammad is Hanafi Muslim and not among the polytheists نور محمد كان حنيفا مسلمان و ما كان من المشركين.' This fully convinced me of my being a true unitarian and follower of the orthodox faith."

He also said, "Once in a dream, someone questioned me, 'What is your genealogy شجره نسب?' I answered, 'Hazrat Sultan ul-Arifin Sultan Bahu (R.A), Hazrat Pir Dastgir Mehbub-i-Subhani, Hazrat Sheikh Abdul Qadir Gilani (may his unique secrets be sanctified), and Hazrat Sarwar-i-Kainat Hazrat Muhammad Mustafa (the peace of God be upon him) are my father, grandfather, and great-grandfather, respectively, and I am the bright attendant and adopted descendant of these three pious personages.'" This answer astonished the interrogator.

He said probably in 1912 intending to leave for Baghdad, "I first visited the brilliant tomb of my spiritual patron, HazratSultan-ul-Arifin (R.A) and obtained his permission to depart.Then I went to Multan and visited the graves of the saints there. Idid the same in

Delhi. Reaching Baghdad, I tarried for about two months at the holy tomb of Hazrat Pir Mehboob-i-Subhani (mayhis unique secret be sanctified)! I derived esoteric blessings from the holy graves of many great religious magnates, the Imams and perfect saints of Baghdad named as follows: Hazrat Imam Abu Hanifa (the greatest imam), Hazrat Imam Abu Yusuf, Hazrat the Two Kazims, Hazrat Usha يوشع, Hazrat Maruf Kirkhi, Hazrat Junaid Baghdadi, Hazrat Siri Saqti, Hazrat Sheikh Shibli, Hazrat Bishar Hafi, Hazrat Hussain bin Mansur al-Hallaj, and Hazrat Sheikh Shihabud-Din Suhravardi, and so on (God's mercy be on them all!).

"Later on, we went to Karbala-i-Mualla and paid homage to the illustrious tombs of all the martyrs of Karbala, especially to the head of the martyrs, Hazrat Imam Hussain (God be pleased with him!). It is worth mentioning that those were the early days of Muharram. Shias from all over the world had mustered in Karbala. There was a huge gathering at the tomb of the king of martyrs. Inside the mausoleum, visitors were flocking to the grave like moths and weeping bitterly. Everyone was shedding tears. I tried to weep. But to weep is not a voluntary act. I could not. I recollected the oppressions of the martyrs of Karbala and made great efforts. I thought it would be an act of wretchedness if I did not weep here. Finally, I stood at the feet of the king of martyrs and beseeched the spiritualism of my esoteric leader, Sultan-ul-Arifin. That very moment, I began to weep involuntarily such as I had never wept before. I heard the sound of my heart like that of a hot boiling kettle, and had that state continued for a little longer, my heart would have certainly burst. In a few minutes, I shed so many tears that my lap was wet and my heart felt an unaccountable esoteric relief."

In the early days, Faqir Sahib had traveled on foot and all alone, hundreds of times to visit the tomb of Hazrat Sultan-ul- Arifin. For about twelve years, he wandered in the sands of Thal (A Desert) and slept on the ground without a pillow or bedding. Being subject to a sort of spiritual intoxication, day and night, he followed no earthly pursuit in those days. It kept him independent and carefree of the world and all its paraphernalia. This state continued for a long time, but later on, his nature gradually pacified, and the intensity of seclusiveness decreased.

On the cessation of this cycle of seclusiveness and state of renunciation, there commenced another one in which he reverted to material senses and began paying heed to worldly affairs, along with the religious one, which still exists. The series of compositions and compilations also relate to this cycle.

In about 1935, he first thought of publishing a book of *Hazrat Sultan-ul-Arifin's Iranian Nur-ul-Huda* with Urdu translation and *Irfan*. But because of "monetary shortage," these could not be published for years. At last, this difficulty was overcome through the spiritual help of two deceased saints. Here are the details.

In 1941, he desired to visit the Asifiyya Library in Hyderabad Deccan and to study its rare manuscripts. He communicated with Abdul Aziz Sahib, one of his college fellows and friends, who was the vice principal in Usmania Training College. So he first went to Lahore and stayed with Hakim Sultan Muhammad Sahib (deceased). The Hakim Sahib was one of his oldest and best friends, and he always stayed with him on visiting Lahore. One night, he intimated his intention to Hakim Sahib, who ordered him to give it up. The Hakim Sahib, who was a very experienced, world-knowing, and discreet personage, said, "What's the good of going so far?"

Faqir Sahib felt hesitant and said, "If this is what you advise, I won't go."

Early the next morning, the first thing that the Hakim Sahib said to Faqir Sahib was, "Don't give up your determination. Do perform this journey; it envelops something good."

Faqir Sahib was astonished on hearing this and said, "Yesterday, you advised me to desist from this journey, and today, you insist on it. How is that?"

The Hakim Sahib said, "Someone told me in a dream last night not to stop you from proceeding on this journey."

So Faqir Sahib set out on this long journey.

On reaching Hyderabad, he stayed with Abdul Aziz, his only acquaintance there. Aziz himself was a man of a retiring nature with only few friends in the city.

One day, Faqir Sahib turned toward the enshrined spirits for help. The tomb of Yousuf Shah Sharif Shah is a public sacred shrine there. His object was realized after visiting the tomb a few times. He found access to Sir Akbar Hydari, the then prime minister, who was an ardent believer in the tomb. On the first meeting, he sanctioned a substantial sum payable in two instalments for the publication of the two books. In this connection, Faqir Sahib had to go to Hyderabad in 1942 again—accompanied by the present writer. This time, he made the acquaintance of Mirza Yar Jang Bahadur, the minister for theology, a believer in Faqir Sahib. He once gave a sumptuous invitation to Faqir Sahib. Jiwan Yar Jang Bahadur, the chief justice, and other dignitaries of the state were also among the invitees. This time, because of the efforts of Mirza Yar Jang Bahadur, Faqir Sahib stayed as a royal guest in Sulh Sarai for two months.

He spent the last five years of his life in the Punjab (Pakistan). In August 1955, like other parts of Pakistan his ancestral city Kulachi was flooded and swept away his house and entire household and belongings. Instead of grumbling over the loss the, he appeared joyful and said we the Sufis always have ruined houses but flourishing mind which is our way and spiritual status. Therefore, he went to Faisalabad and stayed there till end. Although he was quite comfortable there, but the climate did not suit, and many a physical ailment was caused. The disease that proved fatal was inflammation and tumor of liver.

On 16th October 1960 when he became very feeble and said, "I want to make a will and wish to appoint you my spiritual successor." Therefore, a lawyer was called, and he dictated his will signed it and handed over the completed deed of will to me. According to the will he appointed me the spiritual successor and the head of his mystic seat. He said, "I have accomplished the aimed expedition. Now I am awaiting death with great impatience." And he recited a couplet meaning:

I am desirous of death in a manner.
As Sikundar for elixir of life.

After the 16th October, the day of 17th passed all right. On the night of 17th October, the sun of gnosis whose beams have illuminated thousands of obscure minds was to set. The same night the light house was to become extent which had enlightened the path of truth for the humanity stranded in the dark night of infidelity, atheism and skepticism. At one AM he welcomed the death angel and surrendered his soul to the Creator.

"We belong to God Almighty and unto Him we return.

Life waits for ages in the Kaaba and temples
To procure a Gnostic from love assembles

The humblest of all
Sahibzada Faqir Abdul Hameed Sarwari Qadri

Hazart Qabila Faqeer Noor Muhammad Sarwari Qadri (R.A)
and Hazart Faqeer Abdul Hameed Sarwari Qadri R.A (Son)

Hazart Qabila Faqeer Abdul Hameed Sarwari Qadri
First Spiritual Successor

PROOF OF THE EXISTENCE OF GOD

Praise be to God, the Lord of all creatures, and a successful end for the pious men. Benedictions and peace be upon His Prophet Muhammad and his descendants and all his companions.

When we ponder humanity's general and universal faith toward God the Most High, we have to believe that man is connected with the secret essence of his true Creator through a most invisible etheric cord. From the most enlightened scientist and philosopher down to the simple-natured savage of the desert, men of all the superior and inferior ranks agree about a high and superior existence of that Holy Essence possessed of perfection, glory, beauty, power, and knowledge.

His name is carved in every human heart, and consciously or unconsciously, His memory exists in every mind. As you would say, the clay of man has been kneaded with the water of life of His remembrance and commemoration, and human nature and disposition have been leavened with the name of the Creator. Undoubtedly, on the dawn of creation, the clay of Adam was kneaded with the etheric wine of His personal name, Allah—the drunkenness whereof has intoxicated every heart and inhabited every brain. The great poet Hafiz says

دوش دیدم که ملائک در میخانه زدند   گل آدم بسر شکسته و پیمانه زدند

آسمان بار امانت نتوا نست کشید   قرعهٔ فال بنام من دیوانه زدند

(حافظ)

"Yesterday I saw that the angels knocked on the door of the wine-shop. They kneaded the clay of Adam and cast it in the cup of wine. The heaven could not bear the burden of that trust. The dice of omen was thrown in my—the madman's—name."

Undoubtedly, the knowledge of the learned philosopher who has given to man the title of "Seeker of God" has fully realized the reality and nature of man, and absolutely true is a certain poet's remark: "عدم سے جانبِ ہستی تلاشِ یار میں آۓ" "We have come to existence from nothingness merely in quest of our beloved Lord—the Creator."

In short, the belief in the existence of God is so very common, natural, and universal that it would not be improper to call him who denies His existence and repudiates this creed as crazy, insane, and mad. This boundless and unique artisanship of heaven and earth fully indicate its real Creator. This orderly manufactory of the universe is shouting aloud the name of its eternal Artisan. When we look at the manufactory of the universe, we find all its principles based on perfect knowledge and wisdom. Every part of this splendid machinery of the world functions according to a dominant power, so much so, that the small particles of the solid, senseless, and concrete stones are attached to one another according to the most useful and well-arranged law of Providence, and every leaf of the inanimate tree moves according to a potent order of nature. At the sight of this flawless order of Providence, every wise heart and sensible mind is compelled to acknowledge the existence of that learned and wise essence of high attributes, and every seeing eye is bewitched by the imperishable beauty of the real Creator.

برگ درختانِ در نظرِ هوشیار هر ورقے دفتر یست معرفتِ کردگار

(سعدی)

"In the eyes of the enlightened man, a leaf of the green tree is a large book of wisdom to know God, the Omnipotent."

At the sight of this amazing order and unblemished continuance in this wonderful creation, human intellect gets lost in utter astonishment, and understanding and imagination get confounded. Not a single semblance of disorder is visible anywhere. Not a bit of negligence and divergence from arrangement occurs even for a moment. What a powerful and strong supervision. The great Creator is peeping through the curtain of creation, but there is no eye capable of seeing Him. His holy oneness is singing the melodies of unity from behind the veil and cabinet of plurality, but a clear ear and waking heart are wanting. I have a Beloved beyond the curtain, whose facial beauty deserves concealment. The universe is the painter's curtain. All the objects are the pictures on the curtain.

This curtain has separated Him from me. Surely, this is the exigency of the curtain. I behold that separation between us, the true Lover and the Beloved, cannot be affected by the covering of the curtain.

Once upon a time, a simple-minded man of the desert who grazed camels in the jungle was asked by a learned man as to how he knew the God and the Creator of the world. To this, the man wisely answered:

اَلْبَعْرَةُ تَدُلُّ عَلَى الْبَعِيْرِ وَلَاقْدَامُ عَلَى الْمَسِيْرِ فَالسَّمَاءُ ذَاتُ اَبْرَاجٍ وَّالْاَرْضُ ذَاتُ فِجَاجٍ كَيْفَ لَا يَدُلَّانِ عَلَى الصَّانِعِ اللَّطِيْفِ الْخَبِيْرِ۔

"The camel dung indicates the personality of a camel, and the footprints show that a traveler has gone this way. Why not heaven with all its grand signs of zodiac and the solar system; The suns, the moons, the planets, and the earth with all its contents; the mountains, the rivers, the jungles, the plains with their inhabitants; men, animals, birds, fish, insects, and all living and unloving creatures indicate their benign, knowing, and powerful Creator?

ابھی اس راہ سے کوئی گیا ہے   کہہ دیتی ہے شوخی نقشِ پا کی
(مومن)

Some Beloved has just passed this way; the spriteliness of the footprints is self-expressing."

In short, every particle of this elemental chain is alive and resplendent with the light of that world-illuminating sun, and the truth-revealing mirror of the world is shining with the reflection of His light of glory and beauty. All the people of the world endowed with eyesight, the aggregate of those endowed with insight and reckoned as the seers of the age, and all the truthful, just, and sound-minded people of the world give evidence of the single and pure existence of that Mighty, True, and Most Holy Lord and praise His perfect wisdom and mightiness. As the Holy Quran says:

شَهِدَ اللّٰهُ اَنَّهُ لَآ اِلٰهَ اِلَّا هُوَ وَ الْمَلٰٓئِكَةُ وَ اُولُوا الْعِلْمِ قَآئِمًۢا بِالْقِسْطِ ؕ لَآ اِلٰهَ اِلَّا هُوَ الْعَزِيْزُ الْحَكِيْمُ ۞ اِنَّ الدِّيْنَ عِنْدَ اللّٰهِ الْاِسْلَامُ (۳ آلِ عمران ۱۸-۱۹)

"God bears evidence that verily there is no deity except Him and all the angels and learned people are steadfast about the truth; that there is no Allah except Him and verily the true and right religion with God is Islam."

What is the value of the denial of a blind, darkling, owlish atheist, and what is the weight of the obstinacy and infidelity of a darkness-loving, bat-like heretic? If the bat can't see in the daytime and blames the sun, it is through its own defect and is not the fault of the sun, which illuminates the whole world and gives life and light to the whole universe.

The famous poet Hali has very excellent sayings about this:

کانٹا ہے ہر اِک جگر میں اٹکا تیرا   حلقہ ہے ہر اِک گوش میں اٹکا تیرا

مانا نہیں جس نے تجھ کو جانا ہے ضرور   بھٹکے ہوئے دل میں بھی ہے کھٹکا تیرا

O Lord! The thorn of Thy love is sticking in every human heart, and the ring of Thy obedient slavery pierces every ear. The great atheist also recognises the fact of Thy reality, though he does not conform to Thee. The heart astray also fears Thee very much.

ہندو نے صنم میں جلوہ پایا تیرا   آتش پہ مغاں نے راگ گایا تیرا

دہری نے کیا دہر سے تعبیر تجھے   انکار کسی سے بن نہ آیا تیرا

The Hindu discerned Thy splendour in the idol; the Magi seeks Thee in the flames of his fire. Even the materialist and naturalist cannot but interpret Thee in matter and nature. Never, never, O my Lord, can any one denies Thy existence.

طوفاں میں ہے جبکہ جہاز چکر کھاتا   یا قافلہ وادی میں ہے سر ٹکراتا

اسباب کا آسرا جب کہ ہے اُٹھ جاتا   واں تیرے سوا کوئی نہیں یاد آتا

When the ship whirls in the storm, or a caravan is lost in a jungle; when reliance on any external and material provisions is entirely lost; then and then, O my Almighty God! None is remembered and called for help save Thee.

جب لیتے ہیں گھیر تیری قدرت کے ظہور   منکر بھی پکار اُٹھتے ہیں تجھ کو مجبور

خفاش کو ظلمت کی نہ سوجھی کوئی راہ   خورشید کاشش جہت میں پایا جب نور

Encompassed by the manifestations of Thy almightiness, the atheist and the denier are compelled to call upon Thee. The bat, when encircled and surrounded by the sunlight everywhere, can think of no exit to darkness.

جب مایوسی دلوں پر چھا جاتی ہے   دشمن سے بھی نام ترا جپواتی ہے

ممکن ہے کہ سکھ میں بھول جائیں اطفال   لیکن اُنہیں دُکھ میں ماں ہی یاد آتی ہے

When disappointment overtakes the heart, even the atheist is forced to take Thy name by and by. I suppose in pleasure and comfort the children may forget their mother, but in pain and trouble, they cry to their mama.

For the working of the manufactory of the world, the atheists of the world—that is, the naturalists—cannot but believe in an ultimate cause, an omnicompetent power. But it is absolutely inconceivable that the Creator of the universe should be a lifeless matter, senseless nature, and unintelligent body. It is essential for the essence, working such an orderly and regular manufactory based on knowledge and wisdom, to be qualified with personal attributes of life, might, intention, knowledge, hearing, sight, speech, and so on. This is beyond the scope of senseless ether and unintelligent matter. The naturalists and materialists ought to populate a separate populace of fools. Let them appoint a senseless, soulless, foolish, and unintelligent person like mother matter as its supervisor, and then see how it flourishes and progresses in a few days' time. Or let them visit a lunatic asylum and have a glimpse of unintelligence with its attendant results and the chaos that will ensue if it is momentarily deprived of the superintendence of intelligent and sensible people. Look at the factories, firms, and machines of the world, and ponder all the departments of the government; in fact, observe any object, any job, or any faculty of this populated world, and you will find them formulated and regulated under the influence of knowledge, understanding, might, wisdom, and such like attributes. A part is analogous to the whole. Is it possible that this splendid manufactory of the world in a corner of which the sun burns like a candle and every part of which is working according to knowledge and philosophy should not have intelligent, sensible, learned, and wise servants appointed on every ordinary part of it, whereas the entire manufactory of the universe with all its magnitude and spaciousness should exist and work voluntarily without any artisan or superintendent?

In the course of a controversy, Hazrat Imam-i-Azam (RA) defeated and confused an atheist by this solitary argument, saying, "Supposing a boat is put in a large lake. Would it voluntarily, on its own account, without a boatman, come and go to a particular place at a stipulated time?"

"Impossible," interjected the atheist.

Whereupon His Holiness said, "In this large and spacious blue lake of the firmamental space of the heavens, how do the sun and the moon rise daily from a particular place and set in a determined abode at stipulated times without any operator? As the Holy Quran says:

$$وَالشَّمْسُ تَجْرِىْ لِمُسْتَقَرٍّ لَّهَا ۚ ذٰلِكَ تَقْدِيْرُ الْعَزِيْزِ الْعَلِيْمِ ۞ وَالْقَمَرَ قَدَّرْنٰهُ مَنَازِلَ حَتّٰى$$

$$عَادَ كَالْعُرْجُوْنِ الْقَدِيْمِ ۞ لَا الشَّمْسُ يَنْبَغِيْ لَهَاۤ اَنْ تُدْرِكَ الْقَمَرَ وَلَا الَّيْلُ سَابِقُ النَّهَارِ ۚ وَ$$

$$كُلٌّ فِيْ فَلَكٍ يَّسْبَحُوْنَ ۞ (٣٦ يٰسِين: ٣٨-٤٠)$$

'And the sun goes on a set course. This is the measure set by the Most Powerful and Learned God. And for the moon we have determined stages; until it diminishes like an old date-palm branch. Neither can the sun overtake the moon nor the night forestall the day. All are moving in set circles.'"

At this silencing argument of Hazrat Imam-i-Azam (RA), the atheist became penitent and repentant.

How ridiculous of the atheists to say that by establishing the unity of God, religion has circumscribed this magnificence and greatness of the universe. The significance of matter and nature carries a wider sense. These fools have conjectured the peerless, incomparable, unchangeable, eternal, holy, and uncreated essence of God after the manner of their own ignorant, valueless, and earthly body, which cannot understand. He does not know about his house and abode and is unaware of his family and dynasty. Far above their trifling materialistic intelligence, the magnificent being of the Islamic God is an unlimited, all-encircling, omnipresent, and holy existence, beyond the scope of name and fame, encomium and praise, manifestation and concealment, universally partness, generality and particularity, and such like examples and allusions. Nay, He is absolutely free from all such examples, specifications, and annexations. More than that, He is far removed and free from confinement, freedom, and specification; inanimate matter and insignificant nature have nothing in comparison to Him.

Knowledge—a single attribute of Allah the Most High—has encircled the entire space and time and enclosed all the invisible and visible worlds. As He says, "He is the first and the last, the visible and the invisible, manifest and the concealed and He is cognizant of everything." Says the Most High, "Verily the knowledge of Allah surrounds everything." We can truthfully assert on the basis of our own knowledge and experience that when this attribute of Allah the Most High, knowledge, manifests to His special selected spiritual men, they see all the matter and nature, namely, all the created beings and the eighteen thousand creations هجده هزار عالم in the palm of the hand and the nail of the thumb, not to speak of the pious, pure, and holy essence of God the Most High, which is beyond the scope of imagination.

اے برتر از قیاس و خیال و گمان و و ہم   وزہرچہ گفتہ اند و شنیدیم و خواندہ ایم

دفتر تمام گشت و بپایاں رسید عمر   ماہمچناں در اوّلِ وصفِ تو ماندہ ایم

(سعدی)

"O Thou! Who art above conjecture, imagination, fancy, and whim. And all that has been said, heard, and read about. The book of Thy praise will be finished and life will come to an end. But as yet we shall be left in the first step of Thy praise."

If the most irreligious heretic relinquishes his obstinacy for a moment, puts on the spectacles of justice, and peeps toward his mind and reflects, he will inevitably conclude that when if speaking, seeing, and thinking creation like me can exist, why could not a self-existing creator of all? It is curious that the impotent atom should affirm its own existence but negate that of the world-illuminating sun! A tree is judged by its fruit. The craze for political ascendency, the melancholia and worldly greed and ambition, and the insatiable appetite for glory and grace have transformed man into a blind animal. Otherwise, there could not be a stronger proof of the existence of God the Most High than the existence of man himself. Someone has well said:

مری ہستی ہے خود شاہد وجودِ ذات باری کی   دلیل ایسی ہے یہ جو عمر بھر رد ہو نہیں سکتی

"My very existence is the evidence of the existence of God. It is a proof which cannot be refuted life-long."

Should a sound-minded and just-natured person retire even for a few days and meditate and reflect about himself, he would clearly perceive in himself the signs of the knowledge of his Creator and Master, the secrets of His holiness, and the lights of His perception. Says the Most High:

وَ فِىٓ اَنْفُسِكُمْ ۚ اَفَلَا تُبْصِرُوْنَ ﴿٢١﴾

"And His signs are within yourselves but you don't perceive."

مَنْ عَرَفَ نَفْسَهُ فَقَدْ عَرَفَ رَبَّهُ ـ

Tradition says, "He who recognized himself, recognized his Lord."

Moreover, the heretical people advance the following argument in vindication of their heresy: How should we comprehend and believe in His existence when in the world, we can neither see the person of God nor comprehend the substance and reality of His essence nor yet perceive any of His manifest attributes, potent actions, and solid operations? Now, let it be remembered that lack of understanding, finding, or feeling of a thing is no proof of its nonexistence. Profound reason hasn't limited the range of things to only those that can be sensed and felt. What the human species has comprehended and felt through its scientific and intellectual endeavors and applications so far amounts to less than an insignificant particle of the unknown and invisible world. There exist in the atmosphere billions of varieties of germs, thousands of kinds of gases, and innumerable invisible electric waves that cannot be sensed or discovered through the external senses.

A new creed called modern spiritualism is extant in Europe, America, Australia, and so on. For about a century (namely since AD 1848), scores of people have believed in it. In those cities, innumerable persons are members of the societies of this modern doctrine. Those people invoke spirits in their seances, chat with the spirits, and photograph them publicly. The speeches of the spirits are recorded directly. Innumerable journals and newspapers are engaged in imparting correct news of them to the people. This psychic science is progressing daily. Famous scientists, clear-minded philosophers, and eminent personalities, including members of the parliaments, believe in that science and participate in those societies. Though a hundred years ago, not a single man in the whole of Europe believed in life after death and the existence of spirits. But today everyone there confirms the existence of spirits and their life after death because, on thousands of occasions, they have witnessed spirits with their own eyes and experimented on them. The aforementioned spiritual investigation of Europe is sufficient, eye-opening evidence to the heretics who are in the habit of repeatedly saying, "Where are the dead who asserted the eternity of spirits and sponsored spiritual communication? Why don't they return and tell us, the living unbelievers, 'We are alive!'? Why don't they unveil this secret but let us suffer to perpetuate irreligiousness and faithlessness?" Now the dead in the West have revived and are publicly proclaiming, "We are alive." There the veil between the dead and living has been set aside. But the people of the East are still groping in the darkness, heresy, and materialism. Later on, we will narrate the reality and full account of this science. In short, it does not follow that whatever cannot be sensed and felt with the five external senses is nonexistent. Innumerable jinns, angels, and spirits hover about us day and night, and this atmosphere of ours abounds with unlimited mysterious objects. Denial of such etheric objects is proof of the absence of internal senses among the deniers. God with His ample splendor and pure essence, all His holy attributes, names, and acts is effulgent in every particle of the universe and is nearer to man than his jugular vein—nay, his very soul. But what can the savage-like ignorant and blind public see? The sun illuminates the entire universe and burns the brow of the blind, but the blind still roam and wander in the dark.

آنکھ والا ترے جوبن کا تماشا دیکھے

دیدۂ کور کو کیا آئے نظر کیا دیکھے

(داغؔ دہلوی)

"The eyed can enjoy the glory of His grand personality: What can the blind see and what can it feel?"

Now the only objection remaining unanswered is why has God divulged these things to some people and concealed them from the others? In fact, this world is an examination hall. God has created man for trial and examination. At the dawn of the beginning of creation when He created all the spirits, He examined them with the summary question of "Am I not your Lord the Creator?"—that is, He examined them with the oral question of the manifestation of his Lordship and obtained from them the approval of His adoration, so that all the spirits unanimously answered, "Yes"—they answered in the affirmative, saying, "Verily Thou art our Lord the Creator." Later on, God admitted them in the examination hall of the world and required them to write down their answers to the difficult and unsolvable questions regarding His Unity and Lordship on the opaque answer books of matter, which we alive people are doing here. The recording angels on our both sides roll them up every morning and evening and attach them to their file and record, and the results will be declared on the perfect trial day of Resurrection. As says the Most High in His Holy Quran:

$$ \text{الَّذِىْ خَلَقَ الْمَوْتَ وَالْحَيٰوةَ لِيَبْلُوَكُمْ اَيُّكُمْ اَحْسَنُ عَمَلًا (الملك: ٢/٦٧)} $$

"He is the essence who created death and life in order to try and examine which of you acts meritoriously."

Just think of the tremendous attention paid to the concealment and secrecy of the answers to the material and momentary examinations in schools and colleges. The question papers are put forward, but utmost precautions are taken to keep their answers secret, although success in these material examinations results in a transitory, material luxury and comfort. Hence, however great the precaution for concealing the answers to the examination on which eternal bliss and comfort or perpetual deprivation and failure depend, it is inadequate. This proposition of the atheists and materialists, that if the essence of God, His angels, and the acts of His domination exist, we must be able to see them in some form or other, is as foolish and insane as a student in the examination hall asking, "These papers of the examination contain questions and questions only; why aren't the answers given with them?" The fool considers the examination hall to be the playground.

$$ \text{بر سرِ طور هوا طنبور شهوت می زنی} $$
$$ \text{عشقِ مرد لَنْ تَرَانِیْ را بدیں خواری مجو} $$

(حافظ)

- 44 -

You are playing on the guitar of lust aloft the Mount Sinai of passion. Seek not the sight of one, saying, "You can't see me لَّن" "تَرَانِی," so cheaply.

The illumination of the essence and attributes of God and the clear proof of His power and His mysterious invisible creations, for example, jinn, angels, spirits, and so on, are one and all the etheric and invisible things of the etheric world. It is not within the scope of the external senses and material intellect to behold and understand them. Internal and etheric senses are required to understand and feel them. Just as the external senses can not replace one another—the eyes cannot function for the ears and vice versa—the external senses cannot perform the duties of the internal ones. Self-denial and full devotion are conditional on the attainment of internal senses, and a patriotic teacher is indispensable for this. Says the Most High in His holy book, "and to those that strive towards Us, We indicate Our path to them."

در مکتبِ حقائق پیش ادیب عشق

ہاں اے پسرِ کوش کہ روزے پدر شوی

(حافظ)

"In the school of realities afore the tutor of love, take heed, O son, and try hard that someday you may become the father of knowledge."

Through assiduous labor and hard work for etheric educationin the spiritual school, sound intellect and internal senses are obtained to a degree of experimental knowledge, so that in this very world, they are relieved of the apprehension of the great examination of the next world and the grief and pain of failure. Says the Most High in the Holy Quran:

اَلَآ اِنَّ اَوۡلِیَآءَ اللّٰهِ لَا خَوۡفٌ عَلَیۡہِمۡ وَلَا ھُمۡ یَحۡزَنُوۡنَ (۱۰ یونس: ۶۲)

"Verily the friends of Allah have nothing to fear or grieveabout."

In short, esoterically, there are different academies and schools of the soul and heart and different colleges of the spirit. Those who have not even happened to pass by these etheric schools and spiritual colleges, what can those blind materialists know of the etheric sciences, this invisible education department, and its spiritual prospectus and professors?

حیف کیں بے بصراں تا بہ ابد بے خبر اند

زانچہ در دیدۂ صاحب نظراں ے آید

(حافظ)

Alas! The blind are unaware of that which passes before the eyes of those gifted with insight.

In short, this world is an examination hall, testing whether one acts here rightly or wrongly. One is neither immediately chastised nor adequately rewarded, because the time prescribed for declaration of the result is far off yet. That is why immediate and spontaneous punishments are not awarded for moral and religious offenses in this transitory world; neither can full punishment be awarded. For example, a person commits adultery, and there ligious law awards that person one hundred canes as punishment or death through stoning. But another man commits adultery thousands of times and escapes all sorts of worldly chastisement. Or a person deliberately and intentionally commits homicide. The law and shariat sentence him to death. But another man is instrumental in or responsible for destroying thousands—nay, *millions*—of people. Can he who commits adultery thousands of times or murders 100,000 innocent people be adequately chastised in this material world?

Never, such notorious culprits can be fully and adequately punished only in another world erected for them, where there is no time limit, lives are very long, and every offender is given innumerable bodies and lives and is chastised by being killed and revived over and over again.

This cannot be affected in the limited material abode of this world. The endless abode of power and retaliation of the next world must necessarily be set for this purpose. The noble Quran often speaks of serious, painful, and prolonged affliction prescribed for such major offenses. It runs as follows:

وَإِذَآ أُلْقُوْا مِنْهَا مَكَانًا ضَيِّقًا مُّقَرَّنِيْنَ دَعَوْا هُنَالِكَ ثُبُوْرًا ۝ لَا تَدْعُوا الْيَوْمَ ثُبُوْرًا وَّاحِدًا وَّ

اُدْعُوْا ثُبُوْرًا كَثِيْرًا ۞ (۲۵: الفرقان: ۱۳-۱۴)

"And when they will be cast in dark abode oppressed together, they will pray and ask for pray death and destruction. They will be told in reply, not for a single death today; but pray for many deaths."

Elsewhere, it is said, "Says the Most High:

اِنَّ الَّذِيْنَ كَفَرُوْا بِاٰيٰتِنَا سَوْفَ نُصْلِيْهِمْ نَارًا ۚ كُلَّمَا نَضِجَتْ جُلُوْدُهُمْ بَدَّلْنٰهُمْ جُلُوْدًا غَيْرَهَا لِيَذُوْقُوا الْعَذَابَ ۗ اِنَّ اللّٰهَ كَانَ عَزِيْزًا حَكِيْمًا ۞ (۴: النساء: ۵۶)

'Hell-fire will shortly burn those that denied our signs. When their skins are burnt, We will give them new skins (i.e., bodies); so that they may taste the full punishment.'"

Verily, God has dominant wisdom. In short, the abode of power and retaliation of the next world is a necessity, and this world is like an examination hall. No one is told during the examination whether he is acting justly or otherwise. The result will open the eyes of everyone. Alas! There is no cure for the eternal blindness and obstinacy, and there is Allah's curse on those unfortunate ignorant creatures. There are innumerable patent signs and thousands of real marks for those possessed of intellect, the light of faith, and etheric sight. Every particle of the universe is shouting aloud with the unity of God:

May I tell you a true and right story about the Holy one? All is from Him and if you look more nearly, He is all. His beauty is apparent from all the particles of the world. Your fold on fold conceit is your only veil.

VIEWS OF WELL-KNOWN EUROPEAN SCIENTISTS ON THE EXISTENCE OF GOD

Sir William Thomson

Speaking at the annual meeting of the University College, London, in April 1903, Lord Calvin, who was a professor of natural philosophy at Glasgow University in Scotland and made many discoveries in physics and mathematics and many inventions, said,

> Science has full faith and perfect belief in a Creator of the heaven and earth and, compels us to believe in the existence of the Absolutely Powerful Creator, keeper and sustainer of our existences; rather He is a power which creates and guides the things existent. Scientific investigations and revelations insist on us to have full faith in that Eternal existence.
>
> When we ponder over the physical changes, revolutions and the cause of the movements of the things around us, we cannot resist concluding that God the Creator is evident from that wisdom and art of His, which appears in the system of the world and arrangement and composition of things. Science compels, us to have faith in a Power that actuates and guides aright all the physical acts of the world; and that Creator is quite different from physical force, electrical and mechanical power. He has nothing to do with the theory of automatic communication of atoms, which unanimously all the scientists of the day hold as most absurd and irrational. All the learned are agreed on the point that the world and all that therein is not the result of the casual conjunction of atoms. No; the creatures have assumed life through the wisdom and power of an intelligent and willful essence. The changes that continually

take place in the living are not accidental. On the other hand, the things existent have come into being according to the directions and fixed laws of the Creator. For all these acts science confirms the existence of the Creator. Forty years ago I enquired from Germany's famous chemist, Lee Beck, while he was having a walk with me in the fields outside the city, "Are these plants born and nourished through chemical actions?" He replied, "not at all. Just as a book on botany is not composed spontaneously, these plants are not born by themselves. Every act of (divine) intention is a miracle according to physics, chemistry and mathematics. Don't be afraid of thinking and pondering freely. If you think properly, you would be unable to dispense with the existence of God; which is the foundation and cause-root of religion. Science is not the enemy of religion but is its supporter."

Lord Salisbury

Besides a statesman, Lord Salisbury was a famous man of letters. He was appointed the secretary of state for India during the conservative ministry in 1866 and 1874 and was twice prime minister of Britain. There cannot be a greater proof of his learning than that he was selected president of the British Association Meeting in 1840. He had hard discussions with Herbert Spencer on the theory of evolution, and learned articles appeared from both sides in many consecutive numbers of the *ContemporaryReview* in the nineteenth century. In the course of an address at Oxford, he said,

It is my time-honoured opinion that the evolution that has appeared in plants and animals is not found in the theory of physical selectivity and the true theory of evolution is quite foreign to it. After full deliberation I have come to the conclusion that the researchers conducted about the origin and propagation of animals during the last few years no heed has been paid to arguments based on cause and effects. A careful study of the universe reveals that an intelligent and intending essence has created it for a set purpose and special use. In proof there are innumerable arguments all round us. When physical or scientific perplexities cast their veils on our eyes we may temporarily lose sight of these arguments; but they invariably return to our eyes and draw our attention.

On the bases of these signs we are told to believe that an independent and self-willed being has created the universe out of his perfect power. We further learned that all living beings are in need of and are dependent upon the wisdom and power of that eternal essence, unperishing Creator and Unparallel Ruler.

Doctor Wallace

Alfred Russel Wallace is called the old man of the realm of science. He was born in 1822. In 1911, he published his famous scientific work, *World of Life*, and placed before the world the results of his ideas and scientific research of half a century.

This book is very famous. In expounding the theory of evolution through physical selection, the doctor is a cooperator of Darwin. He was a God-fearing and pious man. For the scientists, his word is an authority. In his work, *Natural Selections*, he says,

Man was not born through the act of evolution alone—independent of the power and wisdom of the Omnipotent. Power emanates from the rational soul. Every kind of power is will-power.

If there is anything will-power, it is the power which directs the faculties assembled in the body. It is impossible for any part of the body to follow direction without being affected by power. If we come to know that the minutest power too is the result of will-power and should one know no other primary source or cause of power, we cannot help admitting that every kind of power is in fact will-power. On these premises it can be asserted that the entire world not only depends on superior intelligent beings but in fact consists of them. In other words, He is the highest intellect and philosophy.

All the creatures of the universe, whether animate or inanimate, stones or trees, large or small, celestial or terrestrial, are sincerely and harmoniously singing the songs of the praises and oneness of God, their Creator and Master.

As God the Most High says in the Holy Quran:

$$\text{يُسَبِّحُ لِلّٰهِ مَا فِي السَّمٰوٰتِ وَمَا فِي الْأَرْضِ (١٢ الجمعة:١)}$$

"Every thing in Heaven or on earth praises Allah."

The concord and the object of the universe and the harmony in their composition is a strong proof of the fact that their creator and master is a single, peerless, unparalleled, unique, and unequal essence. Here is the proof. Supposing a man descends into the depths of the underworld and fetches a piece of unique mineral; then he dives for miles into the depths of the Atlantic Ocean and brings out some aquatic shell, and for the third time, he ascends the heights of the skies for crores of miles and picks up a pellet from a very distant star. Now, if the components of all the three things are carefully examined under the microscope, it would be unanimously declared by all the scientists that the same magnetic particles are found in the components of these three objects and are equally present in all the big and small objects and heavenly bodies of the universe. This unity of the constituents of all the things from the moon to fish از ماه تا ماہی and from heaven to earth is an irrefutable declaration of the unity of the Creator. Or, in other words, the objects of the universe unanimously proclaim with the tongue the existence of God: لَا اِلٰهَ اِلَّا اللّٰه "There is no deity except Allah"; that is, our Creator and Lord of the worlds and truthful Deity is a single, solitary, absolute essence. So that objects recovered from the ancient pyramids of Egypt, minerals and pieces of stone shed by shooting stars, pebbles removed from the summits of the highest mountains, and shells and corals brought up from the deepest recesses of the seas are preserved in the various museums of the universe. When their constituents were analyzed and carefully examined in the light of modern science and chemistry, it was unanimously concluded, as already stated, that the composition of all these is alike and all of them are the product of a single Artisan

وَّالنَّجْمُ وَالشَّجَرُ يَسْجُدٰنِ ۝ (۵۵ الرحمٰن:٦) "And the stars and the trees prostrate." All the celestial and terrestrial creation is manifesting His Lordship and their own servitude. The light of His unity is flashing from the twinkling stars of the heavens. The seminaked resplendence of His craftsmanship and wisdom is dripping from the dancing leaves of the trees and the smiling flowers.

His grandeur descends from lofty mountains, singing His anthems. The black, fearsome clouds in the atmosphere and the sighing waves of the awful deep oceans are echoing with His panic and awe. But man, submerged in his imprudence from topto toe, entertains a futile and empty pride of his short intellect and understanding and is unreasonably avoiding and stupidly conniving from the patent signs of God the Almighty.

وَكَاَيِّنْ مِّنْ اٰيَةٍ فِي السَّمٰوٰتِ وَالْاَرْضِ يَمُرُّوْنَ عَلَيْهَا وَهُمْ عَنْهَا مُعْرِضُوْنَ ۝ (۱۲ يوسف:۱۰۵)

"And there are stores of innumerable signs in heaven and earth which they constantly pass by, but they avoid them all."

Blind, ignorant, and foolish man is making imaginary theories about the existence and reality of God the Almighty and does not even know a bit about himself or a worthless atom. Says the Almighty, "He is finding counterparts for Us, while he is ignorant of his own birth."

در ذاتِ خدا فكرِ فراواں چه كنى   جاں راز قصور خويش حيراں چه كنى
چوں تو نه رسى بكنهِ يک ذرّه تمام   در كنه خدا دعوئ عرفاں چه كنى

(ابوالخير ابوسعيد)

Why so much pondering over the essence of God? Why perplex yourself in your failing every moment? Since you cannot even understand the essence of an atom, why boast about knowing the essence of the Lord the Creator?

The European men of learning and knowledge are leaving no stone unturned in exploring and researching the material world. They are trying their best to discern the minute particulars of the worldly objects and the external effects of the universal bodies and are spending their lives in order to discover everything of the material world, to bring into practice their useful qualities. But they have never even unintentionally thought about themselves as to what they are, what they are for, whence they have come, and where they are going, or what becomes the condition of man after death? The mystery of death remains insoluble, and the great secret of the afterlife lies unknown. How unexplorable lies the stupendous secret of the end of life. In the dark ocean of the material world, their intellectual horses have outrun Alexander the Great, but in searching the water of life of the next world, these people are crippled, lame, blind, and deaf. Among the worldly sciences, religion is a great secret. But alas! The Antichrist of the West is blind in the religious eye, though his material eye is all right. He views everything from the worldly point of view and draws material benefit therefrom. He studies a unique, unchangeable, and instructive divine work like the Holy Quran from a historical point of view. Like a blind man, the fool cannot utilize the sun, except for deriving heat; therefore, they have outcast the essential science of religion outside the file of practice and consider its investigation unessential. The superficial and material West has taken the mother pebble of matter in its lap but has paid absolutely no heed to the search for and acquisition of the valuable secret and estimable pearl of religion. In the pride of their material intellect and knowledge of worldly art, they deny the existence of religion and spiritualism, nay, even the existence of God. As regards the modern science of spiritualism through which they invoke the spirits and converse with them, though it is unanimous and well-accepted dogma of all the religions that spirits survive after death and enjoy pleasure or pain and this science corroborates and verifies religion and faith, these people are so averse to the name of religion that they call it a new science and discovery and do not name it as religion. They say that it has no concern with religion, and so far, this new science of ours is dumbfounded and silent as regards the existence of God. In spite of privilege and observation, they have been led astray by God. As the Holy Quran says:

اَفَرَءَيْتَ مَنِ اتَّخَذَ اِلـٰهَهٗ هَوٰىهُ وَاَضَلَّهُ اللّٰهُ عَلٰى عِلْمٍ وَّخَتَمَ عَلٰى سَمْعِهٖ وَقَلْبِهٖ وَجَعَلَ عَلٰى بَصَرِهٖ غِشٰوَةً ۗ فَمَنْ يَّهْدِيْهِ مِنْ بَعْدِ اللّٰهِ ۗ اَفَلَا تَذَكَّرُوْنَ ۩ (۴۵: الجاثيه:۲۳)

"Have you seen the person who made his passions his deity and Allah misguided him in spite of his knowledge, and He sealed his ears and heart and cast veils over his eyes? So who can guide him except Allah? Do not you understand?"

As yet, these people are bent on ridiculing and belittling all the divine books and especially the strong moral principles and the true and solid realities and precepts of spiritualism and Sufism found in the directly descended and true and unique book the Quran. So far, they have acquired only a little portion of the material sciences, and the wise men of the West are puzzled to find out the reality of even the most common things. For example, the scientists are perplexed about the light of a humble fly of God, the Almighty, that is the glow-worm. Because, according to the principles of science, light and heat are inseparable. But in the body of the glowworm, mere light without heat exists. In short, all the principles and theories established by the research of modern science are imperfect and incomplete. They contain innumerable pitfalls and immeasurable imperfections. Most of them are contradictory to each other, and just as modern scientists and philosophers have disproved and falsified the principles and theories of ancient scientists and philosophers, thus people of a hundred years hence will disprove and kick out the theories and principles established by modern scientists, and the range of material science will be proved conjectural and imaginary from one end to the other. Of course, through scientific observations and experiments, men have acquired some knowledge of the close and common objects that lie within the reach of the five external senses. But it is the height of folly to consider it all. A wide dominion of the material world lies unexplored before them. Matter is as small and dark compared to the invisible world as the mother's womb is compared to the material world. They are lying in the womb of Mother Earth in the form of unripe, incomplete embryos, and while unborn in this world, how can they comprehend the reality of the endless and unlimited broad and wide next world?

فلسفی گشتی و آگہ نیستی خود کجا و از کجا و کیستی

از خود آگہ چوں نہ اے بے شعور پس نباید بر چنیں علت غرور

(رومی)

You have become a philosopher but know not where, whence, and who you are. Unaware of thyself, O fool, I pride not over thy knowledge.

Aluminous Argument on the Reality of Spirit

The material objects of this world are found in three states: solid (e.g., brick, stone, and wood), liquid (e.g., water, milk, and oil); and gas (e.g., vapors, smoke, and air). All these three states are present in water. In the state of ice, water assumes the form of a solid. When the ice melts, it turns into liquid water, and when it is sufficiently heated on fire, it turns into vapor and gas. Of all the three forms, that of gas is most highly refined and invisible and intangible. If the component parts of air are analyzed, they will be found to consist of more subtle gases, like oxygen, hydrogen, and nitrogen. Likewise, these gases are also composed of ethereal, electric molecules. But the reach of human senses and scientific and chemical experiments and observations are at this point and cannot proceed further. Therefore, man ends the details of the more invisible things by naming them ether, vacuum, or nonentity. This chain of things terminates at the frontier of the subtleties of the invisible and spiritual world, and beyond that, the subtle world of the invisible world begins. This should not lead us to think that the subtle spiritual world is some other sphere situated above our universe. No, that subtle spiritual world is mixed and joined with the kernel and shell of this world and permeates all its particles like the blood in the human form and soul in the body, or as there is butter in the milk and ghee in the butter. No, their conjunction is more inexplicable than the present example.

In his sleep, a man creates a subtle spiritual world around him, which can be called an imperfect model of the spiritual world. Just as the spirit is connected to the body, the etheric world has an incomparable connection with this world. God the Almighty Creator of all objects has an all-in-all that is particular and general, external and internal, terrestrial and celestial, patent and latent, subtle, incomparable, and most invisible connection with all His creation. That connection and relation consists of the signs and lights of this personal, attributive, nameable, and functional illumination, which manifest in the outside and inside of the universe and on which depend the entire management, arrangement, and establishment of the universe and creation.

ظاہر و باطن توئی چیست وجود و عدم   اوّل و آخر توئی چیست حدوث و قِدم

ظاہر بے چند و چوں باطن بے کیف و کم   اوّل بے انتقال آخر بے ارتحال

"Thou art the first and the last; what is eternity and opacity? Thou art the patent and latent; what is existence and annihilation? Thou art a first without transfer; a last without death, a potent without how much and how; a latent without how and how many."

Alas! It is more difficult to make a materialist understand the subtle and spiritual world of the invisible hierarchy and the innate priceless, uncomparable, unique, ineffable, inaccuratable essence of God the Almighty than to make a born-blind man understand the colors, shape, and appearances of worldly things or the world-illuminating sun. Together with the art of writing, it is a most defective instrument for conveying the real thoughts and ideas of the mind and heart and especially the true particular states of the unaccountable, timeless, invisible, esoteric world. Moreover, the sphere of words and letters is so narrow that in order to explain it, we have no alternative case of the etheric world, besides quoting examples and employing metaphors. But our illusions and metaphors can certainly serve as a guiding post for those in whom the seed of the light of faith is reposed in trust by God on the day of the beginning, who still possess spiritual competency and have not frustrated it through their immorality, insubordination, and intemperance. But there is no remedy for the eternal wretched and blind. They would not believe even if all the curtains and veils were removed and the resurrection day were erected for them. As the Almighty says in the Holy Quran, "And if We reveal all things before them they would not believe except when Allah wishes them to do so."

We have given some account of the connection and relation of the material world with the spiritual one. Now let us explain the direct connection between the human body and soul or spirit, which will sufficiently explain the reality of the soul and spirit. Let it be known that in accordance with the external world, all the three primary things (solid, liquid, and gas) are existent in the human body. To wit, bone, flesh, skin, and the like are solids; the blood and water are liquids; and the respiratory breath, which spreads within, is gas. It is an accepted fact that the air that is breathed plays an important role in the circulation of blood in the heart and lungs, and human existence solely depends on this air. Through the wire of respiration, the electric wave of the human soul emerges from its powerhouse, and by reaching the bulbs of the heart and brain, it heats, illuminates, and starts the entire human machine. Scientists, chemists, physicians, and doctors do not know the reality of this hidden spiritual electrical energy. They designate blood or its fine vapors as soul. Whereas if blood, air, and heat were the soul, the human body could have been revived by reintroducing air or artificial heat or blood in the human body immediately after death. Or, if the soul were merely the fine vapors of the element self, the mutilation of some human limb must cause some loss or decrease in the soul. But it is not so. The soul is a distinct, subtle, and invisible thing of the celestial world. It is an electric wave of the light of the other world, which sustains and finds access to the human body from the powerhouse of that great source of light through the wire of respiration. Says the Almighty:

قُلِ الرُّوْحُ مِنْ اَمْرِ رَبِّیْ وَمَآ اُوْتِیْتُمْ مِّنَ الْعِلْمِ اِلَّا قَلِیْلًا ۞ (۸۵ :بنی اسرآئیل)

"Say, O Prophet! to the people, that the soul belongs to the invisible world of my Lord, and We have given them very little knowledge of it." This solid material world is called the world created, the visible and material world, while the invisible etheric and spiritual world is called the world of the Creator's command, invisible, or the world of spirits. Says the Almighty:

اَلَا لَهُ الْخَلْقُ وَالْاَمْرُ (۵۴ :الاعراف)

"The elemental world and the spiritual world both belong to Him."

He is the protector and master of both these material and spiritual worlds. Elsewhere, God the Almighty says about the soul:

وَنَفَخْتُ فِیْهِ مِنْ رُّوْحِیْ ۞ (۲۹ :الحجر)

"We blew Our soul (breath unto him) (the Adam)."

In short, the illusion and significance of blowing the soul into the human body clearly indicates that the act of blowing and puffing, through which the soul was put in the human body, is something with this wire of respiration and the air, which comes and goes in the human body every moment.

In Arabic, air is called *reeh* ریح, and the word *ruh* (soul) is taken from it. Also, the word *nafas* means "puff," and the word *nafs* is used for the soul or spirit. So, it is apparent that *ruh* and *reeh* and *nafas* and *nafs* are synonymous words and are one and the same thing because soul has an intimate relation and etheric connection with air and is a subtle and invisible object like the air. Hence, the *real* Creator has tied the subtle essence of the soul to the human body by the subtle thread of the air. Or put it thus that the learned and knowing Creator has imprisoned the subtle and esoteric bird of the soul in the grotesque skeleton and elemental cage of the human body by the subtle thread of air. Since the soul is an extremely subtle object of the etheric world and it was impossible for it to get settled and fixed up in the grotesque world of matter except through a subtle connection, therefore, in this material world of elements, the absolutely potent Creator suggested for it the tie and relation of the most subtle object that is the air, and by tying this subtle string to the foot of the abodeless falcon, He confined it in the frame and the cage of the human body. Hence, the soul is confined in the human body through the air, and through the air of the breath or the wire of respiration, it receives the electric wave of the light—that is, its spiritual food and strength comes from the powerhouse of the etheric world. Everything in the world, whether mineral, vegetable, or animal, possesses a sort of soul and breathes. But because of the difference of degrees and grades, there is difference between mineral, vegetable, animal, human, and angelic souls. And every soul enters the world through the subtle aerial connection. Spiritualists are not unaware of the fact that without the instrumentality of reeh (air), the evoking and calling of the etheric and invisible creation of spirits—that is, the jinn, angels, and spirits in this world—is an impossibility. Whenever the subtle beings of the invisible world are evoked in this world, there the gusts of wind are felt in closed quarters and a wind begins to blow. That is to say, these invisible spiritual beings are sent to the opaque space of this world in company with the subtle companionship of air.

The Holy Quran bears testimony to this concerning the science of evoking spirits, about which His Majesty God the Almighty says:

وَلِسُلَيْمَٰنَ الرِّيحَ عَاصِفَةً تَجْرِيْ بِاَمْرِهٖٓ اِلَى الْاَرْضِ الَّتِيْ بٰرَكْنَا فِيْهَا ۚ وَكُنَّا بِكُلِّ شَيْءٍ عٰلِمِيْنَ ۞ وَمِنَ الشَّيٰطِيْنِ مَنْ يَّغُوْصُوْنَ لَهٗ وَيَعْمَلُوْنَ عَمَلًا دُوْنَ ذٰلِكَ ۚ وَكُنَّا لَهُمْ حٰفِظِيْنَ ۞

(الانبياء:٨١-٨٢)

"The wind was subjected to Solomon and in obedience to his dictates, it used to blow towards the earth that We had blessed and We are operators of all things. Among the devils, some used to dive for him and performed other duties for him and We were their guardian." Elsewhere, it is said in the Quran, "We had subjected for him (Solomon) the wind which in obedience to his order used to blow in the direction that he desired. And there were masons and diver demons, and the rest were tied in chains of subjugation." Regarding the descent of the angels from heaven to help His Majesty, the Prophet Muhammad (peace be upon him), and his dignified companions in the battle of Ahzab, God the Most High says in the Holy Quran:

يٰٓاَيُّهَا الَّذِيْنَ اٰمَنُوا اذْكُرُوْا نِعْمَةَ اللّٰهِ عَلَيْكُمْ اِذْ جَآءَتْكُمْ جُنُوْدٌ فَاَرْسَلْنَا عَلَيْهِمْ رِيْحًا وَّجُنُوْدًا لَّمْ تَرَوْهَا ۚ (الاحزاب:٩)

"O you believers, commemorate the bounty of Allah on you, when the enemy attacked you, He sent on them the wind and an army which you could not see."

It is related by His Holiness Hazrat Ali (peace be on him):

> In the battle of Badr there blew a wind so strong that the parallel of which we had never seen before. The strong and fierce wind blew thrice. In the first his Majesty the Jibriel came to our help along with one thousand angels. The second time his Majesty the angel Michael came with a similar number of angels and the third time his Majesty the angel Israfiel along with a thousand angels came to our help.

To wit, whenever there arose a need in this world for such an invisible and etheric army either to help the prophets, saints, or other faithful servants of God and to destroy and annihilate the unbelievers and heretics, it was sent to the world in the subtle companionship of a strong wind or ferocious cloud. Hence, it is proved that the subtle carriage of the air is indispensable and highly essential for lowering and sending the spiritual beings to this world. God the Most High speaks of His own descent into this world in company with the subtle cloud. Says the Holy Quran:

هَلْ يَنْظُرُونَ اِلَّا اَنْ يَّاْتِيَهُمُ اللّٰهُ فِیْ ظُلَلٍ مِّنَ الْغَمَامِ وَالْمَلٰٓئِكَةُ وَقُضِیَ الْاَمْرُ ۖ وَاِلَی اللّٰهِ تُرْجَعُ الْاُمُوْرُ ۞ (۲البقرة:۲۱۰)

"Do they await that God should come to them in the shadow of the cloud with angels and the order should be fulfilled and all things return to God?"

When a woman matures and the soil of her body becomes ready, she demands to obtain the human seed from man, and she naturally remains unrestive. Finally, when the seed of human semen drops in the land of her womb, it begins to nourish in the womb of the mother. The child in the womb receives material food in the form of raw blood through the mother out of her food. Through the material food, its elemental body is nourished within, and by this time, it is endowed with the mineral soul, which keeps that piece of flesh safe and alive. Later on, it is nourished and flourished by the vegetable soul, which is put into it. But after about six months, it begins to move and receive its food through the umbilical cord. But no sooner does the child come out of the womb and the human soul of the invisible world is put into it, and it begins to breathe through the air. The wire of respiration is conjoined to him from the esoteric world in the form of an invisible rope. Similarly, through the medium of respiration, the two nostrils of the nose serve as a passage for the positive and negative electric waves of the etheric powerhouse. Moreover, this wire of respiration serves as the connection and medium for human food as well as thoughts, whose chain is connected with the spiritual and etheric powerhouse of the invisible world, and it illuminates and works the entire machinery of the human heart and body. Ponder the construction of the human body: the two nostrils, two ears, two eyes, two lips, two jaws, two hands, two lungs, and two feet serve as passage and medium for the two sorts of electric wires of the five senses to reach the human heart and brain. The human body is as an electric machine in which different kinds of electricities come and go through various electric wires. This machine is for a definite purpose. The object and goal of this physical machine—that is, the life of the soul—is to provide food for the elementary body of itself and its dependence to protect them and to devise and exercise means of their external and worldly material food. Usually, there is an abundance of such common people in the world. But there are some special high, divine people who are endowed with the angelic capacity and aptitude from the day of beginning. The angelic seed that lies dormant in the soul of their hearts turns restless to sprout up and flourish and to obtain the water of management and nourishment and is impatient and restless to obtain the angelic sperm. It finally joins some perfect spiritual man and obtains from him the luminous sperm. Shaikh-ul-Amr and Shaikh-ul-Ilm, etherically, become his spiritual father and mother and are appointed and deputed for his etheric training and spiritual nourishment. This angelic child is tied to his angelic mother through an etheric luminous navel cord, which is called the tie رابطه of spiritualism. He receives his angelic diet and nourishment through this bright navel. On emerging from the material egg, this etheric bird steps in to the endless universe of the spiritual and angelic world, and like the unbounded royal falcon, the two worlds cannot accommodate this splendid bird. With a slight movement of its invisible and etheric wings, it passes beyond the lines of heavens and earth. To him the entire material world is like an egg, and the whole universe is like its nest. The angelic personalities of these chosen and selected servants of God acquire the generous dispositions of angels, as for example the prophet Joseph when he displayed angelic attributes by overcoming the luxurious and carnal sensual passions and avoiding the contemptible act of adultery. For this, the Egyptian women thus praised him. As the Holy Quran says, "They [Egyptian women] said, God protect us it is not a man but a noble angel." Worship and obedience of God and His remembrance and meditation become the food and drink of such angelic people. Some specially selected and most virtuous persons even surpass this stage and supersede the angels in esoteric merit. God the Most High illuminates such perfect gnostics with His own light and blows into them His special spirit. Such selected and blessed personalities are the true caliphate of God on this earth and deputies and apostles of the Prophet and are rightfully called the true descendants of Adam; angels of God bow to them and respect them.

As God the Most High says in the Holy Quran, "And whenWe blew Our spirit in him (Adam), O Angels! fall prostrate beforehim." Just imagine man's gradual progress through the esotericstates and the place that he finally reaches, from mineral tovegetable, from vegetable to animal, and from animal, he reachesthe stage of man and further that of the divine angel. He then ascends even further. This spiritual progress and esoteric change has been thus depicted by Maulana Room in his Masnavi:

از جمادی مُردم و نامی شُدم وزنما مُردم بجیواں سرز دم

مُردم از حیوانی و مردم شُدم پس چہ ترسم کہ زمُردن کم شُدم

جملہٗ دیگر بسیرم از بشر تا بر آرم از ملائک بال و پر

بار دیگر از ملک قُرباں شوم آنچہ اندر وہم ناید آں شوم

(رومی)

"I passed from mineral into vegetative stage and thence in to animal, and I passed from animal into man; I do not fear this emergence. Once more I want to pass from manhood to become an angel. Then I'd forego angelhood and become the unimaginable."

The aforementioned improvements are attained by pious, pure, and holy spirits. Certainly, the unfortunate, miserable, and impure spirits attain degradation. From man, they degrade into animal and from animal into devil, nay, even worse than them. Hence, man possesses the capacities of both good and evil, andhe has been cast into a stupendous trial and examination. Happy is the man who succeeds in this difficult examination.

گہ ناز کند فرشتہ بر پاکیٴ ما گہ دیو کند عار ز ناپاکیٴ ما

ایماں چوں سلامت بہ لبِ گور بریم اَحسنت بریں چستی و چالاکیٴ ما

(ابوالسعید ابوالخیر)

"Sometimes the angels boast of our purity, and sometimes the devil is also ashamed of our evil deeds. If I could safely take my faith to the bank of the grave. Bravo, my alertness and cleverness!"

In support of our commentary narrated earlier and the various grades of human life, we will narrate some observations and experiments of Western spiritualists, which would in all satisfy and appease the Westernized and science-ridden brains of the present age, and in order to show that our statement is in confirmation with both reason and quotation, we privilege the science of today and the past. Briefly, spiritualists have discovered a new wave of the electricity of life, which is technically called an aura. It is a circle of the etheric electricity of life, which surrounds every object. Eminent scientists have accepted it because the aura can be clearly perceived through clairvoyance. They mention different kinds and colors of mineral, vegetable, animal, and human auras. Their details are very long. Through experiments and observation, it has been proved that at the time of sleep, the animal and human aura escapes the body; while the mineral and vegetable auras stay within. At the time of death, the human, animal, and vegetable auras get out of the body one after the other, and only the mineral aura is left behind, which is the aura of dust, and it combines with its homogeneous source (its color is blue). So it is proved that there are all the mineral, vegetable, animal, and human electricities of life in man, and man is the combination of all these. Minerals, vegetables, animals, and mankind emit one, two, three, and four kinds of auras respectively and breathe according to that.

ESOTERIC CONNECTION BETWEEN RESPIRATION AND THOUGHTS IN MAN

Two systems are constantly working in the body of man. One is that of the visible, external breathing and respiration, which continues incessantly, and the second is that of the etheric, internal thoughts, which are also inseparable from man. These two sets of breath and thoughts are constantly attached to and tied with the body and soul of man. These two have a secret connection with each other. Thoughts greatly influence breathing; more than that, breathing is the gateway of thinking. Therefore, ecclesiastical dignitaries and pious men of the past have devised the system of watchfulness on breathing and breath control for commemorating. The philosophy thereof is that it is a special feature of the heart and that it is always thinking of something or is speaking etherically or, in other words, commemorating something. This attribute of commemoration is constantly present and current in his creation and nature because the foundation and nature of man is based on the act of commemorating Allah, His personal name. The fact is that man constantly thinks of or commemorates something. It indicates that the esoteric reality, real nature, true disposition, and temperament of man comes from commemorating His personal name, Allah, which is the origin and mineral of all commemorations.

The names of all objects, along with their commemorations, are the branches and shadows of His personal name, Allah. And His personal name, Allah, is the original source of all worldly objects. Says the Almighty:

وَسَخَّرَ لَكُم مَّا فِي السَّمٰوٰتِ وَمَا فِي الْأَرْضِ جَمِيعًا مِّنْهُ (١٣ الجاثيه: ١٢٥)

"And We captivated for you all that is in heaven and earth through it (that is His name)."

Because all things took creation from His name, when His Holiness Ibn-i-Abbas (be God pleased with him) was asked about the meaning of this verse, he said:

فِي كُلِّ شَيْئٍ اِسْم مِن اِسْمَآئِهِ

"In every thing there is a name from among His names and the name of everything comes from His name."

In a tradition, it is said the spirit entered Adam (peace be upon him) and entered every man by His personal name, Allah الله, and when the spirit entered the person of Adam and found repose in the frontal bone of the brain, it said, "Oh, Allah!" And when the light of the sun of His personal name, Allah, illuminated the mind of Adam, and he looked at that world-illuminating sun, he sneezed. Then he said, "Praise be to Allah!" And from the words "and We blew our spirit therein," it is proved that the spirit was blown into the body of Adam through the air. From the preceding statements, it is evident what an intimate relation, perfect harmony, and strong connection exists between the spirit and commemoration of His personal name, Allah, and between commemoration of all other things of the universe, that is, the thoughts, breath, and respiration. And the methods of watching breath and retaining breath have been devised for the regulation and intensification of this relation. Hence the human soul is founded on the name of Allah and unification, and commemoration of Allah is the source genius of everything. All the things of the universe and their commemoration are its species and branches. When man remembers God, that is, he commemorates His name, he is, as you would say, on his real destination and eternal nature and attentive to and inclined toward his genius. But when he remembers someone besides God—and since this commemoration is transitory, therefore the commemoration and thought of all other objects of the world besides Allah الله are against and opposed to the real attribute of the human heart, it spoils the real attribute and disposition of the heart.

Like a cloud, the commemoration of other things works as a veil for the sun of His personal name, Allah. Being in search of its material and elemental objects (i.e., food and drink and other material necessities), the animal soul always remembers material objects that are other than God, and through the five senses, the animal soul conveys to the mind the memory of all its requirements of material objects and similar sensual desires and worldly things. The commemoration and thoughts of things other than God grapple with the real object and true disposition of the heart, which is the commemoration of His personal name, Allah, and they verify and disturb the true nature of the heart, commemoration of Allah and do not allow the name of Allah to affect the heart. So the philosophy of retention of breath and watchfulness of breathing is that the commemorator and mediator should sit like a watchman at the gate of the heart (i.e., breath and respiration) not to allow any stranger or any thought other than the name of Allah and to keep it as a passage for the real owner of the house (i.e., God the Almighty and his name).

مرا در دل بغیر از دوست چیزے در نمی گنجد 　　　 بخلوت خانہء سلطاں کے دیگر نے گنجد

درونِ قصرِ دل دارم کے شاہے کہ گرگاہے 　　　 ز دل بیروں زند خیمہ بہ بحر و بر نے گنجد

تنت گر ہمچو موئے شد حجاب جاں بودے را 　　　 میانِ عاشق و معشوق موئے در نے گنجد

حساب صد ہزار عاقل بمحشر بگذرد یک دم 　　　 حساب یک دم عاشق بصد محشر نے گنجد

　　　　　　　　　　　　　　　　　　　　　　　　　(خواجہ غریب نواز)

"Nothing abides in my heart except my beloved. None else can dwell in the king's secret palace. Inthe palace of my heart I have a king; who, if heever pitched his tent outside the heart he cannotbe accommodated in the universe. Be your bodyis like a hair, it is a veil to Him (because) No haircan be accommodated between the lover and the beloved. During the resurrection day the accountsof a hundred sages can be dealt with in a moment. But the account of a lover's moment cannot bedealt with in a hundred thousand resurrections."

In relation to the heart, the similitude of the commemoration of His personal name, Allah, and the extraneous thoughts is like this: Say there is a tank in a city in which sweet and pure water sprouts from the earth involuntarily. But the water of the city sewage drains into it through external channels. Irresistibly, the real, sweet, pure, self-spouting water of the tank will become dirty, disturbed, impure, polluted, and foul-smelling on account of the inflow of the external, dirty, and impure water. If the dirty, impure water of the dirty drains is allowed to pour into the tank for some time, its filthy dregs and dirt will settle in the bottom of the tank and close its original spouting springs, and the fine, sweet tank will be converted into a dirty, impure ditch; those who drink of it will fall ill and die. Exactly the same is the case of the human heart. The name of Allah and His commemoration is like the original, pure, and sweet springs sprouting from within, and the memories of those besides God and sensual thoughts are the dark sources of blackness that fall into the pure spring of life of the heart through the channels of the five senses. Like the dirty and polluted water, they make the elixir of the heart, namely the commemoration of Allah, foul and dirty and later on put an end to it. Therefore, when the inlets of the heart are guarded from these foul channels of external thoughts and the heart is allowed to commemorate the name of Allah in accordance with its original attribute and disposition, the invisible and etheric springs of commemoration of Allah invariably spring up in such a heart, and the secrets of the truth are revealed to such a commemorator.

چشم بند و گوش بند و لب بہ بند   گر نہ بینی سر حق بر ما بخند

(رومی)

Cover the eyes, ears, and lips; if you miss the divine truth, then ridicule me.

Aloofness and determination are essential for concentration on one's idea and thoughts, as are spiritual guidance and cordial might. All spiritual progress depends on it, and etheric travel is based thereon. According to a general rule and well-known principle, the unification and concentration of thoughts and reflections are instrumental in increasing cordial might and esoteric power, and the dispersal and diversification of ideas cause weakness of the heart. When the rays of the sun pass through a lens pitched on a point, they gather so much heat as to burn a cloth or a similar thing. If the same rays are made to pass through the lens diffused and spread up, they lack that heat. Therefore, attention and inclination toward unitarianism is, so to say, increasing the power and might of the heart and directing it toward the immeasurable vastness of the material world to decrease it. Says the Almighty Allah:

ءَاَرْبَابٌ مُّتَفَرِّقُوْنَ خَيْرٌ اَمِ اللّٰهُ الْوَاحِدُ الْقَهَّارُ ۩ (۱۲ يوسف: ۳۹)

"Is it better to have multiple material deities or to have a single omnipotent Allah?" In all religious performances and actions and theological fundamentals, Islam and Islamic mysticism lay stress on the intention of the heart, singleness of purpose, and unitarianism and corroborate and vindicate them. Tradition says, "Man's actions are counted with his intentions" (i.e., the discordance and acceptance and faultiness and soundness of actions depend on intention). This means that if at the time of doing any good deed, your intention is to obey and please God only, it is acceptable, but if the intention in doing an action is directed and inclined toward material and sensual objects, that action is unacceptable and contemptible in the eyes of God. It is therefore said:

$$\text{لَا صَلٰوةَ اِلَّا بِحُضُورِ الْقَلْب}$$

"No prayer except with the presence of mind is acceptable" (i.e., no prayer is correct and right unless the heart is present with God at the time of the prayer). Likewise, in all Islamic fundamentals, it is necessary and indispensable for the heart to be inclined and directed toward God, so that in every act and performance, the heart should be inclined toward God and steepedand engrossed in His concentration and meditation. This causes the aloofness and unity of the heart and the centralization of its etheric senses (i.e., concentration, meditation on a single point) and centers the name of Allah and its commemoration. The same is the cause of the intensifying etheric might of the heart and the power of the spirit. And this is the object and goal of Islamic unitarianism and the purpose of religious and spiritual acts that can be termed "religious concentration."

The yogis, mesmerists, hypnotists, and spiritualists also exercise the concentration and meditation on an imaginary and whimsical dot and thereby implement their etheric powers. The nucleus of concentration of Islamic religion and spiritualism is the name of Allah, the personal name of God, which is the beginning and end of all the universe and creation and which has relation and connection with the unending, imperishable, priceless, and unparalleled Creator and potent essence of Allah, but in yoga and mesmerism, on account of concentration on an imaginary brilliant object or dot, the operator cannot go beyond that dot or his own self. Therefore, the act of the Hindu yogi or mesmerist and spiritualist is confined to the lowest and nearest sphere of the material world. Contrarily, the concentrator on the word Allah, His personal name, has a very wide, endless, and unlimited space of progress. The most important and essential fundamental recitation of Islam and Islamic Sufiism, without reciting which one can neither become a Muslim nor traverse the path of Sufiism, is the reciting of "Kalima لَا إِلَهَ إِلَّا اللّٰه," which means that none is worshipable except God the Allah (i.e., to cast out of the heart allthe false gods and temporary desires for perishable objects and to establish and affirm in the heart the commemoration and thought of a single, real, true, worshipable Master). This is the real purpose of our religion, and spiritualists and everything depend on it.

We have already discussed the intimate connection between cordial thoughts and breath or respiration. The heart of a real gnostic is like a garden, and when the breath passes over it, like the morning breeze, it comes out laden with the sweet odor of the commemoration of the name of Allah and wraps it in heavenly clothes, the angels of Allah take it to the court of Allah as a most precious gift from the gnostic commemorator, and that breath is stored for the gnostic as a priceless jewel in his treasury of the next world. And the breath of the gnostic commemorator that comes back is replied with divine favor and bounty of compassion and kindness. This breath may be called a reward from God the Almighty for that gift of commemoration, and it pours the showers of lights of God's favor and felicity on the heart of the gnostic man and revives the garden of the heart of the commemorator. In the space of the hearts, when the breath of such perfect men of God strike against some alike and sensitive hearts, it also imparts sweet odor to that heart from its own sweet breeze. How well has someone said:

ستم است اگر ہوست کشد کہ بسیر سرو سمن درآ   تو زغنچۂ کم نہ دمیدۂ در دل کشا بجمن درآ

بے نافہ ہائے رمیدہ بو مپسند زحمتِ جستجو   بخیال از سر زلف اوگر ہے کشا بختن درآ

(بیدل کانپوری)

"It is a pity if desire drags you to visit the garden and see flowers therein. You yourself have not blossomed less than the bud; come and open the door of your heart and enter your garden. Suffer no search for musk-pods and their vast spreading smell. Untie a knot from the tipoy of His tresses in imagination and enter the City of Khutan."

In contrast, the heart of a dead-hearted, materialist, sinner, polytheistic, and heretical man is full of worldly and material impurities and filth, like a latrine, when the destructive, foul smelling breath of such a man emerges from the stench of his heart, it is like a bomb full of poisonous Satanic gas, which is stored in the magazine of the devil and issues thence with avarice, greed, envy, pride, lust, and similar evil effects. The heart that such a breath strikes is rendered poisoned, stenchful, and sick and is ultimately deprived of its good odor.

In short, when a man breathes, the breath comes out with the smell and attribute of his heart and spirit, and the thoughts and attributes of the man breathing are found out from his breath. Therefore, when a man commemorates God with his tongue or worships Him with the external organs of his body only, while his heart is busy with its undivine material thoughts and ideas, such a commemoration and worship has no value or weight with God because God only looks at the heart of the commemorator and worshipper, not to his words and the actions of his body only.

إِنَّ اللّٰهَ لَا يَنْظُرُ إِلٰى اَجْسَامِكُمْ وَلَا إِلٰى صُوَرِكُمْ وَلٰكِنْ يَنْظُرُ إِلٰى قُلُوْبِكُمْ وَنِيَّاتِكُمْ (مسلم)

Tradition says, "God does not behold your figure nor actions but peers through your heart and intentions."

بر زباں اللہ و در دل گاؤ خر   ایں چنیں تسبیح کے دارد اثر

"Allah on your tongue and cow and ass in your heart—how can such recitation be effective and approved of?" When the human body is engaged in performing the prayer and his heart is busy with his worldly affairs, his prayer is not acceptable.

دل پریشان و مصلی در نماز   ایں نمازے کے پزیرد بے نیاز
(رومی)

"When the heart is in the shop and the body in the mosque, how can such prayer be acceptable near One Who is all sight and wisdom?" Briefly, the living-minded gnostic can read and discern the quality of man's heart from the etheric and electric wave of his heart (i.e., from the air of his breath). Because, when a man thinks of something or commemorates or remembers somebody, he is, so to say, speaking etherically and esoterically, and this is the voice of his mind, which produces waves and billows in the etheric and esoteric atmosphere, and its circle spreads and passes more rapidly than electricity and even more rapidly than our thoughts through the esoteric atmosphere. That voice contacts and touches every heart and mind and things likewise esoteric that come within its circle. Only the alert, living, and sensitive mind hears that sound. But stiff, inanimate minds, which are solid like stones cannot hear or feel such voices, nor can they see esoteric seances. This esoteric sensation is called telepathy or mind-reading. The holy prophets and the great saints possess this faculty in its high state and full perfection. As for example, when the brothers of Joseph the Prophet set off with the caravan, taking the shirt of Joseph to Kina'n, and then Jacob (Peace be upon him) immediately by his knowledge of mind-reading and telepathy informed his family before hand,

اِنِّیْ لَاَجِدُ رِیْحَ یُوْسُفَ لَوْلَاۤ اَنْ تُفَنِّدُوْنِ ۝ (یوسف: ۹۴)

"I feel the air and receive the smell of Joseph, if you do not befool me."

Prophet Muhammad (peace be upon him) occasionally turned his face to the Yaman and used to say, "I feel the air of God from Yaman," where his lover and devoted Awais Qarni lived. In both these quotations, the word *air* signifies that there is a deep connection between the air and the human heart, the mind and its thoughts. It is also important to explain, at this juncture, that some people think that esoteric revelation of this kind is granted to prophets and saints by God the Almighty for a special important occasions, but this conception is erroneous. Just as in this world, we permanently possess material sensations whereby we can sense and feel material objects when and where we like, similarly God the Almighty permanently bestows esoteric and etheric senses to His special obedient servants as a gift they can utilize when and where they like and wish and profit thereby. But it is quite a different thing that God the Almighty wisely conceals something from His obedient and accepted servants on some occasions. Just as the master of the house keeps something concealed from the inmates of the house or advisedly keeps some affairs secret from them, or sometimes the man looks in one direction, and the objects of the opposite side are concealed from his sight. There lies a difference between the contingent and eternal. The ambit of the sight and feelings of man, whether high sighted, great prophets or benign saints, is always limited, no matter how magnificent and purified a prophet or a saint may be, and it reaches near God and unites with Him to obtain eternity with Him. It is always branded with the blemish of the weakness of the elementary body. This blemish of elementary creation cannot be washed off from him anywhere, and God always remains God and the servant remains the servant. But the special servants of the Protector occasionally receive manifestations of His person, attributes, names, and acts, and in accordance with their status and the capacity of their esoteric utensils, they derive the reflection of His lights. Therefore, in that special state, the special servant of God can be termed God-like, and their special act and performance can be called the special act and performance of God, but the term man can never be applied to God the Almighty. It is a very secret thing to understand; hence it is said in the Holy Quran:

لَقَدْ كَفَرَ الَّذِيْنَ قَالُوْۤا اِنَّ اللّٰهَ هُوَالْمَسِيْحُ ابْنُ مَرْيَمَ (۵ المائده ۱۷:۱۷)

"Verily they are infidels who say that Allah is Messiah—the son of Mary."

God the Almighty has come in the human shape and form of the Messiah. Contrarily, it is now here right if it were put thus: "Filled with divine light and the holy spirit, Messiah the son of Mary performed divine." There is tremendous difference between the two beliefs. The former people like Hindus, Christians, and other religions believe in such erroneous dogmas and wrong theories and say that God sometimes descends to the earth and takes human form and shape, but the Islamic theosophy believes in the faith, which is evident from this tradition of Sahih Bukhari:

يَتَقَرَّبُ الْعَبْدُ اِلَيَّ بِالنَّوَافِلِ حَتّٰى اَكُوْنَ عَيْنَيْهِ يَنْظُرُ بِيْ وَ اُذْنَيْهِ يَسْمَعُ بِيْ وَاَيْدِيْهِ الَّتِيْ

يَبْطِشُ بِيْ وَلِسَانَهُ الَّذِيْ يَنْطِقُ بِيْ (الخ) بخارى

"An obedient servant of God approaches the God Almighty through good acts and virtuous deeds until He becomes his eyes, ears, hands and tongue and he sees, hears, catches and talks through Him."

In the magnificent Quran too, there are verses similar to this tradition. Says the Almighty:

$$وَمَا يَنْطِقُ عَنِ الْهَوٰى ۚ اِنْ هُوَ اِلَّا وَحْىٌ يُّوْحٰى ۚ (۵۳ النجم: ۳-۴)$$

"He (the Prophet) does not talk out of lust but according to the revelation revealed by God to him."

In another place, the Almighty says:

$$وَمَا رَمَيْتَ اِذْ رَمَيْتَ وَلٰكِنَّ اللّٰهَ رَمٰى ۚ (۸ الانفال: ۱۷)$$

"And you (O Prophet) did not throw pebbles when you threw them but it was Allah the Almighty who threw them."

And in another place says the Almighty in the Holy Quran:

$$اِنَّ الَّذِيْنَ يُبَايِعُوْنَكَ اِنَّمَا يُبَايِعُوْنَ اللّٰهَ ۚ يَدُ اللّٰهِ فَوْقَ اَيْدِيْهِمْ$$

"Those who swear allegiance to you do not but swear allegiance to Allah; the hand of God is over their hands." Hence faith of this nature is true and correct according to Quranic verses and the traditions, as Maulana Room says in his Masnavi:

گفتهٔ او گفتهُ اللّٰه بود   گرچہ از حلقومِ عبداللّٰہ بود
ہر کہ خواہد ہم نشینی با خُدا   اُو نشیند در حضورِ اولیاء
اَولیاء اللّٰہ و اللّٰہ اَولیاء   ہیچ فرقے درمیاں نہ بود روا

"His word is the word of Allah. Be it on the tongue of his servant. Whoever desires communication with Allah, say him to sit in company of saints. Saints are all God-like; and God is with saints there is no difference and separation between them." As someone says:

مردانِ خُدا خُدا نہ باشند   لیکن ز خُدا جُدا نہ باشند

"Though men of God are not God but they are no apart from Him."

Another poet says it like this:

Do not call Adam—God; Adam is not God. But Adam is not apart from the light of God.

In connection with His Holiness Jacob the Prophet's discovering and feeling the smell of Joseph's shirt from Egypt, it is also worth mentioning, because some people think that Jacob had absolutely no knowledge of his son, Joseph. If he had any knowledge, why did not he go and pull him up from the well in Kina'n? Now the fact is that Jacob had certainly this much knowledge about Joseph that he had not been killed by the wolves but was alive.

Therefore, giving lie to the false pretension of his sons, he said, "Rather you have fabricated a lie for you." And on the second occasion, while sending his sons to Egypt to fetch grain, he advised them thus: "O my sons! Go and search for Joseph and his brother and do not despair of the mercy of God." And he also added, "It is easy for Allah to give them both back to me." In spite of the knowledge of the unknown and esoteric revelation, Jacob remained fearful and hesitating partly because of his human weakness and partly because he was afraid of God's trial of his patience and endurance; therefore, he continued repeating, "Patience is a praiseworthy act." For otherwise, he always used to talk about Joseph in his family, saying, "Now he is in such a place and in such a state and doing such a job." His sons used to attribute his talk to madness and melancholy, though it was his true revelation. This affair of the examination of Jacob was exactly like that of the mother of His Holiness Moses the Prophet, when God the Almighty revealed to his mother telling her that she should put the baby in the box and put it in the river along with which He promised, "We will return him to you and make him a Prophet." But in spite of the true revelation and esoteric insight, her heart remained uneasy and impatient. As says the Almighty, "The heart of Moses's mother was so impatient that she would have divulged everything if We had not strengthened her heart to make her a believer in God."

Therefore, in spite of true revelation and esoteric insight, prophets and saints entertain anxiety and fear because of their human weakness. The blemish of human weakness can never be removed from man, and this is what distinguishes a servant from the Master and the worshipper from the Worshipped. If the special servants of God had not been advised of esoteric knowledge, why does God the Almighty speak thus through the tongue of Jesus in the noble Quran, "I can tell you what you eat and what you store in your houses."

Hence, you must not conjecture the selected men of God to be like yourselves. As his Holiness Maulana Room Sahib says:

کار پاکاں راقیاس از خود مگیر   گرچہ باشد در نوشتن شیر و شیر

آں یکے شیر است کہ مردم را درد   ویں دگر شیر است کش مردم خورد

گر بصورت آدمی انساں بدے   احمد و بوجہل ہم یکساں بدے

"Conjecture not the deeds of the pious men in your own manner though the word Sher (to mean Tiger) resembles "Shir" (Milk) in writing the one means man-tearing tiger, while the other means milk that man drinks. If only the body of flesh could mean men, Ahmad the Prophet and Abujehl the atheist might have been alike."

Hence, in commemoration, the real act lies with the mind and heart. External figures and mere verbal commemoration are valueless. Many people are engaged in verbal utterances all the night long, while their minds and hearts are absolutely unaware of what they are uttering. There are, however, perfect gnostics who do not move even their tongue in commemorating and reciting the name of Allah at all, but their mind and heart is fully and completely engaged with Allah.

بدل مذکر حق باش ورنہ طوطی ہم   بصوت و حرف خدا را کریم سے گوید

"Commemorate the name of Allah within your heart and mind. Otherwise a parrot too can recite His name with its tongue."

Every breath of the pure and pious gnostic is a spiritual and etheric message of love toward God and divine craving which reaches the holy court of God like a telegram or a wireless wave message and narrates there without sound and letters the loving state and affection of the commemorator. When the breath returns, it brings back the light of God and His blessings to the commemorator. Thus the telephone of remembrance exchanges between the servant commemorating and the Lord, the commemorated. As says the Almighty:

فَاذْكُرُوْنِيْ أَذْكُرْكُمْ (٢ البقرة : ١٥٢)

"Remember Me and I will in return remember thee."

And at another place, it says:

رَضِيَ اللّٰهُ عَنْهُمْ وَرَضُوْا عَنْهُ (٥ المآئدة : ١١٩)

"God is pleased and appeased with them and they are also pleased and appeased with Him."

And this is another like utterance in the Holy Quran:

يُّحِبُّهُمْ وَيُحِبُّوْنَهٗ (٥ المآئدة : ٥٤)

"They love God and God loves them." So thus in every breath the message of commemoration, the telephone of appeasement, and the wireless message of love are exchanged between the obedient-servant and the kind Master. If man remembers only once the name of God in mind, it is far better than remembering Him "with" the tongue a thousand times. A poet, Mir Sahib, says:

ہر چند کہ طاعت میں ہوا ہے تو پیر یہ بات مری سن کہ نہیں بے تاثیر

تسبیح بکف پھرنے سے کیا کام چلے منکے کی طرح من نہ پھرے جب تک میّر

"Though you are grown old in worship, but bear in mind my word; which is very valuable. Nothing can be gained by carrying the rosary in hand and moving; unless your heart within is moved like a bead."

Once upon a time, I was retiring in a mosque to perform etikaf, during the last ten days of the holy month of Ramadan. There was another man also in the mosque sitting for his performance of the etikaf. He kept awake all the night and uttered "Allah, Allah" until morning and did not sleep a moment. When I saw this, I went and said to him, "O man of Allah, what are you doing and saying all the night long?" He said that his spiritual guide had commanded him to repeat and utter the name of Allah twelve thousand times every night. "I have been doing this for ten years regularly." I asked him if he had received any fruit of light or observation or anything like that in the long course of ten years. He replied, "No, nothing have I felt or received of the kind, but I am performing and obeying the word of my guide and master, and the day this order is fulfilled, my heart feels happy within and I am satisfied."

I said to the poor fellow, "Your labor is very hard, but it is fruitless and valueless." It was a pitiful state. Thus thousands of people like him practice ill-placed and unsystematic hard work and devotion without any use or benefit. As the Almighty says:

"They gain nothing except toil and tiresomness."

God the Almighty is alive, and He can hear and see. He is also very near and responsive. He is "not a solid stone idol, that when man calls Him, "O Allah, He should not respond and reply thus: "Here I am, O my obedient servant!" There is no reason that a man may worship Him sincerely and honestly, and in spite of being independent, merciful, and bountiful, He should not favor him with reward and prize. The commemoration, meditation, prayer, devotion, charity, and alms that do not yield immediate effect and result and if the man receives no sign of information through revelation or in sleep from God the Almighty, one must understand that the prayers and devotion performed or the charity and alms given in His name have not been accepted, and some shortcoming or defect has taken place in conditions and requisites of the performance. So for every action and devotion, the pious saints of God receive from Him diverse kinds of tidings and invisible signs. As says the Almighty:

اِنَّ الَّذِيْنَ قَالُوْا رَبُّنَا اللهُ ثُمَّ اسْتَقَامُوْا تَتَنَزَّلُ عَلَيْهِمُ الْمَلٰٓئِكَةُ اَلَّا تَخَافُوْا وَلَا تَحْزَنُوْا وَ اَبْشِرُوْا بِالْجَنَّةِ الَّتِيْ كُنْتُمْ تُوْعَدُوْنَ ۞ نَحْنُ اَوْلِيٰٓؤُكُمْ فِي الْحَيٰوةِ الدُّنْيَا وَفِي الْاٰخِرَةِ

(حٰم السجدة ٣٠:٣١-٣١)

"Those who said, our protector and master is Allah and stick to it, We send them Our angels, who inform them not to fear or worry and give them tidings of the Paradise which is promised to them and say, We are your friends in this world and the next."

Man ought to consider that the presence of mind and heart is necessary in devotion, submission, invocation, commemoration, and meditation. He may be careful and watchful in his breath so that no breath may escape and come out without the remembrance and commemoration and meditation of Allah, because the breath that comes out with the thought and commemoration of Allah is turned into a priceless jewel and stored for the commemorator in His treasury of the next world.

هر دم که می رود نفس از عمر گو هریست   کا نزا خراج عمر دو عالم بود بها

(حافظ)

"Every outgoing breath is a jewel of life more precious than the wealth of the whole world", because the breath that is gone out can never return on any payment and is lost forever and the breath which is to come in future may come or not. In short, the breath of the past and that of the future are both out of our control, and we are only the masters of the breath that is at present in our hands. If this breath of the present bears with it the name and thought of Allah, then be sure that it has become a very precious ethereal jewel, by which you can buy the prosperity and wealth of both worlds. A poet says,

Trust no future however pleasant

Let the dead past bury its dead

Act in the living present

Here within and God overhead

But if this breath goes out in carelessness and negligence, be sure that it was not mere air that escaped your mouth but a heavy mountain of eternal misery and incessant misfortune that will befall you in the next world. Therefore, man should value his breath.

نگهدار دم را که عالم دے است   دے پیش دانا به از عالمے است

سکندر که بر عالمے حکم داشت   در آن دم که بگذشت عالم گذاشت

(سعدی)

"Watch the breath for your world lies in your breath. For a wise sage a breath excels the wealth of the universe. Alexander the Great who once ruled the world, left the world when he left and discharged his last breath."

It is said that a saint, along with his students and disciples, came across some graves. He there uttered some prayers for the dead and afterward attended to their condition in meditation. After a moment of meditation, he drew out a sorrowful sigh and fell in tears. His disciples asked him as to what was the matter. He said that the spirits of these graves were such obedient people of God who had been very pious and had devoted their whole lives to the obedience of God. Now they were so sorry about some moments they had lost in their lives in the negligence and carelessness that if the sorrow and regret of one inmate of the grave is brought out and distributed in the hearts of you all, by God, you will all turn mad and insane. In short, after death, a man is not sorry for having left behind his beloved children, dear wife, brothers, sisters, friends, acquaintances, property, wealth, beloved country, and home. When he comes to know that in the market of the next world no other coin is currency except the commemoration, remembrance, devotion, and worship of God and no object can be achieved without this genuine coin, then if he is sorry for anything, he is sorry for having lost those golden and precious moments of the valuable life and those golden rings of the chain of respiration in every breath of which the real objective jewel of life was strung. Alas! Twenty-four thousand breaths are taken in a day and night, and every breath carries chances of proximity, observation, and unity with God, but not a single one of them can return. Alas, the carelessness and foolishness! Lost is the key now by which could unlock the gate of God the Almighty.

دلا تو غافلی از کار خویش و مے ترسم   کہ کس درت نہ کشاید چو مے کنی مفتاح

"O heart! You are unmindful and careless of your duty, and I am afraid that none will open you the door if you lose the key."

In short, the value and price of this valuable life and its golden breaths will be apprehended after death, when it is lost and the foolish, careless man will cry aloud, "Alas for what I wasted in getting near to God and verily I am one of the great losers." Therefore, O dear ones, think highly of the few breaths and moments left to you in this world. Even if one of these is spent in remembrance of God, it is preferable to the kingdom of the whole world! As Khaquani, a truthful poet, has said:

پس از سی سال این معنی محقق شد بخاقانی

کہ یک دم با خدا بودن بہ از ملکِ سلیمانی

"After thirty years of meditation Khaquani learnt the point that a moment with God. Far better than the kingdom of Solomon the Prophet."

O man of God! Understand and meditate. Do not waste these valuable jewels of your breath in useless engagements of play and sport. Else, you will repent bitterly. The real object of human life is devotion and obedience to the command of the Protector. As God says:

$$وَمَا خَلَقْتُ الْجِنَّ وَالْإِنْسَ اِلَّا لِيَعْبُدُونِ ۞ (١٥ الزاريات:٥٦)$$

"And We did not create Jinn and Man except to worship Us."

It is evident from this divine tradition that the object of human life is to know and reveal the essence of God. As tradition says:

$$كُنْتُ كَنْزًا مَّخْفِيًا فَأَرَدْتُّ اَنْ اُعْرَفَ فَخَلَقْتُ الْخَلَقَ$$

"I was a hidden treasure; when I intended to be known, I created man."

Also on the day of beginning, God the Almighty addressed the spirits of the whole world and said:

$$اَلَسْتُ بِرَبِّكُمْ (٧ الاعراف:١٧٢)$$

"Am I not your Lord the Creator?"

From this oral question of God the Almighty, it is evident that His commemoration and devotion to His obedience is the chief object of human life. Some ignorant and materialistic blind people regard the search for wealth and the acquisition of the livelihood of this world as the real object of life and devotion and utter that to serve man is to serve God. The offering of prayers, fasting, reciting the Quran, commemoration, meditation, and devotion to His obedience is regarded by them as a waste of time and imitation of monasticism. But God the Almighty has loudly repudiated their claim in the second line of the previous verse, saying that "We did not create jinn and men but to worship Us." It is clearly added:

$$مَا أُرِيْدُ مِنْهُمْ مِّنْ رِّزْقٍ وَّمَا أُرِيْدُ اَنْ يُّطْعِمُوْنِ ۞ اِنَّ اللهَ هُوَ الرَّزَّاقُ ذُو الْقُوَّةِ الْمَتِيْنُ ۞$$
$$(١٥ الذاريات: ٥٧-٥٨)$$

"We do not intend that they should provide Us livelihood or feed My servants; but Allah Himself is the sustainer of His people and He possesses great strength."

This means that He is not unable to feed all the creation, whether animals, birds, jinn, or man.

تا تُو نانے بکف آری و یہ غفلت نہ خوری ابر و باد و مہ و خرشید و فلک در کاراند

شرط الصاف نہ باشد کہ تو فرماں نہ بری ہمہ از بہرِ تو سرگشتہ و فرماں بردار

(سعدی)

"The cloud, wind, moon, sun, and stars all are at work. That you may acquire livelihood and may not eat it carelessly; All are busy and obedient for you; It is injustice if you do not obey your Lord the Creator."

God the Almighty has appointed all the universe to feed and nourish the jinn and men, but He has created them only for His devotion. Solely, as He says:

$$\text{خَلَقَ لَكُمْ مَّا فِى الْاَرْضِ جَمِيْعًا}$$

"I have created for you all that is in the earth and heaven."

فکرِ ما در کار ما آزار ماست کار ساز ما بِفکرِ کار ماست

(رومی)

"God the Almighty takes care of our affairs." Our reflection and taking care in our affairs is our own trouble.

$$\text{وَمَا مِنْ دَآبَّةٍ فِى الْاَرْضِ اِلَّا عَلَى اللّٰهِ رِزْقُهَا (هود ٦:١١)}$$

God says, "And there is not a living being on the earth but God provides its food." We have already said before that the spirit was puffed into man through air. When the spirit entered the body of Adam, it said, "Allah."

Therefore, the foundation of man's disposition and creation is laid on the light of His name, Allah, to revert and incline to its origin, to harmonize with its true nature, and to carry itself to its origin (i.e., to reach God the Almighty through commemoration of His name).

Reciting Allah is its true natural act and real object. The constant thought of something and continuation of thoughts and commemoration in man is due to the name Allah. And the light of the name Allah and its commemoration has been placed in human nature as a seed and trust. Man is naturally tied to his Creator and Master through this hidden and esoteric bond and invisible string. Therefore, in all the religions and specially in Islam, all fundamentals and legal acts (i.e., prayers, fasting, Hajj, alms, and the profession of faith) depend upon the name Allah and its commemoration.

Tradition says, "At the time of birth, the nature of every child is Islamic." The following statement of God the Almighty also indicates this:

$$\text{فَأَقِمْ وَجْهَكَ لِلدِّينِ حَنِيفًا ۚ فِطْرَتَ اللهِ الَّتِي فَطَرَ النَّاسَ عَلَيْهَا ۚ لَا تَبْدِيلَ لِخَلْقِ اللهِ ۚ}$$
$$\text{ذَٰلِكَ الدِّينُ الْقَيِّمُ ۚ وَلَٰكِنَّ أَكْثَرَ النَّاسِ لَا يَعْلَمُونَ ﴿٣٠﴾ (الروم: ٣٠)}$$

"So turn your face toward the orthodox religion. It is the nature provided by God, and He created man in this natural religion. The nature of all is unchangeable. This is the steadfast religion, but the majority of people do not understand."

In short, Islam is a special, true, original, and really Unitarian religion. The seed whereof was placed in the nature and essence of man as a trust by God the Almighty on the day of beginning. To keep this original deposit in fact is termed Islam, and to keep this eternal trust safe and sound is real orthodoxy. This nature is referred to in the following tradition:

$$\text{كُلُّ مَوْلُودٍ يُولَدُ عَلَى فِطْرَةِ الْإِسْلَامِ وَأَبَوَاهُ يُهَوِّدَانِهِ أَوْ يُنَصِّرَانِهِ أَوْ يُمَجِّسَانِهِ ۔}$$

"Every baby is born according to Islamic nature, but the parents make them Jews, Christians, or Magians."

People place the yoke of their ancestral and imitative religion on the necks of their children, and the parents so turn them polytheists. This is the greatest trick and deception of Satan that he disfigures the real religious eternal nature of man. As says the Almighty:

$$\text{وَقَالَ لَأَتَّخِذَنَّ مِنْ عِبَادِكَ نَصِيبًا مَّفْرُوضًا ﴿١١٨﴾}$$

وَّ لَاُضِلَّنَّهُمْ وَ لَاُمَنِّيَنَّهُمْ وَ لَاٰمُرَنَّهُمْ فَلَيُبَتِّكُنَّ اٰذَانَ الْاَنْعَامِ وَ لَاٰمُرَنَّهُمْ فَلَيُغَيِّرُنَّ خَلْقَ اللّٰهِ ۚ وَمَنْ يَّتَّخِذِ الشَّيْطٰنَ وَلِيًّا مِّنْ دُوْنِ اللّٰهِ فَقَدْ خَسِرَ خُسْرَانًا مُّبِيْنًا ۞

(النساء: ١١٨-١١٩)

"(Shaetan) said I will get hold of a large portion of Thy servants and turn them astray and subdue them and command them. They will cut the ears of animals and I will command them so they will change the nature of creatures."

The inborn and true religious nature and eternal disposition of man referred to in the verse "Allah's nature is that which man follows" and the tradition "every child is born in the nature of Islam" are evident. This nature is discernible in the nature and senses of the child in its early life. Therefore, the child views every object of the universe in its real nature. Longing for this natural view, some divine persons have prayed thus, "O God, show us the things in their real nature." Therefore, everyone seems to be craving and desiring for the pleasant, beautiful, and picturesque time of childhood. As long as the man is an innocent child, his soul is, so to say, entitled to paradise, the eternal legacy of his father, Adam. Hence streams of milk and honey are made to flow for him from the breasts of his mother. But no sooner does he approach the forbidden tree and begin to partake of wheat then the doors of his natural and eternal paradise are closed on him. Therefore, remembrance and commemoration of Allah is the real and eternal nature of the child. That is why the call to prayers, "Allah o' Akbar, Allah o' Akbar," is pronounced in the ear of every Muslim child at the time of his birth, and he is thus coaxed and conveyed toward his real eternal nature by reminding him of the name of God and commemoration of Allah. In other words, the water of life of Allah's name is sprinkled on the seed of the baby's nature to revert him to his real origin that is the name of Allah in this world. So in the time of death, the name and commemoration of Allah is again uttered and he is reminded when the bird of his soul and spirit is about to fly from the cage of the body, so that he may take the direction of his true destination and real abode of Allah's name and may not be led astray from the right path of Islam by Satan. This is the reason assigned by a tradition to the weeping of a human soul at the time of birth and death. The devil attacks him in order to destroy his real religious nature of remembering the name of Allah and leads him astray from the right path of Islam. The chief enemy of mankind, Satan, makes two vigorous attacks one at the commencement of the life of this world and one at that of the next, to plunder away from man the true jewel of the object life (i.e., the remembrance and commemoration of the name of Allah). Therefore, the poor child of soul and spirit weeps at the time of birth and death:

طفل می گرید چو راه خانہ را گم می کند   چوں نہ گریم من کہ صاحب خانہ را گم کردہ ام

"The child having lost the way to home weeps bitterly, Why should not I, having lost the Master of my home, weep day and night?"

COMPARISON OF SCIENCE AND RELIGION

How ignorant and blind are the people who do not know the value, price, and importance of the name Allah. They assert that it merely invites and leads man toward the word *Allah*, which is a nondescript thing. That is say that religion teaches monasticism, inertia, and idleness, which is a waste of time and suspension of the organs and energies granted and given by the Omnipotent and nature. Contrarily, science invites man toward action and observation of the universe and creation of God the Almighty, which is the main and chief object of life. The materialists and scientists assert that science provides means of comfort and is the cause of progress and welfare of all mankind, while religion stands for ineffective and meaningless works like ablutions, prayers, fasts, reading and reciting the Quran, the pilgrimage or Hajj, almsgiving, commemoration, devotion, and so on, which can render no solid and material gain, except mere waste of time. In short, the people of God are held back, discouraged, and deprived of the devotion, gnosis, nearness, union, and observation of their Creator and real Master, by declaring such innumerable, unprofitable, and absurd lies against religion and spiritualism.

Worldly wealth is a highly deceptive toy in the hand of Satan, whereby he occupies and charms childlike persons in play and sport (i.e., the desires and ambitions of the short, limited life of this material world) and deprives them of and distracts them from the eternal life and real and true etherical pleasures and joys of the next world.

Truly speaking, the name of Allah—His commemoration, devotion, and worship—is the only key to the felicity and pleasures of this world and the world beyond and the exclusive means and source of the unlimited eternal life and continuous pleasure and wealth of the world hereafter because His personal name, Allah, is the cause of creation of the entire universe. This pure name is the origin and destination of the creation. Alas, in the pitch-black and dark night of the whimsical, temporary, brief, and fleeting life, the materialists, sensualists, and dead-minded people are enjoying the deep dream of carelessness under the dirty quilt of the material body and are deeply engrossed in the talismanic world of dream and fancy, careless and unaware of the permanent and eternal pleasures of that true, resplendent, alert, and etherical world, which is the high object and real goal of human life. All the material wealth and its knowledge and the endeavor of labor and exertion for the material, perishable pleasures is merely playing with dust like children, unprofitable and fruitless acquisition. Says the Almighty:

فَاَعْرِضْ عَنْ مَّنْ تَوَلّٰى ۙ عَنْ ذِكْرِنَا وَلَمْ يُرِدْ اِلَّا الْحَيٰوةَ الدُّنْيَا ۙ ذٰلِكَ مَبْلَغُهُمْ مِّنَ الْعِلْمِ ۙ اِنَّ رَبَّكَ هُوَ اَعْلَمُ بِمَنْ ضَلَّ عَنْ سَبِيْلِهٖ وَهُوَ اَعْلَمُ بِمَنِ اهْتَدٰى ۙ (۵۳ النجم:۲۹-۳۰)

"Turn your face from the person who recedes from commemorating Us and intends not except material wealth. This is the reach of his knowledge. Your Lord knows very well those who are astray from His path and he knows those that are rightly directed."

لذّات جہاں چشیدہ باشی ہمہ عمر   بایار خود آرمیدہ باشی ہمہ عمر
چوں آخرِ عمر زیں جہاں باید رفت   خوابے باشد کہ دیدہ باشی ہمہ عمر
(خیام)

"Suppose you have enjoyed the pleasures of this material world through your whole life, and lifelong you have reposed with your beloved; since you quit this world at last, all your pleasures and enjoyments will seem [like a] dream."

Granted that the material talisman of science and the false magic of matter have astonished the world today. Every day, we see that through science, man is flying in the clouds, running on the ground on the horses of wood and iron, swimming and floating in rivers and seas like fish, and hearing the talk of East and West in a moment. Though science has discovered such useful objects, providing means of material comfort and luxury in the world for a few days' life, beside that, science has created many earthquaking and mountain-breaking, dreadful and dangerous instruments of war for the destruction of mankind. It is therefore not unlikely that science, which is regarded as Mecha'eel, the angel of mercy and rain, may one day prove to be the angel Israpheel and would one day cause all the world to sleep in the deep dreams of death and destruction. Science is taking people toward idleness and suspension. The day is not far off when this unnecessary intruder in the power and wisdom of God will cast the human race in the ditch of suspension, idleness, and unemployment.

A large portion of the world is perplexed and aggrieved through its perils today. Because all sorts of goods, handicrafts, agricultural products, and all other occupations that formerly poor and destitute people carried out with their own hands and earned their livelihood by have been taken into possession by the capitalists in the form of machines; lying prey to unemployment and joblessness, the poor and helpless people are crying and groaning as in agony, and there is no one to take care of them and help them. Science has, by making dangerous and dreadful weapons and war instruments, demolished the correct system of rule and true government laid by religion among all the nations, without the distinction of color and caste and has upset the economic, social, moral, and religious standards. No doubt, science is a knowledge and wisdom, but the insatiable greed of the materialist nations has converted this valuable and glorious knowledge of science into a universal peril and curse and is day by day piling curse upon curse. Instead of being serviceable to man, it has been turned into a weapon of universal massacre and destruction. It is assuming such formidable features from day to day that this warlike knowledge of these cruel people will bring resurrection on them and cause their destruction. Supposing the capitalists have conquered the whole world through these weapons and these cruel materialists have amassed the gold and silver of the whole universe, gathered all the unique objects of comfort and decoration, collected the means of the material ease and luxury, and subdued and subjugated their fellow men for a limited time of the worldly life. Then what is the value and weight of such a transitory, temporary, and brief power and might, the foundation of which is weak like the spider's web and which the powerful and revengeful hand of death will suddenly demolish and destroy in one moment?

خون کے دریا بہے عالم تہ و بالا ہوئے

اے ستم گر کس لیے دو دن حکومت کے لیے

(نظیر اکبر آبادی)

"Rivers of blood and streams of tears are flown and the world thrown up and down, Why, O tyrant! for a short momentary rule."

The transitory cruel kingdom of the materialists and the false rule of science and capitalism are established in the world and gain currency when the true powers of religion and spiritualism disappear from the world and people become deprived of moral and spiritual weapons. Blessed was the age when the true Solomon of spiritualism subdued the world by the name of Allah, the world was enjoying peace and prosperity, the life of general brotherhood and universal equality prevailed everywhere, and the safety of faith and the peace of Islam shaded the whole universe. But the day the Solomon of spiritualism lost the ring of rule of spiritualism, the devil of materialism and the Satan of capitalism assumed the reins of the government, and that very day, the cruel, greedy people established their rule, and the clouds of misery and misfortune overwhelmed the whole world.

Everywhere new feats of political magic are being played, and every day, new snares of policy and fresh tricks of propaganda are being used and the chains of human bondage and subjugation are being strengthened. By providing ostensible and material objects of comfort and decoration, science is showing no favor to God's people; on the contrary, it is entangling them in the transitory, perishable, material, sexual, and satanic pleasures and removing them from the worship and obedience of their Creator and Master and rendering them careless of the eternal and perpetual life. Science is connecting man to the empty skeleton of matter and the dead shell, transitory, and material body and covering, but snatching its connection from the real ego (i.e., the spirit and the spiritual world), which keeps him fresh and alive. Religion and spiritualism assure physical and spiritual, etheric and material, and worldly and religious progress in all aspects of life. Religion gives equal right in life to every human being in the world. As says the Almighty God:

$$ \text{إِنَّمَا الْمُؤْمِنُونَ إِخْوَةٌ (٩/٣ الحجرات:١٠)} $$

"All the Muslims are brethren."

Religion is bestowing the natural birthright of independence and equality on all the people without distinction of color, race, and nation and gives service and respect to the fittest. As the Almighty says:

$$\text{اِنَّ اَكْرَمَكُمْ عِنْدَ اللّٰهِ اَتْقٰكُمْ (الحجرات: ١٣)}$$

"With God the most pious of you is the noblest."

Religion bestows rule and kingdom on the ablest and best of all, as the prophetic command says:

$$\text{سَيِّدُ الْقَوْمِ خَادِمُهُمْ}$$

"The ruler of the nation is he who serves them well" (i.e., the true ruler is the true servant of the nation).

Through religion and spiritualism, man obtains the worship, knowledge, union, and observation of his Creator and Master, perfumed with the pure, luminous habits of God the Almighty and qualified with His holy attributes. Gaining exhilaration and existence in the light of his inexplicable, unparalleled, incomparable, unchangeable, and eternal essence, he enters his eternal and perpetual kingdom, and gaining ceaseless life with his living and ever-fixed essence, he enjoys His union, observation, and sight. Science in itself is not a bad thing. No, it is a fine knowledge and art and a very beneficial thing. The fault lies only with the cruel, bloody, selfish, materialistic, and capitalistic nations who used this knowledge in incorrect and evil ways, and instead of providing service and ease to the peoples, they have rendered it as the instrument for the subjugation, starvation, destruction, and annihilation of the weak, oppressed, and helpless people. We are absolutely against this state and condition of affairs. But remember, that getting tired of the bloodthirsty and cruel deeds of the statesmanship, dictatorship, capitalism, and tyrannies of materialism, the world would voluntarily seek refuge in the safe abode of religion, which is the home of peace and comfort and will cast off from its neck the yoke of the governments of the oppressive, aggressive, and tyrannical and cruel statesmen and dictators. The world will thus find shelter and protection under the veil of the courteous, kind, compassionate, and merciful religious leaders and spiritual guides and will attain real peace and true comfort. The day is not far off when science and philosophy, having reached their utmost zenith and extreme perfection in the near future, will affirm and acknowledge the reality and truth of religion and spiritualism, and the world will come under the rule of religion and spiritualism. At that moment, the world will become like a paradise, and its inhabitants will enjoy true peace and real comfort. As some English poet has said,

I live to hail that season

By gifted minds foretold.

When man shall live by reason

And not alone by gold;

When man to man united

And every wrong thing righted.

The whole world shall be lighted

As Eden was old

Twofold Human Construction

Man is composed of two parts: the material body, composed of elemental and material essences, which is a drop of the dirty semen, and the etheric body, which belongs to the invisible world. Says the Almighty:

$$ اَلَا لَهُ الْخَلْقُ وَالْأَمْرُ (الاعراف: ۵۴) $$

"To Him belong both the visible and invisible worlds."

The spirit belongs to the invisible world, as has been said:

$$ قُلِ الرُّوْحُ مِنْ أَمْرِ رَبِّيْ (بنی اسرائیل: ۸۵) $$

"Say, O Prophet, the spirit belongs to the Unseen."

Each body has an inclination toward its origin, and every object reverts to its mine. Since the material body is constructed of material objects and dements, it has an inclination toward the material world and material things, which is the special feature of animals. All these consumers and eaters of material food have been called animals by God the Almighty in the Holy Quran:

$$ وَمَا مِنْ دَآبَّةٍ فِي الْأَرْضِ إِلَّا عَلَى اللّٰهِ رِزْقُهَا (هود: ۶) $$

"There is not any animal on the earth but God provides them with food."

The other invisible body (i.e., the spirit) has its origin in the world above (i.e., heaven and the invisible and unseen world), and it has desire and inclination toward its special spiritual food. Therefore, this food has been thus mentioned separately in the Holy Quran.

وَفِى السَّمَآءِ رِزْقُكُمْ وَمَا تُوعَدُوْنَ ﴿٢٢﴾ (١٥ الزاريات:٢٢)

"Your food is in heavens and that which was promised to you."

This food will be obtainable commonly after death. Just as this material body has a desire for material objects (i.e., eating, drinking, and other necessities of life), the etheric body has an inclination toward its heavenly and angelic food (i.e., commemoration, meditation, worship, devotion, and practicing virtuous deeds). Because the food of all the etheric beings (i.e., angels and spirits) consists of God the Almighty's commemoration, meditation, obedience, remembrance, and so on, as is evident from this tradition, said the Prophet:

اِذَا مَرَرْتُمْ بِرِيَاضِ الْجَنَّةِ فَارْتَعُوْا ـ

"When you pass by the garden of paradise graze therein."

The companions inquired about the meaning of the garden of paradise. He replied, "The assemblies and circles where the name of God is commemorated and recited." In short, the nature of this etheric, heavenly, and invisible body is based on Islam and carries in it the religious and Islamic capacity from the day of the beginning to keep this nature. This capacity is complete, perfect, and unchangeable; nourish and feed it, and take it to the point of perfection and complement. This is termed in Islam faith und union.

رَبَّنَآ أَتْمِمْ لَنَا نُوْرَنَا وَاغْفِرْ لَنَا ۖ اِنَّكَ عَلٰى كُلِّ شَيْءٍ قَدِيْرٌ ﴿٨﴾ (٦٦ التحريم:٨)

"O Lord! perfect for us our lights and forgive us. Verily Thou hast power over everything."

The material and elemental body of man is like a skin or covering for the etheric and spiritual body and is for its conveyance, staying, walking, and working in this material world. The seat of creation, the beginning of creation, and the source of the lower and the material body is situated in the lowest part and basest organ of man, and its propagation also takes place in the basest place of the body. The devil with all his evil forces and Satanic arms and weapons (i.e., ill qualities and contemptible vices) has his seat and abode in this place. This body of man is always prepared to work evil deeds under the command of Satan and against the dictates of the faith and religious fundamentals. When the invisible and spiritual body becomes alive and alert in man, it is always inclined toward virtuous deeds, commemoration, meditation, devotion, and worship and informs and reveals virtues to the soul every moment and accuses it of its vices. Therefore, such a soul is called the inspired or accusative soul نفس لوامه.

Do not you see that the highest and noblest part of man (i.e., his heart and brain) is the inlet and habitation of this etheric, luminous body, and it has descended from the elevated place (i.e., heaven), and when it is ready and complete, the inhabitants of heaven (i.e., the angels), bow to show honor and respect to this blessed body. The very construction of the heart bears testimony to the fact that it is a heavenly object descended from above because when we inspect the heart, we see that its arrow-like head is hanging below, and like the two legs, two thick veins are attached to its large portion from behind.

Hence by way of an examination, there is a conflict and battle between the two etheric and material, angelic and devilish, and invisible and grotesque bodies, and the one that prevails establishes its rule and government in the human body. Says the Almighty:

إِنَّا خَلَقْنَا الْإِنسَانَ مِن نُّطْفَةٍ أَمْشَاجٍ نَّبْتَلِيهِ فَجَعَلْنَاهُ سَمِيعًا بَصِيرًا ﴿٢﴾ (الدهر:٢)

"I created man out of a mixed sperm and nature in order to test him and made him hear and see."

Elsewhere, it is said, "He who created death and life to test you which of you acts virtuously and rightly." In short, by way of trial, there is a conflict and battle in the human body between the two contradictory and opposite beings (i.e., good and evil and invisible and material bodies). The exemplary figure of the lower spermatic body is that of an animal, which is called the animal soul. Because of its baseness and meanness, it is a friend and companion of Satan. Through its companionship, Satan hurls man into the pool of vice and sin. Thus, the higher and etheric body has an exemplary, luminous figure like an angel, which is called the holy spirit or the satisfied soul نفس مطمئنة. On account of its etheric fineness and lightness, this body mixes with angels. This blessed body receives direction and revelation from heaven. So man is composed of these two bodies.

آدمی زاده طرفه معجونیست   از فرشته سرشته و زحیواں

(سعدی)

"The animal soul is strengthened by the material and fed by evil acts and is exported to action by the accursed Satan." The satisfied soul, or the subtle body, partakes of commemoration, meditation, devotion, worship, and so on and so gathers strength from virtuous acts and praiseworthy actions. As says the Almighty:

اِلَیْهِ یَصْعَدُ الْکَلِمُ الطَّیِّبُ وَالْعَمَلُ الصَّالِحُ یَرْفَعُهُ ۚ (۳۵ فاطر:۱۰)

"The pure recitation returns to Him and the good actions ascend to Him."

His Holiness Muhammad the chosen of God (p.b.u.h.) and his other apostles and messengers intimate saints and true sages are the guides of the high and good spirits. Both these varieties of good and evil, with all their companions and appointees, are from God the Almighty. As He says:

وَالْقَدْرِ خَیْرِهِ وَشَرِّهِ مِنَ اللّٰهِ تَعَالٰی

"Evil and good both are from God the Almighty."

It means that from the day of beginning, God the Almighty has created in man the causes of both good and evil in the form of the evil spirit and sacred soul, as well as their means of good and evil in the form of evil passions and bad desires on the one hand and on the other hand the blessed eternal pleasures and bounties of the next world. The inviters and callers to both the sides (i.e., good and evil) have also been appointed and employed. By revealing His books, He has indicated the paths of good and evil and has ordered one to avoid wrong and practice right. He has completed His action and decision by clearly explaining their ways and methods. Now by way of test and trial, man has the choice and power whether to assume the path of evil and vice to hell or enter paradise by taking the right path of goodness and virtue.

$$فَمَنْ شَآءَ فَلْيُؤْمِنْ وَّمَنْ شَآءَ فَلْيَكْفُرْ (الكهف:٢٩)$$

"He who wished became faithful and who wished turned heretic."

The essence of God, the Almighty, cannot be accused or blamed for making man act rightly or wrongly. Everyone understands material food and external victuals. But the internal cordial and etheric victuals (i.e., commemoration, meditation, devotion, worship, virtuous acts, and so on) can be explained only by examples and metaphors. Then let it be known that when man becomes helpless in working and earning his livelihood, his income decreases, and he becomes miserable, weak, sick, and dead because of lack of proper food. Similarly, in the etheric world, when the subtle body of the man is kept back from earning and acquiring its etheric sustenance and livelihood and is deprived of commemoration, meditation, devotion, worship, and so on, his livelihood becomes hard, and it ultimately perishes because of weakness and sickness. As says God the Almighty:

$$وَمَنْ أَعْرَضَ عَنْ ذِكْرِى فَإِنَّ لَهُ مَعِيشَةً ضَنْكًا وَّنَحْشُرُهُ يَوْمَ الْقِيَمَةِ أَعْمَى (٢٠ طه:١٢٤)$$

"He who avoids Our commemoration, his livelihood becomes hard, and on the day of Resurrection, he will be raised blind."

In this verse, avoiding commemorating Allah can never result in external worldly hardships of livelihood and destitution of means. Those who avoid commemorating and worshipping Allah generally possess wealth and pass a luxurious and comfortable life in this world. This creates a great doubt and difficulty in the truthful word of God the Almighty. Sustenance and livelihood are twofold: physical and spiritual.

God the Almighty has separately narrated both sports of livelihood in different verses of the Holy Quran. For example, the animals receiving physical food are mentioned in this verse:

"There is not, any animal on earth but God provides its food."

The spiritual and etheric food is mentioned in this verse. "And in heaven there is food for you and what He has promised." Just as a man is upset by poverty, starvation, and hunger in the material world, when his income increases and his means of food are provided and he receives his food properly, his heart is satisfied, and he feels himself contented and at home. As the Almighty says in the Holy Quran:

$$\text{اَلَا بِذِكْرِ اللّٰهِ تَطْمَئِنُّ الْقُلُوْبُ ۝ (الرعد ۱۳: ۲۸)}$$

"Beware! Commemoration of Allah and his remembrance gives contentment and satisfaction to hearts."

This contentment of the heart is clearly perceived to a lesser degree by ordinary people engaged in daily commemoration, meditation, and worship of Allah. Because, when a man performs his daily commemoration, meditation, and so on, on that very day, he feels himself satisfied, happy, and very jubilant. Though his purse and home be empty of money and provisions, yet his mind is so contented and satisfied as if he has everything. In contrast, those who do not remember and commemorate the name of Allah are extremely disturbed in mind and discontented in spite of wealth and power. But the true worshippers and commemorators of God the Almighty are perpetually happy and satisfied, though they may not possess even a penny of material riches or a grain of earthly provisions.

THE REALITY OF WORLDLY WEALTH

With the material food of the world, we can fill the material stomach for a while, but the vast etheric interior of our heart can never be satisfied with this material substance. By explaining the material wealth as insignificant merchandise, God the Almighty has publicized its calamity and meanness as He says:

$$قُلْ مَتَاعُ الدُّنْيَا قَلِيْلٌ ۚ (النساء:٧٧)$$

"Say the merchandise of the world is very insignificant."

If the reality of the material wealth is contemplated upon, it is a very contemptible and despicable thing in spite of all its means of comfort and luxury. A tradition says, "If the material wealth valued a fly wing, by God, no heretic in the world would have got a cold draft of water." But compared to the perpetual bounties of the next world, this wealth is merely valueless and nothing. Let us explain the reality of this material wealth a bit. Firstly, its pleasures are small and transitory. Secondly, the human life here is very short and brief. Its acquisition necessitates great worries, labors and pains, and its comforts are very few. The merchandise of this material world, whether edible or drinkable or smellable or audible, all are of little value and very mean. The best eatable or edible things are meat, ghee, milk, and so on. These are animal blood and flesh or its juice and refuse, while fruits and vegetables grow out of manure and dirt. Says the Almighty:

$$نُسْقِيْكُمْ مِّمَّا فِيْ بُطُوْنِهِ مِنْ بَيْنِ فَرْثٍ وَّدَمٍ لَّبَنًا خَالِصًا سَآئِغًا لِّلشّٰرِبِيْنَ ۝ (النحل:٦٦)$$

"Animals give you to drink the refuse obtained from within the dung and blood (i.e., milk)."

Among the drinkables, the best thing is honey, which is the saliva of a detestable fly. The best among the smellables is musk, which is the coagulated and condensed blood and dirt of the navel of an animal, namely the deer. The best among the wearables is silk, which is the refuse of a moth and insect. And all the audible pleasures and instruments of music and singing are derived and made from striking the dirty skins, sinews, and intestines of animals. Besides this, there is another thing of pleasure (i.e., the place of touch), which it is against decency and morality to describe, but suffice it to say that it consists of the use of the lowest, meanest, worst, and dirtiest organ of man. In short, these are the sources of all the pleasures of the material world, which we have mentioned.

حال دنیا را بُپر سیدم من از فرزانئ   گفت یا خوابیست یا وہمیست یا افسانئ

باز پر سیدم زِحال آنکہ دل دروے بہ بست   گفت یا دیویست یا غویست یا دیوانئ

(سیمیں بہ بانی)

"I asked about the nature of the worldly pleasures from a wise man. He replied, 'It is like a dream or a wind or a fable.' I asked again about the nature of one who loved it. He answered he is either a demon or a devil or an idiot."

Now consider the time and duration of these material enjoyments.

When a man is hungry and he eats something, for a few seconds, the tip of the tongue derives a little taste and a faint pleasure as long as the delicious and fine foods are on the tip of the tongue. But that faint sensation also disappears when the belly becomes full and one is satisfied, and afterward, the food devoured turns into a weight for the heart and repugnant to the mind. Likewise, the duration of all physical pleasure is very brief, and its ambit is very narrow. Hence, God the Almighty has called all the merchandise and property of the material world insignificant and valueless. For the acquisition of this transitory, despicable, and perishable merchandise, one has to undergo immense sweepings, headaches, and toils; practice tremendous tyranny and cruelty; and shed the blood of innumerable innocent and helpless people. There is also another worthless side of material relishes, namely, that the destitute and the rich both derive equal pleasure. On account of daily consumption of rich dishes, wearing gorgeous clothes, inhabiting lofty houses, and constantly cohabiting with beautiful women and through constant and continuous engagement in the worldly pleasures, the rich people become highly accustomed to them; therefore, their appetite for, relish in, and taste of these things is greatly decreased, rather altogether lost, because real relish lies in starvation and privation, which the rich people lack very badly.

But on account of excessive hunger, the poor, destitute, derive much pleasure from a simple and stale loaf of bread, which the rich people cannot find in numerous kinds of delicious dishes. In short, the enjoyment and pleasure of taste depends on digestion, which is extremely lacking and almost wanting in the case of rich people. The poor possess this unrivaled blessing in abundance and plentifully. Similarly, drowned in worldly worries, the rich capitalists pass restless nights in their magnificent and lofty palaces, changing sides on costly beds and flopping like a fish out of water. In contrast, a poor laborer, tired of the daily toil and labor, sleeps such a deep and pleasant sleep on his pillowless and rough bed that he passes the whole night on one side. The rich aspire for a moment of sound sleep and genuine hunger all their lifelong. Similarly, the rich are absolutely wanting in sexual virility and are always childless in spite of having three or four wives. All other pleasures and enjoyments should also be conjectured after this. The poor and penniless are advantageously placed. The rich can never achieve contentment and satisfaction of mind and heart, and the richer one gets, the more perplexed and discontented he becomes. Even if one were to get all the wealth and luxury of the material world, he would never have peace of mind and satisfaction of heart. Go and ask the rich man. Amirs and traders, nay, even the nawabs, rajas, and kings, ask them, "You possess every gift of God and want nothing. Every moment, you have rich, delicious victuals and fruits to eat; sweet and cold syrups to drink; soft and fine clothes to wear; nice, beautiful, and magnificent houses to live in; fine horses, carriages, and motor cars to travel in and ride on; gardens, orchards, entertainments, radios, cinema, dancing, and music; and beautiful maids and servants to serve you. In fact, you have realized all your worldly desires and luxuries. In spite of this joy and luxury, comfort and bounty, and convenience and ease, are you really pleased, and is your heart satisfied and wanting no more?"

To this, nearly all of them will reply that they are not happy in this world. They will say, "Though our persons and bodies are rolling in ease, comfort, and luxury, but, God knows, why the hearts in our bosoms are dejected and our minds are full of some unknown sorrow and any unperceivable secret grief lies therein. What is the matter, we feel a causeless and endless sorrow in ourselves, and we always sense a nameless and boundless ache in our hearts!" You will certainly find them grumbling and groaning about the dissatisfaction and distraction of their hearts. The reason thereof is that these people are lacking the real food of the heart. Therefore, though their stomachs are full, their hearts are empty of their special etheric food (i.e., the commemoration of Allah). Therefore, the heart remains discontented. The rich and capitalists of those nations, in whom the esoteric food of the heart is absent and where atheism, materialism, and naturalism are rampant and people of the land where the famine of God's commemoration prevails, are always found badly complaining of discontentment of heart, in spite of material wealth and worldly power.

The European nations who have surpassed Qaroon in amassing material wealth and have overthrown the world in capitalism are badly crying from the discontentment of heart. That is, why, in spite of enormous wealth and plenty of power, there are so many cases of suicide in Europe, while in our poor and destitute Asia, you cannot find a hundredth of such cases. Especially in the Muslim nation, which is the poorest and most needy of all other nations, the offense of suicide is very rarely and seldom committed. The reason is quite clear. Although the Muslims have renounced and abandoned their religious commandments and performances to a great extent and a prominent decrease has taken place in their cordial and spiritual deeds (i.e., commemoration, prayers, meditation, devotion, worship, and so on), yet Islam is such a comprehensive, embracing, and prevailing religion that the effects of this pure and true religion are current in the daily actions and works of a Muslim during the whole of his life from the cradle to the grave. Therefore, however hopeless a Muslim may be, he involuntarily and unintentionally draws some portion of his cordial and spiritual food, and though he be deprived of material wealth and worldly luxury, he yet maintains himself through the help of the cordial and spiritual food and does not lose the balance of his mind and heart in extreme distress and perplexity and does not commit suicide. In contrast, when a bit of disturbance appears in the worldly affairs of infidels and atheists, the state of their worldly comforts and luxuries is upset. Then the weak thread of their life gives way like a spider's web and is unable to bear against the conflicting gale of worldly incidents, and the tiny tent of the bubble of their life immediately breaks down and is scattered about. That is why suicides are generally committed by those people whose religious condition is very low and defective and whose hearts are devoid of religious capacity and esoteric food. In Europe, which is the headquarters and center of materialism and capitalism, there prevails a universal famine of God's commemoration, devotion, and worship. This famine-stricken area is generally very tired of life on account of discontentment of heart and extremely perplexed. Some have given vent to their perplexity and discontentment to the extent that going out of control, they have thrown away their clothes like mad and insane people and become absolutely nude and naked. They could not achieve contentment of the heart in their fine and fancy clothes. All these are the signs and results of cordial discontentment and esoteric restlessness that appear from these capitalist nations through various forms. They are feeling the pangs and pains of this esoteric disease in themselves and try to struggle for its cure like madmen. But their material endeavor, outward efforts, external struggles, and empty labors are absolutely useless. The disease increases, the more it is treated. In fact, the only medicine for this disease is the commemoration of Allah. But this medicine is very rare and unavailable in that materialist land. Therefore, without the name of Allah, their material, treatments, and external toil and labor are useless.

Once upon a time, the Lord Jesus Christ begged God the Almighty to show him the material wealth in its real shape and true color. At this, God the Almighty promised him to do so. One day, while walking through a jungle, he saw a veiled woman from afar, whose veil was glittering like gold in the light of the sun, on account of the silken embroidery and golden stitching. He thought to himself that there must be a very beautiful moonlike woman in this dress. In short, she came near and face to face with her. When she lifted the veil, he was astonished to see that through the veil appeared the face of a very ugly, old, ill-shaped, black, frightful woman.

On seeing her, Lord Jesus asked, "Old hag, who are you?"

She replied, "I am a pattern and a model of material wealth."

He asked her, "Old woman, why this beautiful golden glittering garment on this old ugly figure?"

She replied, "O Lord of truth, it is through this fancy, fine, and glittering dress that I captivate and enchant people; otherwise, my real figure is that which you see herein."

When he looked toward her hands, he saw that one of her hands was stained with blood, and it was dripping down from it and her second hand was dyed with myrtle leaves. He asked her, "Why is your one hand stained with blood?"

She replied, "I have just killed my husband because it is my old habit that he who marries me I kill certainly, and you are just seeing the signs of his blood on my hand."

The Lord Jesus then asked, "Why is your second hand dyed with myrtle?"

She answered, "I am now becoming the bride of another husband."

He questioned her, astonished, "Does not your new husband take warning from your bloody hand?"

She replied, "O Lord! Don't be astonished; the moment I murder one brother in a family, the other brother is at once ready to marry and woo me."

Afterward, much other questioning and answering took place between them.

Many gnostics of true insight and real revelation see material wealth in its real shape. While the blind, ambitious materialists die after her external dress and are thus killed and destroyed by her:

عارفے خواب در فکرے   دید دنیا بصورت بکرے
کرد ازوے سوال کائے دلبر   بکر چونی بایں همہ شوہر
گفت یک حرف باتو گویم راست   کہ مرا ہر کہ بود مرد نخواست
دانکہ نامرد بود خواست مرا   زاں بکارت ہمیں بجاست مرا

"A gnostic in a vision and dream saw the material wealth in the shape of a virgin. He asked her, 'Darling, why are you virgin in spite of so many husbands?' She said, 'I tell you the truth, those who desired and married me, they all proved impotent, and those who were real potent men did not desire me at all. Therefore, my virgin hood remains safe."

Now we will relate the sad exemplary ends of a few of the wealthiest men and great capitalists, hoping that some sound minded, fortunate, and wise people might take a lesson and warning and avoid the snare of this bloody, cunning old hag—material wealth.

The Exemplary and Sorrowful Ends of the Great Capitalists of the World

1. "I cannot count my wealth. It is estimated at more than five hundred million pounds, but I will willingly part with all this wealth, if only I can have one full meal according to my desire and appetite." These are the words of the famous American multimillionaire, the oil king Rockefeller, the stories of whose wealth and richness are current in all corners of the Old and New Worlds. Many are envious of his good fortune, and God knows the number of those whose mouths will water at the mention of his material wealth. But the poor fellow, in spite of all his wealth and in spite of all this abundance of gold and silver, craves for a single hearty meal and is ready to forego all his wealth for this one desire. He is now eighty-five years old, but from his early age, he has suffered from indigestion. The amount of money spent by him on his treatment can be well guessed. But with all that, he cannot take more than a little milk and a few biscuits a day, whereas his poor servants and employees eat to their fill every delicious food many times a day. This master of them all craves for a single full meal through his whole life but cannot touch even more than a little milk and a few biscuits. O you poor fellows who envy the worldly life of these capitalists, be thankful of this bounty of God, that the richest man in the world is envious of your state of health.

2. Now, listen another story of an American, the motor king Henry Ford, who has defeated Qaroon in respect of wealth. He cannot eat more than a bit of a cautionary diet. A large number of doctors are always busy attending him. He is absolutely deprived of all the pleasures of life, though his poor servants enjoy themselves before his very eyes, and he watches them with his envious and desirous eyes. His one

confidant relates that this Qaroon of his age is altogether deprived of all the pleasures that a man can have in this material world through wealth and dignity and which by money can be purchased. O you, who consider wealth to be the object of life and money to be the goal of existence! Do you not see the futility and worthlessness of money and wealth?

3. There was another multimillionaire, Mr. Edward Scripps, the owner of newspapers. After years of comfort and luxury, his heart became sick of the adventures of life, and he searched for peace and solitude of mind. But where could he have it in the centers of these busy and civilized cities? Finally, he caused a ship to be constructed at the cost of four million dollars and made it soundproof through various instruments, so that the faintest sound, too, could not be heard. Thus creating a world of silence around himself he thought that now he had acquired peace of mind. He handed over the newspaper business to his son and in that ship set out on a voyage in search of peace. It sailed not around a country or two but sailed around the entire world twice; however, the peace and satisfaction of mind could never be gotten through closing and shutting the openings of all material sounds. Death overtook him in this state of impatience and despair, and his dead body was cast down in the depth of the sea, with accordance to his testament. O you who gather wealth and sacrifice your precious life in search of it, look at the pauperism and helplessness of capitalism.

4. Gobisp Bagiani was a fabulously rich man of Italy, who amassed great wealth in America and domiciled there. This was the beginning. And his end was that he constructed a beautiful residence at the corner of the picturesque Lake Como. One day, he hanged himself from a tree by a rope and left behind the following statement of his suicide. "During my long life, I have found out by experiment that if one desires peace of mind, he cannot have it in piles of gold. I am putting an end to my life, because I am tired and sick of solitude and despair. I enjoyed complete happiness when I was an ordinary labourer in New York, America, but now that I am the master of millions of pounds, my sorrow and distress

know no limit, and I prefer death to such a miserable life." O you, who regard money as a cure of all ailments, behold the helplessness and worthlessness of material wealth.

5. J. P. T. Morgan is today reputed to be the owner of the biggest factory for the manufacture of fine articles. It is difficult to estimate his wealth. He has all the best means of luxury in his home, but he is so sick of intestinal disease that he cannot touch the simplest food. He has spent all his life on a strict cautionary diet and has not taken a single meal according to his desire. He always complains of stomachache, always enviously looks with greedy eyes at the meals of his meanest servants, and sighs helplessly but cannot eat a morsel. O you who are envious of the rich and desire more and more to become rich! Do you see these pathetic scenes, that a man standing in the river yet craves for a drop of water to quench his thirst?

6. Mr. Brenester was a multimillionaire of New York, America. His wife had a fabulous beauty. Ostensibly, none could have had a happier and more successful and fortunate life than this pair of such a rich husband and handsome wife. A large number of people envied the life of this happy pair. They were very fond of each other. In June 1926, they both went to a village in their estate. One day, they were found murdered in their bedroom. Thus the secret of their suicide was buried with their bodies forever. O you who worship wealth and beauty and its features, behold the worthlessness and uselessness of wealth and beauty both.

The preceding are not supposed stories but true facts. They are not mere imaginary and exemplary tales and fables but true adventures of the past. Here, there are immense capitals, large factories, great exchange houses, and estates worth millions, and alongside these are uneasiness, discontentment, disappointment, dejection, and suicide at the end.

On the other side, there is poverty, moneylessness, a broken hut, dry and unbuttered barley bread with some simple vegetables, an old blanket, and a patched garment, and side by side with it is happiness of the heart, contentment of the mind, jubilance of the soul, the treasure of satisfaction, the crownless eternal lordship of the esoteric world assemblies and meetings of the angels and holy spirits, the perpetual endless pleasures unseen by human eyes and unheard by ears and un-thought-of by any human heart, and at the end divine, proximity and union and observation of God the Almighty. Both sides of life are open, and everyone has the choice to choose whichever he likes. If you desire and wish true repose, real composure, and perpetual pacification defeated, tired, and having tested everything, you must ultimately come toward recollecting God the Almighty and His worship and the corner of derveshism and faqirism. But if you want to add to the number of suicides and add to hellish fuel, the doors of the world are lying open.

عُمر برق و شرار ہے دنیا   کتنی بے اعتبار ہے دنیا

داغ سے کوئی دل نہیں خالی   کیا کوئی لالہ زار ہے دنیا

ہر جگہ جنگ ہر جگہ ہے نزاع   عرصہٴ کارزار ہے دنیا

گرچہ ظاہر میں صورتِ گل ہے   پر حقیقت میں خار ہے دنیا

زندگی نام رکھ دیا کس نے   موت کا انتظار ہے

(مومن خان مومن)

"The worldly life is like the flash of the lightning or the spark of fire: How unreliable is the worldly life. No heart is here without a brand; No doubt, the world is like a tulip-bed with the brand of heart; Everywhere there is a quarrel and conflict; The world is indeed a battlefield; Though obviously it has the form of a flower; But in reality it is a thorn Who foolish termed it life. The world is a waiting room for death."

Remember, that God the Almighty's worship, commemoration, meditation, recitation, and virtuous acts are the real food of man's subtle self, namely, the heart and the soul, and through this food, the heart and the mind attain desired contentment and satisfaction. But when the esoteric self, namely, the heart and mind, are deprived of their special food consisting of commemorating and meditating on God the Almighty, they are disturbed by the pangs and pains of hunger and compelled to eat the impure food of the animal self. As, for example, it is commonly observed among the common domestic animals that if they are deprived of their special food consisting of grass, hay, grains, and so on, they are compelled to eat rubbish and dung and make it their special diet whereby their nature becomes like that of dirt-eating animals. Similarly, if the angelic self of the human body, namely, the heart and mind, is deprived of its special food—commemoration, devotion, and so on, it is compelled to make the temporal material opaque food of the animal self (i.e., the dirt and rubbish of the material world) and begins to live on that. The human angelic self assumes the characteristics of animals and is given the bad attributes and vile morals and habits of animals and beasts and hurls down from the high angelic position into the lowest state of animality, savageness, and diabolism. When he dies in this state, he is joined with the dark terrestrial region of the devils and evil spirits, is put into that dark lowest depths of the hell called Sijjin, and is tormented and tortured by the multifarious kinds of esoteric afflictions and various kinds of spiritual punishments. But when the blessed pious people are helped to their eternal fortune, their nature inclines toward its real, high, and angelic luminous sources and their esoteric self requires its especial food of God's commemoration and meditation. It is ready and prepared to acquire that spiritual livelihood and that splendid food in the next world, and having gotten it, they live and thrive on it in accordance with this mandate of God the Almighty:

فَاذْكُرُوا اللّٰهَ قِيَامًا وَّقُعُودًا وَّعَلٰى جُنُوبِكُمْ ۚ (١٢ النساء:١٠٣)

"Remember God while standing, sitting, and sleeping."

Thus he is always engaged in commemoration, meditation, and worship of Allah the Almighty.

The excess of perpetual commemoration and royal glorification encompasses all his bodily organs, senses, and energies and lastly his heart and mind and the whole of his exterior and interior. His heart becomes engrossed and intoxicated by relish, desire, and delight of observation and light of divine commemoration. Then his animal self too, which is a close associate and neighbor of his angelic self (i.e., the mind and heart), on finding the smell and receiving the taste of the angelic food of the heart, becomes fond and desirous of the angelic food of his companion mind and heart and turns his face from the material food and the childish, perishable, worldly pleasures and derives sustenance and food from splendid angelic meals (i.e., commemoration, meditation, and devotion) and attains angelic attributes. As says the Almighty:

$$قَدْ أَفْلَحَ مَن زَكَّىٰهَا ۞ (٩١ الشمس: ٩)$$

"Whoever cleansed himself got off."

$$وَاذْكُرُوا اللَّهَ كَثِيرًا لَّعَلَّكُمْ تُفْلِحُونَ ۞ (٦٢ الجمعة: ١٠)$$

"Commemorate God much, perhaps you may be absolved." Thus, the animal self now gets the angelic color of heart and, uniting there, loses its own animalistic attributes and adopts angelic qualities and spiritual virtues and joins the bright region of the hierarchy of angels and blessed spirits. In that highest, bright, blessed abode, it enjoys the splendid, untouched pleasures and scenes of that holy invisible world forever without any end, which our material eyes have never seen nor our ears ever heard nor material mind ever thought of. Says the Almighty:

$$فَلَا تَعْلَمُ نَفْسٌ مَّا أُخْفِيَ لَهُم مِّن قُرَّةِ أَعْيُنٍ جَزَاءً بِمَا كَانُوا يَعْمَلُونَ ۞ (٣٢ السجدة: ١٧)$$

"None knows of the pleasant reward the sight of which will cool their eyes, that We have prepared and have concealed from them in return for their virtuous actions."

When the doors of this esoteric grace and etheric pleasure opened on the mind of God's pious and favored people, they remained intoxicated and, having left the population, inhabited and occupied mountain caves for scores of years. On tasting the sweetness, some kings and nobles abandoned their kingdom and set off in its quest toward the jungles and deserts and no more thought of their kingdom and wealth. Here are the names of some of them: Gautam Buddha, His Holiness Ibrahim s/o Adham, and Shah Shuja Kirmani (R.A). They all renounced their kingdoms for the eternal and perpetual kingdom of the next world. It is said that whenever esoteric and etheric sparks of light used to rain upon Ibrahim s/o Adham, he used to say, "Where are the worldly monarchs?" By God, if they witness an atom of these bounties and scenes, they will at once renounce their thrones and crowns and run to the desert to obtain it. Sultan of Sanjar once wrote to His Holiness Hazrat Shaikh Abdul Qadir Jilani, the great Pir of Baghdad (R.A), "If Your Holiness could take the trouble of gracing my dominion with your blessing steps and having come to my country give me a chance of your inspiring visit, I will create a trust of the entire kingdom of Nimroz for the expenses of your *langar*" (i.e., charity-house). His holiness wrote this verse on the back of his paper and handed it over to the ambassador:

چوں چتر چنبری رخ بختم سیاہ باد　　بافقر اگر بود ہوس ملک سنجرم

تا یافت خاطرم خبر از ملک نیم شب　　صد ملک نیمروز بیک جونے خرم

"The face of my fortune be as black as the umbrella cloth of your kingdom, Sanjar, were I to desire the kingdom of Sanjar in spite of my Faqr, poverty. Since my mind has found the kingdom of midnight I would not purchase even a hundred kingdoms of Nimroz (midday) for a single barley."

In short, nothing can be said of this perpetual esoteric wealth and eternal spiritual pleasure. Those alone can know the real value and price of that eternal fruit who have tasted its sweetness.

قطع نظر از جمال ہر یوسف کن　　یک بار چراغ آرزو بایف کن

از لذت اگر محو نہ گردی تف کن　　زیں شہد یک انگشت رانم بلبت

(ناصر ناخدا)

Put out the candle of worldly desires once and for all. Remove your eyes from every material beautiful thing. Let me put a bit of this (etheric) honey on your lips. If you don't get mad for pleasure, spit on me."

Highly mistaken are those who consider this elemental body (i.e., this skeleton of flesh and bones) to be everything or call the elemental mixture or its compound vapor spirit or like the physicians call the blood spirit, and extremely foolish are those who believe that the derangement of this material composition or the elemental system is called the end of human life. All the religionists, modern and ancient philosophers, and modern spiritualists agree that the spirit is a thing different and separate from this material body, and it has its own personality distinguished from the elemental structure and existing even after the destruction and death of this material body and the removal of this material cover.

Nowadays, in Europe, the experiments of invoking the spirits and talking to them have reached perfection. Hence, there is no need to adduce further verbal arguments and intellectual reasons.

Highly short-sighted, ignorant, and blind are those who consider this whimsical life a ceaseless and endless system.

تو مے گوئی کہ من ہستم خدا نیست   جہانِ آب و گِل را انتہا نیست
من اندر حیرتم از دیدنِ تو   کہ چشمت آنچہ بیند ہست یا نیست
(زکریا رازی)

"You say, I exist and God does not exist and this material world has no end. I am surprised at your eyes, whether that which you see and feel even really exists or not."

Now if anyone is insistent to say that he cannot believe in the existence of the spirit or soul in the human body, if there is any, he may be shown that, so it is like the question of the followers of Prophet Moses who asked him to show Allah the Almighty in person if there is any. So such blind-born, unfortunate people are incurable and excusable because their minds are wrapped in the thick covering of matter.

ہزار معجزہ بنمود عشق و عقل جہول   ہنوز درپئے اندیشہائے خویشتن است
(حافظ)

"Love showed thousands of miracles, but the foolish intellect still wanders in its own fancies."

Proof of the Human Spirit Being Eternal

Some would say that if there existed anything like the spirit of man before birth on the Day of Beginning, why don't we remember that self and its abode and place and the happenings and surroundings in that esoteric world. So the fact is that on the Day of Beginning, the soul was naked and awake. When it was born in this material world, it wore the quilt of the opaque body and fell asleep and senseless. Then it forgot that living and waking world of the beginning and its place and time during sleep. As, for example, supposing if we are closed up in the world of a dream and not awakened for years, we would never remember this living and wakeful world nor desire to wake up, because we have before us an imagining and like world resembling the world in our dream. Similarly, the hearts and souls of the sensualist people are sleeping carelessly in this world, unmindful and unaware of the living and wakeful next world.

Occasionally in this world, when the senses and material faculties of the soul are lost and taken away during sleep and suffer a kind of death, the heart and soul, through the esoteric senses, sometimes find and feel that world and witness such unseen places during sleep, which previously he has never seen in life. But he is so familiar with those houses as if they are his own homes that he has used for a very long time. Or sometimes he meets such unseen people in dreams whom he had never seen before in his life, but in the dreams, they seem to him to be his friends and relatives. Or a man sometimes sees a saint, a holy man, or a prophet in the dream and knows him already well by face and name and talks to him like an intimate and confidant one, although they have passed long before him. So through familiarity and recognition of the Day of Beginning, the human heart and soul know these men and places of the next world very well.

In short, there are many things like this that indicate that the spirit has an identity separate from the material body that survives after death, and it existed also on the Day of Beginning before assuming this corporal body. The reason for our recognizing unseen familiar places or unseen strange people is that these are the same eternal places and eternal friends that were familiar to our soul and spirit on the Day of Eternity. Man's elemental carcass and material body perish and mix in dust after death. But the esoteric and spiritual body of man, namely the spirit and its senses and faculties and thought, can neither die nor be destroyed by the earth, nor are they perishable and destructible. But it is impossible to exist by themselves without any pot. Therefore, after death, these esoteric senses, faculties, and thoughts are granted esoteric and etheric bodies in the esoteric and spiritual world. Therefore, the object and aim of all worship, devotion, concentration, and commemoration of God the Almighty are that, in this very life, man should prepare such a subtle, luminous, and esoteric conveyance that can carry these esoteric senses and faculties and that he be able to live and dwell and achieve spiritual progress on reaching the other eternal and invisible world. We sometimes see the raw and imperfect model of that body in the dream as an example of the whole. In the dream, a subtle esoteric body of man becomes the carriage and vehicle of human senses, faculties, and thoughts, and that esoteric body sees, senses, speaks, walks, thinks, and performs all other things in an invisible world. In dreams, sometimes the dreamer even understands that what he sees is in dream. But since this body of the sensualist man is raw and imperfect, so far; therefore, he has neither full knowledge nor understanding of that body. Therefore, he interprets the world of dreams as an imaginary world. Though in reality, it is not so, nor is every dream the sum total of the everyday usual work, the worldly perplexed thoughts. The dreams of the virtuous and selected servants of Allah are the true samples of future incidents, the motion pictures of the guarded tablet [1] لوحِ محفوظ and solid realities, and these dreams are true and exact like the twilight of day. When gnostic travelers contemplate, they enter the subtle invisible world of dream with their senses, intellect, and understanding and go wherever they like and do whatever they wish. Since this subtle body of sensualist common folk is lifeless and senseless like an embryo in the uterus, they lack understanding and senses during sleep, but like an invisible child, the esoteric body of the livehearted gnostic is borne from the esoteric womb alive, a whole and hale man in the esoteric world who comes from and goes there (i.e., the land of dream) with full understanding and senses and sees with his eyes

---

[1] In Islamic technology, there is a very vast and wide esoteric tablet *Lauhi-Mahfuz*, in which all that is to happen is to be written.

the states and incidents of the invisible nextworld. In Sufistic terminology, this subtle body is called "Latifa لطیفه."

Like the physical body, this Latifa is a perfect invisible man with all invisible subtle organs and senses. Casting aside the clothes and covering of the physical body, it comes and goes in the invisible world voluntarily. It is quite easy to read of these Latifas in the books, converse about, and discuss them. But to attain that state and become the invisible subtle man and a luminous person of God the Almighty is a most difficult and hard thing.

Tricks of False Preceptors with Ignorant Disciples

After reading the accounts of the said Latifas in books of Sufiism, a number of formal shopkeeping Sufis verbally told their followers that the two Latifas of the soul and heart belong to the material world, and the five Latifas of the spirit روح, the secre سر, (خفی), most hidden (اخفیٰ), and ego (انا)belong to the invisible world. They tell them that the place of the soul is in the trunk, that of the heart and that of another is in the brain, and so on and so forth. They direct them to control the breath and order them to attend toward the heart and perceive in the heart the movements of commemoration and listen to the sound of commemoration. When the simple-minded poor follower attends to the heart, having controlled his breath, he actually perceives the action of the circulation of blood in the heart; nay, he even finds and feels its movements in every vein and artery of the whole body, and simultaneously, he hears the sound resembling "lubtup" of the pumping of the blood by the heart. To the ignorant followers, these movements and sounds of circulation are named as commemoration of the heart and soul, and the simple follower rejoices, taking these movements for the real commemoration and invocation of the Latifas, although these movements and sounds of the material heart are not even remotely connected with real divine commemoration and true esoteric Latifas. This movement and material sound of the circulation of the blood in the heart and other organs is not the real commemoration of the heart because this movement and sound of the circulation of blood is found in all the animals, even in the dogs.

Alas, that the formal, customary, hypocritic "shopkeeper" and sheikhs of today consider Sufiism as children's play, just as young children make toys, play with them, perform their marriage, and sing marriage-songs, while in reality, there is neither marriage nor matrimony. Copies cannot be originals.

حقیقت چھپ نہیں سکتی بناوٹ کے اصولوں سے   کہ خوشبو آ نہیں سکتی کبھی کاغذ کے پھولوں سے

(اسماعیل میرٹھی)

"Artificial things cannot be like real ones, because paper flowers cannot give perfume."

The revivification of the heart through commemoration of Allah and its real movement and motion is a very difficult task and a very great and high thing. When the heart is revived and begins to move with the name of Allah, it causes the high heavens to shake, the angels of the heavens are wonderstruck, and the whole universe becomes like an open book before the living-hearted gnostic. He even sees the whole world on the palm of his hand like an atom.

دل کہ ے جنبد جنباند عرش را   عرش را دل فرش سازد زیر پاء

(رومی)

"When the heart of a real gnostic moves with the name of Allah, the heavens of God move in dance with it and the throne of God the Almighty is under his feet at that moment."

The revivification of the real heart of a gnostic just resembles the birth of an invisible luminous child in the esoteric and etheric next world. The revivification of these personalities through divine commemoration is the ultimate object and aim of Islamic Sufiism. Its semblance is thus described in the Holy Quran, "The luminous candle of His personal name (Allah) is hanging in the globe of the heart of a gnostic by the tree of his material body," and when the danger of that material globe was imminent, its intelligent owner lit another candle from it and put it in that bright, eternal, peaceful, steadfast, and perpetual tree (i.e., the holy spiritual tree (Tuba) of the invisible world), where it is quite immune from breakage and putting out for ever. Maulana Rum Sahib thus expressed it in his masnavi:

باد تند است و چراغ ابترے   زد بگیرانم چراغ دیگرے

گر بادے آں چراغ از جا رود   تابود کز ہر دویک دانی شود

شمع دل افروخت از بہر فراغ   ہمچو عارف کز تن ناقص چراغ

پیش روئے خود نہد او شمع جاں   تاکہ روزے ایں بمیرد ناگہاں

(رومی)

There is a hard gale (of death) prevailing and the candle of material life is most tender and delicate, so I will light another strong and everlasting lamp from it. That perhaps one of the two may suffice if the former is put off by the wind the latter candle may take its place. Thus the gnostic who from the bodies' feeble lamp lit the minds' everlasting durable lamp for light. So that if this one suddenly goes out some day he may place that everlasting spiritual lamp before him.

Here is another example of it: We have been given for conveyance the elemental body to move about in the land journey of this material world, but after death, we have to commence another spiritual life, which exactly resembles a sea voyage, through which our material body is unable to convey us. Now the perfect gnostic, like the Prophet Noah, receives a revelation and information from God the Almighty: that in the material life, the universal flood and destructive deluge of death is about to come. The inspired gnostic like Noah prepares a spiritual ark by the name of Allah and embarks into it with all his family and relatives (i.e., his senses, intellect, memory, and all his faculties). Thus, the gnostic spiritual traveler escapes the terrible and destructive deluge of death, by getting and settling into the spiritual ark of God the Almighty through His personal name, Allah, reciting and saying the holy verse of the Quran:

$$بِسۡمِ اللّٰهِ مَجۡرٜىٰهَا وَمُرۡسٰىهَا ۚ (۱۱هود:٤۱)$$

"In the name of Allah we set sail and voyage." But materialist and ignorant people with their raw material bodies get drowned and destroyed in the infinite dark ocean of death forever.

چوں ترا نوح است کشتیبان ز طوفانِ غم مَخَور ۔۔۔ اے دل ار سیل فنا بنیاد ہستی بر کند

(حافظ)

"O heart! If the deluge of annihilation upsets the foundation of thy existence. Don't fear the deluge when you have a boatman like Noah." Moreover, this invisible etheric body emerges alive from every particle of this elemental body like the chicken out of the egg or butter out of milk, and a more subtle etheric body emerges from another one just as ghee comes out of butter and so on and so forth. This luminous etheric personality of the heart is a royal falcon without an abode and is a (عنقائ ٔ قاف قدس) phoenix of the mountain Qaf. When it breaks the temporal egg of matter and comes out, it cannot be accommodated in the dark and small nest of the material world, and with a slight flapping of its spiritual, angelic wings, it flies beyond the universe and six directions شش جہات. The holy tree becomes its humble house, and it makes its splendid nest on the edge of the Holy Throne کنگرۂ عرش of God the Almighty. Man has come to the world for this elevated objective, and this is the goal and end of human life. O pupil, try to search this real milestone and true destination.

گوہر تو زیور خاکِ آمدہ ۔۔۔ اے بدل از گوہر پاک آمدہ
تا توں بروں آمدی اے دُرِّ پاک ۔۔۔ چنبر نہ چرخ بے بیخت خاک
وانکہ نہ گنجد بیجہاں ہم توئی ۔۔۔ جانِ جہاں و ہمہ عالم توئی
نزپئی بازیچہ پدید آمدی ۔۔۔ گنجِ خدا را تو کلید آمدی
آئینۂ صورت رحمانت ساخت ۔۔۔ چرخ کہ از گوہر احسانت ساخت
آہ ہزار آہ کہ ندہی بزنگ ۔۔۔ آئینۂ سیں کہ گونہ کہ داری بچنگ
آئینۂ صافی اہلِ دل است ۔۔۔ آنکہ بمملک و ملکی قابل است

(نظام قمی)

"O you who are born of the pure essence as regards your soul, your essence is the ornament of the material world. The circle of the heavens sewed much dust, ere you made your appearance, Opure pearl. You are the soul of the world and the entire universe and that which the universe cannot accommodate. You are the key to the divine treasure. You were not created for sport. The heaven modeled you out of the jewel of mercy and made you the mirror of the divine form. With such a mirror in your hand, beware lest you let it rust. Noblest among the two worlds: is the mirror of the hearts of the pious people clear?"

The Perverted Notions of Modern Occidental Scholars about the Spirit

Nowadays, the Europeans, and the English too, believe in spirits and are attracted to spiritual sciences. Although in respect of the esoteric sciences of Islam, these people are like mere schoolboys reading the alphabet compared to our wise and pious men of yore and our present perfect saints. This statement of ours will prove to be a mighty proof for our young generation that is Westernized and fond of the new light and regards every word of European scholars as something more than heavenly revelation. Let our broadminded friends know that entirely changed is the erroneous idea promulgated in Europe about religion and spiritualism by science and modern philosophy sometime back. Now they have full faith in divine revelation, the invisible esoteric existence of spirit, its wonderful supernatural perceptions, and spiritual perfections. By reproducing here the descriptions of modern Occidental scholars, let us tell our ignorant young friends that those who regarded divine revelation and spiritual proclamation as mere folly have admitted its truth at last. In proof of the tremendous revolution in the religious ideology and spiritual outlook of those people, we would briefly narrate the present theories of Occidental scholars. Possibly, it may serve as a caution to those who repudiate religion and spiritualism, and they might take the trouble of reviewing their persistent atheism and irreligiousness and desist from opposing the true facts, which even the European scholars have accepted as true.

Like all the orthodox nations, the Europeans formerly believed in the divine revelation of the prophets up to the sixteenth century. But later on, with the onset of the scientific era, when the people began to drift from spiritualism and incline toward materialism, science and Western philosophy declared revelation as one of the old absurdities that still predominate the human heart and brain because of ignorance, folly, and superstition. Modern philosophy exaggerated the repudiation of metaphysical facts to the extent of altogether denying God and spirit. Revelation was regarded either as an invention of those claiming prophethood, pretended with a view to attracting human attention, or a malady that overtakes patients of nervous disorders during fits of which they visualize certain apparitions having no external reality. European philosophy so vigorously propagated this theory about revelation and other metaphysical things that it became a permanent parcel of philosophy, and to believe in it was necessary for everyone who wished to call himself learned or educated so that a large silly class was swept by the waves of this tide of folly and passed from the world ignorantly. But in the year 1846, there appeared certain signs of the existence of spirits that crossed beyond America and created a commotion in the ideas of Europe as well. People were led to believe in a spiritual world where great intellects are at work. The outlook of the discussion of spiritual theories was completely revolutionized, and revelation and spiritualism were revived. Western scholars began to discuss this theory anew to explore and investigate it. The whole atmosphere of Europe was set ablaze when they published the results of their research a few years later. A committee was set up in London in 1844 with the object of discussing and exploring the spirit and its circumstances. Notable among the scholars of the committee are the following:

1. Professor Jack of Cambridge University, president of the committee and world-famous physicist of England
2. Professor Sir Oliver Lodge, specialist in physics
3. Sir William Crookes, world-famous chemist of England
4. Professor Frederick Mayers, of Cambridge University
5. Professor Hudson
6. Professor William James Herfarel, University of America
7. Professor Bleryub, of Columbia University
8. Kamel Flamerian, famous astronomer and mathematician of France

Besides these, there were also other famous European scholars on the committee. It lasted for thirty years, investigated thousands of spiritual incidents, and made repeated experiments about the human soul and its energies and intelligences, which are preserved in forty stout volumes. This committee constantly published the results of its experiments and proved that man has another esoteric existence besides material body (i.e., that though we are alive in our present life and comprehend things, this comprehension is not the outcome of all the spiritual powers within us but is only a part thereof) that affects the external senses. But besides the life bestowed on us by the five senses, there is another and much superior life no trace of whose greatness is apparent unless this external personality of ours is suspended by sleep or some other means. We found out by experimenting on people who were put to sleep through hypnotism or magnetic sleep that the sleeper obtains an abundant wealth of the spiritual life. In the spiritual world, he sees and hears and gives information about distant and imperceptible objects through an esoteric sense different from his external senses. At that moment, his intelligence and comprehension are fully awakened to perform their duties. The committee is convinced that besides the external personality of a man, there is another personality much more exalted than the aforesaid material and physical personality and which survives after death and is imperishable.

These learned men have also discovered that it is this exalted personality that causes the stabilization of the embryonic matter within the mother's womb, and its influence and reflection shape the human body. The actions of the stomach and other organs beyond the pale of human intention are also due to this exalted personality. In fact, the very fact of a man's being depends on that esoteric personality and not this material personality connected with the five external senses. It is that very personality that creates superb ideas and thoughts within the opaque veils of the body. Divine revelations are also connected with this personality, and this is the force that promoted in the hearts of the prophets the new things called divine revelation. Sometimes, the revelation assumes a personality and becomes visible and is then termed an angel of God, the Most High, which descends from heaven. It is the opinion of these learned investigators that this duplicate personality of man feels through esoteric senses. Because we see in those people who are put to a magnetic sleep through hypnotism the presence of discriminative intelligence, reflection, foresight, and penetration in the hidden secrets of persons, the ability to discover secret things, traveling in the wide expanse of the world, in spite of complete stupid—all these things and other extraordinary capabilities are strong indications of an esoteric personality in man, which is concealed in the curtains of human existence and is visible only when his physical body is engaged in natural or artificial sleep.

Moreover, truthful dreams that come to pass, like the true dawn, whereby man discovers invisible things and coming events or wherein he solves such difficult problems that he could never solve while in his senses or he sometimes commits acts that he could not venture in consciousness, indicate the fact that besides the external personality, man has another esoteric self muchstronger, higher, and progressive than the former one. Besides these arguments, there are numerous other incidents this investigating committee has deeply studied with great pain. They examined the experiments conducted prior to them and have finally candidly admitted the existence of the spiritual world and its subtleties and incidents, and like a spiritual science, this knowledge has prevailed in all the countries of Europe, where spiritual societies and regular committees have been set up, regular colleges and innumerable schools of spiritualism have been started, and numerable books have been written on the science. In this connection, Professor Dr. Maurice, the famous psychologist, who is a distinguished member of this committee, has written a notable book on human personality in the various chapters of which he has fully discussed magnetic sleep, demonology, revelation, and esoteric personality. In the following, we give a few extracts from p. 77 and the following pages of the book. First of all, Professor Maurice has mentioned the mathematicians who give correct answers to the most difficult mathematical problems without any contemplation during magnetic sleep. The beauty of it is that if they are asked as to how they found out the answer, they can only say, "We have solved it, but we do not know how." In this connection, the professor has mentioned a man named Bedlar, who could instantaneously give the multiples of very large sums. Once he was asked about the sums that when multiplied would yield 17,861. He forthwith replied, "Multiplying 337 by 53 wouldyield this answer." When questioned about the method of it, he said, "I can't say." This means that his answer was a sort of natural impulse unconcerned with human intention and intelligence.

The professor says that he is convinced that such incidents were not appearing in the world for the first time, but before this also, similar higher states and incidents had come within the knowledge of ancient people and were the workings of our esoteric self, which has been present in all ages and at all times.

The professor says, "Now I can most positively and confidently assert the certainty of the presence of a spirit in man which extracts force and beauty from the spiritual world, and moreover, I affirm that Great Spirit and a circumambient light permeates the entire world with which the human spirit can obtain a union." Along with his own research, Professor Maurice has quoted from Aibu, a famous professor of France: "The esoteric personality of man is the very thing which the common folk call Revelation. This state has natural attributes and particulars which are peculiar to it."

Lastly, we turn to the testimony of Russel Wales, who is considered an equal and sharer of Darwin in physics. He has written a book on the wonders of the spirit in which he openly admits in the following words,

I was a rank materialist and atheist, I could not guess for a while that some time I will publicise spiritual life or verify an invisible spiritual power working in the world besides matter and its forces. But I am helpless! I have repeatedly sensed such spectacles which can never be falsified. They have compelled me to regard them as true and real. Though for a long while I was not prepared to admit them as spiritual effects, but these observations have gradually affected my mind— not by way of argumentation and reasoning but as a result of the persistent continuation of those observations which I could not escape except through admitting the existence of the spirit.

The investigations of the European professors of modern sciences into the spirit have led them to the conclusions Kamel Flamerian enumerates as follows:

1. The spirit has a permanent identity separate from the body.

2. The spirit is possessed of peculiarities that are unknown to modern science so far.
3. The spirit can be affected without the agency of the senses or can affect other things.
4. The spirit can be cognizant of coming events.

In the light of the preceding, these learned men regard Divine Revelation as follows:

Revelation, in fact, is the name of a particular kind of manifestation to the human spirit that sheds its light on him through his esoteric personality and teaches him things unknown to him, erstwhile. Regarding revelation, this much is common to both the wise men of Islam and Europe, that it is connected with the spirit and not with the body or any corporeal force. But it remains controversial that according to Islam, revelation descends to the heart of a prophet through an angel, while, according to them, angel means an esoteric personality. It is an insignificant difference in terms, not in facts.

This spiritual faith is prevalent in every house of Europe. Day and night, the spirits are invoked and talked to. In every house, there are circles (called home circles) for invoking the spirits. In every circle, the presence of an intermediary (i.e., medium) is essential. The medium is a person naturally controlled by a spirit. In other words, such a person is a link between the spiritual and corporeal worlds.

Through the person of the medium, the spirits come to the circle, enter into conversation, meddle with objects in the rooms, play on instruments without anyone's touching them, and import and export things into sealed rooms. The spirits deliver public lectures that are recorded, and they are photographed. In short, they display innumerable wonderful feats of a kind that science and material intelligence cannot explain. They have numerous colleges of spiritual sciences with various departments and subjects. They are engaged in progressing this science, day and night. In the following pages of this book, we will fully discuss this in the chapter on invocation, if it pleases Allah, and will fully detail and explicitly explain the nature, reality, and truth of the spirits and the particulars of their invocation. After years of research and a prolonged contemplation and meditation, the materialistic scholars in Europe and the scientific and philosophic explorers of the Occident have discovered a meek, humble, temporal, esoteric personality, while our sages and perfect saints have set up a regular chain of these esoteric and invisible personalities. By reviving in themselves the seven (etheric) personalities—each one better than the previous one—whereby they have displayed such wonderful spiritual inspiration and miracles that should the modern scientists and philosophers come to know of an atom of it, they would denounce groping after matter and die for spiritualism, and relinquishing all worldly affairs, they would concern themselves solely with this important, luscious, and present science, day and night.

In Sufistic phraseology, the lowest esoteric personality, recently discovered by the Occident, is called Latifa-e-Nafs لطیفه نفس (etheric personality of self). This etheric personality is present in every man in a raw, incomplete condition. One enters the land of dream through this elementary esoteric personality. This etheric personality of self is covered by the physical body like a dress. The sphere of this body is Nasut ناسوت (the hierarchy of mankind). Jinn, demons, and lower spirits reside here. The magicians and soothsayers of yore displayed feats of magic and auguring through this lowest personality of the self and disclosed them to people. This very etheric personality of self is the fountainhead of all the wonderful tricks and astonishing deeds of mesmerism, hypnotism, and spiritualism. Whatever be the case, it is now unanimously agreed upon by all the learned men and investigators of the past and present that the spirit survives after death and existed in eternity prior to the present life. In the human body, the etheric personality of the self is the elementary esoteric personality at the revival and awakening of which one steps into the invisible esoteric world of the jinn and lower spirits.

There are two methods of reviving and awakening this self, Latifa. One is celestial; the other is terrestrial—virtuous deeds, commemoration and meditation on God the Most High, devotion, prayers, fasts, and concentration on His personal name, Allah, as well as similar practices constitute the celestial method. Through mere opposition and combat of Nafs (the lower self of the etheric personality), ascetic practices, and seclusion, this is revived and awakened in the terrestrial form. In both the celestial and terrestrial forms, it attains subtlety and, on reviving and awakening, enters Nasut—the invisible world of Nafs. Esoterically, the terrestrial self is visited and befriended by jinn, satans, and terrestrial spirits. At this stage, the European spiritualists invoke jinn, satans, and terrestrial spirits. In this very stage, the soothsayers and magicians give performances of their soothsaying and magic, and the hypnotist uses his subject by introducing magnetic sleep in him. In a raw and sleeping state, this etheric personality is present in every man. One dreams through it. It is also called the subconscious mind through which the mesmerist gives mesmeric performances. The wonders of this Latifa are past counting. A detailed account of all will require a separate volume. Through it, the student attains frenzied inspiration and tells the people about the past and future and is celebrated by them as one endowed with inspiration and miraculous powers.

The jinn of the invisible world are subdued in this stage, and the operator can take from them all sorts of services. He can injure his antagonists; through them, he flies and travels over land, creates love and enmity among people, and cures fits of obsession and diseases. In short, through this etheric personality, innumerable terrestrial tricks can be shown esoterically to the commonfolk. Through a single demonic glance, ignorant fools can be driven mad. In Tibet, this art is very prevalent. In short, the wonders of this lowest etheric personality alone are unaccountable. But such a person has no esteem and rank with God the Most High. If an elementary operator of this kind remains stationary and satisfied with this stage, the specialized perfect gnostics do not consider him equal to a fly because even an irreligious yogi or a nonpraying and unorthodox person can also perform such earthly feats. In short, by attaining union with jinn, satans, and lower spirits in this stage, he can perform everything that a jinn, satan, or lower spirit can do. He can fly in the air like a bird, enter fire without being hurt, walk over water, dive here and appear there, and reach in a single breath and a single step from the east to the west. Because of this, His Holiness Junaid of Baghdad (R.A) says:

اِذَا رَاَيْتَ رَجُلًا يَّطِيْرُ فِي الْهَوَآءِ وَيَمْشِىْ عَلَى الْمَاءِ وَتَرَكَ سُنَّةً مِّنْ سُنَّةِ رَسُوْلِ اللّٰهِ صَلَّى اللّٰهُ عَلَيْهِ وَسَلَّمَ فَاضْرِبُهُ بِالنَّعْلَيْنِ فَاِنَّهُ شَيْطَانٌ وَّمَا صَدَرَ مِنْهُ فَهُوَ مَكْرٌ وَّاِسْتِدْرَاجٌ۔

"When you see a man flying in the air and walking over water who has practically relinquished a single tradition out of the traditions of the Prophet of Allah (P.B.U.H.), strike him with your shoes, for he is a satan and what he displays is fraud and deception."

مرد درویش بے شریعت اگر   بپرد بر ہوا مگس باشد

درچوں کشتی رواں شود بر آب   اعتمادش مکن کہ خس باشد

(زکریا رازی)

"If an unorthodox dervish flies in the air, he is a mosquito. And if he walks over water like a boat, trust him not for he is a straw." All the spiritualists and psychologists of Europe, especially the modern spiritualists who invoke the spirits in their circles and seances and talk to them; the hypnotist who introduces magnetic sleep in the subject and employs his esoteric personality, namely, this etheric personality of the self; the mesmerists who display various earthly tricks; and the utmost exertions of all the sorcerers, magicians, and all earthly operators are confined to this lowest etheric personality of the self. They cannot proceed one inch beyond it. And though these terrestrial feats are highly esteemed by the sensualist, materialist brains, the perfect gnostics do not value it as much as a grass blade. That is why all the terrestrial sensualist adepts are engaged in earning ignoble worldly wealth through these feats and tricks. Had they any knowledge of their Creator, they would not have gone about exchanging their acts for the short-lived, perishable, and worthless wealth. In fact, Occidental spiritualism, hypnotism, and mesmerism are the pickers of the bunches of the elementary raw fruits of the Islamic garden of mysticism. Mesmerism is the predecessor in time of hypnotism. In Europe, it was highly celebrated in Hungary and later on in Austria. Mesmerism was founded by Dr. Mesmer, a resident of Austria's capital, Vienna. Out of the whole of Europe, Hungary was chosen by the famous Baktashi Sufis of Turkey as their largest spiritual center. In Budapest, the mausoleum of his holiness Baba Gulshan is still the rendezvous of the public. Not only the Muslims but the Christians as well flock there to ask for their needs. It is generally known about His Holiness Baba Gulshan that the holy man used to cure the diseased by a pass of his hand. There is a small fountain near his grave that is still celebrated as an elixir for repelling maladies. Haji Qandash Baktashi was the most famous miracle man of Hungary in the middle of the eighteenth century. His mausoleum was in Naghi Kanizsa, a village in Hungary. Besides Abyssinians, thousands of other Musalmans and many Christians had joined him as his disciples.

In the memoirs of Haji Qandis, Dr. Zemur, the famous European Orientalist, says that whenever a sick person was brought to Haji Sahib, he used to recite some prayers and blow on him, and making him lie facedown, he used to pass his hand over him. The patient recovered within a few minutes. It is also related about him that a sword, bayonet, or gun could not injure the man who had tied his amulet around his arm. The Haji Sahib used to cure deep wounds of swords, bayonets, and bullets by passing and application of his saliva. It is also said about him that if he stared at anyone, the man fell down unconscious. Hence, the Haji Sahib used to wear a veil around his face.

Dr. Mesmer became famous in the end of the eighteenth century just like many other Christians who had joined the Baktashi order. Dr. Mesmer was a disciple of the Haji Sahib and learned from him the method of paying attention according to Islamic mysticism. Later on, he gave it the color of materialism, called it "animal magnetism," and utilized it as healing power.

Everything in the lap of mesmerism or hypnotism is the faint impression of the elementary etheric personality of self of the Sufis. The only difference between the two is that while Tasawwuf is perfect material, mesmerism is imperfect; the former is light, and the latter is fire; Tasawwuf looks toward religion and mesmerism toward the world; and Tasawwuf turns toward God, and mesmerism toward the material world and all that is therein.

Sometimes, jinn, Satan, and evil spirits inhabit a house and frighten and harm the inmates in sleep and in waking. In the whole world, there is not any city where this invisible spirit does not reside in any house or building. Such houses are commonly called haunted houses. Some jinn are harmless, and far from injuring and harming the inmates of the house, they protect them against other jinn and satans. I have seen such haunted houses with my eyes and found them to be the dwelling places of jinn and satans. Some jinn, satans, and evil spirits possess human beings, which upsets their health, and they fall prey to incurable diseases. But besides physical maladies, the entrance of jinn and satans into the human body also adversely affects the morals and convictions. When some human heart or brain is affected by their hellish and impure effects, he becomes mad and insane.

They are divided into different categories and have separate qualities and functions. One of their categories dwells in mountainous springs and caves. Another group frequents houses and mansions in the cities. A third kind inhabit graveyards. These are natural jinn and satans who live with human beings, separate from men after death, and roam for a while around their graves. Jinn and satans sometimes possess and control the relatives of the dead. It is common news among the Hindus that on his death, the spirit of the deceased converts into an evil spirit and possesses one of his relatives. Therefore, they disguise their dress and features at the time of cremating the dead. Some Hindu clans exaggerate the disguise to the extent of shaving the hair of their head, beard, and moustaches so that the spirit of the departed may not recognize them on becoming an evil spirit and that they may escape their control.

OBJECT OF LIFE AND NECESSITY OF COMMEMORATING ALLAH

Let it be known that on the day of beginning, God the Most High created all the spirits out of the essence and light of his personal name, Allah, by pronouncing the word "Become," bidding all the spirits to His presence, and displaying His majesty. He questioned them, "Aren't I your Lord?" At that moment, since the eyes of all the spirits were lightened with the light of His personal name, Allah, and lightened with the collyrium of gnosis, all of them unanimously replied, "Yes! You are certainly our Lord." Thereafter, the Divine Goldsmith desired to test the worth of their speech and the metal of their assertion by casting these in the melting-cups of actions and states (i.e., the elemental bodies) and melting these in the kiln of the examination house of the world. Therefore, from "the best creation," He lowered them into the lowest depths, and in his lighted nature, he intermixed Satanic fire, the smoke of sensual darkness, and the filth of the perishable world. And he fully tested the power of fulfilment of the spirits, the sincerity of their promise of—Yes—and the force of the assertion of worshipfulness. So He removed them from the paradise of proximity and union and cast them in the unknown and distant desert of the world. He removed the free and spiritual birds of the spirits from the garden of the pure world, thrust them in the cages of earthly bodies, and gave their strings to the hands of powerful hunters, such as the evil passions and Satan.

When weak-natured man was put in the operation room of the world, the chloroform of the impure world made his eternal heart and brain unconscious and immediately made him forget the promise "Aren't I of the worshipful and real beloved." Hadith.

رَوَى جُوَيْرٌ عَنِ الضَّحَاكِ قَالَ اَهْبَطَ اللّٰهُ اٰدَمَ وَحَوَّاءَ اِلَى الْاَرْضِ وَوَجَدَاْرِيْحَ الدُّنْيَا وَفَقَدْ رَائِحَةَ الْجَنَّةِ فَغُشِىَ عَلَيْهِمَا اَرْبَعِيْنَ صَبَاحًا مِّنْ نَّتْنِ الدُّنْيَا۔

"When Allah cast Adam and Eve on the earth and they found the earthly air and lost the air of heaven, they remained unconscious for forty days due to the stinginess of the material world."

Thus man's eternal, natural bright lamp of His personal name, Allah, was concealed in the opaque veils of the worldly sensualist darknesses and Satanic blackness. You would say that the Jonah of the spirit fell into the belly of the fish of matter, whence it is impossible to emerge except by commemorating His personal name, Allah. Says the Most High:

$$
فَلَوۡلَاۤ اَنَّهٗ كَانَ مِنَ الۡمُسَبِّحِيۡنَ ۞ لَلَبِثَ فِيۡ بَطۡنِهٖۤ اِلٰى يَوۡمِ يُبۡعَثُوۡنَ ۞
$$

(۳۷ والصّٰفّٰت: ۱۴۳-۱۴۴)

"If he hadn't turned one of the commemorators, he would have remained in its belly till the resurrection."

Now poor man lies entangled in the chains of relations and impediments, far from the brilliant court of proximity and gnosis. In the black sea of the world, he is striving in search of the fountainhead of the eternal water of life, which lies concealed under the dust of his earthly self. It is impossible to dig out this fountain without the hoe of His personal name, Allah, and without the strong rope of commemoration, it is very difficult for the Joseph of the spirit to climb out of the well of forgetfulness of the material world. In the darkness of the world and the black night of forgetfulness, man has no other friend, sympathizer, or guiding light except the lamp of concentration on the name Allah. Because except for commemorating Allah, there exists no other relationship or medium between the Creator and the created, the Provider and the provided, the Eternal and the contingent, the Master and the slave.

It is this esoteric telephone and spiritual wireless that has interconnected the Master and the slave. Man is tied to his Lord through the string of commemoration alone. This is the meaning of

وَاعۡتَصِمُوۡا بِحَبۡلِ اللّٰهِ جَمِيۡعًا (۳ آلِ عمرٰن: ۱۰۳)

"Stick ye all to the rope of Allah."

One end of this rope lies with the Creator in heaven and the other one with the created in the world. He who vigorously grasped this rope ascended to the bright court of the Creator, and he who avoided it remained blind in the darkness of the world forever.

مل مل کے غیروں سے آشنا کو بھولے   یاں آ کے ہم اپنے مُدعا کو بھولے

دنیا کی تلاش میں گنوائی سب عمر   اِس میں کی طلب میں کیمیا کو بھولے

(اکبر الہ آبادی)

"On coming here we forgot our object. On meeting strangers we forgot the friend. We lost our lives in search of the worldly wealth. And forgot the alchemy in search of the copper."

Don't you see that protracted absence wipes out the memory of a friend or relative from one's mind, and on meeting him after a long time, he fails to recognize him. But the recognition is refreshed after mutual conversation, recounting past occurrences, and recapitulating incidents and episodes. But if, after separation from a friend, one continues to send messages and letters, the mutual friendship sustains, and he does not forget the friend. The same is the case with the eternally estranged spirit that has come out of the paradise of proximity and presence and is lying in the distant deserts of the world—away from the true beloved. Now during this space of separation, if he

$$فَاذْكُرُوْنِىْ أَذْكُرْكُمْ (١٢ البقرة : ١٥٢)$$

"Remember Me and I'll remember thee" or keeps aglow the fire of his love with the wireless of "They love Him and He loves them," he will not, undoubtedly, forget the True Beloved, in accordance with

$$وَالَّذِيْنَ جَاهَدُوْا فِيْنَا لَنَهْدِيَنَّهُمْ سُبُلَنَا (١٢٩ العنكبوت : ٦٩)$$

"And those that strive towards Us will be shown Our path."

The Eternal Beloved will reciprocally arrange to call and unite him with Himself, and mounting him on the fleet steed of His personal name, Allah, He will give His lover the felicity of interviewing Him in His pure and luminous court. "And that is not difficult for Allah." When friends who have been separated in the material world for a short while find it difficult to recognize each other at sight unless there is a mutual conversation and recapitulation of past memories, why should not it be difficult without the help of commemoration to recognize and know the Beloved, separated on the Day of Eternity and lost for a long while?

Apparently then, the eyes stand in need of commemoration and sight is strengthened by speech. The patent عیان is strengthened by narration بیان, and the way to recognition is through the ear. This manifests the importance of commemoration.

بسا کیں دولت از گفتار خیزد   نہ تنہا عشق از دیدار خیزد

(جامی)

"Love isn't kindled through sight alone. Conversation often produces this wealth." Therefore in this world commemoration is highly essential and indispensable to man for refreshing that eternal memory, fulfilling the promise of 'yes' and recognizing his True Beloved."

We have already stated that whenever one is remembered by name, an electric wave from the heart of the commemorator reaches that man. Similarly, the electric wave from the heart of God the Almighty's commemorator reaches Him. Though the Essence of God the Almighty is absolutely incomparable and peerless and without any abode or mark, through His selected and intimate slaves (i.e., the prophets and saints), He has indicated ways and means of meeting Him by saying, "I am very near to man; closer to him than his jugular vein and self. If any one desires to meet Me he can do so by commemorating Me." This, we will presently narrate. So when the commemorator remembers Allah, the Most High, the electric wave of his commemoration flashes to Allah, the Almighty, who responds reciprocally as is evident from the verse.

فَاذۡكُرُوۡنِیۤ اَذۡكُرۡكُمۡ (۱۲ البقرۃ: ۱۵۲)

"Remember Me; I'll remember thee."

Thus, it is clear that the wireless of commemoration runs between the commemorator and the commemorated (i.e., the worshipper and the worshipped). Now we have to scrutinize the utility of the wireless of commemoration and how it avails. Then let it be remembered that since the electric wave of commemoration emanates from the two wires of the heart and brain, the result is that every breath of the commemorator exhaled carries the attribute of the heart of the commemorator to the commemorated and on return brings the cordial attribute and esoteric fragrance of the commemorated to the commemorator. Thus, the attributes of the heart and brain, invisible states, and thoughts of the commemorator and the commemorated are exchanged esoterically. Thus, the imperfect, raw commemorator gets qualified by the sublime and pure qualities of the perfect commemorated and acquires His praiseworthy and pure attributes. So when the telephone of

فَاذْكُرُوْنِىٓ أَذْكُرْكُمْ (٢البقرة: ١٥٢)

"Remember Me; I'll remember you" or the telegraph of

رَضِىَ اللّٰهُ عَنْهُمْ وَرَضُوْا عَنْهُ (٥المآئدة:١١٩)

"God is pleased with them, and they are pleased with God!"

Or the wireless wave of يحبه ـ و يحبونه They love him and he loves them is set up between the Worshipped and the worshipper, frail man, who is fettered in the chain of worldly attachments, tied in the ropes of sensual passions, and imprisoned in Satanic darkness, receives divine aid through this holy chain of commemoration, and his esoteric fetters and spiritual chains begin to snap. If he sticks and adheres to excessive commemoration, he obtains complete liberty, as God the Most High says:

وَاذْكُرُوا اللّٰهَ كَثِيْرًا لَّعَلَّكُمْ تُفْلِحُوْنَ (٦٢الجمعة:١٠)

"Remember Allah excessively, perhaps you may escape."

Through commemoration of God the Most High, the evil habits of the commemorator gradually change into praiseworthy qualities until he is qualified by angelic qualities and rendered fit for God the Most High's affinity, union, and observation. Finally, God the Almighty absorbs him in the light of his interview and esoterically combines him with Himself. In short, commemoration is the sole means of God the Almighty's gnosis, affinity, and union, and out of the commemorations, the best selected and most complete is the commemoration of His personal name, Allah. The Holy Quran is replete with the importance and superiority of commemoration of His personal name, Allah. Utmost emphasis on commemorating Allah is frequently found in the Prophet's traditions. God the Most High says:

$$يَذْكُرُوْنَ اللّٰهَ قِيَامًا وَّقُعُوْدًا وَّعَلٰى جُنُوْبِهِمْ (٣ آل عمران:١٩١)$$

"They remember Allah while standing, sitting, and lying."

Moreover, He says:

$$اِنَّ الصَّلٰوةَ تَنْهٰى عَنِ الْفَحْشَآءِ وَالْمُنْكَرِ ۗ وَلَذِكْرُ اللّٰهِ اَكْبَرُ ۗ (١٢٩ العنكبوت:٤٥)$$

"Perform the prayers in order to commemorate Me. Verily the prayers stop one from evils and detestable and commemorating God is a great thing."

Says the Most High:

$$وَالذّٰكِرِيْنَ اللّٰهَ كَثِيْرًا وَّالذّٰكِرٰتِ ۙ اَعَدَّ اللّٰهُ لَهُمْ مَّغْفِرَةً وَّاَجْرًا عَظِيْمًا ۩$$

$$(١٣٣ الاحزاب:٣٥)$$

"And the men and women who commemorate Allah abundantly have been promised amnesty and a great reward by Allah."

Says the Most High:

$$يٰٓاَيُّهَا الَّذِيْنَ اٰمَنُوا اذْكُرُوا اللّٰهَ ذِكْرًا كَثِيْرًا ۙ وَّسَبِّحُوْهُ بُكْرَةً وَّاَصِيْلًا$$

$$(١٣٣ الاحزاب:٤١-٤٢)$$

"O faithful! commemorate Allah profusely and praise Him morning and evening."

The Holy Prophet once said to his companions:

$$عَنْ اَبِى الدَّرْدَاءِ (رضى الله عنه) قَالَ رَسُوْلُ اللّٰهِ صَلَّى اللّٰهُ عَلَيْهِ وَسَلَّمَ اَلَا اُنَبِّئُكُمْ بِخَيْرِ اَعْمَالِكُمْ وَ$$
$$اَزْكٰهَا عِنْدَ مَلِيْكِكُمْ وَاَرْفَعِهَا فِىْ دَرَجَاتِكُمْ وَخَيْرٍ لَّكُمْ مِنْ اِنْفَاقِ الذَّهَبِ وَالْوَرِقِ وَخَيْرٍ لَّكُمْ$$
$$مِنْ اَنْ تَلْقَوْا عَدُوَّكُمْ فَتَضْرِبُوْا اَعْنَاقَهُمْ وَيَضْرِبُوْا اَعْنَاقَكُمْ قَالُوْا بَلٰى قَالَ ذِكْرُ اللّٰهِ تَعَالٰى ـ$$

$$(مشكوٰة)$$

"Shouldn't I intimate to you the best of actions, best liked by your Master, higher than all your stage, more beneficial than spending gold and silver and more profitable for you than fighting your antagonists when you strike off their heads and they strike off yours?"

They said, "Please do! O Prophet of Allah (P.B.U.H.)."

The Prophet said, "That action consists in commemorating Allah."

Some people would be astonished at this tradition as to how a verbal action like commemoration can be superior to the most difficult and self-sacrificing action of fighting against the infidels. Therefore, we herein recite a verse of the glorious Quran in corroboration of this tradition. Says God the Most High:

وَلَوْلَا دَفْعُ اللّٰهِ النَّاسَ بَعْضَهُمْ بِبَعْضٍ لَّهُدِّمَتْ صَوَامِعُ وَبِيَعٌ وَّصَلَوٰتٌ وَّمَسَاجِدُ يُذْكَرُ فِيْهَا اسْمُ اللّٰهِ كَثِيْرًا (الحج:٤٠) ١٢٢

"Had not some people (i.e., the infidels) been repelled by others (i.e., the Muslims), the former would have demolished the worship places, markets, and mosques (of the latter), where Allah is abundantly remembered."

This verse shows that vindication and defense of mosques, places of worship, religious and spiritual meetings, and functions is the sole purpose of fighting against the infidels. And the final and true object of all these is that which is mentioned at the end, namely the abundant commemoration of Allah's name. And the means can never surpass the end. There is another tradition.

قَالَ عَلَيْهِ الصَّلٰوةُ وَالسَّلَامُ مَا مِنْ عَذَابِ اللّٰهِ مِنْ ذِكْرِ اللّٰهِ قَالُوْا وَلَا الْجِهَادُ يَا رَسُوْلَ اللّٰهِ صَلَّى اللّٰهُ عَلَيْهِ وَسَلَّمَ قَالَ وَلَا الْجِهَادُ وَلَوْ يُضْرَبُ بِالسَّيْفِ حَتّٰى يَنْقَطِعَ ـ

The Holy Prophet once said to his companions, "For removing the punishment of God nothing can be more effective than the commemoration of Allah."

Then the companions inquired, "Not even the Religious War, O Prophet of Allah (P.B.U.H.)?"

The Prophet remarked, "No, not even the Religious War, though you be struck with swords and cut to pieces!"

The Prophet (P.B.U.H.) says:

قَالَ رَسُوْلُ اللّٰهِ صَلَّى اللّٰهُ عَلَيْهِ وَسَلَّمَ لَيْسَ يَتَحَسَّمُ أَهْلُ الْجَنَّةِ اِلَّا عَلٰى سَاعَةٍ مَرَّتْ بِهِمْ وَ لَمْ يَذْكُرُوا اللّٰهَ تَعَالٰى فِيْهَا ـ

"The inhabitants of paradise would not regret anything except the moment which they allowed to pass without commemorating therein God the Most High."

Tradition says:

اِذَا ذَكَرْتَنِیْ شَكَرْتَنِیْ وَاِذَا اَنْسِیْتَنِیْ كَفَرْتَنِیْ۔

"When you remembered Me, you were thankful, and when you forgot Me, you were ungrateful."

کسے کو غافل ازوے یک زمان است

درآں دم کافر است اما نہان است

(رومی)

He who forgets Him for a moment is a heretic at that moment but potentially not forever.

Tradition says:

قَالَ مُوْسٰی یَارَبِّ اَقَرِیْبٌ اَنْتَ فَاُنَاجِیْكَ اَمْ بَعِیْدٌ فَاُنَادِیْكَ فَاِنِّیْ اَحِسُّ صَوْتَكَ وَلَا اُرِیْكَ فَاَیْنَ اَنْتَ قَالَ اللّٰهُ اَنَا اَمَامَكَ وَاَنَا خَلْفُكَ وَعَنْ یَمِیْنِكَ وَعَنْ شِمَالِكَ یَامُوْسٰی وَاَنَا جَلِیْسُ عَبْدِیْ حِیْنَ یَذْكُرُنِیْ وَاَنَا مَعَهُ اِذَا دَعَانِیْ۔

Moses (P.B.U.H.) said, "O my Lord, if thou art nigh I'll address thee slowly and if afar I'll do so loudly. I can hear thy sweet voice but can't see thee. Tell me where art thou?"

God replied, "I am to thy front and rear, right and left, O Moses! I sit with my slave when he commemorates Me and am with him when he calls Me." Once God the Most High sent this revelation to Moses (p.b.u.h.), God said to Moses:

وَاَوْحٰی اللّٰهُ تَعَالٰی اِلٰی مُوْسٰی اَتُحِبُّ اَنْ اَسْكُنَ مَعَكَ فِیْ بَیْتِكَ یَا مُوْسٰی۔ فَخَرَّ لِلّٰهِ سَاجِدًا وَّقَالَ یَارَبِّ كَیْفَ تَسْكُنُ مَعِیْ فِیْ بَیْتِیْ قَالَ یَا مُوْسٰی اَنَا جَلِیْسُ مَعَ مَنْ ذَكَرَنِیْ وَ حَیْثُ مَا الْتَمَسَنِیْ عَبْدِیْ وَ جَدَنِیْ۔

"Do you wish Me, O Moses, to stay with you in your house?"

Moses (A.S) fell prostrate and said, "O Lord! How can you stay with Me in my house?"

He said, "I sit with one who remembers Me, and whenever My slave seeks Me, he invariably finds Me."

From numerous other Quranic verses and traditions, it is proved that the mere commemoration of Allah is the best of all acts. All other acts are inferior to it. The cream of all the revealed scriptures, especially the Holy Quran and the Prophet's traditions, is that devotion, gnosis, proximity, and union of God the Almighty is the real object of human life, and the commemoration of Allah and this name is the sole means thereof. All the religions, especially Islam, provide for taking man through the name of God the Most High to the named God the Most High, as will be presently narrated. All the fundamentals of Islam—the divine precepts—expediently, sayings of the Prophet, and supererogatory acts are the various manifestations of this single act, namely, the commemoration of Allah, and the auxiliaries of this object and the means of perfection of this single act. The whole of the Quran and all the chapters commence with the name of Allah: "In the name of Allah the Most Compassionate, the Most Merciful." It is in the tradition that the entire Quran is imbibed in the opening chapter, and the whole of the opening chapter is contained in "In the name of Allah, the Most Compassionate, the Most Merciful." That is to say that the whole of the Quran is contained in this personal name, Allah, like the tree contained in the seed. And why should it not be so when the Quran is the commemoration of Allah in detail and the name "Allah" is His commemoration in brief?

When the old bishops of the Christian faith are interrogated about the commencement of creation, they invariably repeat this proverb: "In the beginning was the word and the word was with God and God was the word." The bishops are unable to explain this proverb and merely reproduce it like a parrot. Obviously, this proverb is part of the same old revealed text, which means that His personal name, Allah, is the word that was with God the Most High at the commencement—before the creation of the universe—and that word was God the Most High Himself. That is to say, that the name had a unity with the named. And this is the enigma of the name and the named, which the materialistic brains know not. They regard the commemoration of Allah as mere inertia, idleness, and the suspension of bodily limbs. From the similitude of the English words *word* and *world*, a wise man can come to the conclusion that the word *word*, the word *become*, or His personal name, Allah, and *world* (i.e., the entire universe) have the same origin. In short, His personal name, Allah, is the cream of all commemorations, and the entire universe, especially the human body, was in the light of His personal name, Allah.

On the Day of Eternity, God the Almighty secretly deposited the light of His personal name, Allah, in the esoteric human nature by way of trust. His personal name, Allah, is the bright cord wherewith man is attached to his Creator. Through its intermediation, a bright ventilator and esoteric path is opened in man toward the invisible world. This very personal name of Allah is the only key of all the esoteric treasures composed of all the exoteric and esoteric sciences, knowledge, and secrets; all the lights of the Essence (ذات), attributes (صفات), acts (افعال), and names (اسماء); all the hierarchies of man(ناسوت), angels (ملكوت), power (جبروت), and God (لاهوت); all the stages of the law (شريعت), path (طريقت), truth (حقيقت), and gnosis (معرفت); all the commemorations and etheric personalities of the self (نفس), heart (قلب), spirit (روح), secret (سرّ), hidden (مخفى), most hidden (اخفىٰ), and ego (انا); and all the ranks of Islam namely faith (ايمان), certainty (ايقان), gnosis (عرفان), proximity (قرب), affection (محبت), observation (مشاهده), and union (وصال).

The value of commemorating God the Almighty; His personal name, Allah; and religious performances will be realized after death. The value of these esoteric jewels cannot be realized by the blind-hearted sensualist people fumbling in the black sea of the world, who are in the habit of saying, "Religion brings one towards the study of the word Allah, which is mere inertia, idleness, and dry life. It is very difficult to discern the real worth of commemorating Allah." About the name Allah and the fundamentals of religion in the examination hall of the world, there is a famous story: Sultan Sikandar took a fancy for drinking the water of life and becoming immortal. With a few companions, he set out in search of it under the guidance of His Holiness Khizr خضر (A.S). They reached a place where sunlight could not penetrate, which is called the Black Sea, and it is pitch-dark there. Unfortunately, Sikandar and his companions lost their way in the darkness. They were separated from Khizr (A.S) and lost his guidance. After wandering about in the darkness for a while, they regained the company of Khizr (A.S), who had reached the Fountain of the Water of Life and was partaking of it. Since they had run short of provisions, all were agreed on going out of the Black Sea and returning to their country, Khizr (A.S), their guide, was moved by their deprivation and gave them another piece of profitable advice. He said, "Perhaps you were not destined to drink the water of life. But I will tell you another useful thing. The stones and pebbles that you feel under your feet are rubies, diamonds, and valuable jewels. Fill these up in your provision sacks and take them away. These will make you rich in your country."

Believing in the veracity of Khizr, some of his companions filled their portmanteaus with the stones. Some were less credulous and picked up a few stones only. The rest said that formerly Khizr too (A.S) had misguided them by making them wander hither and thither in the darkness and that the unprofitable trouble of picking up the stones would also prove futile. So they picked up nothing. When they left the place, crossed the Black Sea, and opened their portmanteaus in broad daylight, their surprise knew no bounds because they saw that the heavy and useless stones and pebbles were precious stones. Those who had picked up no stones grieved heavily, and those who had picked up only a few were also very sorry. But those who had brought more stones got very rich in the world.

This is a fable that fits with the material life. The world is the Black Sea. The light of His personal name, Allah, is the water of immortality, which is sprouting beneath the stone of the heart (i.e., the invisible world under the heart). The felicitous people are the special selected people who drank their fill of it, became immortal, and were made prophets and saints like Khizr (A.S). Whoever drank the water of immortality of the light of His personal name, Allah, gained eternal life and lived forever through the personal light of God the Most High. Like Khizr (A.S), God the Almighty made them the guides of His creation in this world and the next.

فرق است ز آب خضر که ظلمات جائے اوست

تا آب ما که منبعش الله اکبر است

(حافظ)

"Different from Khizr's spring of life, which is in utter darkness, is our water, the source of which is the name of Allah."

To those deprived of this water of immortality, these guides give this advice: "O men! The outward fundamentals and acts of religion appear to you like heavy and useless stones in the Black Sea of this world. In your real home, the next world, you will find them to be rubies and diamonds, and through these, you will become very wealthy in the next world. Briefly, this story is an exquisite example of the darkness of this world. But when the materialistic sensualist people read such allegorical religious stories in religious books, they take no lesson from them and do not come to the right path but begin to laugh at these. In fact, the melancholia of materialism and labarum of politics have upset the brains of the modern people. Like the blind frog of the well, they regard this world as everything. Proud of their materialistic intellects and external knowledge, they proudly, hotheadedly, but foolishly deny Quranic truths and spiritual secrets. But when the dust of the path will vanish and the hard grip of God the Almighty will hold them fast, they will lose all their sensualist pride and material intoxication. One will know then whether he is riding a horse or an ass.

بروز حشر تُرا ایں ہمہ شود معلوم

کہ باکہ باختہ عشق در شبِ دیجور

On the day of Resurrection, you will know all fully well with whom you have love in the dark night.

THE ENIGMA OF THE
NAME AND THE NAMED

Very few people realize the importance of commemorating Allah and the name Allah. The lawgivers of Islam and the religious elders have told us the commemoration of Allah and the name Allah is the sole means of divine gnosis, affinity, observation, and union. Because the name is the very named and the enigma of breaking up the physical talisman, it is said in a holy tradition, "I used to sit with the one who commemorates Me." Another tradition says, "I am between the lips of the one who commemorates Me." Now it is evident that the magnificent and unbounded Essence of God the Almighty can never be accommodated between the two lips of a mortal. Only the name of God the Almighty can be so accommodated. This refers to the union and unity of the name and the Named, showing not only that there is union between the name and the Named but the name is the very essence and very self of the Named and the same is the very cause of the creation of the people and the universe.

Now we want to explain the meaning of His personal name, Allah. Let it be clear that whenever any object or any person is remembered or mentioned, all praises and things revert to his person or name and all things are directed toward his name in the first instance and toward his person in the second. And when the person talked about is absent, all mention of him is directed toward his name only, and all things end with his name. Names are twofold: personal and attributive. The personal name is that which indicates someone's single person qualified by all his attributes; for example, a person is called Zaid. Now this is his personal name. If that man has acquired learning, he will be called "learned." If he has studied medicine, he becomes a physician, and if he has performed the pilgrimage, "pilgrim" becomes one of his names. If he has committed the Quran to memory, he becomes a Hafiz. In this way, the more attributes this single man Zaid is qualified with, the more attributive names—learned, physician, pilgrim, and Hafiz—will be added to his name. The more the vocations, the more the names. But when we call him by the name Zaid, we will mean thereby the man qualified with all the mentioned attributes—physician, Hafiz, pilgrim, and so on. Hence, Zaid is his proper name, and the rest (learned, physician, pilgrim, Hafiz, and so on) are his attributive names because these were attached to him after he was qualified with these attributes. Now if we refer to Zaid's learning and intelligence and talk about these, all this talk and the story of Zaid's learning is expressed by the word *learned*. Similarly, all the adventures of his expertness in medicine are included in the word *physician*. This proves that the attributive name is the compendium of all the attributive tales while the personal name is the soul and spirit and sum total of all the attributive names. Similarly, "Allah" is the personal name of God the Almighty, and compassionate, merciful, master, holy, almighty, powerful, forgiver, and all the ninety-nine or more names of Allah are attributive. So the various chapters and verses of the Quran indicate some attributes of God the Most High. Thus, all the statements, commemorations, sciences, knowledge, and secrets of the Quran indicate some special attribute of God the Most High. If the verses promise reward, they indicate His lovable names, such as compassionate, merciful, munificent, pardoner, and so on, while the retributive verses indicate God the Most High's terrible attributes, such as powerful, almighty, avenger, and so on. Similarly, the stories of the prophets also aim at displaying some special attribute of God the Most High. All the other thanksgiving eulogisms (تمجید), praises (تعریف), magnifications (تکبیر), sanctifications, and glorifications found in the Holy Quran are the details of God, the Most High's attributive names—pleasant, holy, praised, glorious, and the like. In short, the glorious Quran is like a holy tree; its letters, words, and verses are like flowers, leaves, and tiny buds, respectively. The chapters are like the small branches, the attributive names are like the larger branches, and His personal name, Allah, is like the large trunk with regard to action and like the seed and fruit with regard to power. Though the tree produces abundant fruition, its branches, its own creation and origin, are due to a single fruit. In the same way, though His personal name, Allah, is mentioned in innumerable places in Quranic chapters, the entire Quran is the praise and eulogism of God the Exalted's Essence and his great name "Allah," and His personal name, Allah, is the root and cause of all.

عِبَارَاتُنَا شَتّٰى وَ حُسْنُكَ وَاحِدُ

وَ كُلٌّ اِلٰى ذَاتِ الْجَمَالِ يُشِيْرُ

(حسّان بن ثابتؓ)

"Our phraseology is different, but Your beauty is single. And all phraseology points to your lovely Essence." Therefore, when someone remembers God the Most High with His personal name, Allah, he is, so to say, remembering God the Most High with all His attributes or, in other words, with all the Quranic verses. When the seed of His personal name, Allah, springs up in the person of some perfect gnostic, the whole of the Quran, with all its sciences, knowledge, illuminations, and secrets, gets fixed up and appears in his heart in the form of a tree of light. All the Quranic realities and exoteric and esoteric sciences appear to him through the grace of His personal name, Allah. It is the holy tree that was planted in the blessed person of the unlettered Prophet (may my parents be his sacrifice) in the cave of Hira. Its branches touched the parapets of the High Emporium, far beyond the tree Tuba. Says the Most High:

كَشَجَرَةٍ طَيِّبَةٍ اَصْلُهَا ثَابِتٌ وَّ فَرْعُهَا فِى السَّمَآءِ ۙ (۱۱۴ ابراهيم: ۲۴)

"Like the holy tree with its trunk firmly fixed in the earth and its branches in heaven."

THE FIVE FUNDAMENTALS OF ISLAM ARE DIFFERENT MANIFESTATIONS OF COMMEMORATING ALLAH

Hence, the mention of His personal name, Allah, is the root of all commemorations, and all Islamic fundamentals depend on the commemoration of Allah and the name Allah. This is the key of the gnosis and unification of the essence of the Creator. If carefully viewed, the commemoration of His personal name, Allah, or its concentration is the real object of all Islamic fundamentals and religious acts. All the pious deeds and praiseworthy virtues, especially all the Islamic fundamentals, are the various manifestations of the commemoration of Allah or auxiliary to its completion. Take the five fundamentals of Islam on which the edifice of Islam stands, namely, the formula of faith, prayer, pilgrimage, fasts, and alms. Commemoration of His personal name, Allah, alone is the real object of all these, if their real object is deeply studied. Now, the five prayers constitute the first fundamental of Islam. It is clearly evident that the prayers consist of commemoration of God the Most High solely. As Allah the Most High says:

$$\text{وَ اَقِمِ الصَّلٰوةَ لِذِكْرِیْ} \; \text{(۲۰)} \; \text{(طه: ۱۴)}$$

"Perform the prayers for commemorating me."

Elsewhere, it is said:

$$\text{قَدْ اَفْلَحَ مَنْ تَزَكّٰی} \; \text{(۱۴)} \; \text{وَذَکَرَ اسْمَ رَبِّهٖ فَصَلّٰی} \; \text{(۱۵)} \; \text{(الاعلٰی: ۱۴-۱۵)}$$

"He certainly achieved salvation who purified himself and performed the prayers by commemorating the name of his Lord."

It is narrated in another verse:

$$\text{اِنَّ الصَّلٰوةَ تَنْهٰی عَنِ الْفَحْشَآءِ وَالْمُنْکَرِ ۗ وَلَذِکْرُ اللّٰهِ اَکْبَرُ} \; \text{(العنکبوت: ۴۵)}$$

"Verily the prayers protect one against indecencies and the commemoration of Allah is the great thing."

The elements of prayers, namely, standing, bending, sitting, and prostrating, are the formalities and natural movements of the spiritual pleasures and esoteric enjoyments of commemorating Allah, just as dancing is the natural movement of sensual exhilaration. Recitation of the formula of faith is the second fundamental of Islam without which one cannot be a Musalman in spite of singly discharging all the virtuous deeds of the world. One who recites this formula sincerely once becomes pure and finds a place in paradise though he be a heretic and staunch polytheist, formerly. In Islam, this formula is regarded as the best of commemorations and the root of the whole affair. As it is said, "The best commemoration is "There is no god except Allah, Muhammad is the Prophet of Allah." Elsewhere, it is said, "He who said There is no god except Allah entered paradise without reckoning and undergoing chastisement."

The religious saints have verified that the fundamental which starts at the time of the last examination of death and its pangs is the means of entering paradise without computation and chastisement because this formula which appears at the last moment is the cream of lifelong actions or the result of Islamic education and faith. If this formula comes to the tongue or heart, consider yourself successful in the real examination of the object of life, else not. In short, the start of the formula at the last moment is the butter of the Islamic deeds of the entire life, which appears in the vessel of the body.

كليدِ مُقفل جناں لَآ اِلٰہ اِلَّا اللہ	نجات مردم جاں لَآ اِلٰہ اِلَّا اللہ
ڈرا کہ کرد بیاں لَآ اِلٰہ اِلَّا اللہ	چہ خوف آتشِ دوزخ چہ خوف دیولعیں
کہ بود دور اماں لَآ اِلٰہ اِلَّا اللہ	نہ بود ملک دو عالم نہ دور چرخِ کبود

"There is no god but Allah" is the salvation of mankind. "There is no god but Allah" is the key to the lock of paradise. The fire of hell and the accursed devil frighten not one who said, "There is no god but Allah." The two worlds and the little firmament did not exist when there prevailed the rule of the verse of faith. There is no god but Allah."

It is clearly evident that the formula of faith, the second fundamental of Islam, is solely the commemoration of Allah. The pilgrimage to the noble house of Allah is the third fundamental of

Islam. The pilgrimage has been ordained with a view to dissociate oneself from one's family, home, and all worldly attachments and to be aloof for the worship of Allah. Commemorating Allah is the only sacred occupation during all the stages of the pilgrimage, and it is emphasized in all the verses of the Quran relating to pilgrimage to the House of Allah. As God the Most High says, "When you reach Arafat, commemorate Allah near Muzdalifa." Says the Most High:

$$ فَاِذَا قَضَيْتُمْ مَّنَاسِكَكُمْ فَاذْكُرُوا اللّٰهَ كَذِكْرِكُمْ اٰبَآءَكُمْ اَوْ اَشَدَّ ذِكْرًا (١٢البقرة:٢٠٠) $$

"And when you have performed the rites of the pilgrimage, commemorate Allah as you commemorated your forefathers." And at the end, it is explicitly ordained:

$$ وَاذْكُرُوا اللّٰهَ فِىْٓ اَيَّامٍ مَّعْدُوْدٰتٍ (١٢البقرة:٢٠٣) $$

"Commemorate Allah in the days defined." Therefore, there is only the commemoration of Allah during the pilgrimage. Moreover, the cordial occupation and absorption in commemoration is increased in the heart by seeing the selected holy place. By an account of the holiness of those sacred places, the spiritual effect of the holy spirits there, and the esoteric cordial reflection of the Musalmans of the world and the selected persons among them, the idleness and foulness of the heart is removed and the relish of commemoration is increased and its pleasure doubled. Fasting in the month of Ramadan is the fourth fundamental of Islam. In this also, there is recitation of the holy Quran, supererogation, Tarawih, and commemoration. So that one may retire from sensual and worldly engagements like eating, drinking, cohabitation, and so on and commemorate God the Most High with utmost isolation. Because the real object of commemoration and devotion is frustrated when the heart is entangled in the sensualist desires of eating and drinking and worldly attachments. But commemoration reaches the commemorated when one commemorates God the Most High along with meditation and presence of mind in isolation and with singleness of purpose. Moreover during the last ten days of the month of Ramadan, the prophetic act of retiring in the mosque is observed with the object of complete seclusion for the purpose of commemoration.

Zakat, or the giving of alms, is the fifth fundamental of Islam The secret involved in the giving of alms is also the same because the destitute disturbed in mind on account of hardship of livelihood and worry for a living cannot commemorate God the Most High and pay Him homage with peace of mind. Distracted in their livelihood, they are distracted in mind. Therefore, Islam has made it obligatory on the well-to-do to help the needy Musalmans and to enable them to commemorate God the Most High with a contented mind. However, a man may trust in God and be a recluse; his contentment and forbearance are shaken by the presence of a family and children. Besides, in the mystic path too, it is not very profitable to put this unnecessary burden on the weaker sex and the innocent children.

A poor householder in his night prayers thinks thus:

چہ خورد بامداد فرزندم
شب چوں عقدِ نماز بر بندم
(سعدی)

"When I am engaged at night in prayers, I think, What will my children eat in the morning?"

Sheikh Sa'di has truly remarked that the anguish for the livelihood of the children and the worries about meals cast down the esoteric traveler flying in the higher abode below his angelic stage.

دگر آزادگی مبند خیال
اے گرفتار پائے بندِ عیال
باز دارد زِ سیر در ملکوت
غم فرزند و نان و جامہ و قوت
(سعدی)

Another philosophy of Zakat is that excess and shortage of everything is bad. Moderation in everything is commendable.

خَيْرُ الْأُمُوْرِ أَوْسَطُهَا وَشَرُّ الْأُمُوْرِ تَفْرِيْطُهَا وَإِفْرَاطُهَا

"Moderation is the best of things, and excess and paucity are the worst of them."

The excess of worldly riches is also injurious for religiousness, devotion, and commemoration of God the Most High. Says the Most High:

وَلَوْ بَسَطَ اللّٰهُ الرِّزْقَ لِعِبَادِهٖ لَبَغَوْا فِى الْاَرْضِ (۲۷: الشوریٰ ۱۴۲)

"Were Allah to increase the livelihood of His servants, they would certainly rebel on the earth."

In another place in the Quran, God the Most High speaks through the mouth of Moses (A.S) as Moses (A.S) requested God the Most High, saying, "O Allah Thou hast provided Pharaoh and his nation with worldly riches and means of pomp and glory due to which they have gone astray from Thy path. O, Allah! deprive them of their riches and fasten their hearts in the chains of destitution and starvation so that they may believe." This proves that abundance of worldly riches and means of comfort and luxury lead one astray. It is said in a noble tradition:

حُبُّ الدُّنْيَا رَاْسُ كُلِّ خَطِيْئَةٍ

"Love of the wealth is the head of all sins."

In short, wealth is a dreadful calamity and an incurable malady that a man can hardly escape.

Sa'di سعدیؒ has expressed the nature of wealth in this verse:

اگر دنیا نہ باشد درد مندیم   وگر باشد بمہرش پائے بندیم

بلائے زیں بلا آشوب تر نیست   کہ رنج خاطر است، ارہست درنیست

(سعدی)

"If there is no wealth in our hand we are distressed. If we have it we are fettered to its love. There isn't a more tumultuous calamity than wealth, whose presence and absence both are painful."

It is a fact that when riches increase, they take hold of one's skirt and hold him back from God the Most High. The excess of poverty and starvation also cast him in infidelity. As it is said, "Nearly poverty leads to infidelity." Hence to establish equality among the people and to bring down the excess of the world to moderation, Islam has made it incumbent on the wealthy to pay alms, so that they too may not be deprived of commemorating Allah with singleness of purpose and presence of mind. Shortly speaking, what is Islam? It is the commemoration of Allah with the outward tongue, discharging the ceremonies of commemoration through bodily limbs and taking down the commemoration of Allah to its real abode, namely, the heart, through the help of the five senses. When the commemoration of Allah is transposed from the external body to the heart, the esoteric figure of faith appears in the body.

قَالَتِ الْأَعْرَابُ اٰمَنَّا ۗ قُلْ لَّمْ تُؤْمِنُوْا وَ لٰكِنْ قُوْلُوْٓا اَسْلَمْنَا وَ لَمَّا يَدْخُلِ الْإِيْمَانُ فِيْ قُلُوْبِكُمْ (۲۹الحجرات: ۱۴)

"The Arabs said we have become the true believers. Tell them: 'You have not believed but say that you adopted Islam. That will be when the faith enters your hearts."

Hence it is evident that the heart of the faithful and not his body is the particular abode of faith. Faith, in fact, is the bright light of His personal name, Allah. The fourteen spheres are revealed to the faithful when this bright light is lit in the globe of the human heart of the faithful.

اَللّٰهُ نُوْرُ السَّمٰوٰتِ وَالْأَرْضِ ۗ مَثَلُ نُوْرِهٖ كَمِشْكٰوةٍ فِيْهَا مِصْبَاحٌ ۗ اَلْمِصْبَاحُ فِيْ زُجَاجَةٍ ۗ اَلزُّجَاجَةُ كَأَنَّهَا كَوْكَبٌ دُرِّيٌّ (۲۴النور: ۳۵)

"Allah is the light of the heaven and earth the likeness of His light is like a niche with a lamp in it, the lamp is in a globe, the globe (not to mention the lamp) is like a shining star."

It is incorrect to translate the verse as this: "The Essence of God the Most High is light because it necessitates the vessel ship of the essence of God the Most High and His magnanimous, unlimited Essence is bounded within the firmaments of heaven and earth—whereas Allah the Most High is the Creator of the heavens and earth and all that is in these and beyond these." Here, Allah means His personal name, Allah, the light of which illuminates the heaven and earth and is a glow in the globe, shining like a bright star. On account of the lamp of His personal name, Allah, this globe is attached to the olive tree or the elemental body of the gnostic. Those who are unaware of the enigma of the name and the named will be certainly surprised at this new explanation of ours. But we are obliged to divulge the truth, though the stereotyped may get annoyed at the publication of their incorrect explanation. Some will be surprised that we have given the name of His personal name, Allah, to faith, which is firmly established in the heart of the faithful in the form of the light of certainty. Then let readers ponder over the purport of the following Quranic verse and impartially see how true is our explanation and commentary. God the Most High says:

اُولٰٓئِكَ كَتَبَ فِیۡ قُلُوۡبِهِمُ الۡاِیۡمَانَ (۵۸ المجادلة: ۲۲)

"Those in whose hearts faith is written."

Now faith can be written only if it is in the form of a sentence or word. What else can the word and sentence be except His personal name, Allah?

هزار معجزه بنمود عشق و عقل جُهول

هنوز در پئے اندیش ہائے خویشتن است

(حافظ)

"Love has shown a thousand miracles, but the idiot's intellect still follows its own imaginations!"

We have already proved that the five fundamentals of Islam, namely, the word of faith, prayers, fasting, pilgrimage, and alms, are the different manifestations and methods of commemorating Allah and His personal name. When this Islam or commemoration of Allah is transferred from the outward actions of the limbs to the etheric personality of the heart and gets inscribed in the heart in the form of His personal name, Allah, its light is called the light of Faith (نورِایمان). On the Day of Eternity, God the Most High has placed this light of the faith on His bright personal name, Allah, like a seed in the hearts of the faithful. When in this world that seed is irrigated by the sermon teaching attention or favor of some pure, selected godly man, it springs up into a holy tree. Hence, for the perfection of the tree of Islam and faith, the bounteous eternal seed of guidance and the water of guidance and education by a perfect gnostic (generous like the cloud) are mutually indispensable. Irrigation is useless when there is no seed. God Almighty says:

یٰۤاَیُّهَا الَّذِیۡنَ اٰمَنُوا اتَّقُوا اللّٰهَ وَابۡتَغُوۡۤا اِلَیۡهِ الۡوَسِیۡلَةَ وَجَاهِدُوۡا فِیۡ سَبِیۡلِهٖ لَعَلَّكُمۡ تُفۡلِحُوۡنَ
(۵ المآئدہ: ۳۵)

"O you who believe fear Allah, seek an intermediator towards Him and struggle in His path, perhaps you may find salvation." Elsewhere, it is said:

$$ اِنَّكَ لَا تَهْدِيْ مَنْ اَحْبَبْتَ وَلٰكِنَّ اللّٰهَ يَهْدِيْ مَنْ يَّشَآءُ (القصص:٥٦) ﴿١٢٨﴾ $$

"You cannot guide everyone whom you like but those will be guided whom Allah has chosen for guidance on the Day of Eternity." Again, it is said:

$$ يَٓا اَيُّهَا الَّذِيْنَ اٰمَنُوا اتَّقُوا اللّٰهَ وَكُوْنُوْا مَعَ الصّٰدِقِيْنَ ﴿١١٩﴾ (التوبة:١١٩) $$

"O faithful fear Allah and remain with the saints."

Now, in the commentary of another verse, we will explain how the tree of Islam and faith grows from the seed of his personal name Allah.

Super Commentary of the Quranic Verse: "He Whose Heart Is Opened …"

God the Most High commands:

$$ اَفَمَنْ شَرَحَ اللّٰهُ صَدْرَهُ لِلْاِسْلَامِ فَهُوَ عَلٰى نُوْرٍ مِّنْ رَّبِّهٖ فَوَيْلٌ لِّلْقَاسِيَةِ قُلُوْبُهُمْ مِّنْ ذِكْرِ اللّٰهِ اُولٰٓئِكَ فِيْ ضَلٰلٍ مُّبِيْنٍ ﴿٢٢﴾ (الزمر:٣٩) $$

"He whose heart is opened for Islam by Allah he is on light from his Creator. Alas for those whose hearts are hardened towards commemoration of Allah! They are evidently astray."

There are two sentences in this munificent verse. Every sentence consists of two parts. Every part carries an import absolutely contradictory to the opposite part. The first part of each sentence is a cause, and the complementary one is a sequence. The first sentence mentions a blessed person whose heart has been opened for Islam by Allah. The sequence is that he has received light and guidance from his Lord. The other sentence mentions the evil-hearted people whose hearts are hard like stone toward commemorating Allah. The commemoration of Allah cannot effect their hearts. The sequence is said to be that these people are in evident depravity. In this noble verse, the readers should try to grasp the following delicate point. In the first sentence, there is a man whose heart has been opened for Islam by Allah. He is properly guided. The second sentence ought to have been put thus: Sorry for the people whose hearts have hardened on account of infidelity and consequently are lying in evident depravity. Because in contrast to the word *Islam*, the word *infidelity* would have been appropriate. But here God the Most High has clearly divulged the hidden secret that depravity stands for hardening of the hearts toward commemoration of God the Most High and the non-entrance of the name of Allah therein. And Islam is this that a person's heart opens for Islam and His personal name, Allah, name. But in another way, it means that the person whose heart has been opened by the name of Allah for Islam is on the bright and right path. In other words, the blessed person the earth of whose heart is so soft as to be permeated by the water of guidance and teaching of the Prophet and the saints and where the seed of His personal name, Allah, sprouts up and tears the soft earth of his breast, appears, and grows in the form of the tree of Islam will certainly be guided toward his Lord. But if the heart of a man is like a hard stone without an inlet for the water of guidance and a chance for the seed of His personal name, Allah, to shoot up, the seed of His personal name, Allah, will certainly be wasted in the rocky ground of such an evil-hearted man, and he will certainly go astray. Now, if in the verse already quoted, the word *Allah* is used for the named instead of the name as it is generally translated, it will mean, "The man whose breast has been opened for Islam is especially guided by his Lord." This creates the great difficulty that God the Most High forbids; there is strange justice in the House of God that He opens the breast of some special person for Islam and guides him to Himself and leads the rest astray. What is, then, the fault of those who go astray? The defect and difficulty of this verse can never be removed, and no correct interpretation can be put on it unless the word *Allah* is interpreted to mean the name. Therefore, it is proved that the name *Allah* is like a seed, which when drenched with the water of guidance and invocation, tears the earth of the soft and capable breast, and the holy tree of Islam springs and grows from it. Hence, here and in most of the munificent Quran, the word *Allah* is used in the sense of the name and indicates the essence. Because the name is the named itself, and this is the enigma of the name and the Named:

سبک ز جائے نہ گیری کہ بس گراں گہر است

متاع من کہ نصیبش مباد ارزانی

(عرفی)

"You cannot pick it up and buy it easily, for my property is a very weighty jewel. May it never grow cheap!"

This is the hidden secret of commemorating the name *Allah* and remembering Him, which the material intellects are absolutely ignorant of. This is the real need for commemorating His name and the true object of the human life, which the heretical class dubs as inertia, unemployment, and asceticism. Like the soul in the blood and the blood in the body, the light of His personal name, Allah, is prevalent in the construction of every man. The light of His personal name, Allah, is, so to speak, the soul of the soul, and it keeps the human frame hot and resplendent, fresh and alive, and bright and shining. This holy name is the link one end of which is attached to the human heart in the visible world and the other end of which is attached to God the Most High in the invisible heaven. It is the strong rope of Allah, which hangs to the earth of devotion from the heaven of divinity by holding which man can reach the holy court of his true Creator. It is impossible to reach His lofty, uncreated, and holy palace without the lift of His personal name, Allah. God the Most High has made it the means of His guidance, unity, and union. This is the sun that shines on the earth of devotion from the heaven of divinity and imparts light to the eye of the universe. It has illuminated the entire candle of the world. That is why His personal name is called Allah, and it is the last source of universal salvation, the spring of life, the secret of the secrets, and the marrow of the entire universe.

نواخت تشنۂ لباں را ز لال نام خدا

چوں ہم نشیں تو باشد خیال نام خدا

بشرط آن کہ بہ پری بہ بال نام خدا

تو در تجلّیٔ اسماء کمال نام خدا

ربود جان و دلم را جمال نام خدا

یقیں بداں کہ تو با حق نشستۂ شب و روز

ترا سزد طیراں در فضائے عالم قدس

میانِ اسمِ مسمّیٰ چوں فرق نیست بہیں

"The beauty of the name of God has kidnapped my soul and heart. The pure water of God's name has entertained the thirsty. Be

- 151 -

sure that you are sitting with God day and night. When the thought of the name of God is your companion, flight in the atmosphere of the holy world befits you, provided you fly with the wings of the name of God. Since there is no difference between the name and the Named, behold the perfection of God's name in the illuminations of names."

What is the name Allah? It is the best substitute for the word "Become" uttered by Allah while creating the universe. It is therefore said that the name Allah uttered by a saint is like the word "Become" uttered by Allah. This means that just as God the Most High created the entire world by pronouncing the word "Become," similarly, when a saint utters this great name Allah for any affair, it certainly takes place sooner or later.

When a man remembers God the Most High with His personal name, he is, so to say, remembering Him with all His attributes or all the Quranic verses as we have already stated. It is a covenant of Allah: "Remember Me" and "I'll remember thee." Now, it is clearly evident that we remember God the Most High with the external tongue or heart or thought. But how does God the Most High remember us reciprocally as He promised? How does He respond to our commemoration? In what way and what manner? We will divulge this veiled secret today. God the Most High shines toward a man with the name and attributes with which the man remembers Him. Says the Most High:

$$ \text{أُجِيبُ دَعْوَةَ الدَّاعِ إِذَا دَعَانِ (١٢ البقرة: ١٨٦)} $$

"I respond to the invocation of the invoker when he invokes Me."

$$ \text{وَاللّهُ الْمُسْتَعَانُ عَلَى مَا تَصِفُونَ (١٢ يوسف: ١٨)} $$

"Allah has power to appear with the attribute with which you remember Him." Tradition says, "I treat my slave according to the conception that he entertains about Me. Let him then entertain about Me any idea that he likes." The capacity for His personal name Allah and all the attributive names of God the Most High is eternally, naturally, and expressly present in man. Therefore, he practically circulates in himself the capacity for the attribute manifest in himself of the Name with which he remembers God the Most High, and by way of reflection, he derives in the mirror of his heart the light of that name. For example, when the light of the sun appears in the mirror, the attribute of the heat and light of the sun appear in the mirror by way of reflection. We can see with our eyes the light and heat of the sun in mirrors and lenses. When the rays of the sun pass through the convex glass of the lens, they radiate heat enough to set a cloth on fire. Similarly, when the light of the sun falls on the surface of the moon, on account of the large expanse of the latter, its light illuminates half the universe on the night of the full moon. Photography has further proved that the exact figure of the object reflected appears as in the glass. In addition to the figures and forms of the object reflected by the biscope, the movies have recorded in the reels of the film and projected on the screen the movements, actions, deeds, and even the voice of the things reflected. On the film screen, the people witness past occurrences daily. Had there been such photography that by way of reflection could reflect the very essence and attributes of man in addition to his figure and movements and voice, that photography would have lucidly explained our purpose.

THE PERFECT MAN IS THE TRUE IMAGE AND REAL MIRROR OF GOD

The perfect man becomes such a superb manifestation and perfect mirror of God the Most High that, in measure with his capacity, he reflects in himself the lights of the essence, attributes, and names of God the Most High. When the adept gnostic attains perfect purification of the soul, cleanliness of the heart, brightness of the spirit, and seclusion of the secret, he becomes a clear, transparent, and perfect mirror of God the Most High. He is qualified with all the qualities of God the Most High and imbued with all His virtues. He becomes the true emblem of "He taught Adam the names of all things," that is, the true progeny of Adam, and deserves to be called man in the true sense of the word. Else, there are many people of the kind: "They are like beasts," as they are outwardly men and inwardly beasts. God the Most High with all His names and attributes is manifest in Adam (A.S) and his true progeny, and this is the true significance of "He taught Adam the names of all things," that is, God the Most High taught all His names to Adam (A.S). The inability of the angels to know all these names signifies that the angels are the manifestations of His special names. They have been qualified by some special attributive names of which they are the operators. For example, Izrail (A.S), who is appointed to take the souls, has the capacity for a few terrible names of God (اسمائے جلالی) the Most High, for example, powerful, avenger, taker, killer, and so on. He is the operator of these very names, qualified with their qualities, and works them. He has absolutely no capability for other names, especially the lovable names (اسمائے جمالی). Similarly, Gabriel (A.S) has been made the manifestation and worker of the lovable names. The other angels should also be conceived in the same way. But according to the size of his pot and his esoteric capability, the perfect man derives in himself both the terrible and lovable perfect names and attributes. This is the true significance of "He taught Adam the names of all things." It does not at all mean that God the Most High had taught Adam (A.S) some lexicon containing the names of all the objects in the world, which He had concealed from the angels; that He examined them by naming some of the objects; and that, thus, the inability of the angels and the superiority of Adam

(A.S) came into view. This is far from the just, magnificent, and holy essence of God the Most High. The tradition says:

$$خَلَقَ اللّٰهُ آدَمَ عَلَىٰ صُوْرَتِهِ$$

"He created Adam like His own form" lends support to the contention that the capability to be qualified with all the attributes of God the Most High and to imbibe His virtues exists in Adam. Else, God the Most High has no figure, form, or semblance. In short, a perfect man is the perfect mirror and complete manifestation of God the Most High. And in accordance with "Commemorate Me," "I will commemorate thee." With whichever name a man remembers God the Most High by, He shines to that man with the same name reciprocally. For example, if a man remembers God the Most High with the name Merciful, God the Most High illuminates through the name merciful and the light of that name permeates inside the commemorator. And the attribute of the mercifulness of God the Most High prevails over the whole world; it is through this mercy that compassion and affection exist among the jinn, mankind, animals, beasts, quadrupeds, and birds of the entire world. In accordance with his capacity, the commemorator takes his full share of the action and power of this general universal attribute of mercifulness of the name merciful God the Most High, and he is qualified with God the Most High's attribute of mercifulness and becomes the operator of the actions of the name merciful in the visible and invisible worlds. This is called:

$$تَخَلَّقُوْا بِاَخْلَاقِ اللّٰهِ تَعَالىٰ$$

"Verify yourself with the virtues of God the Most High."

Similarly, when a commemorator remembers God the Most High with the name "Hearer" or "Seer," he partakes of God the Most High's attribute of hearer or seer in proportion to the extent of his capacity, and in addition to the external senses of hearing and seeing, the commemorator acquires esoteric hearing and seeing through the bounty and gift of God the Most High. He hears unheard of things through inspiration and sees unseen esoteric places and invisible spiritual incidents. All the attributes should be conjectured in the same way. And when a person remembers Allah with His personal name, God the Most High gives illuminations to that person with His Essence, comprising all the attributes and names, and the commemorator observes the personal illuminations of God the Most High in himself and is favored and distinguished by the personal display and observation of God the Most High. The person of the commemorator is illuminated with the personal lights. This does, not mean that (God forbid) God the Most High transmigrates into the slave (commemorator). But as the light and the heat of the sun is reflected in a mirror, water, or other transparent things, although the sun remains where it is, or as the fire affects the iron, which acquires the quality of the fire by turning red-hot, similarly the slave derives the lights of the Essence, attributes, names, and acts of God the Most High. The seeing, hearing, and speaking of the man then is the seeing, hearing, and speaking of God the Most High and so on and so forth. In short, God the Most High shines toward a slave with the same name with which the slave remembers Him. The symptom of it is that the very name of God the Most High gets impressed with bright letters of nature inside the commemorator, and at the time of absorption, that commemorator sees it shining on the invisible sky like a brilliant star. Esoterically, the lights of the names appear in the form of stars, that of the attributes like the full moon, and that of the Essence appears in the form of the sun. So that when any name of God the Most High gets written in brilliant words inside the commemorator, the commemorator gets filled up with the light and electric power of that name and exercises his influence, in both the worlds, through the light and power of that name. It can then be said that so and so is the operator of such and such a name or prayer. For example, when His Holiness Jesus (salutations be on him) wanted to cure some leper or lunatic possessed by an evil spirit, he used to commemorate in his heart or concentrate on God the Most High's name Quddus (قدوس) (Holy), and he supplicated and attended God the Most High's attribute of holiness. At that moment, in accordance with the promise "Remember Me and I'll remember thee," God the Most High cast the light of His name holy and the light of attribute holy on Jesus (salutations be on him), and the bright form descended from heaven in the form of a dove sometimes. At moments, he used to be filled up with the light of the name Holy, the holy ghost. Since an evil spirit enters the leper and lunatic, which distorts their exoteric and esoteric nature, the name Quddus (holy) is the opposite of all esoteric and exoteric evils—as the one is light and the other is darkness, and the one is truth and the other false. Therefore, when full of the light of the Holy Ghost, His Holiness Jesus (salutations be on him) touched a leper or lunatic, and the evil spirit would fly from the leper or lunatic because of his power of the light of holiness. The darkness always flies from the light of truth. Says Allah:

$$\text{وَقُلْ جَآءَ الْحَقُّ وَزَهَقَ الْبَاطِلُ ۚ إِنَّ الْبَاطِلَ كَانَ زَهُوقًا ۞ (۸۱ :ابنی اسرائیل)}$$

"The truth has come and the falsehood has vanished; verily falsehood is vanishable."

The stories of his looking toward the heavens—that is, his supplication of God the Most High's attributes of holiness—the descent of the Holy Ghost in the form of a dove; his being filled up with the Holy Ghost; and the driving away of the evil spirits from the lepers, lunatics, and blind; and curing them are amply recorded in the testaments and other historical works.

Whenever some prophet or saint intends to see the attribute, or the place of beginning, he attends to the name "First (اوّل) of God the Most High." Submerged in the light of that name, he reaches the place of beginning. Similarly, through the names Last (آخر), Exoteric, and Esoteric, he visits the places of eternity without an end, the place of the world, and the place of the next world respectively. Similarly, he derives the lights of all the attributive names and amply enjoys them esoterically. But to become the operator of the names of God the Most High and to be qualified with His qualities is not so easy a job that by repeating a name for a few days, one becomes a perfect operator. Not until one fully annihilates one's contingent and worldly attributes and acquires purification of the soul, cleanliness of the heart, polish of the spirit, and unification of the self and acquires eternal life through the innate light of the personal name of God the Most High can one derive the benefits of any name of God the Most High. Nor can he become the operator of any name; this operation cannot be acquired without a teacher.

When, through the mercy of God the Most High and the favor of a perfect guide, the gnostic traveler becomes a perfect operator, he derives, in accordance with his capacity, the lights of the names, attributes, and essence of God the Most High. But the everlasting essence and eternal attributes and the names always belong to Allah the Undefied and Most High. There is no decrease or increase in Him. Always, He is as He was before. Through His special favor, the sun of His essence, the moons of His attributes, and the stars of His names shine on the mirror of a perfect person, and in accordance with his capacity, he derives exoteric and esoteric favors from the universal divine favors. As says the Most Holy:

$$وَرَحْمَتِیْ وَسِعَتْ كُلَّ شَیْءٍ ۚ (الاعراف:۱۵۷)$$

"My mercy spreads over all things."

حق کجا همزار هر احمق شود   دیدهٔ بینا از لقائے حق شود

آنچه اول آں نبود اکنوں نشد   حق ز ایجاد جہاں افزوں نشد

درمیان آں فروان است فرق   لیک افزوں شد اثر ز ایجاد خلق

هر که در پوشد برو گردد و بال   هست الوهیت ردائے زوالجلال

The eye gets light and sight through the name of God and God does not confide in every fool. The Creator didn't increase by inventing the creation. What He wasn't erstwhile, He didn't become now. But His influence increases with the production of the creation. There is a lot of difference between these. Divinity is the only mantle of the Majestic God. It is a calamity for any one who wears it.

We have already said that the esoteric senses of the commemorator open through commemoration, and the veils between the commemorating slave and commemorated worshipped Lord are removed. Satan and the forces of Iblis have pitched their tents in the heart, brain, and other important centers of man; constructed their fortifications of darkness; and locked them with slothfulness. Through the bright key of His personal name, Allah, the commemorator opens the locks of slothfulness and strikes away Iblis and his false forces with the bright sword of commemorating Allah, and constructing therein the bright fortifications of the lights of divine names, he posts therein the bright creation, forces, and armies of Allah. Transformed into the great Ka'ba and holy Qiblah, the heart of such a commemorator becomes the temple of the holy spirits, angels, and bright creation and the abode of commemoration, meditation, recitation, praising, glorification, magnification, thanking, unification, pious acts, gnosis, proximity, union, and divine secrets and lights.

دل بدست آور که حجِ اکبر است   از ہزاراں کعبہ یک دل بہتر است

کعبہ بُنُ گاہِ خلیلِ آزر است   دل گذر گاہ جلیلِ اکبر است

(رومی)

Conquer the fort of the heart, for this is a great pilgrimage or Hajj. A perfect heart is better than a thousand Ka'bas. Ka'ba is the dwelling of Abraham, son of the Azar, while the heart is the passage of the Glorious Great God.

When a man declines from commemorating Allah, the evil passions and satanic attributes take possession of his person and control his heart and mind. Then surrounding the whole body, like the ivy surrounding a tree, Satan enters every vein and capillary of the man and occupies his heart, mind, ears, nose, tongue, and eyes (all the five senses) and every particle of his body like the blood and life. He makes a passage in every part of the body and comes and goes into the person of a man with every breath. Esoterically, the clouds of satanic darkness spread over the heart, brain, and seats of the five senses (namely, the eyes, ears, nose, tongue, and all the limbs of the body) of such a person. The heart and mind of such a man lose sight of discerning between right and wrong. Through this darkness and slothfulness, a person forgets death, the day of resurrection, and computation. Virtue and vice, good and evil, lawful and unlawful appear to him alike. The tear of God escapes his heart.

He altogether forgets the promises and warnings of God the Most High. Whatever he thinks, he thinks evilly because his heart and mind are slaves to Satan. Such an unfortunate man likes and approves of vicious deeds and satanic inclinations; as Allah the Most High says:

$$ وَزَيَّنَ لَهُمُ الشَّيْطٰنُ اَعْمَالَهُمْ (٢٩ العنكبوت: ٣٨) $$

"Satan beautifies their actions for them." Such a man dislikes pious people, and their ways and loves the sinners, infidels, polytheists, and hypocrites and their evil customs and manners.

Such a man becomes a rational brute, nay, he even excels the brutes in the immoderations and evils of sensual and sexual vices, though apparently he may be a Galen of the age or a Plato of the time. On the day of resurrection, he will rise in the form of an animal or permanently blind, crippled, lame, invalid, sick, bankrupt, and destitute and will be subject to everlasting chastisements of various sorts. All these are the results of neglecting the commemoration of Allah and His name.

$$ وَمَنْ اَعْرَضَ عَنْ ذِكْرِىْ فَاِنَّ لَهُ مَعِيْشَةً ضَنْكًا وَّنَحْشُرُهُ يَوْمَ الْقِيٰمَةِ اَعْمٰى (١٢٣) $$
$$ (٢٠ طه: ١٢٤) $$

"He who turned away from commemorating Me will find his (esoteric) livelihood decreased and on the day of resurrection We will raise him blind."

Therefore, it behooves a person to kindle the bright light of the name Allah in all portions of his body, especially the heart and brain so that the false darkness may vanish through the true light of His personal name, Allah. In Islam, the philosophy of the obligatoriness of various manifestations of commemoration— namely, prayers, fasts, pilgrimages, alms, and words of faith—is to expel everything besides God from all the limbs of the human body and to invest there the commemorations and light of God the Most High. Don't you see that in performing the prayers, the entire human body and all its limbs move and work with the commemoration, and more than that, at the time of making the ablutions, every limb is simultaneously irrigated with the commemoration of God the Most High and concentrates on His name? Then again at the time of offering prayers, every particle of one's body from the top to toe is engaged in devotion, commemoration, and the concentration on God the Most High. Particularly speaking, the prayer is imperfect until the heart and brain are emptied of extraneous thoughts and invested with the commemoration and concentration of Allah. Hadith:

$$لَا صَلٰوةَ اِلَّا بِحُضُوْرِ الْقَلْبِ$$

"There is no prayer without the presence of mind."

Therefore, during the prayers, it is essential to safeguard all the senses and limbs (especially the heart and brain) against commemoration—that is, to think about and heed things other than God.

Says the Most High:

$$حٰفِظُوْا عَلَى الصَّلَوٰتِ وَالصَّلٰوةِ الْوُسْطٰى ۚ وَقُوْمُوْا لِلّٰهِ قٰنِتِيْنَ ۞ (البقرة: ٢٣٨)$$

"Safeguard your prayers and the middle prayers of the inner brain and heart and stand to God with complete attention of heart."

All the limbs of the body are bowed down in commemoration of Allah; because the slightest movement or attention toward non-God renders the prayers invalid and even void. Whenever thought of a non-God, for example, thought of the bounties of the next world, occurred to His Holiness Bayazid of Bustam, he performed the prostration of forgetfulness (سجدۀ سہو). If a worldly thought of a lawful thing occurred to him, he used to break off the prayer by returning the salutations to begin anew. If a worldly thought of a doubtful or unlawful object occurred to him, he performed the ablutions and prayers anew.

Somebody asked him as to why he refreshed the ablutions at the thought of a non-God. He replied that to the righteous person, the thought of the world is a greater enemy of ablutions and destroyer of the prayers than forting. In short, at the time of the prayers, a man should be the perfect model. Enter the realm of God the Almighty.

$$وَاذْكُرِ اسْمَ رَبِّكَ وَتَبَتَّلْ اِلَيْهِ تَبْتِيْلًا ۞ (المزمل: ٨)$$

"Commemorate the name of your Lord, and be perfectly absorbed in that."

Then is the duty of performing the prayers fully discharged. From this, it should not be taken that if one cannot perform the prayers wholeheartedly, there is no need for the customary external prayers full of worldly, alien thoughts. At this juncture, Satan waylays many a seeker, leads him astray from the path, and makes him renounce the prayers. But remember that the protection and perfection of the external prayers is called wholehearted prayer, and the form of esoteric prayers comes out of the adequate discharge of the external prayers. The external prayers with all their fundamentals are like the milk, the human frame is like the earthenware, and the human heart is like the churn staff. The man who secured pure milk, skimmed it properly, put it in the pot of his body, continued working the churn staff of the heart through commemoration and presence of the heart, and continued churning the milk will certainly acquire the butter of the esoteric prayers performed wholeheartedly and acceptable to God. But what will he churn who has no milk, and whence will he get butter? He who performs the external prayers gains this much at least that if he cannot get unadulterated milk, if something has fallen in the milk, or if it has not been curdled properly, then if no butter and fine ghee is obtained, there will be at least some simple and ordinary whey. He fares better than the idle pretender, who tries to get butter without milk.

We are obliged to be confronted with alien thoughts during prayers. Thoughts of the things dearly loved usually come to the mind. The prayers should be freed from the thoughts of others, as far as possible. For this very reason, the Takbir-e-Tahrima has been made essential and obligatory at the commencement of the prayers. When one says, "God is Great," one admits that all the other things in the universe are small compared to God the Most High. All extraneous thoughts should be cut off with the sword of "God is Great." Then alone is the Takbir-e- Tahrima perfect. A man truly flies toward God the Most High and makes esoteric ascent if he properly performs the prayers. That is why at the time of descending from the zenith of prayers and returning from esoteric flight and spiritual journey, the man performing the prayers salutes his companions on the right and left. On the night of ascent, our praiseworthy master,

Prophet Muhammad the chosen (p.b.u.h.), journeyed to his Master. On the way, he saw many angels of the seven heavens—the Arsh (عرش), Kursi (کرسی), Lauh (لوح), and Qalam (قلم)—and the holy spirits of the earlier prophets in their particular places engaged in various ways of worship, commemorations, and recitations of the Word of Allah. Some were singing the songs of His praises while standing; some were playing the tunes of thanksgiving and glorifying Him while sitting. Some were busy praising Him in the bending position. Some were praising His unparalleled beauty and magnifying His imperishable glory while prostrating. Then he desired to have for himself and his followers a collective and perfect mode of worship, including the methods of worship of all the prophets, messengers, cherubim, and all the earlier and later people. After observing all the major signs of God theMost High, when his holiness (P.B.U.H) reached the place of the "two bows and nearer"

$$قَابَ قَوْسَيْنِ اَوْ اَدْنٰى ۝ (٥٣ النجم: ٩)$$

and was graced with the unique sight of God the Most High, the robe of being chosen and the crown of "great gracious glory" was placed on his head, thus entrusting to him the treasures and blessings of the two worlds. He said to him:

$$اَلْيَوْمَ اَكْمَلْتُ لَكُمْ دِيْنَكُمْ وَاَتْمَمْتُ عَلَيْكُمْ نِعْمَتِيْ وَرَضِيْتُ لَكُمُ الْاِسْلَامَ دِيْنًا (٥ المآئده:٣)$$

"This day We have perfected for you your religion and furnished Our bounties on you and chosen for you Islam as religion."

Among the bounties of divine grace, one conspicuous favor bestowed on His Holiness (P.B.U.H.), in accordance with his heart's desire, was the grant from the Court of the Grandeur to him and his followers of a collective and perfect method of worship in the form of the present prayers, which include the different modes of worship of all the angels of the seven heavens, such as standing, bending, sitting, prostrating, and so on, and all the methods of thanking and praising God, such as praying (دعا), sanctification (تسبیح), thanking (تحمید), glorification (تمجید), unification, magnification, and so on. In accordance with the verse, "Whatever is in heaven and on earth praises Him," the Omnipotent has engaged all the creation, namely, minerals, vegetables, and animals to praise and sanctify Him. The natural praising of their devotion and worship is included in the five timely prayers. Just as our Holy Prophet— the best of the messengers—and his followers are the choicest of all nations, similarly God the Most High has given them a method of worship that is the best and nicest of all methods of worship. In the four fundamentals of the prayers, the prayer makes the figures of the four letters (A.L.L.H.) of His personal name, Allah (الله), and in the prostration, he makes the form of distance of two bows the name Muhammad (محمد) in his two sides and discharges the obligation of prostrate and approach

$$ وَاسْجُدْ وَاقْتَرِبْ ۩ (۱۹ الْعَلَقِ:۱۹) $$

In short, the prayer is the manifestation of one's humbleness, helplessness, and humiliation through his heart and brain and all the senses and limbs of the body. It is the eternal remembrance of the Creator, gratitude for the innumerable favors of the real benefactor, praise of His unparalleled beauty, and the affirmation of the grandeur and unity of this imperishable glory and the cry of the spirit separated from that Eternal Beloved. This is the worship of the body and soul and submission of the eternal feelings in the holy court of our Master and Benefactor, the Ruler of the two worlds. This is the eternal plaintive tune of the instrument of our spirit. This is the chain of love and the means of introduction between the Creator and created. It contains the consolation of the spirit restless from eternity, the pacification of the soul agitated in the world, the satisfaction of the lonely and dejected heart in the grave, and salvation for the spirit sorrowful and fearful on the day of resurrection. This is the outcome of man's daily life and the fruit of his dear existence. It seems that there is a hidden instrument in the depths of the heart that is played by the invisible fingers and exultation and pleasure of which creates in the human spirit this natural zest of worshipfulness. This is the perfect answer and the best solution to the difficult question, "Aren't I your Lord?"

Similarly, the five fundamentals of Islam are the complete manifestations of the worship of God the Most High. They contain innumerable lustrous gems of wisdom, a detailed explanation of each would require a separate volume. Therefore, we briefly present a sample of the whole. Take the formula of faith—the second fundamental of Islam (there is no God worshipable but one). There are two parts of it: (1) negatory and (2) affirmatory. Ostensibly, it appears a brief and simple sentence, and the verbal recitation of it is quite easy, but its grandeur is very weighty and its action is prevalent in the remaining four fundamentals. You have seen the manifestation of its negatory and affirmatory orders in the prayers that are not corrected unless non-God is negated and His concentration is fixed upon the mind. That is to say that full action on the negation and affirmation of the formula of faith is necessary in the whole of prayers on which the entire prayer depends.

Now take the second fundamental—the fasts of the month of Ramadan. During fasts, all sensual pleasures and physical food is negated, and in its stead are the esoteric pleasures of the heart and spirit and spiritual food; namely, commemoration, meditation, recitation of the Holy Quran, praising, sanctification, and virtuous deeds are affirmed. When we ponder the philosophy and wisdom of the month of fasts, we observe the negative and positive of this pure formula in force. Moreover, abstention from eating, drinking, copulation, and other extraneous engagements of sexual desires have been prescribed to cut the material food of the elemental body with the sword of order. "There is none to be worshipped" to disconnect the spirit from all relishes other than Allah and connect it with the eternal relish of God the Most High. The negation and affirmation of this pure formula seems to prevail in the twenty-four hours of the fast in the day and keeping awake in the night. It is in two fundamentals of Islam, prayers and fasts, that you have seen the action of negation and affirmation from the human body and soul and the frame and heart of the sensualist relations from non-God and the spiritual favors and blessings toward God the Most High. Now for man is left only two kinds of bondages in this material world. One is the bondage of the love of country, family, relatives, and friends. This is negated by the third fundamentals of Islam—that is, pilgrimage to the Holy House of Allah. Instead, the love for the real home of eternity thickly populated the eternal abode, and proximity, union, and observation of the eternal beloved is affirmed. The second restriction is the love for worldly wealth. This is negated by alms—the fourth fundamental of Islam—and instead, the thought for wealth and provision for the next world is affirmed. Thus, we see how the effect of this small and brief fundamental, the holy formula, has been proved to permeate the four big practical fundamentals of Islam. Hence at the time of a man's initiation into Islam, he is taught, first of all, the holy formula:

There is none to be worshipped except Allah.

Muhammad is the Prophet of Allah (P.B.U.H.)

The Dignity of the Holy Prophet

This small and little lustrous jewel includes the large oceans of the entire Islamic world, and this brief confirmation of unity and prophecy comprises answers to all the religious and spiritual questions in the next world. Since, in this world, the generous person of the Prophet; his blessed life, and the memories of the pleasant virtues, good deeds, and acts of his life and all his movements constitute a model of all the fundamentals of Islam, without following him, it is impossible to carry out the fundamentals of Islam and the mundane tasks of negation and affirmation therein; therefore, the two sentences are components of the holy confession of faith: (1) the affirmation of Unity or negation or affirmation, "There is none to be worshipped except Allah, and (2) the affirmation of prophecy or obedience to the Prophet—"Muhammad (P.B.U.H) is the Prophet of Allah," and are equally significant. Says the Most High:

$$ قُلْ اِنْ كُنْتُمْ تُحِبُّوْنَ اللّٰهَ فَاتَّبِعُوْنِيْ يُحْبِبْكُمُ اللّٰهُ (٣ آلِ عِمْرٰن: ٣١) $$

"O my Prophet tell your followers that if you claim to love Allah pursue me—for this—Allah will love you."

The faith of piety and fearing God and faith of love are different:

$$ اَلَآ لَا اِيْمَانَ لِمَنْ لَّا مَحَبَّةَ لَهُ $$

"Beware he lacks faith who lacks love."

Tradition says:

$$ لَا يُؤْمِنُ اَحَدُكُمْ حَتّٰى اَكُوْنَ اَحَبَّ اِلَيْهِ مِنْ مَّالِهِ وَاَوْلَادِهِ وَاَقَارِبِهِ وَمِنْ نَّفْسِهِ $$

"None of you is faithful unless he loves me more than his own riches, progeny, relatives, and self."

Some cynical people consider that the mere negation and affirmation and the simple affirmation of unitarianism suffice in Islam and overlook the importance of the second part—Muhammad (P.B.U.H) is the Prophet of Allah—and do not believe in the true faith of love and guidance. How ignorant are these people who attach more importance to the path than the leader and the mere program than the solid model and sample! Because there are diverse paths and innumerable pitfalls in the wilderness, I think that the second part of the formula ("Muhammad is the Prophet of Allah") is more important than the first one (There is none to be worshipped), namely, the affirmation of unitarianism and negation and affirmation. Because you go and ask the follower of any faith, "Do you believe in God?" All will reply in the affirmative. If you ask them if they believe in one God, they will be ready to affirm even that. Now enumerate the various attributes of God—Greater Master, Provider, and so on. They will affirm all. But the moment you ask them if they believe in Muhammad (P.B.U.H) as the Prophet of Allah, they will be confounded. Talk of unitarianism and virtuous deeds before any infidel, hypocrite, polytheist, and faithless man, and he will admit everything. But the moment you mention the blessed name of His Holiness Muhammad the Prophet of Allah (P.B.U.H), he will be thunderstruck. If mere affirmation of unitarianism and virtuous deeds were the real things, all religions would be true. Thus, it is apparent that the confirmation of the prophethood of Muhammad the Prophet of Allah (P.B.U.H), obedience to him, and his love, in fact, is the real touchstone of faithfulness. He who does not love him is faithless; he who is without his guidance is astray; he who cherishes envy, hatred, and enmity toward him is outcast from the divine court, though, like the devil, he may excel the whole world in learning, abstinence, and devotion. This is the Muslim's capital of Islam and the believer's wealth of faith, the riches of the religion of the religious. Religion and faith are nothing without him.

Dr. Iqbal says:

بمصطفیٰ برساں خویش را کہ دیں ہمہ اوست

اگر بہ او نرسیدی تمام کہ بولہبی است

(اقبال)

"Betake yourself to the Holy Prophet for this is all faith. If you cannot betake yourself to him, you are an obstinate unbeliever."

How well has some saint said about the Holy Prophet:

اے صبح صادقاں رُخِ زیبائے مصطفیٰؐ   وے سرو راستاں قدِ رعنائے مصطفیٰؐ

آئینهٔ سکندر و آبِ حیاتِ خضر   نورِ جبیں و لعلِ شکر خائے مصطفیٰؐ

معراجِ انبیاء و شبِ قدرِ اصفیاء   گویئے روئے پوش و کمر سائے مصطفیٰؐ

ادریس کو مدرسِ درس است   لب بستہ پیش منطقِ گویائے مصطفیٰؐ

عیسیٰؑ کہ دیر دائر علوی مقام اوست   شد دار دُر وہ علیائے مصطفیٰؐ

بر دُر دۂ دنیٔ فتد لۓ کشیدہ سر   ایوانِ بارگاہ معلّائے مصطفیٰؐ

از جام روح پرور مازاغ گشتہ مست   آہوئے چشم دل کش شہلائے مصطفیٰؐ

خیاط کار خانہ لولاک دوختہ   پیراہن اُبیّتٔ بلائے مصطفیٰؐ

شمس و قمر کہ لو لوٕ دریائے اخضر اند   ازروئے مہر آمدہ لا لائے مصطفیٰؐ

قرصِ قمر شکست بریں خوانِ لاجورد   وقتِ صلائے معجزہ ایمائے مصطفیٰؐ

کحل الجواہر ملک و توتیائے روح   دانی کہ چیست خاک کفِ پائے مصطفیٰؐ

روح القدس کہ آیتِ قربت بشانِ اوست   قاصر ز درک پایۂ ادنائے مصطفیٰؐ

خواجہ گدائے درگۂ او شد کہ جبریلؑ   شد با کمال مرتبہ مولائے مصطفیٰؐ

"The beautiful face of the Prophet is the morn of the truthful. His upright stature is the cypress of the rightfulness. The light of forehead and sweet lips of Mustafa are the mirror of Sikandar and the life spring of Khizer. The face covering and back brushing hair of the Prophet are like the sacred night of Qadr of prophets and saints. Prophet Idris, the teacher of the school of science of psychology, is silent before the speaking logic of the chosen Prophet. Jesus, who has his place on the high revolving temple of the sky, is the chamberlain of the high pinnacle of the chosen Prophet. The sublime courtyard of the chosen Prophet has reached the summit of divine nearness. The beautiful deer-like eyes of the chosen Prophet are intoxicated with the soul-nourishing divine wine of "mazagh (مازاغ)." The Divine Tailor of "Lolak (لولاک)" has sewn the selected garment of "Abit (ابیت)," the person of the chosen Prophet. The sun and moon, which are the pearls of the green river of heaven, have affectionately become the slaves of the chosen Prophet. On the azure (sky), the disc of the moon broke at the time of the miraculous word of the chosen Prophet. Do you know what is the collyrium of the angels and tutty of spirits? It is the dust of the feet of the chosen Prophet. The Holy Ghost, in whose honor there is the verse of proximity, is unable to comprehend the lowest rank of the chosen Prophet. Khwaja turned a beggar at his court because Gabriel, with all his high rank, became a slave of the chosen prophet."

We will close the present topic with a final brief point about the confession of faith and then revert to the former subject of His personal name, Allah. It is a very important and weighty point. In spite of writing about the negation and affirmation of the confession of faith, the real difficulty is always there. The point is this: What should be negated in the formula of faith, and what should be affirmed? If it is said that all other deities should be negated and only the True God should be proved, there arises the objection that in their own knowledge, the followers of every religion prove their own God and reject the deities of all other religions. Hence the process of negation and affirmation is, then, prevalent in every religion. Is the God of every religion, therefore, true? If it is said we have to prove that True Deity about whom we were told by his great Prophet Muhammad (P.B.U.H) and about whom we have been informed by his truth—interpreting tongues through the Quran and tradition, as Sa'di says:

$$آں ذات خداوند کی مخفی است بعالم$$

$$پیدا و عیاں است به چشمانِ محمدؐ$$

"The Divine Essence of the God Almighty which is hidden to the world, is visible and unveiled in the eyes of Muhammad (P.B.U.H)."

This shows that without the intermediation of His Holiness (P.B.U.H), our God remains doubtful, and without him, we can have no real deity as Pharaoh declared at the time of his drowning: "I believe that there is no diety that in whom the bani Israeil believe and I am of the Muslims" Pharaoh found out that the gods appointed by him had been proved false. In the confirmation of faith, we have to prove the Lord of Muhammad (P.B.U.H) and disprove the deities appointed by all the different religions, thinking them to be false. But yet there remains a subtle difficulty about this negation and affirmation. It is this: We have negated the deities of the other false religions and proved through the confession of faith one deity established by the lawgiver of Islam (P.B.U.H). But whatever deity we prove would yet be an establishment of our thought and imagination. Now, we can think of the created, but God the Most High is an innate essence free from figure and shape, body and form, and all features, whereas we and our thoughts are created things. Therefore, every one of us will have an imaginary god. Again, human thought differs. So everyone will have a different god, and as many gods will be proved as there are people. But this can never be correct. Or if one thinks as some holy men have said, "Whatever is visible, audible, or comprehensible should be negated," and Sa'di (RA) has also said accordingly:

اے برتر از خیال و قیاس و گمان و وہم

وز ہر چہ دیدہ ایم و شنیدیم و خواندہ ایم

"O superior than thought, conjecture, imagination, and whim: And all that we've seen and heard and read of."

This is to say that whatever we have seen, heard, and read should be negated. In this way, we have "negated in our mind the deities seen, heard of, and read about, but the process of affirmation has remained a chaos as before, and we have proved nothing. If it is said that deity should be considered true and be proved, the attributes and names of which have been told to us by Islam, then only one attribute or name can come to our heart and brain at a time. Or if a compound mixture of all the attributes is prepared and taken into mind, it is an impossibility in the first instance. Even if it were possible, it would be an imaginary deity. Hence, His personal name is the only representative of God the Most High, all his attributes and names, which we have in our thoughts and can comprehend. Though the name also resembles the created idol composed of letters and sound, there is no other way besides making the name an example of Unparalleled Essence. Let it be a big idol, but without it, the negation of all the other created idols is an impossibility. In short, these innumerable idols are never broken without the negation. "There is none to be worshipped" is taken hold of like the greatest Unitarian, His Holiness Abraham, and placed on the shoulders of the great idol. The name is taken in the sense of the Named. This talisman can be broken through the name alone. This enigma can be solved by combining the name and the named; that is, when we have proved the name to be a substitute of the Named (without thoughts, imagination, and conjectures), the true deity is established by the Lawgiver of Islam, qualified with all His attributes and names within it. This negates all the thoughts. The manifestation of all the attributes and names from this personal name, Allah, at any time and any place will be true, and there will be no need for the interference of our thoughts in that. This is the true discharge of the Confession of Faith of Islam and the correct negation and affirmation without the interference of our thoughts and imaginations.

ہم اسم توئی و ہم مسمّی   عاجز شدہ عقل زیں معمّے

"You are the name and the named. This enigma has rendered the intellect helpless."

The author says that these royal pearls drop from the spring showers of prophecy. These lustrous jewels are derived from the treasury of prophecy. These sciences and secrets are not acquired from books and are not the result of studied subjects. They are neither hearsay nor stolen but the creation of divine grace and come from prophetic mercy. The just-natured and sound-minded people can cast critical looks on this in their study houses and verify their truths and appreciate them:

کوثر چکد از لبم بایں تشنہ لبی   خاور دمد از شبم بایں تیرہ شبی

اے دوست ادب کہ در حریم دل ماست   شاہنشۂ انبیا رسول عربیؐ

(گرامی جالندھری)

"With all this thirstiness, Kausur drops from my lips. With all this darkness of the night, the sun shines from my night caution, O friend, for in the sanctuary of my heart, there abides the greatest of the Prophets—the Rasul Arabi Muhammad (P.B.U.H)."

Now we revert to our original topic. The commemorator ought to light the lamp of His personal name, Allah, in all the parts of his body so that its true light may dispel the darkness of falsehood.

With whatever part a person remembers Allah or performs virtuous acts, God the Most High, in accordance with "Remember Me; I'll remember thee" manifests with the same name in the same place, and the seeker finds the same name written in brilliant letters. Supposing a man repeats "Allah" with his tongue thousands of times a night, the heart also attends toward the thought of commemoration of Allah now and then, he hears the name of Allah with his ear, the brain commemorates Him, and the hand is busy in writing His personal name, Allah. In short, whatever limb of the body is engaged in that commemoration, the result of excessive commemoration is that the light of His personal name, Allah, manifests in that place and is written down there in brilliant letters by the power of God the Most High. So to speak, the external exertion in commemoration of Allah and obeying the order "Remember Me" is like making curd of the milk and churning it. The inscription of the name of Allah in brilliant letters esoterically is like the butter on the reciprocal promise of "I'll remember thee." In short, the result of all commemoration and pious deeds is that with whatever limb the name is commemorated or a pious deed performed, God the Most High revives and illuminates that limb with the light of that particular name by way of the promised reciprocal commemoration or as a reward for the pious deed. The more sincerely and attentively the name is commemorated or the pious deed performed, the more beautifully inscribed and brilliant is the name. If the Holy Benediction (Darud) (درود) is excessively indulged in, the name of Muhammad (P.B.U.H.) becomes illuminated and written.

Every name, sentence, and action should be similarly conjectured. This bright name is, so to say, the esoteric reciprocal message that comes to the commemorator from God the Most High for the satisfaction and pacification of his heart. Says the Most High, "Those who say 'God is our Lord' and then stick toit—angels descend to them and tell them, 'Don't fear and worry and have tidings of the paradise promised to you.'" The common folk can not know of it, and even the special people of this age are ignorant of this secret because it is a hidden mystery. Only the perfect saint concentrator on His personal name, Allah, can see there splendent written name. The other commemorators feel only its affects, for example, heat, cold, pleasure, sound, light, or the like. The bright letter of the written name of Allah the Most High is the electric wire to which the bulb of the esoteric etheric personality is attached. In Sufistic technology, it is termed the etheric personality of the place of commemoration, where the esoteric movement,sound, heat, energy, and light of commemoration comes and disseminates. The bright inscription of the name Allah is the root and the external occupation of commemoration, and its essentials are the species. The written name Allah is the esoteric kernel and butter, and the external occupation in commemoration is, so to say, the milk. External commemoration is like taking food or medicine by the mouth, and commemoration on the written picture of the name Allah is the injection of the essence of that medicine or food. Therefore, if instead of verbal commemoration and external occupation, the commemorator adopts its pitch and writes the name Allah in the special places of the body through concentration and meditation, he has, so to say, adopted the kernel. That is to say he has acquired the butter and is free from the worries of acquiring milk, making it into curd, and churning it. Because when His personal name, Allah, gets written down in any part of the body through concentration and meditation and is established there through constant practice, that place or limb becomes alive, lighted, and extended through the light of His personal name, Allah; the esoteric sense of that limb is revived; a bright aperture and esoteric path from the invisible world is opened in that limb for the commemorator. And an esoteric bright limb of the commemorator or concentrator is born in the invisible world. Through practice of concentration on His personal name, Allah, the esoteric personality of the concentrator is gradually prepared in the esoteric world, and the seats of the senses and esoteric limbs are gradually prepared for the eternal spirit in the mother's womb. Supposing the name Allah is written in the eye through concentration; the esoteric eye gets opened, and the concentrator begins to see the esoteric objects of the invisible world and achieves the degree of inspiration, trance, and observation.If the name Allah gets written in the ear with bright words of meditation, the esoteric ears, that is, the ears of the heart, get opened, and the concentrator begins to hear the esoteric sounds,and the stage or rank of inspiration opens to the commemorator and concentrator. If the word Allah is written in bright letters on the tongue, the commemorator's word becomes the word of God, and his tongue becomes the tongue of the Compassionate and is blackened with the ink of the "Holy inkpot." He talks to the invisible spiritual world through that tongue, and whatever he utters with the tongue is accomplished sooner or later, by the command of God the Most High. If the name Allah is written on the palm of the hand, he begins to shake hands with the angels, spirits of the prophets and saints, and the people of Genesis (that is, Ghauth (غوث), Qutab (قطب), Autad (اوتاد), and Abdal (ابدال). With that bright hand, he begins to control and work in the invisible universe of the esoteric world, and so on and so forth. With every limb that is enlightened with the inscription of His personal name, Allah, he begins to work esoterically.

Finally, when the entire body of the concentrator is painted through concentration of His personal name, Allah, a perfect, bright personality of the commemorator is born and established in the esoteric world. The seeing, hearing, talking, walking, catching, and so on of this bright spiritual personality is through the light of His personal name, Allah, and he is a true representation of "He sees, hears, talks, and works through Me." When such a traveler attends toward the invisible world in a trance, his external senses get closed up, and his internal senses open, and with that bright, esoteric personality, he gets drowned in the invisible world. Entering the bright esoteric world, he walks, sees, hears, talks, and performs divine duties with that esoteric personality. He becomes a perfect member of the eternal spiritual world. But the inscription of the name Allah in bright letters in the person of the seeker is a very difficult task. There are conditions, essentials, laws, and regulations for this task, and there are teachers and tutors of this science. In the esoteric world, there are spiritual schools and colleges of this science. But the occupation of concentration and meditation should be continued. One should never despair of this blessed business because (1) the body of a person is quickly cleansed through this occupation, and his esoteric capacity increases. When the land of the heart becomes prepared and irrigated, the cultivator appears to cultivate it at once. Everybody avoids useless saline land. O blessed seeker, if you become an edible bird. You will find many hunters to hunt you. But if you are like an inedible corpse-eating kite, crow, or vulture, who would care for you? In short, through concentration and practice of His personal name, Allah, a person's esoteric capability increases rapidly. (2) Sometimes when the breeze of love—that is, the air of divine grace—blows in the atmosphere of hearts and spirits, the veils of ignorance and darkness are involuntarily removed from the mirror of the heart. At such a juncture, some future incidents of the invisible world, namely, the fortune book Lauh e Mahfuz (لوح محفوظ), are reflected on the heart before their occurrence. In this stage, a person sees true dreams as is said in this tradition: "The wind of Divine grace blows in the world sometimes; therefore, you ought to create concord with it." If at the time of the blowing that wind, your hearts are alert with the commemoration of Allah, the mercy of God the Most High will cover you. A person should therefore regard those times as a boon and should not be negligent of the commemoration of Allah and concentration on His personal name, Allah.

Because the mercy of God comes suddenly, at odd times and to the alert heart, a person ought to be prepared for it and keep crying at the door like a beggar. The negligent man has no right to it. The door opens for one who knocks at it. The straight pots get filled up at the time of rain; the inverted pots remain empty.

چو حسن تربیت گردد با پاکئ گوہر   زرشحہ آب خیزد ڈر زمشت خاک زاید زر

سرشتِ خاک کاں یا آب نیساں گرچہ پاک آمد   ولے از فیض خورشیداست کاں زرگرد و ایں گوہر

بے زحمت برد دہقاں کہ در زیر زمیں تخے   بریزد بیخ یا بد شاخ و گیرد برگ و آرد بر

(خیام)

"Refined breeding and purity of essence combined produce pearls out of rain water and gold from a handful of dust. Though the essence of the mineral dust and spring shower evaporate, but through the grace of the sun, that becomes gold and this one a pearl. The cultivator bears much hardship so that the seed cast in earth throws roots, jets, and leaves and produces fruit."

When through the grace of God and attention of the perfect guide, a perfect personality of the gnostic is established in the esoteric world through concentration on His personal name, Allah, it is first of all like an invisible bright child. It cannot understand the esoteric occurrences that it sees because as yet it has not attained intelligence. Later on, when this spiritual child receives esoteric nourishment and progresses, it sees and hears the doings of the spirit world and partially understands them. Progressing gradually, it begins to understand the talk of these esoteric assemblies. Then it talks to those assembled, becomes a member, and acquires a right to vote. Lastly, he is appointed as a teacher in some esoteric school or as a servant in some spiritual department and given some office. The etheric personality of this esoteric child is inscribed with God's names in bright letters and is a complete sentence of bright written names. For example, God the Most High has explained faith as a scripture:

$$ أُولَٰئِكَ كَتَبَ فِي قُلُوبِهِمُ الْإِيمَانَ وَأَيَّدَهُمْ بِرُوحٍ مِّنْهُ (٢٢:المجادلة ٥٨) $$

"The faithful are those in whose hearts God the Most High has written the word of Faith in their minds and added them with His spirit," and Jesus (AS) has been called a Word.

$$ إِنَّمَا الْمَسِيحُ عِيسَى ابْنُ مَرْيَمَ رَسُولُ اللّٰهِ وَكَلِمَتُهُ أَلْقَاهَا إِلَىٰ مَرْيَمَ وَرُوحٌ مِّنْهُ (٤ النساء:١٠١) $$

"Verily Jesus Christ, the son of Mary, is a prophet of Allah and his word whom He has cast towards Mary and he is a spirit from Him."

Giving the tidings of a son to Prophet Zakaria, God the Most High has said:

$$ أَنَّ اللّٰهَ يُبَشِّرُكَ بِيَحْيَىٰ مُصَدِّقًا بِكَلِمَةٍ مِّنَ اللّٰهِ وَسَيِّدًا وَّحَصُورًا وَّنَبِيًّا مِّنَ الصّٰلِحِينَ ۞ $$

$$ (٣ آل عمران:٣٩) $$

"Verily God gives you the tidings (of a son called Yahya)—He will verily be the word of God and he will be a perfect innocent and a prophet amongst the pious people."

In another place too, God the Most High says, "When the angels said, O Mary, God gives you the tiding of His word called Jesus son of Mary." The reason for God the Most High's calling the faith and Jesus (AS) as the Word is that esoterically the forms, the divine personalities in the invisible world, are composed of bright names of God the Most High. Similarly, the existence of an entire esoteric world (also called the Word of Allah) and the invisible world is established and apparent in the form of bright words. About this Word of Allah, God the Most High says:

قُلْ لَّوْ كَانَ الْبَحْرُ مِدَادًا لِّكَلِمٰتِ رَبِّيْ لَنَفِدَ الْبَحْرُ قَبْلَ اَنْ تَنْفَدَ كَلِمٰتُ رَبِّيْ وَلَوْ جِئْنَا بِمِثْلِهٖ مَدَدًا ۝ (١٨الكهف:١٠٩)

"Say, O Prophet, if the ocean had become ink for writing the words of my Lord, it would have dried up before the words of my Lord had ended; although We had created and added more ink like that."

When God the Most High manifested Himself in the world of plurality from the world of unity, He descended from the essence toward the attributes; then the names appeared from the attributes and the acts came out of the names, and the apparent appeared from acts. The world in which the names appeared after the attributes of God the Most High is called the world of command (i.e., Amr عالم امر). The forms of the objects of that world are compounded of divine names composed of bright letters. Since God the Most High created the universe by pronouncing the word "become (کُن)," and *become* is in the imperative mood, it is therefore called an imperative word, and because *become* is the word, that world exists in the form of words. As words form into sentences and sentences are written with wet ink on dry paper, this wet, wordy world of the imperative world has been written by God the Most High on the dry paper of the opaque and gross material world with the pen of power. Therefore, in the benevolent Quran, the esoteric world has been compared to the ocean (i.e., water) and the material world to the land. Elsewhere, the universe of the esoteric world has been interpreted as a wet thing and the material world as a dry thing. So the esoteric worlds and the material worlds combined have been termed as a perfect book. Says the Most High:

وَّلَا رَطْبٍ وَّلَا يَابِسٍ اِلَّا فِيْ كِتٰبٍ مُّبِيْنٍ ۝ (١٦الانعام:٥٩)

"There is nothing wet or dry, but it is contained in the divine book."

The same is the meaning of collecting and enumerating everything in the person of a perfect Man (i.e., Evident Imam). Says the Most High:

$$\text{وَكُلَّ شَىْءٍ اَحْصَيْنٰهُ فِىْٓ اِمَامٍ مُّبِيْنٍ ﴿١٢﴾ (٣٦ يٰس:١٢)}$$

"We have confined everything in an Evident Imam."

Here, the evident leader and the evident book prove to be an identical written thing. The highest abode of the pious spirits has also been called the written book in the benevolent Quran:

$$\text{وَمَآ اَدْرٰىكَ مَا عِلِّيُّوْنَ ﴿١٩﴾ كِتٰبٌ مَّرْقُوْمٌ ﴿٢٠﴾ يَّشْهَدُهُ الْمُقَرَّبُوْنَ ﴿٢١﴾ (٨٣ المطففين: ١٩-٢١)}$$

"O (My Prophet) what do you understand by the highest abode? It is a written Book which the favorites will see and (read)." We have already stated that in the benevolent Quran, the invisible esoteric world is compared to a wet thing that is to an ocean. Hence the time when God the Most High had not yet created the material world out of the esoteric world. It is thus mentioned in the Quran:

$$\text{هُوَ الَّذِىْ خَلَقَ السَّمٰوٰتِ وَالْاَرْضَ فِىْ سِتَّةِ اَيَّامٍ وَّكَانَ عَرْشُهُ عَلَى الْمَآءِ (١١ هود:٧)}$$

He (is the Essence who) created the heavens and earth in six days. At that time, His throne was on water. Here, also, water means the invisible and the esoteric world, since everything of the opaque world, that is, the material world, is created from the ocean of the esoteric world and its refined matter.

God the Most High says:

$$\text{وَجَعَلْنَا مِنَ الْمَآءِ كُلَّ شَىْءٍ حَيٍّ ط (٢١ الانبيآء:٣٠)}$$

"We enlivened everything from water."

Although not everything exists because of water alone—there are also other elements among its constituents. A tradition says, "Our earth stands on the back of an ox which is standing on the back of a fish which is floating on an ocean of water."

When the gnostic endowed with esoteric insight looks toward his elemental body, He sees this dusty body borne by the animal soul, the esoteric form of which is that of an ox. The ox of an animal soul is borne by the fish of the spirit soul, which floats on the ocean of the invisible world. The part applies to the whole. Similarly, the esoteric animal soul of the entire world has the form of an ox, which is called the animal of the earth (دابته الارض). It will appear on the last day after the destruction of the dusty body of the earth. This universal soul (i.e., animal) of the earth rests on the fish of the spirit world, which floats on the ocean of the esoteric world. Hence, the spiritual world and the material world are two parts of the book of the universe. The former is, so to say, its inscription or text written in the ink of "become," while the latter is like a paper. Or take it like this: There are two letters in God the Most High's order "Be (كُن)." On the Kunto Kanzan (كُنتُ كَنزا) (I was a hidden treasure) of the book of the universe, the world of spirit and matter was created from the Kaf (ک) form of a pen. And Noon, the form of which resembles an inkpot, is ever brimming with the ink of the command "be" with which the scribe of K. N. (كُن) is writing the book of the world of command with the pen of power.

نَ وَالْقَلَمِ وَمَا يَسْطُرُوْنَ ۝ (١٦٨ القلم:١)

"N—and the pen what it writes."

It is strange that the origin of paper, pen, and ink is the same. Paper is prepared from the pulp of trees. Most of the pens are twigs of trees. The ink is prepared from vegetable matter (charcoal, gum, and so on). Just as their origin is the same, the creation of the first growth of the book of the universe is also from one matter, which was in the form of a cloud of dust, like matter, ether, or air. God the Most High caused the world to appear in this form of cloud first of all. Then he threw on it the light of His attributes of Creator and Painter, and that dust appeared in the form of the world of command and the world of matter or the book of the universe. As is said in a tradition, "The world was like cloud. He threw His light on it, and it appeared." Both the worlds (that is, the world of Command and the world of Creation) appeared from a fine element like air. Because our material world is a reflection of the first growth of the invisible world, the two worlds of command and matter were similarly formed. And in our world, a mental world of the world of command and an outside world of the world of matter were created from ether and air. It is an accepted principle of science that all the solid objects in the world were formed from different combinations and variations of these fine etheric elements. At the time of talking, on account of the different motions of the parts of our mouth, different elements (i.e., single letters) are formed. Words are formed from the combinations of the element of letters, and they form the different languages of the world. In short, in this material world, there appeared the material solid, external world of matter and the mental world of command. Says the Most High:

$$وَ مِنْ اٰيٰتِهٖ خَلْقُ السَّمٰوٰتِ وَ الْاَرْضِ وَ اخْتِلَافُ اَلْسِنَتِكُمْ وَ اَلْوَانِكُمْ ۚ اِنَّ فِيْ ذٰلِكَ لَاٰيٰتٍ لِّلْعٰلِمِيْنَ ۞ (۳۰الروم:۲۲)$$

"And amongst His signs or the creation of the heavens and earth and the difference in your languages and colors. In these there are signs for the people."

The origin of both has appeared from ether or air. Now to our minds, these languages composed of letters and words are the means of understanding the names of the outward solid objects, their properties and realities. Without the languages, the out side world lies in an atmosphere of ignorance. If the realities of objects did not reach our mind through languages, the existence and nonexistence of the world would be alike. Now as the elements were composed by the different movements of ether or air in the out side, the different objects of the world came into existence through the combination of the elements, and the material world came into existence in the outside where trees, plants, vegetables, fruits, flowers, gardens, orchards, and innumerable other things came into existence, similarly, the different elements of the letters appeared from the different movements of ether or air. From the combination of the elements of the letters, words and sentences were formed, which gave rise to the different languages of the world and the various books were written through the languages, among which are the revealed books. In short, opposite to the opaque material world, there appeared a mental world like the world of command composed of their realities, attributes, and meanings, and different books of science and art were composed. Thus mental orchards, rose gardens, millions of proverbs, and books were composed. Outwardly, man is composed of material elements—a dusty frame of flesh and bones surrounded by thematerial world. Occasionally, his elemental body avails itself of these material things as need arises. But the esoteric personality of a man, namely, the spirit, which is an invisible creation of theworld of command, avails itself of the object of the imperative world and derives mental benefit and food. In short, esoterically, all the prophets, messengers, and perfect saints are granted are fined personality inscribed with the name and the holy sentences of the bright letters of God the Most High. Like the spirit and soul, when this refined personality enters the elemental body of the gnostic, it colors his real spirit in its own color, and through that bright personality, he involuntarily acquires all the spiritual sciences and arts, esoteric favors, and blessings and spiritual powers (i.e., revelations, miraculous powers, inspirations, events,manifestations, flight, and travel on earth and in heaven) andnine firmaments (نه فلک) (emperean, chair, stratum, and so on).God the Most High has called this bright personality (کلمه طیبه) theword of faith.

Now the question arises how does this bright esoteric personality inscribed with the name of God enter a person's body, and what are the conditions of its entrance and the means of acquiring these bright esoteric personalities? Let it be known that there are many ways of acquiring it (i.e., all the virtuous deeds— piety, renunciation, trust in God, humility, patience, gratitude, submission, satisfaction, generosity, politeness, kindness, affection, and so on) and all kinds of worship and devotion (prayers, fasting, pilgrimage, alms, recitations, and so on. The correct discharge of all these prepares the ground for the bright esoteric personality in the body of man and for the cultivation of the holy tree of His personal name, Allah, and the folio of the heart and the tablet of the spirit is cleansed for the inscription of these bright sentences. Then there is a need for throwing the seed of commemoration of His name Allah and His name Allah in the field of the heart because the field is useless without the seed. When the field is arranged, it requires irrigation, which consists of the company and attention of the perfect guide. No matter how well the tablet and paper of the heart of the seeker are prepared through virtuous deeds and worship, a perfect scribe is indispensable for writing on it. If the ploughman is perfect, he converts inferior saline land into cultivable land by application of manure, and by sowing in it the seed of His personal name, Allah, and irrigating it with the water of his attention, he converts the fallow land into a garden of paradise. The perfect scribe clearly and easily writes on it the words of Allah with his pen and ink. But in this world such a perfect guide is rare like the phoenix. The presence of a perfect guide is an invaluable bounty: "His body is, so to speak, a litho-plate of perfect block permanently inscribed with the name of God and His evident signs. No sooner the block of the heart of the guide touches it, than he immediately imprints with the sentences of Allah and unites himself with God.

How fortunate are the people who become the bright mandate of the word of faith and reach the exalted court of God the Most High or become the holy trees and perpetually swing in the paradise of affinity and union. Says the Most High:

$$\text{اَلَمْ تَرَ كَيْفَ ضَرَبَ اللّٰهُ مَثَلًا كَلِمَةً طَيِّبَةً كَشَجَرَةٍ طَيِّبَةٍ اَصْلُهَا ثَابِتٌ وَّفَرْعُهَا فِى السَّمَآءِ تُؤْتِىْ اُكُلَهَا كُلَّ حِيْنٍ بِاِذْنِ رَبِّهَا (ابراهیم:۲۴-۲۵)}$$

"Don't you see how God relates parables? The word of faith is like a holy tree with firm roots and its branches in heaven which yields its edibles at all times by the permission of its Lord."

آناں کہ زیرِ سایہ مہرت مقام شانست   در دل چرا تخیل بال ہما کنند

شوریدگانِ حسن و جلال و جمال یار   تسکینِ دل بملکِ دو عالم کُجا کنند

دیوانگانِ بادیہ پیمائے عشق اُو   ہفت آسماں بچشم زدن زیرِ پا کنند

(حافظ)

"The people who have abodes under the shadow of your love, why should they think of the feather of Huma? The true lover of the beauty and glory of the Beloved does not satisfy the heart with the dominion of the two worlds. His desert-traversing mad lovers cross the seven skies in the wink of the eye."

Some ignorant people consider this matter very easy and regard the perpetual paradise and divine proximity as child's play. A person can never become a true Muslim by merely being born in the house of a Muslim and coming into the fold of Islam by way of a legacy from his forefathers. Moreover, it is the height of shortsightedness to formally obey the external fundamentals of Islam blindly and to regard it as everything or to regard mere verbal confession and a bit of physical exercise and monetary sacrifice as a sufficient price for eternal paradise and divine proximity! This bargain with God the Most High is not so cheap!

ہر دو عالم قیمتِ خود گفته ٔ

نرخ بالا کن کہ ارزانی ہنُوز

(امیر خسرو)

"O Lord! Thou hast asked the two worlds as Thy price: Raise up the bid for Thee are still cheap." Remember that God the Most High cannot be understood through mere discussions or blind following and external acts, and the external verbal knowledge can give no clue to the prophecy and messengering of the Prophet and his special spiritual power or miracles or the reality of the revelation of the Prophet or his spiritual flight or ascent. It is on this account that all the times the verbose scholars keep quarrelling about the Prophet's knowledge of the unknown, observation of God in this world, the reality of the essence, miracles, and other problems. A true follower is one who follows in the footsteps of his leader. Therefore, unless a person follows in the footsteps of the Prophet of Islam and acquires some of the special virtues of prophethood, he can never truly be a Muslim and a faithful follower, a pure, sincere man of faith. Things heard cannot be like things seen. Unless a person receives revelations or at least sees true dreams, which are admitted to be an ordinary part of prophethood, the reality of revelations cannot be understood through mere discussions and reading the accounts of revelations in books. Or unless a person himself acquires miraculous or supernatural powers, he cannot form a correct idea of the miracles and the true signs of the prophets through mere intellectual argumentation and verbal proof. And unless a seeker acquires the degree of esoteric flight and travels in the spiritual world, he cannot understand the reality of the ascent of the Prophet through mere narrations; nor can he solve physical and spiritual differences of the ascent and its difficulties of dreaming or waking. A handful is a sample of the stock, and a tree is judged by its fruit.

چراغ مُردہ کُجا زندہ آفتاب کُجا

ببین تفاوت رہ از کُجا است تا بہ کُجا

(حافظ)

"A dead candle stands no comparison with the living sun. Behold the great difference between the two."

Truly speaking, to be a true follower is a very difficult task. A sincere follower is one who follows the Prophet step by step and reaches his esoteric stage, and the Prophet (P.B.U.H) calls him a follower with his truth-interpreting tongue. It is no use being a follower in name only. Different is the lion painted on the carpet from the lion in the reeds.

Some people on failing to acquire this rank console themselves by denying these esoteric stages and spiritual ranks or lay interpretations on them. These people take in pride the external form of Islam and bookish and "acquired knowledge":

خونِنا بہ خور کہ شرابے بہ ازیں نیست دندان بہ جگر زن کہ کبابے بہ ازیں نیست
در کنز و قدوری نتواں یافت خدا را بر صفحۂ دل بیں کہ کتابے بہ ازیں نیست
(سرمد)

"Drink the blood of the heart for there is no better wine. Bite with the teeth at your liver for there is no better roasted meat (Kabab). God cannot be found in Kanz and Quduri (religious books). Read the folio of the heart for there is not a better book than this."

Religious mentality has disappeared from the world, and truth and falsehood are indiscriminate. By writing a few books, some people have laid false claim to prophethood, and the blind idiots have become ready to believe in them. God be praised! What an ordinary thing was made of prophethood that a decent shop has been opened by writing a few ordinary books and thousands of idiots and fools desired to purchase this imaginary merchandise without weighing it:

ہر چند زمانہ مجمع جہال است در جہل نہ حال شاں بیک منوال است
کو دِن ہمہ لیک از یکے تا دگرے فرق خرِ عیسیٰؑ و خرِ دجال است
(خیام)

"Although the world is a congregation of fools. But in foolishness they are not all alike. All are idiots but from the one to the other, there is the difference between the ass of Jesus and that of Anti-Christ, Dajjal."

In the world, we cannot find a follower in the true and real sense of the word. God the Most High is my witness that in order to become a follower, I had to roam in jungles and mountains for many years, to drink the liver's blood and turn the blood into perspiration. I had to adopt many hard journeys in this thorny and difficult path in the search of God. Should these be narrated, the hearts would tremble and the livers would shiver. The beauty of it is that in this path, there has been found eternal wealth every moment and a stage and place at every step. Yet it does not befit me to claim this with my own mouth. Alas! What a big claim it is that by merely studying books, people have become saints, nay even prophets by sitting in their houses. But it is the age of independence. Who is there to ask him even if a man claims to be a God? As long as there is an abundance of fools in the world, crooks and cheats will enjoy it to the full. When people begin to pay for useless bits of glass as jewels, why should not the worldly crooks think a boon of such golden chances and open a jeweler's shop and the real jewelers should close down their shops?

سرگین گاؤ و عنبرِ سارا برابر است   امروز قدرِ گوہر و خارا برابرا است

"Alike is the value of a jewel and flint today, Alike are the cow's dung and pure amber."

How much folly it is that with nothing in their house to eat and dying of starvation, they are inviting to meals thousands of people from outside, calling them to the house saying, "Come, everything is ready."

زیرا کہ بزیرِ خرقۂ سالوس دراند   آں قوم کہ سجادہ پرستند خراند

إسلام فروشند و ز کافر بتر اند   دیں از ہمہ طرفہ ترکہ در دیدۂ زہد

(خیام)

The people who worship only the carpet of saint-seeming are donkeys because they are prey to fraud and deceit. But this is strangest of all that under the garb of piety, they sell Islam while they are worse than infidels.

Now, first of all, it is very difficult to find a perfect guide. If one comes across one, it is still more difficult to recognize him because, to the best of their capacity, the real men of God conceal themselves behind curtains like houri-faced beauties and fairyfaced beloved and don't open shops of nudism and lewdism in the streets like prostitutes.

پری نہفتہ رُخ و دیو در کرشمہ و ناز

بسوخت عقل ز حیرت کہ ایں چہ بو العجبی است

(حافظ)

The fairy has covered her face while the demon is in display and coquetry. My intelligence burned down in astonishment at this wonder.

CONCENTRATION ON HIS PERSONAL NAME, ALLAH, IS THE REAL THING

Therefore, it behooves the seeker "after God to continue the commemoration of Allah and concentration on his personal name, Allah, day and night because nowadays truth and lawful food are nowhere to be found in the world. People lack the grace of the former pious people to engage in virtuous deeds, hard labors, and self-denial. There is a great reduction in discharge of prayer, pilgrimage, and alms. All that happens takes place in the form of customary display. Therefore, concentration on His personal name, Allah, is the best occupation in these days of dearth of men, actions, and reforms. The seeker very soon succeeds through it. The seeker ought to light the lamp of His personal name, Allah, in every limb of the body and enlighten the entire body with its light.

The concentrator on His personal name, Allah, is a man of gain without pain. He who always keeps himself busy in concentrationon His personal name, Allah, attains the secret without laboring and observation without self-denying. Al1 the prophets, saints, religious leaders, companions, scholars, faqirs, dervishes, and men of genesis and power have reached the highest stages through His personal name, Allah. All the prophets (A.S) and munificent saints have got their miracles, revelations, and miraculous powers through the blessing and meditation of His personal name, Allah.Concentration on His personal name, Allah, was the manifest light that Gabriel the trustworthy put in the form of a bright seed in the breast of his holiness the prophet Muhammad (P.B.U.H) in the cave of Hira by pronouncing the words "Read in the name of your Lord," which later on came into view in the form of the tree of the Quran from his truth-interpreting tongue. It was the spiritual Rafraf and esoteric Buraq that took his holiness to the seven skies, Empyrean (عرش), and chair (کرسی) on the night of ascent; got for him the rank of the place of "two bows space

$$\text{قَابَ قَوْسَيْنِ أَوْاَدْنَى ۝ (۵۳ النجم: ۹)}$$

and confronted him with the great signs of the bright spectacle of God the Most High. It was the bright hand and staff whereby Moses

(A.S) relieved his nation from the tyranny of Pharaoh and his premier, Haman. It was the inscription in the signet of Solomon (A.S). It was the blessed letter of His name as it came in the Holy Quran:

$$اِنَّهٗ مِنْ سُلَيْمٰنَ وَاِنَّهٗ بِسْمِ اللّٰهِ الرَّحْمٰنِ الرَّحِيْمِ ۙ (٢٧ النمل:٣٠)$$

"This is from Solomon and this is in the name of Allah the Most Merciful, the Most Compassionate."

It had esoterically enchained Queen Bilqis, all the jinn, men, animals, and birds in the chain of his subjugation. It was this holy name that sailed the Ark of Noah in the great ocean with the oar of

$$بِسْمِ اللّٰهِ مَجْرٰىهَا وَمُرْسٰىهَا ۚ (هود ٤١)$$

"In the name of God, it starts and stops" and saved it from the deluge. In short, all the prophets and saints receive the esoteric electricity from the powerhouse of His personal name, Allah. Now too all these pious beings swim in the ocean of the purgatory of this holy name like the brilliant fishes. He who wants to meet them ought to dive in the river of light of His name and see them. His personal name, Allah, is the world-revealing mirror of Sikandar. In the telescope of this name, the concentrator studies the fortune book and views the spectacle of the innumerable worlds on the nail of the thumb or on the palm of his hand. The concentrator enjoys undisturbed secrecy in his breast. The bridal chamber of his heart gets independent of the parlor of the water and clay (i.e., this world). He enjoys secrecy in public and publicity in secret (namely, spiritual assemblies); in his breast (خلوت در انجمن اور نیز انجمن در خلوت). Verses by author:

کھُل گیا مشتق و تصور کا معمّے آخر	اسم میں دیکھ لیا ہم نے مسئلے آخر
پھر اَنَا اَنْتَ کہو اور سُنو اَنْتَ اَنَا	اسم کو جسم بنا جسم کو کر اس میں فنا
جامِ جم کی طرح دل سینہ صفا ہوتا ہے	اسم اللہ کے تصور سے لقا ہوتا ہے
صوفی درویش ہوں یا شیخ و قلندر و زہاد	ہر نبی اور ولی غوث قطب اور اوتاد
سب تصور سے ہوئے واصل و عامل کامل	سب کو جو معرفت و قرب ہوا ہے حاصل
برکتِ اسم سے سب ناظر و منظور ہوئے	نیّر اسم کے انوار سے سب نور ہوئے

"We saw the Named in the name at last. The riddle of exerciseand concentration was solved at last. Make a body of the nameand annihilate your body in it. Then say, "I am Thou," and hear, "Thou art Me." The visage is acquired through concentration on the name, Allah. The heart and breast are cleansed like a worldrevealing cup of the king Jamshed. All prophets, saints, ghaus (غوث), qutub (قطب), and autad (اوتاد)-sheikhs, Sufis, dervishes, qalandars, and exotics, all had gnosis and proximity that they enjoyed through concentration and became united operators and perfect by it. All lights come from the light of the sun of the name. Through the blessing of the name, all of them saw and were seen. Concentration is the key to the treasures of the two worlds, O friends! If fortune helps you, believe it, O friends."

The mesmerists, hypnotists, and spiritualists in Europe have copied Islamic concentration on His personal name, Allah. They practiced fixing their gaze on a particular thing (e.g., a crystal, the flame of a lamp, or an electric bulb)—in short, they practiced fixing it on some bright object. They call it concentration. Thus, through practicing concentration and meditation, they acquire an electric power and power of attention through which the operator pays attention to his subject and makes him unconscious. He makes him sleep a magnetic sleep and works in his subconscious mind through his (operators) willpower and suggestion. Whatever he orders, the subject obeys. But since this power is a creation of the elemental body and a raw, imperfect process of the terrestrial self, the operator of this science astonishes unintelligent and ignorant people by showing them mere terrestrial incidents, material tricks, and exoteric shows in the place of the hierarchy of man. Some mental and nervous diseases can also be cured by it. But it cannot yield any permanent and real spiritual profit because the fields of the spiritualist, mesmerist, and hypnotist are confined to the lowest hierarchy of man and cannot proceed further. It has no access to the hierarchy of angels. Hence, elemental man in it remains confined to matter. The philosophy of this raw and imperfect power is as follows:

When all the human senses and power of imagination are concentrated on one object, the illumination of an electric energy is produced in it. As when the rays of the sun are collected on a point after passing through a lens, they acquire heat that can burn other things like fire. Similarly, when human thoughts and senses are focused on a point, an electric power is generated whereby a weak person (the subject) can be rendered unconscious. But the object of concentration of the men of this science is a material thing and imaginary dot utilized for the concentration of thoughts only. Hence, the whole affair of the spiritualist, mesmerist, and hypnotist is confined to this material world and lowest place of the hierarchy of man. It has no connection with the spiritual world. But if instead of an imaginary material dot, one focuses his thought on the noble figure of His personal name, Allah (i.e., incessantly practices writing His personal name, Allah, in the heart and brain), he will thereby acquire an imperishable esoteric electric power directly connected to the ocean of light of that unparalleled, everlasting, and imperishable essence who is the beginning and end of the entire universe and whose bright spark is the source of all creation, whose smallest attribute is this:

$$\text{(٨٢ : يٰسٓ ٣٦) اِذَآ اَرَادَ شَيْئًا اَنْ يَّقُوْلَ لَهٗ كُنْ فَيَكُوْنُ}$$

"When he desires, He says to it become and it becomes into existence," and whose ordinary rank is

$$\text{(٢٠ : البقرة ٢) اِنَّ اللّٰهَ عَلٰى كُلِّ شَىْءٍ قَدِيْرٌ}$$

"Verily God is Omnipotent."

By practicing meditation and concentration on His personal name, Allah, in the eyes, the light of the observation of the Named comes into the eyes, and in the bright telescope of His personal name, Allah, a terrestrial man can see the illuminations and senses the hierarchy of God and the esoteric world because the sun of the Named with all the colors of the names and attributes is shining in the royal mandate of His personal name, Allah. If concentration on His personal name, Allah, is practiced in the ears, the esoteric ears are opened, and one begins to hear the spiritual and angelic sounds and becomes a man receiving inspiration.

When the concentrator writes His personal name, Allah, in his heart, brain, or other particular places of the body, the electricity of the light of His personal name, Allah, is produced in the concentrator. That electricity is connected with the Named (i.e., the mind of the light of the essence of the Creator from where the heart and brain of the concentrator receive the electric waves of the unseen light, brilliance, sound, and other attributes of the esoteric electricity). The body of the concentrator is filled up with the electricity of the spiritual light. The seeker disseminates the waves of the light of the brilliance, power, sound, and other attributes of the esoteric electricity in both the worlds. Today, we see that through the material electricity, every kind of power, light, sound, and so on are transmitted to places thousands of miles apart in the twinkling of an eye so much so that light is changed and the forms of the speaker also appear clearly. The way that this material electricity can be the source and medium of transmitting power, sound, light, and so on from one place to another, the esoteric and spiritual electricity can be the source of transmitting the waves of light, brilliance, energy, and other lights of attributes and names from the powerhouse of the breast of a perfect guide into the bodies and souls of millions of followers. Through these esoteric waves, various divine incidents and doubtless victories descend on the gnostic, and he builds in himself the radio station of inspiration, television of revelation, machinery of miraculous powers, and electric powerhouse of illuminations. Thus, the esoteric telegraph offices, telephones, radio stations, wireless, and television are fixed in every prophet and saint. His personal name, Allah, is the origin of the entire universe. All favors and blessings of God are acquired through it, and it is the source of all lights and secrets. When instead of verbal commemoration, it is written through concentration and meditation in the particular places of the body, all the bright names that are the origin of all the favors and blessings illuminate within the person through which his inner self (i.e., heart) becomes alive. Because commemoration of God is the commemorator's attribute, "Remember Me," and the writing of His personal name, Allah, is its natural bright inscription of God the Most High's illumination, "I'll remember thee." The human heart is the real seat of commemoration and the true internal stomach for this spiritual food. Therefore, there are many dangers in transferring the commemoration from the tongue to its real seat, namely, the heart. Because when a man engages in verbal commemoration, the devil does not allow its effect to reach the heart and overfloods the heart with worldly sensual and extraneous thoughts to produce a tumult of Satanic doubts and reminds him of innumerable forgotten things. Turning away the face of the heart from God the Most High, he sets it toward others and does not allow the commemoration to affect the heart because the heart can think of only one thing at a time. "God has not put two hearts in the breast of a Man." Hence, the experts have devised a few conditions and essentials, different regulations, and some laws for transmitting the verbal commemoration to the heart. For example, eating the lawful and speaking the truth have been put forward as the foremost essential conditions of bringing into practice the divine names, verses of the Word of God, Quranic chapters, and other sentences. The other different conditions and essentials for the various holy verses and recitations prescribed are the alms, lock, expenditure, seclusion, fixing of time and place, abandonment of animals' flesh (namely, recognition of the auspicious and inauspicious times), perfect permission, practical exertion, and the cleanliness of person, place, and clothes. If any of these conditions for external recitation remain unfulfilled or there are some shortcomings in discharging it, the recitation becomes ineffective, and the deal is upset. For this reason, many people put in exhaustive labors but cannot derive any benefit from recitation and finally deny and disbelieve the effect of recitation of the divine names and the Holy Book. But if instead of verbal recitation, the commemorator writes this name with his mental finger of imagination on the heart or some other important parts of the body, he is relieved of all the troubles and retreats of external and verbal recitations and of all the conditions and restrictions, and thus the commemorator reaches the real destination of commemoration (i.e., the light of the commemorator God). O seeker, if you have understood our talk and the riddle of the name and the Named, believe that you have filled your skirt with the desirable jewels because we direct you toward a water of immortality in search of which thousands of seekers have spent their lives and for a drop of which the seekers have been facing hardships and troubles for years and have been yearning for but could not get. Verses are by the author (God forgive him).

سر آب باتو گویم نہ رہ سراب پویم   بدر از چہ آب جوئی بہراست آب جویم

من ازاں شراب مستم کہ بداد در الستم   نہ بخواب اندر استم کہ حدیثِ خواب گویم

O boy! I am leading you to the spring of the water of life and not toward the mirage. Why do you seek the water outside? The source of it is in my breast. I am intoxicated with wine, which He gave me on the Day of Eternity. I am not dreaming so as to relate the story of a dream.

There are two methods of commemoration: (1) verbal with the tongue and lips and (2) mental with the mind and thought. One is the commemoration with the tongue and lips. The second is the commemoration through concentration and imagination (i.e., the eye of insight). God the Most High mentions both these methods in the magnificent Quran thus:

$$ \text{(١٠-٨: البلد ٩٠) } \text{اَلَمْ نَجْعَلْ لَّهُ عَيْنَيْنِ ۞ وَلِسَانًا وَّ شَفَتَيْنِ ۞ وَهَدَيْنُهُ النَّجْدَيْنِ ۞} $$

"Didn't We give him two eyes, and a tongue, and two lips and We have shown him two paths?" Thus, the path of the tongue and lips is that of the external commemoration with the tongue. The path of concentration and meditation is that of commemoration with the eye. Therefore, when the seeker practices concentration on His personal name, Allah, and it gets fixed up in the heart of the seeker, an electric spark of illumination of lights comes out of His personal name, Allah, whereby the seeker is drowned in that flame of the lights of observation, and the esoteric personality of the seeker is traversed and quickened in that personal light. The course of interview and observation is permanently opened for the seeker. So the sublimest, highest, most perfect, most complete, and most collective of all commemorations is that of the eye (i.e., concentration on His personal name, Allah, is the pith of all commemorations). All the other methods of commemoration are its branches.

Some people will say that His personal name, Allah, is a word composed of four letters—A, L, L, and H (الله). When we utter this word with the external tongue or write it on paper or see it with the eye, we see in it no weight or any sort of heat, coldness, or some other kind of effect, pleasure, power, and so on. How should we know that it has influence, light, brilliance, and power enough through which veils and shadows of the soul sin and slackness be removed and that it has esoteric heat enough through which the terrestrial egg of a person is incubated and the divine bird of the heart becomes alive or that there is an esoteric electricity concealed in it by riding in the lift by which the commemorator and concentrator reaches the holy and high court of God the Most High.

Pronouncing the name of Allah with the external tongue or writing it on paper or merely beholding it with the eyes is like a person's holding medicine (e.g., quinine) or a piece of arsenic on the palm of the hand or beholding it. Thus what effect of the medicine or arsenic can be felt in this way? Because a medicine exercises its influence in its particular place, such as the stomach or liver, and especially by mixing with the blood. For example, if it is desired to feel the effect of arsenic, it should be taken down the throat to the stomach. Then it will be clear that the white piece of arsenic that appeared a harmless thing like lime on the palm of the hand proved to be an atom bomb for the body and soul and shattered it into pieces on going down the throat and reaching the stomach and liver. Similarly, a useful and beneficial medicine (e.g., an antidote) shows its effect on entering the human body. A thing is effective in its appropriate place. Moreover, if the essence of a medicine is extracted and infused into the blood through an injection or subcutaneous syringe, it quickly produces a useful or harmful revolution in the body. In short, concentration on His personal name, Allah, is the extract of the entire glorious Quran and great names of God. The human heart is its stomach and esoteric womb. If it is repeatedly recited with the external tongue and taken to the esoteric stomach or the heart with all the conditions and essentials of commemoration, it will most certainly manifest its influence. Or if it is written and taken to some other particular place of the body through the injection of concentration or meditation, it will be found out that the word *Allah* composed of the four letters, which appeared a very ordinary and ineffective thing when placed on the palm of the hand or expressed by the tongue or seen by the eye after reaching the esoteric womb proved itself to be a dynamite of esoteric power that dispelled all the sensual and Satanic darknesses of the body and made it eternally alive, illuminated with the innate lights of God the Most High. The part of the body in which His personal name, Allah, gets written in bright letters through concentration or meditation is thereby esoterically revived. When all the essential parts of the body of the seeker are inscribed with the bright writing of His personal name, Allah, a bright, invisible personality of the seeker gets alive in the esoteric world, and the seeker-traveler is, so to say, reborn with the bright, esoteric personality in the invisible world and the world of spirits. Then he receives nourishment and training at the hands of the spiritual parents until he becomes a proper, bright child. Bright education is imparted to him by the spiritual teachers in the esoteric school. There are different schools of souls (نفوس), colleges of hearts (قلب) and spirits (ارواح), and universities of the innermost self (سر). The alphabet, as well as the language, curriculum, system of education, and books of the bright science, is also different. The earth, sky, and universe there are quite different. Things heard cannot be like things seen:

دل گفت مرا علم لدنی ہوس است　　　تعلیمے کن اگر ترا دسترس است

گفتم کہ الف گفت دگر گفتم ہیچ　　　در خانہ اگر کس است یک حرف بس اس

"The heart said I desire esoteric knowledge."

Teach me if you have the power to do so!

I said the letter "A." It said "further." I said, "Nothing but the letter A. If there is one intelligent, a word is sufficient."

It means that this is the path of the esoteric body and its esoteric senses. The elemental body has no access there:

پائے ظاہر رو ہمیشہ راہ ظاہر میرود

قطع راہ باطنی ہاکار پائے دیگر است

"The external foot always travels the external load. To cross the esoteric path is the task of other feet."

The fraudulent priests and pirs have highly defamed Islamic mysticism and spiritual science. This science was the rightful legacy of the Oriental, whereby they could rightly boast over the Europeans. In fact, the Orientals possess nothing if they do not possess this eternal wealth and perpetual felicity. With regard to this science, the only claim of our so-called Sufis is that of a glorious ancestry, or at places, the empty dress and fables of spiritualism are left behind. The Europeans are acclaiming this science anew, and these notorious and self-sacrificing people are stacking their heads and lives in search of it. Though they are in its initial stages at present, the day is not far off when they will find out this felicity and treasure of the two worlds because life signifies practice and exertion. Mere claim of legacy and right are vain:

زندگی جُہد است استحقاق نیست

جُز بعلم انفس و آفاق نیست

(اقبال)

"Life means exertion, not a right. The real life is achieved by the knowledge of the visible and invisible worlds."

The great merit of this nation lies on this if one of them undertakes a new adventure or begins to investigate a new invention, discovery, or science, the entire nation encourages him. Even the government supports him. But look at the evilheartedness of the East. If a man in simple clothes brings down and shows them stars of the high empyrean or diving into the deep sea of the invisible worlds brings out those invaluable pearls that are unique in the world, they wouldn't look at these in the first instance. But if they see that he is being respected, the whole world will turn out to be his enemy out of jealousy, and he will be disgraced so much that he will be compelled to hide himself in a corner of seclusion and solitude. In face of the bodily and property stakes that the Europeans are risking, we Muslims ought to die of shame. In this connection, we will submit a few incidents of those people by way of an example.

Mrs. Ray Nobles, a Christian woman, made a testamentary gift of twelve hundred thousand dollars to be expended in religious and national charities. The dispatch of a mission for religious propaganda to New Guinea Island—thousands of miles away from Jerusalem—was under contemplation. A Christian traveler was sent there in 1771 to survey the condition. In utter dejection, the traveler sent the following report to the London Biblical Society: "This place is inhabited by large and dangerous crocodiles and highly venomous snakes. The inhabitants are so cruel and bloody that one should not think of stepping between them."

He got the following answer from London: "It is sufficient information that men also live there and where there are men the missionary must reach."

So that a mission was sent there from London on which the London Biblical Society spent thirteen million pounds in connection with propaganda. This is an ordinary example of the monetary and physical sacrifices of those people, in religious and spiritual matters. Look at the sacrifices of others and easelovingness of ours in religious matters.

THE DIFFERENT ESOTERIC PERSONALITIES IN ISLAMIC THEOSOPHY

In the terminology of our ancient munificent Sufis, the lowest esoteric personality or elementary essence of life that Europe has just come to know about is called the etheric personality of the soul. This etheric personality is present in every man in a raw and incomplete state. A man enters into dream through this personality. With our ancient perfect faqirs and true gnostics, the lowest esoteric personality is that of the soul. Higher personalities than this are gradually born in a man though traveling the esoteric path; they are called the etheric personalities of the heart (قلب), spirit (روح), secret (سر), hidden (مخفی), most hidden (اخفی), and Ego (انا). The Europeans have no knowledge of these other higher personalities. They have only come to know the etheric personalities of the soul, which is wearing the elemental body like a dress. When it enters the world of dream, it assumes an esoteric resembling form. The hierarchy of man is its domain. In this domain, the soul also encounters lower spirits, jinn and satans, because these lower spirits of the invisible worlds also live in this domain. The place of this esoteric personality is shariat or the religious law. This is to say that it acquires esoteric progress and spiritual elevation through obeying the religious law. Its esoteric flight and travel is "Toward Allah" (i.e., in this place only one's direction and inclination is toward God, the Most High). In this place, the affair of the traveler is confined only to conversation, commemoration, saying, and hearing. The state of such a traveler is only an inclination toward God the Most High. The color of this esoteric personality is blue and its commemoration is "There is none to be worshipped except Allah. Muhammad is the Prophet of Allah. The name for its concentration is Allah."

The soul is continually cleansed through observation of the religious law, attention, and affectionate glances of the perfect guide and austerity and self-denial in commemoration and meditation. Then the self becomes accusative (لوامه) from depraved (اماره), inspirative (ملهمه) from accusative, and tranquil (مطمئنه) from inspirative. Thus, there are four stages of the self.

Every self is identified by its demeanor. So that the soul depraved (اماره) always contemplates and inclines toward evil, sin, and satanic doings. It is always engaged in sexual and sensual thoughts, like eating, drinking, sleeping, cohabitation, and the like. He can never think of death and has no faith in the day of resurrection and reckoning. He is so engulfed in his sensual and worldly ideas that he cannot spare time to think of religious things.

The esoteric semblance of such a soul is that of an unlawful animal or bird. Now and then, God the Most High shows him the resemblant form of His soul in the esoteric world of dream by way of admonition and information. As He says:

وَمَا مِنْ دَآبَّةٍ فِي الْأَرْضِ وَلَا طَٰٓئِرٍ يَطِيرُ بِجَنَاحَيْهِ اِلَّآ اُمَمٌ اَمْثَالُكُمْ (الانعام:٣٨)

"There is no animal on earth or bird flying with its two wings, but they are groups of your resemblances."

To the man with depraved self (اماره), the esoteric malady or vicious character of the self is shown in the resemblant form of some particular animal, in a dream. In a dream, he sees himself in the form of a swine, dog, monkey, wolf, jackal, snake, mouse, scorpion. flea, louse, and so on or among the birds, as a vulture, kite, crow, and so on. He sees his place and stage in the form of a latrine, drinking pub, or gambling house and his food in the form of dirt. In short, these are the esoteric resemblances of the self that continually change, and every form is known by its character and habits. For example, the form of a swine indicates the self eating unlawfully and as a pimp. The form of a dog indicates greed, ambition, and love of worldly wealth. A snake is the quality of injuring the people with the mouth and tongue. The sight of a monkey indicates the disease of mockery and criticism and so on and so forth. When a fortunate-seeker cleanses his soul through observation of the religious law, commemoration, meditation, and austerities, his soul makes progress and becomes accusative (لوامه) instead of depraved. Then his resemblant form is that of a lawful animal (e.g., a camel, goat, and so on) or a fish and lawful birds. Accordingly, he sees his place and stage as superior. In the third stage, the soul inspired (ملهمه) comes out of the stage of animality and steps into the place of humanity. But as long as he does not attain perfection in this stage and is not relieved of all the deformities and defects and animal diseases, he sees his soul in the form of imperfect persons like the defective, diseased, crippled, ugly, destitute, ignorant, and so on. In the fourth stage, when the soul becomes tranquil (مطمئنة), the traveler sees his soul as beautiful, healthy, in the form of a rich man, qazi, official, or some pious man; in a dream or trance among the buildings, he sees a court, a mosque, a hermitage, a house of Allah, Mecca the sacred, and Medina the illuminated. Also remember that it is not essential that the person with the soul depraved should invariably see a swine, dog, donkey, and so on in a dream or that the man with the tranquil soul should always see good things. No, our statement means that if it is desired to show someone his esoteric resemblant form in dream or trance, he sees his soul in its real resemblant form on particular occasions. Otherwise, the common fools and people ignorant of God neither have any sense of their esoteric ailments, nor can they see them. Generally, these resemblant forms are seen in some mirror. They are especially shown at a time when a person is engaged in their reformation. For example, if a person begins to cleanse the soul depraved through prayers and supererogation, he will most probably see the soul in this way! He has entered a mosque, and a dog or donkey is standing there, or he is offering prayers but in an unclean place or building. Or if a man is cleansing his soul through recitation of the Quran, he will see the resemblant form of his soul in a place where the Quran is being read. Or if one has got a patron guide, he will see the resemblant form of his soul in the presence of his guide, in a dream or trance. To sum up, the aforementioned persons have seen the resemblant forms of their souls in the different mirrors of prayers, Quran, patron, and so on.

The personality higher than the personality of the self is that of the heart, which possess great vastness, grandeur, and power of wisdom. Just as the etheric personality of the self is the marrow and essence of life of the elemental body, the etheric personality of the heart is the real marrow and essence of the life of the etheric personality of the soul. When this etheric personality is revived in the body of the traveler through the mercy of God the Most High and the kindness of the perfect guide, the traveler comes out of the hierarchy of man and steps into the hierarchy of angels. The vastness and expanse of the hierarchy of angels compared to hierarchy of man is like the entire material universe compared to the narrow and dark womb of the mother. To put it otherwise, the relation of the mother's womb to this material world is like the relation of this material world to the hierarchy of man, and the same is the relation of the hierarchy of man to the hierarchy of angels. In short, the hierarchy of angels is the domain of angels. In the domain of angels, the pure spirits of the people of heart also dwell. Its place is Tariqat (طريقت), the Path. In the religious law (شريعت), the seeker is nearly a man of conversation (i.e., that is to say that he confines himself to a mere narration of the attributes and states of his God, and hearing them, he is pleased at a future promise of union after death; consoles himself with a mention of His rewards and bounties, namely, the paradise, houries, and palaces; and keeps sitting in expectation of them). But in the Tariqat Path (طريقت), the traveler begins to walk toward God the Most High in this very world. The man of the shariat (شريعت) religious law is a man of talk while that of the path is a man of action. His travel is Lillah i;e whatever he does, he does it for God. In his gait, he employs intention and presence of the heart instead of external physical actions. The intention and presence of the heart enjoy a special importance in the path. His state is changed from inclination (ميل) into love (محبت). The color of the light of this etheric personality is yellow. Its commemoration is "None is to be worshipped except Allah," and the name for its concentration is "Lillah" (لله). In this stage, the traveler meets the angels. Occasionally, he sees the recording angels coming and going to him, and they give him inspiration and information about good and evil.

Whenever some person is about to die in his house, street, or city, he sees the Angel of Death (ملك الموت) with all his other assistant angels descending from the heavens, removing the soul and taking it to heaven. Through this, he can also find out the blessedness or wretchedness of his soul. Sometimes, at the time of commemoration and recitation of the Quran, he can see the angels descending from the heavens in various forms. He greets and meets the angels, who derive sustenance and prescribed meals from the extra light of the commemoration and recitation of the man and visit him. In this stage, the angels please the seeker with their esoteric tidings and spiritual signals day and night from which his heart receives consolation and pacification, as is the divine command:

اِنَّ الَّذِيْنَ قَالُوْا رَبُّنَا اللّٰهُ ثُمَّ اسْتَقَامُوْا تَتَنَزَّلُ عَلَيْهِمُ الْمَلٰٓئِكَةُ اَلَّا تَخَافُوْا وَلَا تَحْزَنُوْا وَ
اَبْشِرُوْا بِالْجَنَّةِ الَّتِيْ كُنْتُمْ تُوْعَدُوْنَ ۞ (٢١ حٰم السجدة: ٣٠)

"Verily those who said: 'God is our Lord' and then stuck to it—we descend on them Our angels who greet them not to fear and worry and make joys for the paradise promised to you." No doubt is left in the eyes of the traveler when his heart is revived with the commemoration of God and his eyes are brightened with the light of truth.

"The heart never blunders in what he sees (esoterically)."

There is a vast universe in the heart that is compared to the Empyrium of Allah. The sensualist people who consider the heart as a coagulated piece of flesh know nothing about its grandeur and vastness. It is related in a tradition that when Adam (AS) was born, his head touched the Empyrium. Then Gabriel (جبرائیل) (AS) put a handful of dust on his head, and he assumed the present small dusty form." In short, this also refers to the angelic esoteric personality of the heart of the seeker. It is said in another tradition,

> When a faithful falls asleep during commemoration. God the Most High creates fromhis commemoration under the high empyrium abird with seventy thousands heads and seventy thousand tongues in each head. With every tongue the bird commemorates God the Most High like the commemorator and he receives his reward.

This also means that when a commemorator falls asleep during commemoration or enters into a trance, through excess of commemoration, the senses take that commemoration to the etheric personality of the heart and the commemoration is transferred from the soul to the heart. And since at the time of sleep or trance, the tongue along with the other senses is suspended of commemoration, the esoteric personality of the heart immediately takes up that commemoration during sleep or trance and the heart begins to commemorate Allah. Sometimes the commemoration is transferred from the etheric personality of the heart to that of the spirit, and the latter begins to commemorate Allah. The bird under the Empyrium referred to in this tradition means the etheric personality of the spirit. The rank and the reward of the etheric personality of the heart uttering "Allah" once is equal to that of the external tongue pronouncing it seventy thousand times. Similarly, if the esoteric personality of the spirit pronounces "Allah" once, its rank and reward is equal to the etheric personality of the hearts pronouncing it seventy thousand times. Hence, in the tradition, the spirit has been compared to a bird that has seventy thousand heads with seventy thousand tongues in each head. In this tradition, how fine is the calculation of the true amount of the commemoration of the divine bird of spirit compared to that of the external tongue! In comparison to the external tongue, this nightingale commemorates by seventy thousand into seventy thousand tongues (i.e., in comparison to the material tongue, the rank and reward of the commemoration of the etheric personality of the heart is seventy thousand times more). Just think what a fine relation has been established between the external commemoration and that of the heart and spirit by this tradition. Some blind sensualist people consider such metaphors and examples in the verses and tradition as exaggeration and falsehood and ridicule them. What do the material-minded people know of Allah, His Holy Prophet, and divine revelation? The blessed person is he who has tasted a drop of this water of life and wept for it forever.

یا رب چه چشمه ایست محبت که من ازاں

یک قطره آب خوردم و دریا گریستم

(حافظ)

"O Lord what a spring is the Love that there from I drank one drop and wept a river!"

In another tradition of the kind, it is related that, when a faithful falls asleep commemorating, a pillar under the Empyrium begins to move, which sets the high Empyrium of God the Most High into motion. The wailing of the commemorator reaches God the Most High, and his prayer is accepted in the holy court of Allah. This pillar also means the bright pillar of the heart of which a material end is fixed in man and the other esoteric end touches the high

Empyrium. When the esoteric seed of the etheric personality of the soul sprouts into the bright tree of the etheric personality of the heart, it produces seventy thousand million fruits like the soul in a single season. And when the breeze of the affection of God the Most High blows against the holy tree of the heart, all its leaves, fruits, and flowers come into motion and become articulated with the commemoration of Allah.

The heart is a very expensive and grand thing. When the heart moves and becomes articulate with commemoration, the high Empyrium of God the Most High is moved thereby and the converse and residents—in short, all the angels of the high Empyrium—are astonished. God the Most High proudly says to the angels about that man, "Come hither, O Angels! Behold the pomp of the commemoration of my earthly slave. He is one of my earthly slaves at the time of whose creation you objectionably said, 'What is the need for the creation of these! We are enough for your thanks, praise, and glorification." Then the inhabitants of heavens would enviously say, "Would that we had been earthly men like them and had remembered God the Most High in this manner:

آسماں سجدہ کند پیش زمینے کہ برو

یک دو کس یک دو زماں بہر خدا بنشیند

"'The sky prostrates before the earth on which one or two people sit for a moment for God commemorating.'"

The heart is not merely the oblong piece of flesh which hangs in the breast to the left side and incessantly pumps the blood into the body. This is but a material abode of that bright invisible etheric personality of the heart in the visible world. As the life of the entire elemental body depends on that piece of flesh and its actions, the esoteric body depends on the bright candle of the heart, about which God the Most High says it is "the resemblance of his light."

The physical action of the whole world combined together cannot equal a moment's reward of the commemoration of the heart. It is therefore said:

تَفَكُّرُ سَاعَةٍ خَيْرٌ مِّنْ عِبَادِةِ الثَّقَلَيْنِ

"A moment's meditation is better than worship of the two worlds" (i.e., a moment's true meditation from the heart of the commemorator is better than the worship of jinn and mankind).

دل بدست آور که حج اکبر است

از ہزاراں کعبہ یک دل بہتر است

(رومی)

"Secure a heart for it is the great pilgrimage. A heart is better than a thousand Ka'bas." It is a commandment of our guide, leader, and religious pattern, His Holiness, Pir of the gnostics, Sultan Bahu (may God sanctify his secret) that, if the heart says, "Allah," once, its reward is equal to finishing the Quran with the external tongue seventy thousand times. In another place, he says, "If the etheric personality of the spirit says, O Allah, once it has the rank of the etheric personality of the heart saying O Allah seventy thousand times. Its further explanation is that the light of the entire munificent Quran is included in the name Allah, as the tree is within a seed. Hence, the same is the meaning of finishing the munificent Quran with the external tongue seventy thousand times or pronouncing O Allah seventy thousand times. The other explanation is that the etheric personality of the heart permeates the body like butter in the milk, and just as the particles of butter are present in every particle of milk, the etheric personality of the heart is present and contained in all muscle, vein, blood, flesh, and marrow of the human body. When the heart of the commemorator becomes articulate with the commemoration of Allah and sometimes when that commemoration affects the entire body, every particle of the body utters "Allah," and all the hair of the body begins to commemorate. Every hair on the body of the commemorator comes into motion and patently begins to shout, "Allah! Allah!" (الله الله). The commemorator hears it with his ears in full senses and a state of wakefulness.

Dream, imagination, whim, and fancy have absolutely no hand in it. Therefore, on account of the inclusion of all the limbs, particles, and hair of the body in the commemoration of the heart, this commemoration is seventy thousand times higher in rank and reward than the commemoration with the external tongue.

For further satisfaction of the reader, the author proposes to relate one of his own incidents. I cannot resist mentioning that in the first edition of *Irfan*, I had included some of my spiritual incidents and ocular observations hesitatingly, lest people should ascribe it to my ostentation. God is my witness that in this respect, I am neither a liar, nor a cheat, nor the one cheated. But I am reproducing here some of my previous adventures and ocular observations by way of an example with the sole object that their study may perhaps prove to be the cause of increasing the faith and satisfying the minds of the readers.

Here are the details of the commencement of my heart's commemoration. Once I was engaged in concentration on His personal name, Allah, when a sort of esoteric grandeur and awe of commemoration overtook me, wherein I was completely absorbed and perfectly tranced. Then I observed that all the hair on my body along with the skin was rotating around the roots and moving like the grass at the time of a severe storm. Simultaneously, every hair was loudly and clearly shouting, "Allah Hu! Allah Hu!" (اَللهُ هُوَ اَللهُ هُو). I was watching this natural and strange movement of all the hair of my body at the time of the relish of illumination while I was in perfect senses and fully awake and hearing with my ears the unusual and most pleasant noise of their commemoration. Dream, imagination, whim, and fancy had no hand in it. Rather, it was a solid reality of the heart's commemoration and Sultanulazkar (سلطانی ذکر) (commemoration of the entire body), which I heard with my ears and saw with my eyes. The description and its true relish and real state is beyond the pale of writing. The external intellect and material mind is unable to comprehend it.

In short, it would be proper to call the heart as an ocean of spiritual light or a mountain of holiness because, when through divine grace, the etheric personality of the heart becomes alive, being illuminated with its invisible and bright grandeur, it begins to utter commemoration of Allah. The angels crave for it. The commemorator of the heart attains so much grandeur that whole universes appear to him like a mustard seed.

عرش است پردهٔ حرم کبریائے دل   چرخ است حلقهٔ در دولت سرائے دل

نہ اطلس سپہر بگرد قبائے دل   دل آنچناں کہ ہست اگر جلوہ گرشود

گرُگے که زیرِ پوست بخونِ تو تشنه است   یوسفؑ شود زیرِ تو نورِ صفائے دل

ما خود چه ذرّه ایم که نَه محملِ سپهر   رقص الجمل کنند زبانگِ درائے دل

دست از کتاب خانهٔ افرنگیاں بشو   صد شہر عقل گرد سرِ روستائے دل

The sky is the ring of the door of the treasure-house of the heart. The empyrean is the curtain of the door of the magnificent court of the heart: were the heart to manifest as it is. The nine brocades of the heavens would become the buttons of the garment of the heart. The wolf which is thirsty for your blood, beneath your body would become Joseph by the reflection of the light of the heart. What an atom are we for the nine palanquins of the spheres, dance like camels at the sound of the bell of the heart. Wash your hands from the library of the occidentals. A hundred cities of wisdom cannot compare even the dust of the village of the heart.

Hence, the real object of the creation of man is the gnosis (معرفت) of God the Most High. And the eye is the best and truest instrument of knowing a thing which is completely "known through being seen. The other senses are imperfect instruments of identification. Therefore, the commemoration of the eye is most superior, higher, and nearest God. The commemoration of the eye is the marrow of commemoration. And this alone is the means of knowledge and meditation of the Nourisher. God the Most High generally calls His words' commemoration as eyes. Says the Most High:

قَدْ جَآءَكُمْ بَصَآئِرُ مِنْ رَّبِّكُمْ (۱۶ الانعام:۱۰۴)

"You've received eyes from your Lord."

هٰذَا بَصَآئِرُ لِلنَّاسِ (۴۵ الجاثیة:۲۰)

These are eyes from your Lord. "These are the eyes for the mankind" (i.e., this Quran and commemoration of God the Most High is like eyes to you from God the Most High). Loss of commemoration is called blindness: "Whoever hurried away from my commemoration will receive scanty livelihood and on the day of judgment we will raise him blind." Thus, the inscription of His personal name, Allah, with the esoteric eye, namely, concentration, meditation, and the commemoration affect the real marrow and esoteric personality of the person and revives it. In this way, the commemoration is commemorated in its true place; so to say, by practicing commemoration in the other ways, the commemorator is very far off from his real aim and true object. In short, opening of the esoteric eyes is the real object of commemoration. When the esoteric eyes of the seeker are opened, he becomes a perfect gnostic.

The story of the elephant and the blind men is applicable to that of the men with the other senses. There is a famous story. Some people were sitting in a place. An elephant turned up there, and the blind men desired to know its structure. They gathered around the elephant and began to touch it. The blind man whose hand touched the back of the elephant cried out, "The elephant is like a wall."

The other one placed his hand on the foot of the elephant and cried out, "No! You are wrong. The elephant is like a pillar."

The third one touched the ear of the elephant and said, "No, Both of you are wrong. The elephant resembles a huge fan."

In short, there were as many opinions as there were men. Because of his defective understanding, every blind man formed a wrong opinion and believed the other blind man wrong, and the recognition of the animal took the form of a controversy. Exactly like this, esoteric blindness is the real cause of the recession and negligence of all the false religions from truth. Says the Most High, "He who is blind in this world, will be blind in the next world";

کور از خواب محال است که بینا خیزد نمایت نمایت ہر کہ زشت است ہمال زشت بعقبیٰ خیزد

"He who is ugly here will arise ugly in the next world. It's impossible that the blind should arise from the sleep with eyes." Says the Most High:

فَإِنَّهَا لَا تَعْمَى الْأَبْصَارُ وَلَٰكِن تَعْمَى الْقُلُوبُ الَّتِي فِي الصُّدُورِ ۝ (الحج: ٤٦) (١٢٢)

"Because (through slothfulness), not the eyes but the hearts within the breast get blind."

جنگِ هفتاد و دو مِلَّت همه را عُذر بِنه

چوں ندیدند حقیقت رہ افسانہ زدند

(حافظ)

"Find an excuse for the battles of the seventy-two classes of religion. Since they did not see the truth, they invented fables."

Gnosis of God the Most High is the real intention of the entire religion and the true aim of the revelation of the Quran. The esoteric eye is the real instrument of gnosis, and the commemoration of Allah is its light. The commemoration of His personal name, Allah, is the compendium of all commemorations, and the eye is the real seat of commemoration. Its best method is inscription of His personal name, Allah, within oneself through concentration and meditation. All the other religious acts are inferior to it. In those occupations, some retreat and hindrance thwarts the seeker. The way to the illumination and life of the heart (انشراحِ صدر), proximity (قرب), observation (مشاہدہ), union (وصل), and interview (دیدار) with God the Most High can never be achieved without concentration on His personal name, Allah. Though the seeker may bear severe austerities and exertion all his life long and languish like a hair, the heart remains dead and dark because external worship and physical acts may cleanse the elemental body, but the path of the heart is quite apart and its method is quite different.Now the question arises: How are we to know that the name Allah is the personal name and all the other names are the attributive names of God the Most High and that this name "Allah"is the compendium of all names and the Most Glorious Name (اسم اعظم). We have partially narrated it. Now we will narrate the literary compendiumship and personalness of the name Allah as a sample of the whole for the satisfaction of the readers. A consideration ofthe pronunciation of the word *Allah* reveals that it is composed ofthe four letters Al, LJ, LJ, Hо. If the first letter Alis removed, three letters are left there: LJ, LJ, and Hо. It becomes lilah, and there is no change in the meaning. Rather, it shows the mediation and means for the divinity of God the Most High. If the other letter ل is also removed, the word Lahu لهو is left. which indicates the relation of the personal pronoun. If the second L is also removed, H هis left, which points at the essence; in short, in every case, this name is unchangeable and constant in meaning and all its four states, Allah, Lillah, Lahu له, and Hu هوare themselves most great names. And every name is like a key for a revelation and traversing of the four places of the path—the religious law (شریعت), the path (طریقت), the truth (حقیقت) of gnosis (معرفت), and the four worlds, Shariat, Tariqat, Haqiqat, and Ma'rifat (that is, the hierarchies of man (ناسوت), angels (ملکوت), power (جبروت), and Godhead (لاہوت). Through the commemoration and concentration of these four names, the traveler passes all the veils, stages, and places and becomes one with God the Most High.

از دوئی بگذشتم و یکتا شدم   چار بودم سه شدم اکنوں دوم

(آتش)

"I was four; then I became three; now I am two: I passed duality and became one." Now this thing is not found in any other name except this one. That is to say that the meaning of its divinity is not lost by separating any letter of it and by removal of every letter, the separate feature of it is retained for a particular place of the travel. That is to say that the name Allah is reserved for the etheric personality of the soul; its world is the hierarchy of man. Place the religious law of travel toward Allah. The second name, lillah, is reserved for the etheric personality of the heart; its place is the path, the world, the hierarchy of the angels, and travel for God. The etheric personality of the third name, Lahu, is the spirit; place of the truth; world; and hierarchy of power and travel with God. The fourth name is Hu. Its etheric personality is the secret place, gnosis, and world of the hierarchy of God and travel from God. The experts of this science and ancient sheikhs have presented seven etheric personalities of the esoteric travel. Every etheric personality has a different world, place, state, and commemoration. On the next page, we give the chart.

Moreover, if one letter is removed from the middle of this name, Ilah is left, which is also a name of God. The different forms and parts of this name, Aali, Lahi, Ali, and Ahi, have been the names of God in different languages and at different times. As it is said about Jesus (p.b.u.h.), in the ancient books, his last words on the cross were, "Ihli! Ihli I Lima Sabaqtani" (i.e., "O God, why hast Thou forsaken me?").

نام مقام	نام لطیفہ	عالم	سیر	حال	مقام	رنگ	ذِکر	اسم تصور
مقام اوّل	نفس	ناسوت	الى اللہ	میل	شریعت	نیلا	لا الہ الا اللہ محمّد رسول اللہ	اللہ
مقام دوم	قلب	ملکوت	للہ	محبت	طریقت	زرد	لا الہ الّا اللہ	اللہ
مقام سوم	روح	جبروت یا حقیقتِ محمدی	علَی اللہ	عشق	حقیقت	سرخ	یا اللہ	لہ
مقام چہارم	سِرّ	لاہوت	مَعَ اللہ	وصل	معرفت	سفید	یا حیّ یا قیوم	ھو
مقام پنجم	خفی	یاہوت	فی اللہ	فنا	مقام منتہی	سبز	یا واحد	محمّد
مقام ششم	اخفی	یاہوت	عن اللہ	حیرت	باز شریعت	بنفشی	یا احد	فقر
مقام ہفتم	آنا	ہوئیّت	باللہ	بقا	مقام جمع الجمع	بے رنگ	یا ھو	اللہ محمّد

In those days, the word *Ihli* was used in the sense of Allah, and it would require a separate volume to give the details of all the three letters A, L, and H.

In short, there a thousand secrets in its A. In its L, there are the lights of A, L, M (الٓم), the doubtless books, and the invisible world. The H contains that He is one of the essence and directions for proximity of interview. The second reason for its being the personal name is that every name of God the Most High is qualified by some qualifications, and every name indicates some special attributes and has no scope for any other attribute so that the prayer for a particular attribute is made through a particular name. For example, we say, "O Merciful, have mercy on me," or "O Provider!

Give me provision," or O Honorer! Give me honor," or "O Forgiver, forgive me," or "O Knower! Give me knowledge." But we can never say, "O Knower, give me provision!" or "O Provider, give me knowledge." But the name Allah is the compendium of all the attributes of God and indicates every attribute, and help of every attribute of God the Most High can be sought through this name. Says the Most High:

$$\text{وَاللّٰهُ الْمُسْتَعَانُ عَلٰى مَا تَصِفُونَ ۞ (١٢ يوسف: ١٨)}$$

"Help can be sought from Allah with whatever attribute you qualify Him." For example, we can say, "O Allah, give me knowledge," "O Allah, bestow provision on me," "O Allah, forgive me," and so on. In the munificent Quran, this name is used instead of every attributive name. For example, it is recorded there (1) "Verily Allah is forgiver and merciful"; (2) "Verily Allah is glorious, wise"; (3) "Allah is hearer and knower"; (4) "He [Allah] is the Creator, independent, and painter"; (5) Allah is hearing and seeing. That is to say that individually the name Allah contains every attribute, and collectively, it is the manifestation of the different names. This is clear proof of its being essentially His personal name. The third proof is that the Arabs derive a root from every name. But this name cannot be derived from. Neither it is derived from any noun, nor is any noun derived from it. The fourth reason is that all the fundamentals of Islam are founded on this noun, and on its affirmation, a man becomes a Muslim, and by its verification, one becomes faithful. For example, in the word of faith, "There is none to be worshipped" except Allah, there is affirmation of this holy name. In all the holy formulas (on the formulas of testimony (کلمه شهادت), glorification (کلمه تمجید), and unification (کلمه توحید) and word of faith, this holy name is mentioned. All the chapters of the Quran begin with this name: "In the name of Allah, the Most Compassionate, the Most Merciful." Pronouncing at the commencement of every act lies in this name. This name is recited in the glorification of killing a lawful animal—"Allah is Great"—at the time of commencement of prayer. The succor of this name is solicited at the time of fighting a religious war with the infidels by pronouncing, "Allah is Great" (الله اکبر), and when a child is born, this name is read in his ear. This name is proclaimed in the call to prayer. The opening chapter (سورة فاتحه),

verses of the chair (آیت الکرسی), the chapter of Sincerity (سورۀ اخلاص), and other Quranic chapters owe their superiority to this name. In short, the value and rank, honor and grandeur of all the holy verses and sacred formulas is due to this name. It is the personal and greatest name.

Every prophet and his followers of yore had been granted an attributive name (صفاتی اسم), which in accordance with their attributive capacity served for them as a personal name. That (attributive) name was the source of favors and perfection for them, and the traversing and revelation of the lights of that name used to be the utmost end of their ascent. At the time of their supplications, God the Most High manifested to every prophet and to every saint among his followers through that name. When God the Most High created our Perfect Master, His Holiness Muhammad the Prophet (P.B.U.H) kneaded his holy being with the light of the water of life of His Essence. The Quran says:

اَلْیَوْمَ اَکْمَلْتُ لَکُمْ دِیْنَکُمْ وَاَتْمَمْتُ عَلَیْکُمْ نِعْمَتِیْ وَرَضِیْتُ لَکُمُ الْاِسْلَامَ دِیْنًا (المائدة:۳۵)

"This day We have perfected for you the religion and completed on you Our bounties and chosen for you Islam as religion."

The crown of the perfect religion was put on his head, and he was honored with the role of completion of bounties and the mantle of God's eternal satisfaction with him. And because his light was personal, he and his followers were granted the personal name. Also, because his creation ended the chain of prophecy and he was made the last of the prophets, his religion and book abrogated all the former religions and books respectively. Similarly, on account of the manifestation of the sun of his personal name, Allah, on Him, all the stars of the names of the Acts and all the moons of the names of all attributes were annihilated and the road of the names of all the religions toward God the Most High were blocked. So much so that the languages of the ancient religious books too were removed and annihilated from the world and the acceptance and effect of all those names at the time of prayer and supplication were dismissed forthwith. Don't you see that when in a country a new king is enthroned in the world, all the coins, stamp-deeds, stamps, and so on of the former kings are discontinued, and the coins and so on are struck in the name of the last king? Though this name was present in its partial and distorted form in the ancient languages and like the world-illuminating sun, it was illuminating with its invisible rays the world of existence from the horizon of nonexistence, it was displayed in its real true form and illuminated with the light of the lightning of essence with the Prophet's birth. Just as the land of the house of Ka'ba was held in reverence somehow or other at all times from the beginning of creation, in the days of His Holiness (P.B.U.H), its honor and holiness reached the zenith of perfection. Similarly, every faculty of the religion reached its utmost height in the Prophet's time.

Every human body receives the lights of God the Most High in accordance with its spaciousness and aptitude.

$$\text{لَا يُكَلِّفُ اللّٰهُ نَفْسًا اِلَّا وُسْعَهَا} \quad (\text{۲البقرة:۲۸٦})$$

"Allah does not trouble any one beyond his capacity."

The nature of all the prophets of the past had the ability and aptitude for attributive names, and their lights were attributive. Hence, they had the power and endurance for the lights and illuminations of attributive names. They lacked the aptitude and ability of withstanding the personal lights. The personal light of God the Most High comes in view at the time of interview and meeting. Just as the light of stars and moon vanishes at the time of the rising of the sun, the lights of the stars of acts and moons of the attributive disappear at the time of the appearance and aspect of the Majesty of the Essence. That is why no other prophet or messenger besides His Holiness Muhammad the chosen had attained the rank of interview and seeing (Him) Allah the Most High. Although some of them have expressed the desire of seeing Him and in accordance with their request, God the Most High had cast a bit of illumination on them, at the time of manifestation of the light of the essence, they could not retain even their bodily lives—not to mention senses. But since the light of His Holiness (P.B.U.H) was a personal one and his eyes were brightened with the personal collyrium of "His eyes did not fault," he witnessed the personal manifestation of God the Most High riding the lift of his personal name, Allah, and was graced with a personal interview.

By putting on the spectacles of his personal name, Allah, on the Night of Meraj (ascent), he alone was honored and singularized by God the Most High's personal great signs, sciences, and knowledge:

موسیٰ ز ہوش رفت بیک جلوۂ صفات

تو عین ذات سے نگری در تبسمی

"Moses lost his senses through a single flash of attribute. You are beholding the very essence and are smiling."

MANIFESTATION OF THE LIGHT OF THE PERSONAL NAME, ALLAH

Just as the childhood of a person is according to the natural religion (i.e., Islam), the childhood of the times (i.e., the earlier times) was very much nearer to religion and spiritualism. Therefore, all the prophets were raised and numerous saints were born in that age. That is why the pious men of yore naturally believed in religion and spiritualism and were inclined toward it with heart and soul. As a man grows older, Satan deforms his religious capability and Islamic nature and completely destroys it by the time the person matures. As time passed on, Satan, like Samari, decorated the calf of silver and gold in numerous ways and enchanted the people by the magic of its love and washed away the memory and love of God the Most High from their hearts and brains. So much sothat though the world, today, appears to be civilized, religiously, it is almost obliterated and leading an animal life. What can be a more manifest proof of religion being a natural thing than that in some dark ages when no prophet had been raised and people were absolutely ignorant of the essence, attributes, and names of God the Most High, the thoughts of their Creator, Master, and true Deity involuntarily and naturally struck the people? But because of blindness and ignorance, the people lost the special place of the name, namely, the Named. Since they had not received insight and the light of guidance, they grappled in the darkness in search of Him and in whatever object they sensed a smell of the grandeur and power of God the Most High, they bent before, worshipped, and made a deity of it. So that some nations of that age worshipped heavenly bodies, such as the sun, moon, and stars. Some carved idols, and some worshipped rivers, mountains, and wild trees. Some took to the distinguished personages and kings of their age.

There still exist in Africa some wild nations immune to the ravages of the times. A careful study of their religious record clearly reveals that though no prophet has been raised among them so far and hitherto no spiritual leader or religious guide has invited them to religion, they haven't even heard the name of God the Most High. Yet we find in them a firm conviction about their Creator, Master, and true God, whom they worship in some way or other. The spiritual powers of these wild nations are much ahead of the so-called civilized and enlightened citizens of today. This shows that human nature is brewed with the fermentation of the name and commemoration of God the Most High.

For seeing and knowing a thing, man stands in need of two kinds of lights: (1) the light of the invisible world and (2) the light of the visible world. In the invisible world, he sees through the light of vision, and in the visible world through the light of the sun and moon. Similarly, the seeker stands in need of twofold lights esoterically: (1) the light of the esoteric insight, also called light of certainty and light of faith, and (2) the light of the invitation and guidance of the prophets and saints. The sun is the greatest mine and store of light that illuminates all the material world, and our blessed master His Holiness Ahmed the chosen (P.B.U.H) is the greatest source of light of the esoteric world. The two suns of the two worlds have been expressed by the single term of the *brilliantlamp*, in the Holy Quran by God the Most High.

إِنَّا أَرْسَلْنَاكَ شَاهِدًا وَّمُبَشِّرًا وَّنَذِيرًا ۞ وَّدَاعِيًا إِلَى اللّٰهِ بِإِذْنِهِ وَسِرَاجًا مُّنِيْرًا ۞

(الاحزاب: ٤٥-٤٦ ۱۳۳)

"We have sent thee (O Prophet) as a witness and one who gives the tidings and warns and invites men toward Allah by His Command and a brilliant lamp."

For worldly objects, the two lights (the eyes), and the light are mutually indispensable. The eyes are useless without light, and without eyes, all the bright world is dark. Says God the Most High:

قُلْ هٰذِهِ سَبِيْلِي أَدْعُوْا إِلَى اللّٰهِ ۚ عَلٰى بَصِيْرَةٍ أَنَا وَمَنِ اتَّبَعَنِي (يوسف: ۱۰۸ ۱۲)

"Say O Muhammad (P.B.U.H): This is my path of Islam [i.e., natural religion]; I and my followers invite people toward Allah by esoteric insight."

In the dark ages of ignorance, when these esoteric and brilliant lights were wanting, people worshipped solid material gods, such as the sun, moon, and stars, because of the natural urge. For example, when a man smells the fragrance of something in a dark building, he lays his hands on this thing and that in search of it. This was the condition of the creation in the absence of guides and prophets, in the dark ages. As the light of the name of the Creator is inherently concealed in the creation, it was naturally restless in his search in all times. Therefore, compelled by eternal love and merciful attraction, mankind is intoxicated by the thought of God the Most High, dies after the material semblances of the lamp of His beauty, and blindly embraces the minerals, animals, men, and heavenly bodies in which he finds a smell of His beauty and glory. He fulfils his natural desire by worshipping them. That is why men in the dark ages named the different manifestations of nature and material magnates after the holy names of God the Most High and worshipped them. For example, his internal nature and desire and the natural heat and thirst of His personal name, Allah, compelled His Holiness Ibrahim (AS) to turn toward the sun, moon, and stars. Says the Most High:

فَلَمَّا جَنَّ عَلَيْهِ الَّيْلُ رَاٰكَوْكَبًا ۖ قَالَ هٰذَا رَبِّى ۖ فَلَمَّآ أَفَلَ قَالَ لَآ أُحِبُّ الْاٰفِلِينَ ۝ فَلَمَّا رَاٰ الْقَمَرَ بَازِغًا قَالَ هٰذَا رَبِّى ۖ فَلَمَّآ أَفَلَ قَالَ لَئِنْ لَّمْ يَهْدِنِى رَبِّى لَاَكُوْنَنَّ مِنَ الْقَوْمِ الضَّالِّينَ ۝ فَلَمَّا رَاٰ الشَّمْسَ بَازِغَةً قَالَ هٰذَا رَبِّى هٰذَآ أَكْبَرُ ۖ فَلَمَّآ أَفَلَتْ قَالَ يٰقَوْمِ اِنِّى بَرِىٓءٌ مِّمَّا تُشْرِكُوْنَ ۝ اِنِّى وَجَّهْتُ وَجْهِىَ لِلَّذِى فَطَرَ السَّمٰوٰتِ وَالْاَرْضَ حَنِيْفًا وَّمَآ أَنَا مِنَ الْمُشْرِكِيْنَ ۝

(الانعام:٢٦-٦٩)

"When the night (of the atmosphere of idol and element worship) spread (on the heart) of Ibrahim (AS), he looked toward a star (taking it for a deity); he said (in his heart in imitation of the people), 'This is my Lord.' But when it set, he said, 'I do not like to worship what sets and disappears.' Thereafter, he saw the moon shining and said to himself, 'Perhaps this is my Lord.'

"But when it also set down, he said, 'If I make a God of a thing that sets and should not my true Lord guide me to Himself, I will certainly be led astray like those who worship elements and idols.' Then he saw the sun shine; he said, 'This is very large. This is my Lord.' But when that also set, he said, 'O nation of fools! I hate all your created and perishable deities whom you associate with God the Most High. My heart, now, attends toward a magnificent Being who has created the earth and heaven and what is between them. I have taken that single essence for my God, and I am not a polytheist.'"

From the Day of Eternity, the thought of his Creator naturally surges in a person, and the light of His name and commemoration is kept as trust in man's nature. If his internal capability and esoteric capacity had not been reposed in man from the beginning, it would have been very cruel on the part of God the Most High to invite people to Himself through the prophets. And He does not trouble any man beyond his capacity and capability. This throws off the veil from this false notion of the naturalists and atheists that religion and worship of God is based on fear and that life after death and the idea of the survival of the soul have been manufactured out of a person's own shadow and reflection. In fact, it is not at all like this. Human nature alone in itself is the primary mover of religious beliefs and spiritual thoughts. Fear and hope are the unavoidable results of certainty and faith in God. When God the Most High saw the restlessness of His Creation because of its natural desire and thirst, out of his slaves, He mercifully made some selected personages with the manifestation of His power and sent them as guides and leaders of His Creation, and through them, he introduced the creation to his essence, attributes, and names and gave them information about His name and whereabouts. So that time after time, He raised prophets and messengers in different times. As God the Most High says:

$$ لَقَدْ مَنَّ اللّٰهُ عَلَى الْمُؤْمِنِيْنَ اِذْ بَعَثَ فِيْهِمْ رَسُوْلًا مِّنْ اَنْفُسِهِمْ يَتْلُوْا عَلَيْهِمْ اٰيٰتِهٖ وَيُزَكِّيْهِمْ وَ يُعَلِّمُهُمُ الْكِتٰبَ وَالْحِكْمَةَ ۚ وَاِنْ كَانُوْا مِنْ قَبْلُ لَفِيْ ضَلٰلٍ مُّبِيْنٍ ۝ (٣ آلِ عِمْرٰن:١٦٣) $$

"Allah showed great kindness to the faithful when He raised among them a prophet from among themselves who reads to them His verses and purifies them and teaches them the cooperation and wisdom though formerly they were in manifest error."

It is against the rule and wisdom of God the Most High to deal separately with every individual when the following general rules have been devised: In every age, God the Most High first of all illuminates a perfect person with the light of faith and the sun of His personal name, Allah, and sends him, making him the light of guidance. Then He lights innumerable lamps from His light. Through this perfect omnipotence, he first grows the natural seed of his personal name, Allah, in the field of the heart of a perfect person. When that becomes a holy tree and fully flourishes, he creates innumerable other trees from the fruits thereof and makes a rich garden of the established religion. First of all, from the seed of His personal name, Allah, God the Most High caused the tree of the lights of the Quran to appear in the bright breast of his Holiness Muhammad (P.B.U.H) and illuminated the whole world therewith. Here are its particulars: when the seed of His personal name, Allah, began to grow in the blessed person of His Holiness (P.B.U.H), he felt the signs of revelation in himself (i.e., like Her Holiness Mary, he felt in his esoteric womb the conception of revelation without intermission and in accordance with

$$فَحَمَلَتْهُ فَانْتَبَذَتْ بِهٖ مَكَانًا قَصِيًّا ۝ (١٩ مريم: ٢٢)$$

"Then she conceived and retired herself to a distant place".He took to the desert and retired in a mountain cave called Hira, far from the populace. He often used to go and sit there in expectation of the incubation and shooting of the esoteric seed and birth of the spiritual Jesus. Finally, in order to irrigate that brilliant seed of His personal name, Allah, Gabriel the trustworthy angel brought in his breast the fountain of life from the sea of light of God the Most High.

The great angel embraced and forcibly pressing his holiness said, "Read."

His Holiness says, "I replied: I am not literate."

Gabriel the trustworthy pressed him to the breast thrice, ordering him to read, and every time, he said, "I am not literate." By the expression "I am not literate," he meant that the water was available, but the bright tree of the Quran did not seem to shoot up. When finally Gabriel the trustworthy pressed him to the breast, the earliest verse of the Quran thus issued from his truth-interpreting tongue:

$$اِقْرَأْ بِاسْمِ رَبِّكَ الَّذِى خَلَقَ ۝ خَلَقَ الْاِنْسَانَ مِنْ عَلَقٍ ۝ اِقْرَأْ وَ رَبُّكَ الْاَكْرَمُ ۝ الَّذِى عَلَّمَ بِالْقَلَمِ ۝ عَلَّمَ الْاِنْسَانَ مَالَمْ يَعْلَمْ ۝ (١٩٦ العلق: ١-٥)$$

Read (the Quran, O Muhammad) through the blessing of the name of your Lord, who created (the creation): created man out of coagulated blood. Read on. Your Lord is the most generous who taught (the common, all the acquired sciences) through the pen and (directly taught the selected) people (of the esoteric sciences) which they did not know.

In short, this earliest verse of the Quran, "Read in the name of your Lord," clearly indicates that what Gabriel the trustworthy repeatedly pressed him to read was the bright inscription of His personal name, Allah. On this occasion, many people object that His Holiness was illiterate, there was no trace of the Quran at the time, and Gabriel had nothing readable with him—what was it then the reading of which Gabriel repeatedly stressed by uttering, "Read"? Now it was the bright writing of his personal name, Allah; the concentration (reading and writing it esoterically) was taught and tutored by Gabriel to His Holiness (AS). The words in the name of your Lord in the quoted passage clearly point at His personal name, Allah, meaning, "O Muhammad (P.B.U.H), His personal name Allah has sprung up in your breast and is forming into the Quranic tree. Now read the Quran, enjoy the fruit of its knowledge, sciences, and lights—you and your followers up to the doomsday."

كَزَرۡعٍ اَخۡرَجَ شَطۡـَٔهٗ فَاٰزَرَهٗ فَاسۡتَغۡلَظَ فَاسۡتَوٰى عَلٰى سُوۡقِهٖ (٢٨ الفتح: ٢٩)

"Thus the tree of the Quran grew in the blessed person of His Holiness (P.B.U.H) through the bright seed of His personal name, Allah. As the plants first shoot up in tender branch and then strengthen it. Then growing into a big tree it stands firmly and straight on its trunk."

Thus, this great trust of the Quran was transferred from Allah, the Most High, into the bright breast of His Holiness Muhammad (P.B.U.H) through the intermission of Gabriel the trustworthy. It is the heavy and the weighty trust that the earth, heaven, and mountains refused to bear. As says the Almighty:

إِنَّا عَرَضْنَا الْأَمَانَةَ عَلَى السَّمٰوٰتِ وَالْأَرْضِ وَالْجِبَالِ فَأَبَيْنَ اَنْ يَّحْمِلْنَهَا وَاَشْفَقْنَ مِنْهَا وَ
حَمَلَهَا الْإِنْسَانُ ۖ إِنَّهُ كَانَ ظَلُوْمًا جَهُوْلًا ۝ (٣٣ الاحزاب:٧٢)

"We offered Our trust to the heaven, earth, and mountains to see which of them can bear it—and all of them refused to bear it and (the perfect) man picked it up."

Verily man is tyrant and ignorant (toward his soul). Holy tradition says, "The earth and heaven cannot accommodate me except the heart of the faithful slave.

من دریں فکرم کہ اندر سینہ چوں جا کردہ   پر تو حسنت نہ گنجد در زمین و آسماں

The armies of your beauty cannot be accommodated in earth and heaven. I wonder how you have made an abode in my breast." Says the Most High:

لَوْ اَنْزَلْنَا هٰذَا الْقُرْاٰنَ عَلٰى جَبَلٍ لَّرَاَيْتَهٗ خَاشِعًا مُّتَصَدِّعًا مِّنْ خَشْيَةِ اللّٰهِ ۚ
(٥٩ الحشر:٢١)

"If We had descended this Quran on the mountain you would have seen it fall into pieces" (from the weight and grandeur of the Quran). Elsewhere, it is said, presently:

إِنَّا سَنُلْقِيْ عَلَيْكَ قَوْلًا ثَقِيْلًا ۝ (٧٣ المزمل:٥)

"We will reveal to you a weighty speech [that is, the Quran]."

At the time of descent of the Quran, His Holiness Muhammad (P.B.U.H) used to faint and lose his color, and in severe winter also perspiration used to drip from his blessed face. If revelation came to him while he was riding, the animal ridden upon used to sit down under the weight of the Quran. His Holiness Ali (may God sanctify his face) relates the following:

"Once upon a time, His Holiness (P.B.U.H) was sleeping with his head on my thigh when there appeared the signs of the coming down of the revelation. My thigh began to break down under the weight of revelation and the burden of the Quran."

In short, those alone understand the weight and grandeur of the noble Quran whose hearts have the ability and capability for the light of the Quran. To bear this heavy weight was the task of that perfect man (P.B.U.H); otherwise, what do the brute-like common folk know of the grandeur of the Quran because it never goes down their throats! Many people recite the Quran while the Quran curses them. In short, the noble Quran with all its sciences, secrets, and lights is so contained in His personal name, Allah, as the tree is in the seed.

The perfect gnostic in whose person this personal name, Allah, gets established becomes the direct student of the Compassionate and bears the Quran by heart. Hence, the religious potentates have made the commemoration of His personal name, Allah, and its concentration the only objective of esoteric travel.

O seeker, we have shown you the easiest, nearest, and safest way to the holy court of God, the Most High, through logical and textual arrangements, verses, and traditions and shown you the true, most secret, nearest, and easiest way to the wealth and blessings of the two worlds. If your fortune helps you and you believe us, you will very soon reach the destination of life by acting on it.

بایں زلفِ پریشان ہر نفس چو شانہ آویزی	چہ در طول امل از حرص بے با کانہ آویزی
ہماں بہتر کہ ایں ناقوس در بتخانہ آویزی	بقیل و قال نتواں در حریم کعبہ محرم شد
اگر یک بار در دامانِ شب مردانہ آویزی	نخواہی شدد گر محتاج دامن گیرئ مردم
چو زاہد تا بکے در سبحہ صددانہ آویزی	بہ ہمت گوہر یکدانہ چوں مرداں بدست آور

"Why do you carelessly hang in lengthy hopes through greed? Every moment you stick in this disheveled tress like the comb. You can't become the confidant of the sanctuary of Ka'ba through mere talk. Better hang this bell in the idol temple. You will no more stand in need of begging the help of people. If you once hang in the skirt of the midnight prayer like a man of God, magnanimously acquire the essence of a single pearl of His name like a man of God. Why hang in the hundred beads of the rosary like the ascetic?"

The Need for Preceptor and Guide

As a rule, every path obviously necessitates a companion, guide, or leader, and thus a teacher is needed for every science. Therefore, an experienced leader and perfect guide is highly essential for traversing the long journey and distant and unknown path toward God the Most High. An esoteric teacher is highly essential and is indispensable for teaching the gnosis of God and the inspired knowledge. The story of Moses and Khizar (P.B.U.H) in the chapter of the cave (سورة كهف) in the Quran is well known. In spite of being a resolute prophet, Moses (P.B.U.H) made a request to Khizar (P.B.U.H) for esoteric and occult science (i.e., inspired knowledge) and adopted his company. For a Muslim, nothing can be a greater proof than the Holy Quran. The existence of this secret science is proved from the benevolent Quran.

$$ طَلَبُ الْعِلْمِ فَرِيْضَةٌ عَلَى كُلِّ مُسْلِمٍ وَّمُسْلِمَةٍ $$

"Since the acquisition of the inferior acquired worldly sciences is incumbent according to (acquisition of) knowledge is obligatory on every Muslim man and woman," the acquisition of the superior inspired knowledge must be incumbent in the first degree. The teachers of this science exist in the world openly and secretly. The Holy Quran tells us about the existence of these esoteric teachers. No period of time is without them. Pity for the people who are bent on denying the gnosis of God the Most High and the esoteric sciences! When some fortunate seeker determines to walk on the path, these people act like the will-o'-the-wisp and create the difficulties of diverse doubts in his way and vainly try to keep him back from the path. They become the seduced and seducer, and neither themselves travel the path nor allow others to do so. But who can lead astray those whom God the Most High guides toward Himself?

$$ اِنَّ عِبَادِئ لَيْسَ لَكَ عَلَيْهِمْ سُلْطٰنٌ (١٥ الحجر:٤٢) $$

"You will have no power over My slaves." God the Most High said to Satan, "You shall never predominate My selected slaves;

$$ وَمَنْ يَّهْدِ اللّٰهُ فَمَالَهٗ مِنْ مُّضِلٍّ (١٣٩ الزمر:٣٧) $$

He who is guided by God cannot be led astray."

Though from the Day of Eternity, God the Most High has laid the trust in man, the capability for religion and faculty for being guided (i.e., the seed of His personal name, Allah), the actuation of the faculty of capability and the irrigation of the seed of His personal name, Allah, stands in dire need of a cultivator and patron. Every faculty naturally exists in the body of a person, but another perfect person is needed to revise that faculty and bring it into action. For example, God the Most High has placed the faculty of speech in the nature of man from the Day of Eternity, but the mother is highly needed for bringing it into display through her nourishing and training. The child learns the language the mother speaks. Supposing a child is brought up without a mother or entrusted to a dumb mother and there is none to speak in its presence, the child will certainly remain dumb and lose the faculty of speech, although it did possess the faculty of speech. But the faculty is lost because of a lack of a patron. The story of the dumbsanctuary in the time of Emperor Akbar is well-known. As a test, some children were placed under the custody of dumb nurses and brought up and trained by them. All the children turned up dumb. Consequently, another person is needed to bring into action the stock of nature and omnipotence, the faculties and capabilities. Man was created to meet this demand of nature and omnipotence. For this very perfection and capability, man is honored with the vicegerent on earth. In short, God the Most High has prescribed this as a general law for the nourishment and training of the esoteric, natural capability. Accordingly, this bright fruit and seed was nourished in His Holiness the noble Prophet (P.B.U.H) through Gabriel. His Holiness (AS) was made the teacher and intermediary for the respected companions (صحابه) of the Holy Prophet and the system of tutorship and studentship, seekership and guideship, discipleship and preceptorship continued in the followers, followers of the followers, and later on in all the perfects, gnostics, faithful, and Muslims. The system of this esoteric and exoteric knowledge and gnosis will continue up to the last day. He who acts against this law of nature turns his face from human intermediary and deals directly with God shall certainly come to a loss and stand deprived of the light of faith and the wealth of gnosis. In the world, no science or art can be acquired without a teacher, and no man can have access to the gnosis, proximity, and union of God the Most High without a preceptor and guide.

ے نزوید تخم دل از آب و گل   بے نگاہے از خداوندانِ دل

اندریں عالم نیرزی با خے   تا نیا ویزی بدامان کے

Some blind, eternally condemned fellows deny the path of knowledge of God and esoteric science and consider mere verbal affirmation, the acquired bookish knowledge, and formal Islam as everything. Their affair is confined to mere verbal talk and hearsay things. They deny reaching, seeing, and finding God in this world, whereas things heard of stand no comparison with things seen.

وَمَنْ كَانَ فِى هٰذِهٖٓ اَعْمٰى فَهُوَ فِى الْاٰخِرَةِ اَعْمٰى (۲: بنى اسرائیل ۷۲)

"He who is blind here shall be blind in the next world." Through mere hearsay of things about an object, a man can never have the conviction that he can attain it by reaching and getting that thing. Satan invariably and very speedily destroys and steals the capital of the faith of those who rely on hearsay things. None can compete with Satan in verbal talk and intellectual arguments because in knowledge and scholarship he has been the professor of the angels. In the field of learning, no person has carried the ball of religion from the accursed Satan. Great learned professors and intelligent philosophers have thrown the shield and acknowledged their defeat in knowledge and learning. The how and why of intellectual arguments cannot reach that peerless science. For this peerless knowledge, perfect guiding teachers are needed. Bookish learning is absolutely useless here. What is needed here is intermediation. Satan is rich with the wealth of verbal knowledge and independent of all with regard to the holdings of learning, but from the point of view of the capital of intermediation, he is absolutely destitute and a pauper. In the world of knowledge, he was the tutor and chief of all the angels, but when the examination of intermediation of prostrating before Adam (p.b.u.h.) took place, this accursed one lagged behind all and lost the game.

The unworthy infidels of the former times were deprived of guidance because of the arrogance of this raw notion and used to say:

اَبَشَرٌ يَّهْدُوْنَنَا (۶۴ التغابن: ۶)

"What—a man to guide us?" To the prophets, they used to say:

- 226 -

$$\text{قَالُوا مَا أَنْتُمْ إِلَّا بَشَرٌ مِثْلُنَا وَمَا أَنْزَلَ الرَّحْمٰنُ مِنْ شَيْءٍ (٣٦ يٰس:١٥)}$$

"You are not but man like us, and the Compassionate has not sent anything to you (nor do you deserve it more than ourselves)."

Sometimes, the infidels used to raise this objection: "What sort of Prophet is this that partakes of food and walks in the streets"—meaning that the prophet ought to be a supernatural, exalted, and distinguished being. Sometimes, they remarked:

$$\text{لَوْلَا أُنْزِلَ عَلَيْنَا الْمَلٰئِكَةُ أَوْ نَرىٰ رَبَّنَا (٢٥ الفرقان:٢١)}$$

"Why don't angels come down to us, and why don't we see God?"

So that the matter of guidance may be clarified, in response to them, God the Most High says:

$$\text{وَلَوْ جَعَلْنٰهُ مَلَكًا لَّجَعَلْنٰهُ رَجُلًا وَّلَلَبَسْنَا عَلَيْهِمْ مَّا يَلْبِسُونَ ۞ (١٦ الانعام:٩)}$$

"Even if We had sent an angel We would have sent him in the form of a man and dressed him as you are dressed."

So the infidels lacked guidance because of entanglement in doubts of this kind. Says the Most High:

$$\text{وَمَا مَنَعَ النَّاسَ أَنْ يُّؤْمِنُوا إِذْ جَآءَهُمُ الْهُدىٰ إِلَّا أَنْ قَالُوا أَبَعَثَ اللّٰهُ بَشَرًا رَّسُولًا ۞}$$

$$\text{(١٧ بنى اسرائيل: ٩٤)}$$

"Nothing retarded mankind from bringing faith except that whenever guidance came to them, they kept saying, 'Has God sent a man as a prophet?'"

In short, though the special selected servants of God the Most High, namely, the prophets and saints, are forms of clay in outward form and appearance and elemental people like us, actually, they are bright angels, nay possessing more exalted and higher personalities.

$$\text{قُلْ إِنَّمَا أَنَا بَشَرٌ مِّثْلُكُمْ يُوحىٰ إِلَيَّ (١١٨ الكهف:١١٠)}$$

"Say, O Prophet, I am a man like you but revelation comes to me."

The former is a confirmation of the outward form, while the latter is a manifestation of the esoteric personality and reality of Muhammad (p.b.u.h.). On sight of the dusty body of Adam (p.b.u.h.), Satan refused to respect it and prostrate before it and was cursed on account of egotism of self-complacency. Similarly, those who looked at the outward body of the Prophet and saints and remained ignorant of their reality were deprived of their guidance, blessing, and favors. In short, man is guided by man and receives every kind of blessing, favor, restitude, education, and instruction from another man. Without a teacher, patron, and perfect guide, a man can learn nothing.

هیچ کس از خود بخود چیزے نشد   هیچ آهن خنجر تیزے نشد

هیچ حلوائی نشد استاد کار   تا که شاگرد شکر ریزے نشد

مولوی هر گز نشد مولائے روم   تا غلام شمس تبریزے نشد

(رومی)

"None became anything by himself. No iron itself became a sharp dagger. No confectioner became a master of the art, until he became a student of his sweetmeat-maker. Maulvi never was the Maulana of Rum until he became the slave of the Shams of Tabrez."

On account of their satanic envy, pride, and egotism, some people disacknowledge the instructions of religious teachers and spiritual guides, seek esoteric help from them, and call it unitarianism. They assert that God is nearer us than the jugular vein. He is omnipresent, hearing, seeing, near, and accepting. He is Himself a guide. We have no need for other mediums, intermediaries, guides, and leaders. God is sufficient unto us. They conceal this egotism, arrogance, envy, and enmity toward religious saints under the cover of satanic unitarianism, and alongside this, they claim themselves to be Unitarians and dub those who believe in prophets and guides as polytheists. They deal directly with God the Most High. They are worthless infidels of yore about whom God the Most High says:

$$\text{لَوْلَا يُكَلِّمُنَا اللهُ اَوْ تَاْتِيْنَآ اٰيَةٌ ۗ } \quad (\text{١٢ البقرة:١١٨})$$

$$\text{لَقَدِ اسْتَكْبَرُوْا فِيْٓ اَنْفُسِهِمْ وَعَتَوْ عُتُوًّا كَبِيْرًا} \quad (\text{٢٥ الفرقان:٢١})$$

"The deniers of the Prophet said why does not Allah talk to us (directly) and give us His signs? Verily they were very arrogant in themselves and had adopted serious insubordination."

In short, in the world, there is no science or art, trade or business that man has acquired from God the Most High directly without the mediumship and intermediation of another man. It is 239 the mere envy and arrogance of the sensual, blind, dead-hearted, eternally unfortunate people that keeps them back from treading the path of God and meeting a leader and guide. Satan did not prostrate before Adam (AS) out of envy and conceit and made unitarianism an excuse for it. He said, "I do not prostrate before anybody except God" (I am a Unitarian). Thus, though the accursed claimed unitarianism and disowned polytheism, on account of arrogance and egotism, he was making himself a partner of God. Although God the Most High says, "Arrogance is my mantle and I allow in it none besides myself."

چنداں کہ با اہل کبر محشور شوی   از رحمت کردگار خود دور شوی

گر بادہ خوری و بعد ازاں توبہ کنی   بہتر کہ کنی نماز و مخمور شوی

(حافظ ابن کثیر)

"The more you be one of the arrogant. The further you will be far from God's mercy. Better drink and then to repent, than pray and then get drunk with arrogance."

What can the blind. sensual people know of this polytheism that appears like unitarianism? Who can treat the patient who regards malady as the best of health. A drop of vinegar of arrogance curdles a great deal of the milk of knowledge; one spark of envy burns to ashes the stock of devotion of a thousand years. Tradition says:

$$\text{مَنْ كَانَتْ فِيْ قَلْبِهٖ ذَرَّةٌ مِّنَ الْكِبْرِ لَا يَدْخُلُ الْجَنَّةَ}$$

"He who has a particle of arrogance in his heart cannot enter paradise." Egotism and God can never combine. Alas for people who uplift arrogance and please the devil!

گیا شیطان مارا ایک سجدے کے نہ کرنے سے

اگر لاکھوں برس سجدے میں سر مارا تو کیا مارا

"Satan was cursed for not performing one prostration before Adam. What was the good of prostrating before Allah for lakhs of years?"

Bayazid Bustami (RA) once questioned God the Most High, "What is the way to union with thee?" He received the answer: "Quit thyself and you will meet Me." God the Most High "bestows honor on the person who bows to another and practices humility" for the sake of God the Most High. He is uplifted. He who is vain and proud falls headlong. The grain or seed flourishes and springs up after destroying its existence and vanity in the earth. Its safety and soundness is a hindrance in its growth and progress.

This is the philosophy of intermediation: Excess of both religious and worldly wealth and possessions results in arrogance and egotism. When a man's mind becomes tipsy through the intoxication of wealth like Pharaoh's, he begins to beat the drum of "I am your most exalted god." Hence, most of the worldly kings have laid claim to deityship because of this intoxication and rivalry. The intoxication of the wealth far exceeds that of wine.

باده نوشیدن و هشیار نشستن سهل است

گر بدولت برسی مست نہ گردی مردی

It is easier to get drunk and remain in senses. If getting rich and not getting intoxicated it manliness.

Moreover, knowledge and eminence, piety and devotion to God are esoteric and religious wealth and the merchandise of the next world. The owner of the wealth of the next world is also prone to the antworms of vanity and the defect of egotism.

Because of this intoxication, Satan, the greatest capitalist of this wealth, expressed his arrogance and egotism by uttering the words, "I am better than him," meaning Adam (AS). Many capitalists of this kind of valuables of the next world (i.e., most of the seeming impracticable scholars, dry ascetics, and hypocrites) from day to day lay false claims to be prophets, Mahdis, and Mujadids because of the pride of acquired bookish knowledge and showy devotion. Through His eternal knowledge, God the true goldsmith discerned this inevitable alloy of arrogance and egotism in the pure gold of knowledge and devotions of the angels and strongly forbade this metal of arrogance to enter His holy and sacred Court of Unity. To expunge the gold of the knowledge and devotions of the angels from the inevitable alloy and defect of arrogance and egotism, God the Most High desired to examine and cleanse it in the fire of the insult of prostration before Adam (AS). He ordered all the angels, "Prostrate before Adam." Now it is a well-known fact that arrogance and insult are opposite and two opponents can never unite and also that everything is known by its opposite. Therefore, by way of a test, God the Most High wanted to examine the gold of knowledge and devotion of the angels in the fire of prostration and insult. All the angels unanimously cast aside the mantle of arrogance and egotism from their shoulders and prostrated before Adam (AS). But since Satan the accursed possessed counterfeit merchandise, his nature was full of arrogance and self-worship, and his body was stiff with the metal of arrogance and egotism, he could not bend down to prostrate and pay homage to Adam and flatly refused to do so.

$$ اَبٰى وَاسْتَكْبَرَ ۗ وَ كَانَ مِنَ الْكٰفِرِيْنَ ۝ (١٢ البقرة: ٣٤) $$

"He refused and was arrogant, and he was one of the infidels." In short, he was cursed and driven off from the courtyard on account of arrogance alone. Though he prostrated before God the Most High for millions of years and claimed to be a unitarian, on account of arrogance and egotism, he was associating himself with God the Most High. Hence, the false claim to Unitarianism did not at all avail Satan, and he failed at the practical examination of unitarianism. The stocks of his millions of years of knowledge and devotion were reduced to ashes by a single spark of arrogance, and he was eternally cursed and condemned to hell. Therefore, O Seeker of God, check the shoes of the pride of the knowledge and devotion, and like Moses (p.b.u.h.), enter the august courtyard with the bare feet of meanness and supplication. Pay no heed to knowledge, accomplishment, devotion, and piety. In God's treasures, these things are very common and cheap. God the Most High desires worship, submission, and supplication from His servants, and He is a customer of this rare merchandise.

بہوش باش کہ ہنگام باد استغنا   ہزار خرمن طاعت بہ نیم جو نہ خرند

"Beware for during the gale of the great God's glory and independence, a thousand stocks of devotion do not value a grain of barley."

اَنِیْنُ الْمُذْنِبِیْنَ اَحَبُّ اِلَیَّ مِنْ تَسْبِیْحِ الْمُقَرَّبِیْنَ

Holy tradition says, "I love the weeping of the sinners more than the praises of the great saints."

کہ چوں پیدا شود اشراق خورشید   مشو اے عاصی بے چارہ نومید

ہم افتد نیز بر کنج گدائی   اگر افتد بہ قصر پادشاہی

بروے تابد ایں خورشید درگاہ   کسے کو برہنہ است امروز در راہ

گنہ گاراں برند ایں گوئے چالاک   چوں کار مخلصاں آمد خطرناک

انین المذنبین باید خدارا   نہ زیبد مرد خودبیں بادشاہ را

تن لاغر دلے باید شکتہ   دریں رہ نیست خود بینی نجستہ

"Don't despair, O helpless sinner, when the luster of the sun appears. If it falls on the royal palace, it also touches the huts of the poor. This sun of the court shines on the one who is naked on the path today since the affairs of the pious ones are dangerous. The sinners carry away the ball. A self-conceited servant smartly does not suit a king. The weeping sinners are liked more by God the Most High; self-conceit is inauspicious in this path. A lean body and broken heart are wanted."

Ostensibly, the prostrations of the angels before Adam (AS) was an unpalatable form of polytheism and a very bitter medicine for the angels, who were the embodiment of knowledge and devotion. But since it had to prove beneficial as an antidote for the disease of arrogance and egotism, therefore receiving the command of the Eternal Physician, the wise and farsighted angels closed their eyes, and mustering up their courage, they took this unpalatable and bitter medicine of intermediation and degradation and got rid of the fatal disease of arrogance and egotism.

آن راچہ کنی کہ نفس کافر داری   گیرم کہ ہزار مصحف از برداری

آن رابہ زمیں بنہ کہ در سرداری   سر رابہ زمیں چہ می نہی بہر نماز

"Granted you have a hundred Qurans learned by heart, what would you do with the infidel soul you have? Why place your head on earth in prayer? Place that arrogance that you bear in your head on the earth."

When Satan was cursed for not prostrating before Adam (AS), he undertook the enmity of Adam (AS) and his progeny. Satan said, "O God, by Thy honor I would seduce them all." He, the cursed of all, seduced Adam (AS) toward the heavenly tree of egotism, whereby egotism and sensualism were created in him. It began thus: when first the effigy of Adam (AS) was being made in paradise, the angels asked, "O Allah! What is it that Thou art making?" God the Most High replied, "I am making a vicegerent of Mine."

This kindled the fire of enmity and jealousy in Satan. He said to himself, *I deserve to be the vicegerent; where is this new onebeing made?* Then coming close to Adam, he began to inspect him. Discerning the curious creation and future pomp and grandeur of Adam (AS), the Satan spat at his effigy out of envy and selfworship at the time of departure. That Satanic spit of egotism and self-worship fell at the navel of Adam (AS), which set the foundation of self in Adam (AS). From now onward, a link was established between Adam and his progeny and Satan, and the seed of depravity was sown in the person of man.

In short, the four elements of Satanic envy, egotism, sense of honor, and selfish egotism appeared in the body of Adam, and from the mass of these, the existence of the self was established in Adam (AS) where Iblis the accursed pitched his residence, trenches, and ambush. With the same, he assured Adam the imaginary verdant paradise of the paradisiacal tree of egotism, made him eat the fruit of the forbidden tree, and brought him out of the highest paradise. Since God the Most High desires examination of His creation, He has allowed Satan up to the time of Doomsday, reinforced him by a large fighting army of Iblis (i.e., Satanic forces), and armed him with various kinds of weapons. Of these self-worship and egotism are the strongest and most effective weapons. It is his real, oldest, most natural weapon, and he is very expert in its use. Self-worship and egotism first turned out to be the cause of his own depravity and the accursedness. He constantly shoots these poisonous arrows from the trenches of the soul in the body of every man, telling him that none equals him and turns him against the religious saints and leaders. The fatal germs of envy, self-worship, and arrogance against Adam (AS) killed Satan the very first day, and then putting this destructive venom in the body of Adam (AS) through his spittle, in the form of self-worship and turning him (i.e., Adam) out of the paradise of proximity, Satan imprisoned him in the prison of the remoteness of the world. These fatal germs of selfworship, egotism, and envy continued in the progeny of Adam generation after generation. On account of this hereditary envy and egotism, the worthless infidels, irreligious polytheists, and blind enviers remain eternally suspicious of the prophets and saints of Allah. Because of self-worship, God can never unite.

There are different trenches and pitfalls of Satan in the body of the man. The seat of the soul depraved and self-worship is in the place of the navel. The second trench in the left side of the heart is that of Khannas, the spiritually impure child of Satan. So Satan puts the persons of arrogance and egotism in the heart of man through his cursed son Khannas. The foundations of the accursed Khannas were laid through the semen of "I" and the impure seminal fluid of "I am better than he" self-worship and egotism. Its resemblant figure is that of an elephant. When like the mosquito it thrusts its venomous trunk, full of the germs of arrogance and egotism, into the heart of a man, the man is so overtaken by the severe fever of arrogance and egotism that like the proud Pharaoh, the man begins to beat the drum of "I am your High Lord," and he attaches no value to the saints and religious potentates—nay, even the prophets and messengers. In short, this bloody eternal enemy kills man with the knife of arrogance and egotism.

بکری کرے مَیں مَیں مَیں گلے چھری پھراوے   مینا کرے مَیں نہ مَیں نہ سب کے مَن کو بھاوے
(سرشار)

"The goat says main (I) and gets itself killed. The bird maina says *main nah* (I am not) and is liked by everybody."

Tradition says, "Whoever praised his Muslim brother in his face has killed him without a dagger," so to say. Briefly, arrogance and egotism is such an effective trick of Satan that it is "impossible to escape it" without the intermediation of the guide, and for this fatal disease, the medicine of intercession proves to be the greatest antidote and elixir. But let it be also remembered that moderation is commendable in all things. Excess and shortage are never right. Though humility and submission are good things, there must be a limit to these. It is not proper to magnify and glorify the Prophet above God and to prefer the saint to the Prophet. There is a limit to the respect paid to the parents and teacher, and there is a particular place of the guide and saint. It is incumbent to respect them in accordance with their ranks. And though the rank of a messenger and prophet is above all the creation of God, they should never be placed above God the Most High. No man should be included in magnification and glorification, that is, the prostration for the sake of the display of servantship particular to God the Most High.

گر حفظِ مراتب نہ کُنی زندیقی

"If you don't observe ranks, you are heretic."

To make an unnecessary habit of unreasonable and misplaced humiliation on all occasions degrades a man in his own eyes and in those of others and thus annihilates the useful sense of self-reliance and self-respect and makes a man spiritless and unhonorable."

تواضع گرچہ محمود است و فضلِ بیکراں دارد

نباید کرد بیش از حد کہ ہیبت رازیاں دارد

"Though humility is commendable and has unbounded excellence. It should not be practiced beyond bounds for it damages grandeur."

Supplication and humility are of two kinds. One is praiseworthy, the other censurable. Magnification and glorification of an irreligious, wealthy man, a rich and worldly tyrant, an adulterer, or an insincere official for the sake of worldly greed and derivation of benefit is improper—nay absolutely unlawful.

It is recorded in tradition: "Whoever paid homage to a rich man for his riches, undoubtedly lost two-thirds of his faith." What a great admonition! The ancient pious men were very circumspect in this respect and considered it a very great sin to respect and glorify any rich man. In contrast, they treated the wealthy people and rich rulers with great disregard and carelessness. It is said, "Arrogance toward the arrogant is a worship." It is a commendable and blessed act to show humility and supplication to the parents or an elderly relative or to respect the teacher or some pious elderly man or some pure-pedigreed Sayyed or noble Qureshi or guide or preceptor, with the sole object of attaining the salvation or pleasure of God the Most High. To ridicule and show contempt to God the Most High's poor and indigent slaves on account of their pauperism and destitution throws down a man from the eyes of God the Most High and subjects him to His anger and terror. There are innumerable instances of this in the munificent Quran, and traditions of the prophets and the compositions of the ancient saints are replete with such incidents. It is a warning that His Holiness Muhammad the chosen (P.B.U.H) is the beloved of God, the Most High. But on two occasions, God the Most High has expressed His disapproval of him. Two such instances are recorded in the munificent Quran. One is this: One day, His Holiness the Prophet (P.B.U.H) was sitting among the peers and chiefs of Quresh. A blind companion named Abdullah son of Maqtum entered the assembly and for want of eyesight thought His Holiness (P.B.U.H) to be alone; he intercepted his speech and put to him some questions about religion. His Holiness (P.B.U.H)took it ill and turned away his face without answering Abdullah, who left the assembly hopeless and dejected, whereupon Gabriel (AS) brought the following verses from the divine court:

عَبَسَ وَ تَوَلّٰی ۙ اَنْ جَآءَهُ الْاَعْمٰی ۙ وَ مَا یُدْرِیْكَ لَعَلَّهٗ یَزَّكّٰی ۙ اَوْ یَذَّكَّرُ فَتَنْفَعَهُ الذِّكْرٰی ۙ اَمَّا مَنِ اسْتَغْنٰی ۙ فَاَنْتَ لَهٗ تَصَدّٰی ۙ وَ مَا عَلَیْكَ اَلَّا یَزَّكّٰی ۙ وَ اَمَّا مَنْ جَآءَكَ یَسْعٰی ۙ وَ هُوَ یَخْشٰی ۙ فَاَنْتَ عَنْهُ تَلَهّٰی ۙ كَلَّا اِنَّهَا تَذْكِرَةٌ ۚ (۸۰ عبس:۱-۱۱)

"Muhammad (P.B.U.H)knitted his brow and turned away his face when a blind man came to him. What do you know (O My Prophet) perhaps he might have been reformed and guided and he might have profited thereby? But you are very attentive toward one who is independent of you. (Although your advice and attention do not benefit those wretched and careless people) you are not responsible if one is not guided. But he who came to you running (that is, Abdullah) while he was fearing (God) and you turned aside from him and are careless."

When these verses were brought to His Holiness (P.B.U.H), his blessed color turned pale and leaving the assembly he started after Abdullah, embraced him, brought him back to the Prophet's mosque, and spreading his blessed mantle for him, respectfully and honorably made him sit thereon, and tried very much to please him. He always used to honor him, and twice, he appointed him his caliph, assistant, and ruler of Madina in his absence. He said that "when Gabriel (AS) began to recite those verses, a great fear and the terror of God the Most High overtook my heart, which was much frightened and shaking until I heard the verse, Beware, it is only an advice for all and my heart was pacified." This verse means that this Quran is a general invitation of advice to the very big and small from God the Most High in which there is no particularization and discrimination for anyone.

Another incident of this kind is also thus related in the munificent Quran. A sufficient group of destitute and poor companions, called the Companions of Sufa (اصحاب صفه) were present near his Holiness (P.B.U.H). These people had left behind their country and homes and assembled around His Holiness (P.B.U.H) in order to learn the divine commandments and accomplish the spiritual knowledge. As they had no place to dwell in, they had constructed a large earthen estrade for their residence. Because a projection of the kind is called *sufa* in the Arabic language, some elders of the religion are of the opinion that the word *Sufi* is derived from the word *sufa*. In short, these people had completely renounced the world and had full faith in Allah. They had no worldly possessions. Each one had hardly a mantle or patched garment to cover his nakedness. They lived on bare subsistence. Remembrance of God and interviews of Muhammad (P.B.U.H)and his company and attention, day and night, constitutued their food. When His Holiness (P.B.U.H) came to them, they fell like moths on the lamp of his beauty and gathered around him. It is an established law that the rich and wealthy people loathe the poor and indigent and consider it below their dignity to sit with them. So that when the elders and chiefs of Quresh came to see His Holiness (P.B.U.H) and saw him sitting in the assembly of those unshaven of hair and dusty dervishes, they felt ashamed of sitting with them. One day, these chiefs and peers said to His Holiness (P.B.U.H), "Whenever we come to see you, we find you surrounded by these dirty and naked beggars. Whenever we come to you to hear your talk, you ought to get out of them and sit with us in a separate place where these people should have no permission to come. Or, at least, you ought to turn your *face* from them and attend to us." Because the Prophet was zealous in the matters of religion and inviting others to the faith, he was about to make some proposal in this respect when in the meanwhile Gabriel (AS) came with these verses:

وَاصْبِرْ نَفْسَكَ مَعَ الَّذِينَ يَدْعُونَ رَبَّهُمْ بِالْغَدَاوةِ وَالْعَشِيِّ يُرِيدُونَ وَجْهَهُ وَلَا تَعْدُ عَيْنَكَ عَنْهُمْ تُرِيدُ زِينَةَ الْحَيوةِ الدُّنْيَا وَلَا تُطِعْ مَنْ اَغْفَلْنَا قَلْبَهُ عَنْ ذِكْرِنَا وَاتَّبَعَ هَوٰيهُ وَكَانَ اَمْرُهُ فُرُطًا ﴿٢٨﴾ (١٨ الكهف: ٢٨)

> O Prophet! content your soul with (the external dirtiness of) these (people of the Sufa) who keep invoking their Lord day and night and desire to see Him. Do not remove your eyes from them unless you desire decoration of the worldly life. Do not listen to those whose hearts are unmindful of commemorating Us and who follow their desires and their affair is naught.

Under these circumstances, the ancient saints used to be excessive in disrespecting and belittling the worldly chiefs and respecting and glorifying God's pious, poor, and destitute servants. They did not consider the wealthy, moneyed, or even kings as equal to a fly or a louse. Because they were sincere in their intentions and their object was to raise and elevate the name of God the Most High, their spiritual powers reached the highest heaven. God the Most High had made the worldly kings their slaves and subordinates. Because to the pious kings of those times, it was more evident than the sun that the stability of their kingdoms was due to those holy-natured beings. Hence, the kings of those times used to visit the court of dervishes in the capacity of supplicators and beggars, and through the agency of their prayers, they used to get the difficulties solved from the court of God the Most High. The historical books are full of such instances. Of these, we will reproduce for the readers some brief ones.

MEMOIRS OF SOME RELIGIOUS SAINTS (MIAN MIR SAHIB AND OTHERS)

It is said that His Holiness Mian Mir Sahib was sitting on the roof of his parlor along with his dervishes one morning. At the time, he was reclining his blessed head on the thigh of a dervish and taking rest; the other dervishes were busy removing lice from their patched garments when one of his dervishes saw the emperor of India, that is, the Emperor Shah Jahan, with his eldest son, Dara Shakoh, coming to see His Holiness, Mian Mir Sahib, and laughed. He asked the dervish for the cause of his laughter and exhilaration. He submitted, "Sir, the Emperor Shah Jahan and Dara Shakoh are coming to see you."

At this he retorted, "O ignorant fool! I thought you were making joy at finding some fat louse in your patched garment. You idiot! Are you showing teeth at the advent of the emperor?"

In short, in their eyes, the reality of the worldly kings was less than that of a louse and fly. In their persons, there used to be so much reverence, magnificence, respect, and greatness of the name of God the Most High that the emperors used to shiver out of fear and terror of them and considered it their blessing and honor to carry their shoes. It is said that after kissing the feet of His Holiness Mian Mir Sahib, Shah Jahan and Dara Shakoh crouched in a corner along with the other poor men. His Holiness Mian Mir Sahib was chewing cardamoms at the time and used to spit the refuse out of his mouth, which the Emperor Shah Jahan gathered in a corner of his royal mantle, considering them more useful than diamonds and jewels.

The following incident is related in the book *Tadhkirat-ul-Awliya*.

One night, the Caliph Harun-ur-Rashid said to Fazal, the Bermicide, "Take me to some Godly man. I am tired of the worldly pomp and show and the worries of the government. My heart might perhaps find some peace in God the Most High." Fazal took him to the door of Sufian Ainiyya and knocked at the door. Sufian inquired, "Who is there?"

Fazal told him, "The ruler of the Muslims has come to the door."

Sufian said, "Why did not you inform me beforehand so that I should have myself come to the court?"

On hearing this, Harun said, "This isn't the man that I am in search of."

When Sufian heard this, he said, "If he is in search of a godly man, take him to Fazeel son of Ayaz."

Then both of them repaired to the hut of Sheikh Fazeel the son of Ayaz. The sheikh was reciting this verse of the Holy Quran at the moment: "Do those who have made a hobby of sin consider that We will make them equal to the faithful?"

Harun said, "Had I needed advice, this verse alone would have sufficed." This verse served as a whip of warning to the heart of Harun. Then he knocked at the door.

Sheikh Sahib inquired, "Who is there?"

He said, "The ruler of the faithful (امیر المومنین)."

He replied, "What business has the ruler of the faithful got with me, and what have I to do with him? Don't distract me from my work, and don't waste my time."

Thereupon, Fazal the Bermicide replied, "The king of Islam has also got some rights on the people."

He said, "Don't disturb me."

Fazal the Bermicide insisted and asked, "Should we come in by permission or by force?"

The answer was, "There is no permission, and if you come in by force, that is your own concern."

When Harun entered, the sheikh put out his candle so as not to see the face of Harun. The caliph advanced in the darkness until his hand touched that of the sheikh; thereupon, the sheikh remarked, "How soft is this hand! Would that it escape hellfire!" Seeing this, he started to perform the prayers. Harun began to weep and supplicated him to say at least something. When Sheikh Sahib finished the prayer, he said, "Your grandfather requested the

Prophet of God (P.B.U.H.) for the rulership of some country whereupon His Holiness (P.B.U.H.) said, 'I instruct you to be the ruler and chief of your soul (i.e., keep ordering your soul to obey God the Most High). This is more beneficial to you than ruling the people and administrating justice for a thousand years.' Verily, Rulership is a disgrace for all the rulers on the Day of Resurrection."

Harun requested something more. He said regard the old men, young men, and boys among your subjects as your father, brethren, and children respectively. Harun began to weep bitterly and requested he utter more. He said, "I am afraid about this handsome face of yours lest it gets distorted and ugly on account of vicious deeds on the Doomsday because many rulers will come captives there."

Harun burst into tears and again made a request for something more. He said, "Fear God the Most High and be prepared for the last day and resurrection. Because on that day, God the Most High will question you about every Muslim and interrogate you about the justice delivered to each. Should in this vast dominion of yours an old woman sleep without a meal in the night, she will get hold of your skirt that day."

Harun fell senseless, weeping. Thereupon, Fazal the Bermicide submitted, "Hold your speech, O Sheikh! You have killed the ruler of the faithful."

The sheikh replied, "Keep quiet, O Haman! For you and your associates have killed him (spiritually)."

This increased the lamentation of Harun, who afterwards said, "Truly! O Fazal, you are Haman, and I am Pharaoh."

Then Harun said to him, "I have heard that you owe some debt?"

The sheikh said, "Yes, I am highly indebted to my Master. Avow for me if I do not discharge this debt in my lifetime."

Harun said, "I ask you about the debt to the people."

The sheikh replied, "Thanks I to God, the Most High, I possess an abundance of his bounty and wealth."

Placing a bag full of a thousand dinars before the sheikh, Harun said, "I inherited this as a legacy from my mother. It is pure and lawful. If you utilize it in your expenditure, there will be no harm."

The sheikh drew a cold sigh and said, "Alas! All this advice of mine has been wasted, and you have not been affected. You have begun tyranny and injustice even here. I am drawing you toward salvation and God's forgiveness while you are preparing means for my destruction and ruin. I tell you to give your possessions to the rightful owners, and you are giving the property of another to one who is in no way entitled to take it. O Harun, have shame and fear God!"

With these words, he got up from before Harun and closed the door. Harun left in tears and said to Fazal the Bermicide, "The Godly people are like Fazeel the son of Ayaz."

VALUE OF A PERFECT GUIDE

In short, the saints of the past used to be such true seekers of God the Most High, virtuous travelers. They were overrich with esoteric wealth and spiritual populace. Hence, they had neither love nor value of the wealth in their hearts nor respect and reverence for the wealthy. They were always busy in studying death. The worldly life appeared merely as a perishable, futile dream and imagination to their truth-discerning and far-sighted eyes.

The eternal abode of the next world and that alive and waking world was truly manifest in their eyes. The imaginary dream life and perishable existence stands no comparison with the living, waking, and eternal life.

The preceding few stories have been related by way of a sample. From these, readers endowed with certainty can very well guess that ancient Sufis and faqirs showed to the world such wonderful feats, supernatural revelations, and miraculous powers of their spiritual signs, which put the entirety of humanity of the age into astonishment until all the concerned and common people, big and small, from the beggars to the kings, turned to be their lovers and mad after them, and everyone was ready to sacrifice his soul and property on them and became a wholehearted buyers of the invaluable jewel of Faqr and Gnosis. The faqirs of yore also knew very well the worth and value of their valuable merchandise and considered it an entirely losing concern to exchange it for the kingdom of the whole world. The seeker faqirs and true owners of the gnosis of that age were the true bankers and shopkeepers of these diamonds and lustrous jewels. The seeker disciples of that age were also true in their search and wanted to purchase this precious valuable merchandise with their wealth and souls, nay, even with both the worlds, which they gave up for it.

When the people of the later ages saw this prosperous market of Faqr and dervishism amid the eternal honor and chieftainship of both the worlds therein, many people flocked toward it with the single and solitary object of acquiring material gain and dignity and honor. All the true seekers and saints of the past were the embodiment of belovedship, and amiability dropped from every detail of their actions, every word of their speech, and even from every string of their particular robe of Sufi dress. The rosary, stick, prayer mat, cap, and so on were regarded as the emblems of piety. Hence, the later hypocritical and cunning Sufis and false faqirs began their trade in these, reaped great profits from these things, entangled many simple-hearted birds in their nets, plucked them into shreds, and devoured them. But falsehood is unsubstantial, and the trick of falsehood and treachery at last gets divulged. So that the world came to know of their knavery and roguery, their veil was rent asunder, and the putrescence of their acts became manifest.

If a perfect faqir or true lover of God Almighty is met within the world, any amount of respect and reverence paid to him is insufficient. The soul and property should be sacrificed in their service. The dust of their footsteps should be made the collyrium of the eyes. Their rights have priority over all other rights and are discharged by discharging their rights, because these are the people who unite one with God the Most High and His Prophet and make one acceptable in those courts. The keys of the blessings and treasures of both worlds remain in the hands of these people. The man on whom they cast a favorable glance is rendered prosperous in both the worlds, whereby they discharge the rights of all the rightful.

تمنا درد دل کی ہے تو کر خدمت فقیروں کی   نہیں ملتا یہ گوہر بادشاہوں کے خزینوں میں

نہ پوچھ ان خرقہ پوشوں کی، ارادت ہو تو دیکھ ان کو   ید بیضا لیے بیٹھے ہیں اپنی آستینوں میں

(اقبالؒ)

"If you desire the heart's light, serve the faqirs. For this jewel is unobtainable in royal treasuries. Don't inquire about these in patchy rags. If you have faith, see them. They are sitting with the bright palms in their sleeves, like those of Moses."

Satan betrays the people from the right path and puts them on the satanic road of arrogance, egotism, and envy and intimidating them of polytheism makes them the associates of Allah on account of their arrogance. Plainly speaking, those who believe in the friends of Allah respect them for the sake of Allah the Most High, make guides and friends of them in the path of God the Most High, and respect and obey them in this path; they certainly believe in and know God the Most High a million times better than those false claimants. One man lays a mere verbal claim from a distance to be loyal to a king and to respect him. Another man dies like a moth on the candle of his (i.e., the king's) beauty, runs to him in accordance with "Fly towards Allah," renders service to fellow travelers, guides his path, and salists their help in the journey so much so that he applies the dust of his lane to his eyes like collyrium. Now tell me who cherishes in his heart a greater respect for the king—the first man or the second? As their souls are not crushed and degraded by paying respects and reverence to God the Most High (that is, worshipping without seeing Him), they continue in it, pride in it, and fatten their souls and Satan. But if at any time, His Holy Essence appears before them in visible form, they would at once begin to deny Him:

$$ يَوْمَ يُكْشَفُ عَنْ سَاقٍ وَّ يُدْعَوْنَ اِلَى السُّجُوْدِ فَلَا يَسْتَطِيْعُوْنَ ۞ خَاشِعَةً اَبْصَارُهُمْ $$

(القلم ١٦٨: ٤٢-٤٣)

"When He will show His Calf of the leg and invite them to prostrate to Him, they would not be able to prostrate themselves and their eyes will fear (on account of doubt)."

In short, the egotism and pharaohism can never be crushed, and the selfishness does not die without the intervention of a guide.

نفس نتواں کشت اِلّا ظلِّ پیر   دامنِ ایں نفس کش را سخت گیر

کیمیا پیدا کن از مشتِ گلے   بوسہ زن بر آستانے کاملے

گر تو سنگِ خارا یا مر مر شوی   چوں بصاحبِ دل رسی گوہر شوی

یک زمانہ صحبتے با اولیا   بہتر از صد سالہ طاعت بے ریا

(رومی)

"The shadow of the preceptor alone can kill the selfishness. Hold fast the skirt of this self killer. Make alchemy out of a handful of dust. Kiss the threshold of a perfect one. Be you a flint or a marble. On contact with a saint, you will become a jewel. A moment's companionship of the saints is better than a century of unhypocritical devotion."

The seeker must take hold of the skirt of an instructor and guide because it is indispensable. Helpless and excusable are the people who are contented with their blindness considering a mere verbal affirmation to be all in all and who are happy in the darkness like a bat and have no need of the world-illuminating sun because their hearts are besieged in the darkness of matter and wrapped in the covering of negligence. It is difficult to travel on this path without the company of a guide. Says the Most High:

$$يَٰٓأَيُّهَا الَّذِينَ ءَامَنُوا اتَّقُوا اللَّهَ وَابْتَغُوٓا إِلَيْهِ الْوَسِيلَةَ وَجَاهِدُوا فِي سَبِيلِهِ لَعَلَّكُمْ تُفْلِحُونَ$$

(المَائَدة: ٣٥) ۝

"O you who are faithful! fear Allah and find out an intermediary towards Him and exert in His path — perhaps you may realize salvation."

Some people say that intermediation stands for virtuous deeds. But God the Most High is addressing the faithful to exercise fear of God and piety and to exercise asceticism and austerities in His path. But besides these take hold of an intermediator toward Him. Now it appears that intermediation is something other than faithfulness, piety, and asceticism, which God the Most High particularly commands and conjugates to them. So it is clearly evident that here intermediation means neither faith nor knowledge nor piety nor fear of God but an instructor and a perfect sheikh who can act as a companion and guide to the path of Allah. In this verse, God the Most High has commanded all the four things: 1) knowledge of faith, 2) exercise fear of God and piety, 3) appoint an intermediator, and 4) to practice asceticism. Exercising asceticism and austerities is mentioned after intermediation because some people feel proud of the intermediation and intercession and sit idle and remain so without any action. Taking the appointment of a preceptor or the intercession of some religious leader for a certificate of their salvation, they do not act themselves.

Reliance on intermediation alone, without knowledge, action, and asceticism, throws one in the ditch of depravity. The correct and true path is between the two, like the bridge across hell— thinner than a hair and sharper than a sword—covered by the veil of test and severe darkness of trial. This right path is between the exertion (کوشش) of "We worship Thee" and the attraction (کشش) of "We seek help from Thee." This mystery is unknown even to the chosen people, not to mention the common folk.

اِيَّاكَ نَعْبُدُ وَاِيَّاكَ نَسْتَعِينُ ۞ اِهْدِنَا الصِّرَاطَ الْمُسْتَقِيمَ ۞ (۱۲ البقرة: ۴-۵)

فَاُولٰٓئِكَ مَعَ الَّذِينَ اَنْعَمَ اللّٰهُ عَلَيْهِمْ مِّنَ النَّبِيّٖنَ وَالصِّدِّيْقِينَ وَالشُّهَدَآءِ وَالصّٰلِحِيْنَ وَ حَسُنَ اُولٰٓئِكَ رَفِيْقًا ۞ (۴ النساء:۶۹)

Says the Holy Book, "We worship Thee and seek help from Thee. Show us the right path."

He who acts merely on the worship is like Satan and is the object of divine wrath and oppression. And sitting meditatively with crossed legs at the thresholds of the saints in pride of "We seek help from Thee" alone hurls one into the pit of depravity. Hence, the path of the chosen and accepted people of God the Most High, whom God the Most High has shown bounties, is neither the path of the wrathful (مغضوب) nor that of those who havegone astray (الضَّآلِّيْنَ)." The companianship of and obedience to these people is the real true path and the way to salvation. And they are the people mentioned by God the Most High: "They are those to whom God has been bountiful." They are prophets, the truthful, martyrs, and pious people, and they are fine people for friendship." So the right way and straight path to salvation and paradise is to pursue those whom God the Most High has shown bounties, and they are prophets, the truthful, martyrs, and pious people. They are very good people for companionship and leadership on the path of paradise. So, "O satisfied soul, turn to your Lord and join My selected servants and enter My paradise merrily." Both the wings of "We worship Thee" and "We seek help from Thee" are essential to the traveler for flying in the holy courtyard of God the Most High. It is true that the bird that flies on one feather flies headlong for a while and then falls down. The bird with two wings flies straight ahead.

On the path of Allah, the seeker of God stands in greater need of circumspection and discernment between truth and falsehood, perfect and imperfect, than a perfect guide. Because treacherous, man-shaped but devil-natured, false, impersonating and hypocritical trading sheikhs have infested the world like pests. The seekers ought not to be like one collecting wood in the darkness.

Else he might touch a serpent, taking it for wood and get himself killed. In the world, the special perfect persons of God are rare like the phoenix while there are innumerable liars, professionals, cunning hypocrites, and hunters who spread the net and entangle simple-natured birds.

پس بہر دستے نباید داد دست ۔ ۔ ۔ اے بسا ابلیس آدم روے ہست

(رومی)

There are many men who are Adam-faced and devil-natured. Hence, the hand must not be placed in every hand.

Falsehood is very popular nowadays. When people began suffering from bankruptcy of the religious intellect and lacked discernment between truth and falsehood, genuine and counterfeit, original and imitation, and began to purchase imitation and pieces of glass at the price of diamonds, the owners of genuine diamonds and jewels wound up their shops and the false imitation-selling shopkeepers decorated their stalls and liberally plundered the foolish purchasers. These false shopkeepers confined their claims to prophethood alone. If they had acted a bit more courageously and claimed to Godhood before these enemies of intellect, in this age of religious liberty, millions of fools would have come forward to believe in them. Alas! Those who are ignorant of their own faith are accepted as veracious in all the baseless claims of being the incarnation of His Holiness Ali (may God glorify his face) and simultaneously being a prophet, renewer, the promised Massiha and Krishan, and so on. One ought to lament at this wisdom.

باد سموم و باد مسیحا برابر است ۔ ۔ ۔ امروز قدر گوہر و خارا برابر است

سرگین گاؤ و عنبر سارا برابر است ۔ ۔ ۔ چو در مشام اہل جہاں نیست امتیاز

"Alike is the worth of jewel and flint today. Alike is Samoom and Messiah's breath, since there is no distinction in people's smelling. Alike are the cow's dung and pure amber."

Man is very crafty and ease-loving. In every religion and nation, there are cycles of tide and ebb (i.e., progress and decline). When the age of decline sets in, a nation and its followers become infirm of faith. Then they are split up into two groups. One adopts the skin of the religion on account of their dry piety and performs all the fundamentals of religion in a customary and formal way. They consider mere verbal affirmation, ordinary physical exercise, and a little monetary sacrifice as an adequate price for the everlasting paradise, divine gnosis, and observation. In return for this insignificant act, they firmly expect paradise and desire to attain it gratis. But since the skin of religion tastes indifferent and odious wherein they can find no constant pleasure and progress, they finally begin to loathe it step by step or perform this act only hypocritically, and by way of ostentation, in the discharge of religious duties, they keep material interest in view. It is a special feature of these people that there is a superabundance of the habit of investigation and questioning in their minds. Their eyes are highly fault-finding. These people consider the prophets, saints, and all the pious people equal to themselves and regard none of them superior to themselves. Hence, they always find faults with the religious leaders and spiritual guides and are inimical towards them. They disbelieve the miracles of the prophets' revelations, the miraculous powers of the saints, and all supernormal spiritual accomplishments or put on them highly improper interpretations. Because religion has come down to us through these holy beings (namely, the prophets and saints), their respect and reverence is interconnected with that of religion. By looking contemptuously at these founders and propagators of religion, they invariably begin to think lightly of the religion that has come to us through them. Gradually, this contempt and disregard of religion results in negation and hurls them in the pit of infidelity and heresy.

Since the second group is predominated by forming favorable opinions, they foolishly attach much importance to an ordinary thing. Their eyes always seek the meritable points. They start to accept everything even if it is unreasonable. They consider the religious leaders and spiritual guides to be despotic masters of exoteric and esoteric treasures of both the worlds, the sole lessees and contractors of paradise and all the bounties of the next world. Therefore, on the basis of their pride of their intercession and recommendation, they lay strong claims to paradise and, discarding all fundamentals of religion, consider themselves relieved of all the religious restrictions. More than that, on account of their pride of intercession, they are encouraged in the commission of all the sins and indulgence in things prohibited. Taking advantage of the frailty of this group, Satan generally snares them in the net of imposture of impractical scholars and imperfect, fraudulent sheikhs. Since the hypocritical sheikhs and imperfect scholars make a prey of wealth under the ambush of religion, those bogus shopkeeping guides generally give false consolations to those foolish people in order to please their hearts and keep them entangled by narrating to them false accounts of revelation, miraculous powers, and high-sounding boasts and tell them, "Pay our tribute and gifts from year to year and keep visiting us. You have touched our skirt, now you need not fear the next world. We are responsible for you. You have no need to act."

These people regard these heretical methods as a boon, and the paying of the annual taxes as gifts and kissing the guide's feet as everything. Compared to performing the five prayers daily, dying of hunger and thirst by keeping the thirty annual fasts, paying the alms every year, undertaking long and perilous journeys for performing the pilgrimage, being fettered in religious restrictions every moment, and performing acts of asceticism, austerities right up to death, they consider this easy intermediation and intercession of the guide as a very congenial and cheap bargain of attaining salvation and paradise at the end. Hence, all their lives they sit idle in this hope. In fact, there are two fountainheads of the intellectual depravity of a person. One is to be so deprived of intellect and knowledge as to accept everything thoughtlessly and to tread every path blindly. The second is to immediately falsify whatever fact appears beyond the reach of intellect or that cannot be harmonized with the material intellect and to believe that what his intellect or that of a few persons cannot comprehend in fact does not exist. The first is called depravity and the second heresy.

O Man, God the Most High does not demand from you only a belief. His commandment is

$$\text{فَفِرُّوٓا اِلَى اللّٰهِ ۗ (١٥ الذاريٰت:٥٠)}$$

"So run toward Allah."

Also it is laid down,

$$\text{اَتَصْبِرُونَ ۗ وَكَانَ رَبُّكَ بَصِيرًا ۞ (١٢٥ الفرقان:٢٠)}$$

"Are you waiting patiently while God is looking toward you?"

يَـٰٓأَيُّهَا الْإِنسَانُ إِنَّكَ كَادِحٌ إِلَىٰ رَبِّكَ كَدْحًا فَمُلَـٰقِيهِ ۝ (الانشقاق:٨٤)

O Mankind! You are to strive toward your Lord and then meet Him."

There isn't a lengthy journey between God the Most High and Man, and no mountains, forests, and rivers intervene between the two. There is no distance of space and time between the slave and the Lord. God the Most High says, "I am nearer Man than his jugular vein." Therefore, only the esoteric veils of darkness intervene between God the Most High and His slaves. As in sleep and deep dream, a person becomes unaware of the world, his close associates, and even his own body, similarly, the human spirit fallen in the deep dream of eternity is at a distance from its Master and True Lord nearby. This distance is traversed by the cardiac and esoteric steps alone. It is not the work of the elemental body.

Nowadays, there is a great dearth of perfect men. The existence of a perfect gnostic and sincere seeker is like a phoenix. The spirit of religion and spiritualism has escaped the world. The marrow has been lost. Only the skin and the covering of the faith is left behind. Black clouds of darkness have covered the hearts. In this dark and blind world, the true and sincere lovers of God the Most High have covered themselves up in the mantle of obscurity and anonymity and concealed themselves. The devil-natured people have donned Solomon's dress, seated themselves on the throne of sheikhs, and are ruling the hearts of ignorant and simple-natured people. These cunning shopkeepers deceive the people through various kinds of coquetry and blandishments. Some through the mere dress of Faqir, some through Sufistic appearance and bearing, some through mere chitchat (e.g., Sufistic theories and fables and stories of the ancient saints), while some on the strength of their dynastic holiness and pedigree have made a brisk business of being sheikhs and saints. In short, for the construction of the Jerusalem of sainthood, some have set up the lion like skeleton of Suleman, some have dressed it, some have put the staff in his hand to make him stand, some have hung the rosary, some have spread the prayer-carpet in front of him to give the appearance of the living Suleman, and so like the captive jinn, the plain, simple-hearted, and credulous seekers should render wholehearted services in the construction of this visionary Jerusalem. The blind-hearted people take the dead corpse of sainthood for the living Suleman and serve it with their hearts and souls day and night. When by passage of time the staff of sainthood is devoured by white ants and the lifeless Suleman of bones falls down, then do these foolish jinn begin to realize at last that they have been wasting their precious lives in obeying a spiritless and soulless Suleman. Then these plain, simple-natured jinn find freedom from this chain of deception of subjection.

در جامهٔ صوف بستهٔ زُنّار، چه شُود   در صومعه رفته دل به بازار، چه شُود

آزار کساں راحتِ خود ے طلبی   یک راحت و صد هزار آزار، چه شُود

(ابوالقاسم رافعی نیشاپُوری)

What good is trying an infidel's thread under the garment of coarse cloth of sainthood? What good is going to the monastery and thinking of the market? You are seeking your comfort in the pain of others. What good is a single comfort and a thousand pains?

In short, it is a very difficult and hard task to walk safely over this very fine and very dark bridge across the hell of the path and to enter the paradise of proximity and union. In the world, man is engaged in a severe test and difficult examination. Hardly one magnanimous and fortunate seeker out of millions sweeps away the ball of precedence from this ground.

MEN OF THE PAST AND PRESENT

The Western education and new light has spread the poison of heresy and materialism in the hearts of many people of today. People altogether disacknowledge the existence of God the Most High and disbelieve in the Day of Judgment, assembling and reviving, reward and retribution, paradise and hell, angels and spirits, in short, all the invisible creation and life after death. They think that the world exists from ancient times and will continue to do so. There is no end to the material world. There is an inherent and particular power in matter to gradually evolve vegetables out of minerals, animals out of vegetables, and men out of animals. They support Darwin's theory of evolution. Their geologists adduce a few intellectual arguments and some scientific experiments and observations in support of this theory. They think that monkeys and apes have progressed into man and that the first advanced ape was called, God forbid, Adam (p.b.u.h.). They vigorously advance arguments in proof of this theory. These people have squandered away their natural human faculty and lost that bright capacity on account of their slothfulness and misdeeds. Virtually and morally, they have fallen down from the high rank of humanity into the lowest hell of animalism and apeism. Says the Most High:

$$ أُوْلَٰٓئِكَ كَٱلْأَنْعَامِ بَلْ هُمْ أَضَلُّ \quad (الاعراف:١٦٩) $$

"They are like animals—nay they are even worse."

On the strength of the absurd, baseless, and ridiculous theory of evolution of their leader Darwin, the ape-minded people consider themselves great philosophers, sages, and statesmen and consider the ancients as simpletons, superstitious, and ignorant. The theory of evolution is not a result of the intellectual modernity and literary hairsplittings of this age. Materialists and naturalists have inhabited the world from the beginning up to now. The munificent Quran thus repeats this famous saying of the atheists of the time that they also used to say, "None but the world kills us" (i.e., the world creates, keeps, and kills us independently). The atheists think that the people of the earlier times used to dwell in mountainous caves and hollows of trees like savage animals, and they lived naked or covered themselves with the leaves of trees and skins of animals. Just as they were unaware of material industry and craftsmanship and material arts and sciences, they were simple, unintelligent, superstitious, ignorant, and foolish. Religion and spiritualism are the mental invention and the congregation of the self-made, incorrect, and imaginary thoughts of that superstitious and ignorant age.

Remember, that from the very first day, God has cast human nature in a special mold. The physical construction of man has been uniformed from the beginning of creation up to now. There has been no change in human limbs, energies, and senses. Because from the mummy corpses of the Pharaohs of Egypt (who died three or four thousand years ago) discovered from the pyramids of Egypt, it has been proved that they were of the same type as we are. There is no difference between the types of men of that age and today. Similarly, the human heart and brain have been the same from the beginning of creation. But there certainly has been this much difference that, just as the creation and nature of a child is according to the Islamic faith, similarly the state of childhood of the age (i.e., the primary age of the ancients because of its consonance and conformity with the nature of religion— was naturally more inclined toward religion and spiritualism. Therefore, instead of the temporary and superficial sciences and arts of matter, the ancients naturally turned toward the real and essential knowledge and sciences of religion and spiritualism. Because God the Most High has placed only one heart and brain in the human trunk as Allah the Most High says:

$$\text{مَا جَعَلَ اللّٰهُ لِرَجُلٍ مِّنْ قَلْبَيْنِ فِيْ جَوْفِهٖ } \left(\text{١٣٣ الاحزاب:٣}\right)$$

"Allah did not place two hearts in the human trunk," so that he may be able to think of two things or acquire two sciences simultaneously.

The two opposite phases of the religious and physical sciences, the mixture of the body and the spirit, naturally create for man a complexity and entanglement that it is impossible for him to deal with at the same time. If he attends to one, the other remains unaccomplished. In ancient times, the necessary sciences of religion and spiritualism had taken hold of the hearts and brains of people, and they thought of a single Creator, who had rendered them needless of the superficial sciences of matter. They were so engrossed in the desire and love of God the Most High that they had absolutely no time for attending to material progress. They were busy with the original matter (i.e., religion and spiritualism). They had no mind for the short-lived and temporary material arts and sciences. Else from the beginning of creation, Man—the carrier of the burden of the trust and the true caliph of God the Most High—has been a wonderful thing. Every time that he charged the horses of practical and theoretical resolution in the exoteric and esoteric ground of the invisible and visible worlds, he displayed a perfection that astonished the angels. Instead of the skin of matter, that is, the temporary superficial sciences, the ancients had turned their faces toward the marrow of sciences and the root of arts—religion and spiritualism. Just as the cash-loving, unpremeditating, exoteric-sighted Europeans have devoted their lives and entire energies toward finding the details of matter and superficial sciences and progressing therein, flying at the highest heaven of matter, farsighted intelligent ancients of the primitive age, which was in harmony with nature, had applied their hearts and brains in the solitary use and essential object of life and the only essential goal of human existence (i.e., the gnosis, proximity, and acquisition of their True Creator). In order to find leisure in time for this essential and original business, the ancients paid very little heed toward the exoteric material sciences, so much so that the Lawgiver of Islam (on him be salutations) has reprimanded pondering material, visible, unimportant, perplexing wonders and lengthy philosophical dogmas. It is said in a noble tradition,

> When the nature, rotation, or lucky and unlucky effects of the sun, moon, and stars are discussed in your presence, you should adopt silence. If there starts a discussion about the theory of predestination, you should absolutely desist from pondering over and discussing it. Or whenever there is a conversation about the quarrels or the household differences of my companions about the caliphate or their superiority and inferiority etc., you should avoid those discussions.

Instead of these unnecessary sciences, you should acquire the mother science and origin of science (i.e., the key of commemoration of Allah) with which you will open the gates of all the esoteric and exoteric sciences, and all the sciences and secrets of the world will be revealed to you." Says He of honorable commemoration:

وَمَنْ يَّعْتَصِمْ بِاللّٰهِ فَقَدْ هُدِيَ اِلٰى صِرَاطٍ مُّسْتَقِيْمٍ ۞ (٣ آل عمران:١٠١)

"Whoever strongly clutched the name of Allah found guidance towards the right path."

The eye of the heart should be lighted with the gnosis of an essence comprising all the attributes that through knowing all the unknown become known, the unheard becomes heard, and the unseen becomes seen; the figures of the guarded table (لوح محفوظ) get impressed on the glass of the heart; the great secret of life and the ancient mystery of the unknown is revealed because there are countless faculties of superficial sciences in the visible world of plurality. The chain of exoteric science is very long without an end and is unperishable, but human life in this world of decay is very short.

آنچه ضروری است بدان تغل گیر علم کثیر آمد و عمرت قصیر
(قرة العین طاهره)

Art is long, and life is short. Engage in what is essential.

Therefore, far-sighted and wise is the man who adopts the real and essential business and avoids the unessential, temporary, and perishable ones.

هر چه گیرد مختصر گیرد کار دنیا درازئ دارد

"Long is the business of life. So be brief in everything."

Therefore, from the very first day, instead of sweeping matter, Islam has directed man toward his real spiritual work (i.e., in observation of the created and matter, he has been reminded of the Creator, and in the craft of the universe, he has been made to picture the real artisan). Says the Most High,:

اِنَّ فِىْ خَلْقِ السَّمٰوٰتِ وَالْاَرْضِ وَاخْتِلَافِ الَّيْلِ وَالنَّهَارِ لَاٰيٰتٍ لِّاُولِى الْاَلْبَابِ ۞ الَّذِيْنَ

يَذْكُرُوْنَ اللّٰهَ قِيٰمًا وَّقُعُوْدًا وَّعَلٰى جُنُوْبِهِمْ وَيَتَفَكَّرُوْنَ فِىْ خَلْقِ السَّمٰوٰتِ وَالْاَرْضِ ۚ رَبَّنَا مَا خَلَقْتَ هٰذَا بَاطِلًا ۚ سُبْحٰنَكَ فَقِنَا عَذَابَ النَّارِ ۩ (٣ اٰل عمران: ١٩٠-١٩١)

Verily in the creations of the skies and earth and the changes of day and night there are signs for the intellectuals who remember God while standing, sitting and sleeping and think over the creation of the skies and earth and say: O our Lord! Thou hasn't created all this in vain; praise be to you. Save us from the chastisement of fire.

In short, Islam has set mankind on the real and true object of life (i.e., worship and gnosis of the Lord). The pure teaching of Islam has delivered mankind from the darkness of material sciences and directed him toward the supreme worship, gnosis, proximity, affection and love, union, and existence with the roots of the sciences and cause of causes, lord of the lords, the first, the last, the exoteric, the esoteric, the knower of the invisible and visible, Creator of the earth and heavens (i.e., the single, pure essence of God the Most High (الله بس ماسوى الله هوس). God is great. All else is greed. Says the Most High, "Tell them there is Allah, then let them play wherever they like."

When concentration on His personal name, Allah, becomes firmly fixed in the heart of the seekers, the heart and the brain of the concentrator are dyed in the color of Allah. Then he sees the Painter in every painting, and in every piece of art, he sees the form of the Artisan; the universe becomes his Holy Quran, and the created thing becomes a visible sign to him.

The materialistic fools think that the former people were ignorant, simpletons, superstitious, and unaware of the material sciences and arts. If the modern geologists discover the stone instruments and crude utensils of the people of ancient times in some mountain caves, it does not mean that all the people of that time similarly lived in caves. Do not some wild people live in mountain caves in the advanced and civilized world of today? Now, if in these mountain caves and underground chambers, they find old-fashioned utensils and instruments, these must be the things used by some wild people of the time and not by the civilized people of that age. Because archeologists have found the remains of high-class industries and manufactured goods of the time to which these crude instruments and utensils are attributed. They are surprised on finding the very fine and excellent instruments and things of that time. To sum up, in the realm of science and art in spite of the religious and spiritual engagements, the truthful and pious people of that time in no way lagged behind the modern, ambitious, childish, and sensualist people of today. If we probe into the reality, we find that all the modern materialists are progressing in all sorts of sciences, manufacturing, and trade on the foundations and principles set up by the ancients because it is difficult to set up the foundations of new science, but it is quite easy to develop it up. The standard works of the ancients on the different sciences and arts clearly indicate their mental superiority and excellence of intelligence and understanding. The modern people are their plagiarists (خوشه چین).

Readers have read of the intellectual perfections in regard to sciences, arts, manufacturing, and industries, as a sample of the whole. The standard of morality of the ancients was so high and excellent that supposing the ancients and the moderns are made to stand in spacious grounds, stripped naked of their physical dress, and displayed in the esoteric form of moral acts, as will be the case on the Day of Judgment, the ancients will appear as angels, and the moderns will appear in the form of beasts and savages. As God the Most High says, "They are like animals; nay even worse." In short, one should not be misled by the external appearances of a person. Material beauty, glittering garments, external appearances, and the worldly beauty of the features are unreliable. Material intellect, external wisdom, worldly pomp and show, rank, and glory are nothing. Many a time, many a destitute, dusty, disheveled, shabbily garbed dervish, which your external seeing eyes contemptuously spurn, is esoterically very civilized, handsome, wise, independent, and well-to-do in the eyes of God. Not only that, but some of them are amirs, chiefs, and crownless kings of the time.

خاکساران جہاں را بحقارت مہ نگر

تو چہ دانی کہ دریں گرد سوارے باشد

(اقبالؒ)

"Don't despise the humble ones of the world. There may be a rider in the dust—who knows?" Different is the esoteric eye, which can see the real esoteric figures of persons and can differentiate between the true and real king and the puppet.

مرد آں باشد کہ باشد شہ شناس

ے نشاسد شاہ را در ہر لباس

He is a man who can recognise a king; and recognise him in every dress."

Contrarily, you may see a person, very richly dressed, possessing comely features and a commanding personality, unequalled by anyone in worldly riches and outward pomp and show; in worldly and material wisdom, he may be a Plato and Galen of the time, but morally, religiously, and spiritually, he may prove to be a brainless brute and a bloody beast. From the worldly aspect, he may be very respectable and honorable, but his rank with God the Most High may be less than that of a louse and fly. In short, the outward appearance, worldly status, and material intellect of a man is nothing. The esoteric figure of the morality, religious status, and spiritual understanding is a different thing. The Holy Prophet (p.b.u.h.) has therefore said, "Simple-minded people shall abide in Paradise (i.e., most of the dwellers of the Paradise will be the people whose hands are short of the devilry and cleverness of worldly intellect; who would give no consideration and importance to worldly riches and pay no heed to its profit and loss." His Holiness the Prophet (p.b.u.h.) has been called "illiterate" because he was unfamiliar with the Satanic knowledge of wealth and tricks of acquiring it. From the point of view of worldly intellect, most of the wealthy, crooked, and philosophical heretical kafirs used to call the simple-natured, truthful, clean-hearted Musalmans believing in prophets as idiots, unintelligent, and ignorant. As God the Most High says, the "infidels, used to say, should we believe as these foolish people have believed?" In response to them, Allah says, "Beware! These infidels who pride at worldly riches and material intellect are themselves foolish and mean but they do not know it." So high was the standard of morality of the ancient pious men that the wealthy, rich men and kings of that time were more pious, God-fearing, chaste, abstinent, and devoted than the Sufis and sheikhs of this later age.

At the death of His Holiness Khwaja Qutb-ud-din Bakhtyar Kakai Aushi, it was proclaimed with his testament that his burial prayers should be led by one who has never in his life missed the first takbir (تکبیراولیٰ) and sunnats of the afternoon. The readers will find it difficult to believe that the person who could lead the burial prayers in accordance with the testament of that distinguished personage was not a learned scholar, a God-fearing and abstinent Sufi dervish, a pedigreed Sayid, or a Qureshi, but Sultan Shamsud-din Altamish. The ruler of the vast tract of India turned out to be the one to lead the burial prayers. Emperor Aurangzeb (p.b.u.h.) and Sultan Nasir-ud-din transcribed the Holy Quran for fifty-two and nineteen years of their reigns respectively. That is to say that for seventy-one years, India witnessed the spectacles of the transcription of the holy Quran over the royal throne and under the royal umbrella. This relates to kings of a period who were most entangled in worldly connections, drowned from top to toe in worldly affairs, and bound down in national and political strife. From this, you can guess the high standard of life, of the pious, good-natured dervishes and faqirs of that age. It will require a separate volume were we to reproduce examples of their pure morals and commendable manners. In short, we have already stated that in spite of esoteric, religious, and spiritual engagements, the ancient pious people were in no way inferior to the modern nations in any science or art. The Taj Mahal at Agra, the pyramids of Egypt, the Palace of Jamshed, the Peacock Throne, and the Great Wall of China bear witness to the height of the magnanimity and the power of perfection of manufacture and industry of the ancient people. The scientists of the present age were highly astonished to find the mummies recovered from the pyramids of Egypt (where they were buried three to four thousand years ago) so well preserved after the lapse of such a long time. They believed that these were not the real bodies of the pharaohs of Egypt but idols cast from some minerals. But when through all chemical actions and scientific experiments, they were found out to be the true bodies, their astonishment knew no bounds. Up to the present day, they cannot explain the secret and mystery of the chemicals and process and art through which these bodies have been preserved up to the present day because modern scientists and chemists have only two things for preserving such objects for a long time, ice and spirit. Now it is apparent that the people of three to four thousand years back, whom they call savage, jungle dwellers, and foolish were much more advanced in all sorts of sciences and arts than the so-called civilized, wise, and broad-minded people of today. Can the modern age produce equals and examples of the ancient people, such as Avicenna, Plato, Galen, Aristotle, Rhazes, Imam Ghazali (R.A), Sa'di (R.A), Hafiz Shirazi, Firdosi, Maulana Rum, and so on, in medicine, logic, poetry, astronomy, philosophy, arithmetic, prosody, and other exoteric sciences? All the wise sayings; proverbs; nice and famous poems; moral, religious, and spiritual rules and regulations prevalent in the civilized worlds up to the present day are the production of the bright-minded people of the ancient age!

The observations and experiments of mesmerism, hypnotism, animal magnetism, and spiritualism have proved that there is a tremendous spiritual and esoteric power in man, which if properly practiced and developed can enable a man to perform such perplexing and astonishing feats in the material world that render speechless great sages, philosophers, and materialist wise men. Science and philosophy are deaf and dumb to explain them. In the phraseology of the ancient mystics, these spiritual powers are called extraordinary things and miracles. The uncommon, unnatural, and unusual powers of this nature are of two kinds: (1) celestial and (2) terrestrial. Since the miracles of the celestial powers are manifested through the celestial and invisible creation, angels, and holy spirits, we will explain them at some other time. We will produce here as an example three-hundred-year-old standard historical evidence of the terrestrial but very rare perplexing and astonishing feats that cannot be refuted at all. From this, a sound-minded and just person can guess the reach of the esoteric sciences and spiritual powers of the ancients. History bears evidence that the world is still astonished at the feats displayed by some jugglers and magicians of Bengal in the court of Jahangir. The most wonderful of these is the rope trick, which still perplexed and surprised the Europeans.[2]

---

[2] This fact is thus narrated in the *Memoirs* of Jahangir composed by the emperor himself in his lifetime. Some Bengali jugglers came to the court of the Emperor Jahangir. Besides the wonderful feats, the rope trick was unparalleled. Here are the details. A magician came forward, paid homage to the emperor, and submitted, "Your Majesty, an enemy of mine has ascended to heaven. I will fix a ladder and go to fight him there. God willing, I will kill him and return victorious."

Seating a beautiful young girl near the emperor's throne, he said, "This is my beautiful, beloved wife. I entrust her to Your Majesty. Your Majesty may keep her safe until my return." Then standing in the open, the magician threw a rope toward the heaven, so that its end could not be seen. It was suspended in the air. Arming himself, the magician went up the rope like a ladder and disappeared from the eyes of the spectators. After a while, the rope began to move. Later on, a stream of blood flowed down it from heaven's side. The spectators were eagerly watching the strange movements of the rope and the flow of blood from it when suddenly the amputated and the groaning hands, feet, and all other parts of the magician successively fell from heaven onto the ground near the rope. Lastly, his head crashed onto the ground. At this, the wife of the magician, who was sitting near the emperor's chair, cried and rose up. Coming to the dead body, she said, "This is the corpse of my husband. The enemy has killed him in heaven, cut him into pieces, and thrown him down." Addressing the magicians of her clan, she said, "Provide fuel. I will burn myself alive with my dear husband." The magicians forthwith gathered fuel and prepared a pyre. The king, his ministers, and peers stopped them at length to desist from doing so, but the magicians placed the woman on the pyre and set it on fire. The pyre and the woman burned into a heap of ashes.

At the sight of this awful scene, the king and the spectators were sitting breathless in amazement when the magician appeared descending the rope above, healthy and armed. Immediately, he came up to Jahangir and addressed him thus, "Your Majesty, through Your Majesty's good fortune and felicity, I have murdered that enemy. The corpse that fell here in pieces belonged to my enemy." Then he demanded his wife of the king, saying, "Please return my wife to me."

The king expressed great regret saying, "She has been burned alive with your corpse by your brethren and companions. We are prepared to pay her blood money."

The blood money was being fixed when the magician's wife came out of the smoldering ashes and standing by the side of her husband, said to the king, "Your Majesty need not take the trouble of the blood money. I am alive and whole and hale." At this wonderful scene, the king, the peers, and ministers burst into applause and richly rewarded the magicians. The spectators also amply rewarded the magicians in cash and the kind. A few years ago, a conference of all the sorcerers, magicians, and jugglers of the world was held in London. It was one of the items on the agenda that the magician who could give a performance of the aforementioned rope trick of the court of the Emperor Jahangir would be awarded a prize of £20,000. All the magicians tried their utmost to get the prize and with the help of science and chemistry provided many instruments in order to give this performance but in vain. From this, you can guess the difference between the scientific and exoteric and esoteric perfections of the moderns and ancients. A look at the record of the spiritual perfections of the modern Negro and jungle nations of Africa collected by European travelers surprises one. Up to the present day, it surprises one to see the effects of the spiritual perfection of the old age in those old nations that are immune from the darkness of this new light and the curse of modern civilization. Human intellect is surprised at the spiritual influence and esoteric perfections of the people of that time attached to the old bones, rosaries, and other instruments and utensils and soulless things recovered from old Egyptian graves and cellars. From this, a sensible person cannot help inferring that when so many

Our object in narrating this true and historic fact (of the rope trick) is this that the esoteric sciences and spiritual powers of the ancients of that time had reached the highest heaven. Just as the people a hundred years ago could not guess the material progress of today, the heretical materialists of today cannot guess the spiritual feats and esoteric perfections of the ancients. How curious that even today, in their places of worship and devotion, the irreligious civilized world eulogizes and praises religious leaders and founders of faith of the olden time and regard it as the means of salvation. God be praised! Willynilly the irreligious West is so proud of its material powers, it obeys the superiority of their Israelite prophets. The European churches echo with the songs of their praises day and night. So the spiritual claws of the former people have gripped the hearts of the materialist people of today and fastened them to chains of subjugation esoterically. But they do not know how these esoteric strings fell on their necks. They want to get out of them but cannot. Just as in respect of material power and outward strength, an elephant is more powerful than man, but through intelligence and education, man has subjugated and empowered animals stronger than himself and makes use of them similarly, however wise and clever the dead-hearted and sensualist people may be in respect of material intellect and outward knowledge, before men of esoteric knowledge and spiritual powers, they are like animals whom they hold by the esoteric hair of their heads with hands of light. Saysthe Most High:

$$مَا مِنْ دَآبَّةٍ إِلَّا هُوَ اخِذٌ بِنَاصِيَتِهَا \quad (الهود:٥٦)$$

"There isn't an animal on the earth. But he has caught it by hair on the forehead."

Just as animals are caught by their horns, or hair on the forehead and led wherever desired, men of angelic spiritual powers easily catch hold of the mental hairs of those materialist animals and lead them wherever they like.

Though scientific and material progress is taking Europe to the high roof of heaven today, moral and religious negligence is

---

spiritual powers are attached to these soulless solid objects of the ancients, how great must be their own powers.

dragging it posthaste to the lowest strata of sensual darkness, sex, passionate negligence, and ignorance. Instead of taking pride in over their material progress, they ought to mourn the loss of their spiritualism. If material and political supremacy is elevating them one yard, spiritual ignorance is pressing them miles below. Though Europe of today is a sample of Shaddad's paradise on account of material luxuries and worldly fabulence, morally and spiritually, it is a most destitute, poor, and faminestricken land. Though there is great abundance of material riches and outward victuals there, esoteric food and spiritual meals, commemoration, meditation, devotion, and divine worship are scarce, like the phoenix, there. Everywhere, dancing and singing parties are afoot day and night. There are drinking bouts. There is an abundance of adultery, immorality, debauchery, and sin. Wine and pork are the common drink and food. They are sitting with ladies in one arm and dogs in the other. Satanic merrymaking and sensual playfulness is the only occupation there. Who has the guts to take the name of Allah in the face of this superabundance of the ignorance of the ignorant and Satanic passions? The day that the world has walked toward the material progress and worldly advancement and entirely turned its face in that direction has marked the commencement of the moral, religious, and spiritual degradation. Men are turning unmindful of the essential, true, and real side of religion, so much so that though the world, today, has reached the highest heaven of material progress, it has fallen in the lowest hell of spiritual and moral degeneration.

صفائیاں جتنی ہو رہی ہیں دل اتنے ہی ہو رہے ہیں میلے

اندھیرا چھاجائے گا جہاں پر اگر یہی روشنی رہے گی

(محمد اسمٰعیل میرٹھی)

The more the cleanliness the dirtier the hearts. Darkness will overtake the world if this light persists.

Alas! The materialists are spending time in the detail of physical sciences and wasting their precious lives to the entire neglect of spiritual science. The hobby of amassing the means of enriching the brief worldly life is indispensable to them, but absolutely no attention is being paid to the acquisition of eternal life and the brilliant esoteric wealth. Utmost arrangements are made for decorating and furnishing the spider's web, but no care is paid to the world of the hierarchy of angels.

چند در فکرِ سرائے و غم منزل باشی
گذرد قافلهٔ عمرو تو غافل باشی

کعبه در گام نخستیں کند استقبالت
از سرِ صدق اگر ہم سفرِ دل باشی

گر در آرائش ظاہر دگراں مے کوشند
تو درآں کوش کہ فرخندہ شمائل باشی

کشتئ تن بشکن چند دریں قلزمِ خوں
تختۂ مشق صد اندیشهٔ باطل باشی

(فیضی)

"How long would you worry about a material house and worldly abode? The caravan of life goes on, and you are slothful. Ka'ba will welcome you on the very first step. If you sincerely accompany the heart in travel, let others strive in decorating the outward form, but you should strive in that which will make you of lovable character. Break the boat of the body; in this sea of blood, how long would you be prey to a hundred false ideas?"

Let the Europeans measure the summits of the mountains and depths of oceans; examine the mouths, depths, lengths, and breadths of rivers; find out the vicissitudes of the seasons by constructing underground stations in the North and South Poles; subdue fire, air, water, and earth; and make merry at the idea of reaching the stars through rockets. May they enjoy this material dust-play. Tidings to you, O martyrs of coquetry blandishments and oppressions of love that, for your object and ambition you have the Greatest Sun of the light of beauty and glory, an atom of whose light has illuminated the sun and moon, who gives colors and smell to the flowers, to whose generosities the lips of the beauties of the world we their smiles, the Omnigood, Omniscient, All-seeing, All-light, soul of beauty and comeliness (i.e., the Praised Truth is your object and goal). Auspicious are the august persons through whose blessed personalities the rains pour from the heavens, the earth bears fruits, and various kinds of calamities and misfortunes are warded off from the earth. Great adventures of the world are achieved through a single moving of their eyebrows. One movement of their esoteric hands upsets the crowns and thrones of kings. Half a blandishment of their kindness bestows crowns and scepters on destitute beggars. They are seen to be unemployed because they are the crownless kings of the eternal universe. The greater a man in the world, the lesser his occupation. Kings always pass on hints and are not supposed to work assiduously day and night, like ordinary employees. Though ostensibly, these people appear to be destitute and unprovisioned, but esoterically, they are the real masters of the world. The true lovers of God are the real model of the following verse:

سی پارهٔ کلام و حدیثِ پیمبری — نانِ جوین و خرقهٔ پشمین و آب شور

در دیں نه لغو بو علی و ژاژ عنصری — ہم نسخهٔ دو چار نعلمے کہ نافع است

بیہودہ ہمتے نہ بُرد شمع خاوری — تاریک کلبہ کہ پے روشنیٔ آں

در پیش چشم ہمت شاں ملک سنجری — بایک دو آشنا کہ نیر زدہ نیم جو

جویائے تخت قیصر و ملک سکندری — ایں آں سعادت است کہ حسرت برد بر آں

For a pious, godly saint, dry barely bread to eat, a coarse woolen garment to wear, a simple draft of water to drink, thirty parts of the Holy Quran with some traditions of the Holy Prophet to read, three or four beneficial religious books to study instead of useless gabblings of Bu Ali Sina and meaningless pratings of Ansary, a dark cabin independent of even of the light of sun to live in, and one or two godly companions in whose supreme sight the kingdom of Sunjar weighs and values not even a single barley are such a grand esoteric wealth that invites the envy of one who seeks the throne of Qaisar and the kingdom of Alexander.

Modern Schools and Colleges Are Spiritual Butcheries

Alas, the spiritual sciences and esoteric arts have disappeared from the world and the spiritual doctors, heart healers of esoteric diseases, have left the world. It is a scene of "Islam in books and Muslims in graves."

The doors of theological education and spiritual instruction are closed. What are the modern schools and colleges? These are butcheries of human nature and religious conscience where thousands of innocent herds of human hearts are sacrificed before the Kali Devi of heresy and infidelity and innumerable pure souls are sacrificed at the threshold of the goddess of materialism and irreligiousness. Ostensibly, they are acquiring education, but actually, they are being butchered esoterically.

As says God the Most High:

$$وَلَا تَقْتُلُوٓا اَوْلَادَكُمْ خَشْيَةَ اِمْلَاقٍ ۗ نَحْنُ نَرْزُقُهُمْ وَاِيَّاكُمْ ۚ اِنَّ قَتْلَهُمْ كَانَ خِطْاً كَبِيْرًا ۝$$

(بنی اسرآئیل:۳۱)

"Don't murder your children for the fear of livelihood. We provide them and you. Verily murdering them is a major offense." Remember that this verse means that many people impart worldly education to their children instead of religious instruction because they see no chance of acquiring worldly riches through religious education. By admitting them into schools and colleges, the parents hope that the boys will capture some posts and earn freely. The old interpretation of this verse that the Arab infidels of yore time used to bury their daughters alive or kill them is unadoptable here, because they did so out of sheer disgrace and fear of someone becoming their son-in-law, not out of fear of hunger and poverty. This has been thus mentioned in another place,

$$وَاِذَا الْمَوْءٗدَةُ سُئِلَتْ ۝ بِاَيِّ ذَنْبٍ قُتِلَتْ ۝ (التكوير:۸-۹)$$

"And when the alive-buried daughters are asked for what sin they were killed." In short, there are many people who get their innocent children admitted in school out of fear of starvation and poverty, kill them with their own hands esoterically, and destroy their religious nature and capability. How well the late Akbar has expressed this idea in a verses:

یوں قتل سے بچوں کے وہ بدنام نہ ہوتا

افسوس کہ فرعون کو کالج کی نہ سوجھی

"He would not have been thus defamed of slaughtering children. Alas that Pharaoh did not think of opening a college."

Are these colleges or mints of heresy and atheism, where after mingling the alloy of irreligiousness and immorality with the pure gold of conscience and nature, the seals of heresy and atheism are impressed on the clear tablets of human hearts and the current coins, minted according to Western customs and values and fixed according to vocations? Thus hundreds of Josephs are sold for these counterfeit coins. That is why people have lost their religious mentality. If rarely religious conscience is to be found somewhere in the world, Western education or European civilization has disfigured and frustrated it. From the religious and spiritual points of view, most of the hearts are without any sense of religion. The few confined hearts that are partially alive are involved in very serious esoteric maladies. The effect of these manifests in the hearts of these people in the form of serious heretical thoughts, atheistic misgivings, and objections. Now there are no doctors of hearts and spirits in the world. Most of them are unaware of their sickness. Now who can treat a patient who considers himself hale and healthy? By way of example, we will quote here some of the materialistic suspicious and heretical thoughts that have spread in the world as a result of Western education and have polluted and poisoned almost all the religious world: There are some who altogether deny the existence of God by saying how can we believe in an intangible God and his invisible actions? How can we know and believe in an incomprehensible God? They are blind of heart. It is impossible to make a born blind understand sunlight and the color of things.

Some of them are political heretics and are overpowered by the political devil. The devil put it in their heads that religions and faiths have been devised for man's existence, worldly betterment, economical and political progress, and reformation of civilization, culture, and society. All the religious leaders (e.g., the prophets, saints, and so on) of former times have been mere worldly reformers and political leaders of their nations in their time. Through intellectual intelligence, they invented religions for the sole object of the worldly reformations and political advancement of that age and have been leading like children the simple-hearted peoples of those times on the by-paths of religion and roads of religious dogmas with the desire of imaginary pleasures of paradise and the whimsical fears of hell. The bounties of paradise, houries, and palaces were mere children's consolation and mazes, and the chastisement of hell was a mere imaginary scarecrow created for the simple and superstitious brains of that time. The real object and end in view was the present paradise of political advancement and territorial conquest. The independent and victorious nations enjoy here peace and comfort and indulge in luxury in the paradise of governments and kingdoms.

The subjugated and vanquished nations are bearing torture and pain in the hell of slavery and degradation, destitution, and poverty. This is the only import of religion. There is no other paradise or hell, life after death, settlement of accounts, reward, or retribution. (In vindication of this political infidelity and worldly good, they also utter the following fallacious thoughts and absurdities that all these outward rules of religious law and fundamentals of religion have been devised for worldly progress and political advancement. Every order of religious law and fundamental of religion embodies some secret of worldly good and political advancement. For example, the Confession of Faith is a formal manifestation of national unity. Prayers and fasts of the month of Ramadan are a practice of self-negation and ethics (i.e., the practice of habituating the self to hunger and thirst and controlling passions and desires to be availed of at the time of the shortage of provisions during battles). Congregational prayers denote the obedience of the commander. Prayers are a sort of military parade and exercise. Ablutions merely mean cleanliness. Mosques are five-timely assemblies, for consultation and exchange of ideas for political congregations, worldly affairs, and worldly reformations. They think that all the scholars, learned men of yore, pious men of after times, leaders of the firm faith, expounders of traditions, and all juris consults and commentators have erred in understanding the real object and meaning of the Quran and traditions and that what we have understood is the real object of religion.

"One ought to lament at this intelligence and wisdom." In short, these people think that some material and political profit lies at the root of all the religious fundamentals and laws. Some blind heretics thus interpret prophethood, messengership, and the reality of revelation: The prophets and messengers were sympathetic leaders and well-wishing reformers of their nations who naturally possessed emotions and feelings of betterment and sympathies for their nations. On account of the excess of those emotions and feelings, they were predominated by such thoughts. During the predominance of those thoughts, their imaginative powers accumulated some topics so that under the excess of that predomination, they also heard some sound or other that they call revelation. Sometimes, some imaginary form also appeared to them, which they called angel; though outwardly, there used to be no such invisible form or angel. These were the imaginary creations of their natural imaginary powers. In short, these fools think that the prophets were either cheats or cheated. They regard the revelation, inspiration, and miracles of all the prophets, messengers, and perfect saints as the creation of the excess of their imaginations and consider themselves great philosophers and wise statesmen.

سُبْحٰنَهٗ وَتَعٰلٰى عَمَّا يَقُوْلُوْنَ عُلُوًّا كَبِيْرًا ۝ (بنی اسرائیل: ۴۳)

"God be praised! He is Most High of what they allege."

The infidels of the modern age think religions are the outcome of the Dark Ages, while now it is the age of enlightenment and science. The old religions and the ancient methods befitted the old superstitious age and should perish with that age. Now, by the Grace of God, the world is far advanced. The old religions and ancient methods are incompetent to control the present civilized and alert age and to put it on the highway of progress. Hence, there is need for new reformers and novel fashions. To piss, while standing, continuously emit smoke from the mouth while standing and sitting, whistle, dance in mirthfulness, and sport like monkeys and jump like frogs are the signs of civilization and indications of progression.

اب نظر آتی نہیں ہے مسجدوں کے فرش پر

قوم نے اتنی ترقی کی کہ پہنچی عرش پر

(اکبر الہ آبادی)

"Now, it can't be seen on the floor of mosques. The nation has progressed so much that it reached heaven."

If religion and ethics are mentioned to them, they retort that "these people wish to push us back to the old, rotten, and antiquated age." The world has progressed much now.

Some people deny the miracles of all the prophets and the supernatural powers of all the saints and assert that the laws of nature are unchangeable, and there is no cause or invisible mover or actor besides the chain of causes and effects that we perceive in the world. The world consists merely of the universe of causation sensed and felt within the ambit of senses. There can be no change in the nature of things. The sun comes out in the east, the fire burns, and water flows toward the slope. In support of their atheism and materialism, they quote this verse: "The nature of things does not change

$$\text{لَا تَبْدِيْلَ لِخَلْقِ اللّٰهِ} \quad (٣٠ : الروم ٣٠)$$

," which we have explained, saying that here "nature" means "religious nature" and that the wordscan never mean that the nature of matter cannot be changed. On the contrary, we observe that matter changes every moment, and the nature of things changes constantly. It is also incorrect that nothing can happen against the law of nature. Nay! God the Most High has power over everything. He is not subordinate to His own laws. How can He be a God if He is subject to rules and regulations made by Himself? In that case, matter and its laws and regulations could have their own way in the universe. "God is beyond comprehension and imagination. How can the comprehensible be God?"

In cases of emergency, the fleeting national governments of this world can also now and then frame ordinances against the law. It is impossible to keep Allah the Most High, the Ruler of rulers, who acts how He likes, subject to His own law. God the Most High clearly expresses in His own pure book:

$$\text{يَمْحُوا اللّٰهُ مَا يَشَآءُ وَيُثْبِتُ ۖ وَعِنْدَهٗ أُمُّ الْكِتٰبِ} \quad (١١٣ : الرعد ٣٩)$$

"God erases (from the guarded tablet) (لوح محفوظ) what He likes and keeps firm and established what He likes. He has the mother book of knowledge." It is an established principle that

$$\text{يَفْعَلُ مَا يُرِيْدُ} \quad (١٢ : البقرة ٢٥٣) \qquad \text{يَحْكُمُ مَا يُرِيْدُ} \quad (٥ : المآئدة ١)$$

"He acts what He likes and orders what He intends" (i.e., God the Most High does what He likes and orders the fulfillment of what He desires; none can thwart Him).

"The commandment changes but the knowledge does not" (i.e., the mandate of Allah changes, but his knowledge does not). However, knowledge can change the order. For example, water flows toward the slope, but through the knowledge of the pump and fountain, water can be taken from below upward. Similarly, all other orders can be changed. In another place, God the Most High says,

وَاللّٰهُ غَالِبٌ عَلٰى اَمْرِهٖ وَلٰكِنَّ اَكْثَرَ النَّاسِ لَا يَعْلَمُوْنَ ۝ (۱۲ یوسف:۲۱)

Again, it is explicitly laid down. God the Most High has power over every order (and law of His and has the power to change it), but many people do not know this." Moreover, if you see carefully the rise and fall, change and transformation, and exceptions to all principles and rules, they clearly indicate the powerfulness of this authority and excess of command, and nothing takes place in accordance with our conjecture and expectations. No true opinion can be formed about the occurrence of a thing. However, the hand of the omnipotence is working inside the sleeve of causation, and it generally works behind the curtain of causes. But sometimes, in cases of emergency, Omnipotence tucks up or removes the sleeves of causes and begins to work nakedly. Thus, the miracles of the prophets (p.b.u.t.) and the miraculous powers and extraordinary habits of the benevolent saints are merely the wonders of the uncovered hands of Omnipotence and are, so to say, ordinances against the established law to meet the demands of momentary emergencies. The foolish, sensual, and blind people whose looks are confined to material causes and who, like the frog in a well, consider the material well to be the whole universe, cannot understand the supernatural and unusual deeds of the Omnipotence. To bring them in consonance and harmony with their own material intellect and conjecture, they effect curious changes and high, unlawful interpretations in the meaning and imports of those verses of the Quran where mention is made of such supernatural and unimaginable miracles. We think these blind people excusable and helpless.

کہ نکتہ داں نشود کرم گر کتاب خورد   زاہل مدرسہ اسرار معرفت مطلب

"Don't inquire the mysteries of gnosis from a scholar. Because a worm cannot become a scholar by eating a book."

خدا ہے دور حدِ دوربیں سے   نہیں ہے سائنس واقف کار دیں سے

"Science is not acquainted with religion; God is far from the range of the telescope."

Some people differentiate between religion and politics. They think that religion is confined to worship and beliefs alone. They assert that politics is the relation between men themselves. Religion creates obstacles in worldly and political progress. Hence, they allow it no space in the world of practice. They consider it an imaginary thing. They say that the ultimate aim of religion is to accept and consider God the Most High as One. This we can achieve in imagination. What is then the need for practical and legal obligations? Some say that there arose a need for a change in the mandates and laws within five hundred years from the time of Moses (A.S) to that of Jesus (A.S). But if the same religion and one sort of laws should continue for 1,370 years, it is highly unjust. Some repudiators of prophethood acclaim salvation and say, "The prophets were raised for unification. We also had the orders of the knowledge and practice of the same unification. So the denial of the superfluous is unlawful for one who has achieved the real object. Hence we are Unitarians by belief. Devotion and deeds are various manifestations of the unification and essentials of its wholesomeness. With the attainment of the real object, the need for the means disappears." Thus becoming an embodiment of "they intend to cause separation between God and His messengers," these unfortunate people consider themselves unneedful of the Prophet and his religious laws.

Another section designates itself Ahl-i Quran (people of the Quran). It confines the commandments to the Quran and asserts that the traditions are prone to corruption and hence unreliable. The Quran itself is a perfect thing. In its presence, there is no need for anything else. Interpreting Quranic verses according to their purpose, they become the example of

$$يُضِلُّ بِهِ كَثِيْرًا ١٢) (البقرة:٢٦)$$

"Mislead therewith many." Some repudiate the theological decisions and jurisprudence of religious leaders and call themselves Traditionists (اہل حدیث). Every one of them, according to his own wishes, makes a schism and separate religion for himself out of Quranic versesand traditions, and creates chaos, dissension, and depression in the unity of the established religion and consensus of the followers. Since man, by birth and nature, is quarrelsome, hasty, ease-loving, lazy, and work-shunning, he automatically invents innumerable devices and exercises to get freedom from religious restrictions and to create facilities by making shortcuts. He endeavors to harmonize divine commandments with his own likings and sensual desires by distorting them. These people are slaves of passions and subjects of desire. Says the Most High:

اَفَرَءَيْتَ مَنِ اتَّخَذَ اِلٰهَهٗ هَوٰىهُ وَاَضَلَّهُ اللّٰهُ عَلٰى عِلْمٍ وَّخَتَمَ عَلٰى سَمْعِهٖ وَقَلْبِهٖ وَجَعَلَ عَلٰى بَصَرِهٖ غِشَاوَةً ۚ فَمَنْ يَّهْدِيهِ مِنْ بَعْدِ اللّٰهِ ؕ اَفَلَا تَذَكَّرُوْنَ ۞ (٢٣:الجاثية ٤٥)

"Have you seen the man who made a god of his passions and whom, in spite of his knowledge, Allah has made astray, sealed his ears and heart and put veils over his eye? Who is there who can guide such a person except Allah? Don't you understand?"

To be brief, Western education has rammed down the venom of infidelity and atheism into the hearts and brains of the educated classes. From the religious point of view, most of the hearts are dead. They are devoid of religious feelings, and there can be no hope of bringing them to the right path. The few hearts left behind are entangled in highly fatal diseases, and the doubts and misgivings enumerated earlier have tightly encircled their hearts. Most of them cannot spare any time from worldly and sensual thoughts to give serious consideration to religion and faith and to think what we are after all, why we are so, where we are, whence we have come, and where we are bound to go. They have so completely forgotten the essential, unavoidable, and inevitable journey of death as if they haven't had to face this lengthy, very difficult, soul-languishing, and spirit-failing journey. If perchance the great adventure of death inadvertently comes to the minds of some of them, they brush it aside, saying, "We will see to it when death comes. Why worry beforehand? So many people have gone ahead. If they can manage, we will also do so." In short, through such childish consolations, Satan taps them into the sleep of carelessness and keeps them back from providing for themselves for the journey to the next world. They come to their senses when it is past redress and they are pushed toward the next world empty-handed, destitute, sick, crippled, blind, lame, badly distressed, and afflicted. Then they remorsefully rub their hands, but it is useless to cry over spilt milk.

From the study of our book, some people may think that the object of the book seems to be that a man should renounce all worldly engagements, retire to the jungle, or sit in a corner and remember Allah all his life and remain perpetually lost in the commemoration and concentration of God the Most High. Asceticism seems to be the aim and object of this book, although it is said, "There is no hermitism in Islam." Those are the preachings of Christianity, the followers of which retired to jungles and mountain caves to remember God the Most High (i.e., Jesus (p.b.u.h.) was a man of the caves, whereas our Prophet was a swordsman and fighter). The other nations of the world, especially the Europeans, are soaring to the highest heaven of political and temporal progress, while the Muslims are falling into the ditch of degradation and destitution. Islam stands in need of organization, unity, education, worldly riches, advancement, and political superiority. Alas! Most of our so-called politicians have gone mad after acquiring the worldly wealth, animal pleasures, and sensual joys of Europeans.

And when they find that God and the prophets do not help them in their sensual objects, they are cross at heart and variously scandalize Islam. By writing this book, we never mean that Muslims should retire to jungles and mountains or spend their lives in corners remembering Allah and attend to no worldly affairs. This is an impossibility. But our aim and object in canvassing the Muslims toward commemoration of Allah and the name of Allah is that first and foremost Muslims become really Muslims. Acquiring the light of faith, certainty, and gnosis from the commemoration of Allah and His personal name, Allah, they should imbibe the pious virtues of Islam and qualify themselves with the bright qualities of faith. After this, when they will step into the field of practice with an Islamic grandeur, divine assistance will accompany them in every walk of life and every worldly act. As says God the Most High:

$$\text{(٢٢:المجادلة ١٥٨) أُولَٰئِكَ كَتَبَ فِي قُلُوبِهِمُ الْإِيمَانَ وَأَيَّدَهُمْ بِرُوحٍ مِنْهُ}$$

"Those are the people in whose hearts faith is written down and He helps them with a spirit of His."

Both the worldly and religious, outward and inward, exoteric and esoteric, political and moral, physical and spiritual sides of the lives of such faithful people are highly successful and pleasant. Such a man is the source of untold comforts and blessings for himself and for others, his household and nation—in short, the whole world, here and in the hereafter. Just as at the time of killing an animal it becomes lawful by saying, "God is greatest," similarly, a person becomes clean and pure by the commemoration of Allah and the light of His personal name, Allah, and is truly ennobled and exalted by the degrees of Islam (اسلام), faith (ایمان), certainty (ایقان), gnosis (عرفان), and so on. God never changes the collective condition of a nation unless all its individuals cleanse individually themselves by commemorating Allah and through the name Allah and change the conditions and particulars of their souls for the sake of Allah. As says God the Most High:

$$ اِنَّ اللّٰهَ لَا يُغَيِّرُ مَا بِقَوْمٍ حَتّٰى يُغَيِّرُوا مَا بِاَنْفُسِهِمْ \ (١١:الرعد١٣) $$

"Verily God does not change the condition of a nation unless they change themselves."

Didn't our glorious Master, Muhammad the Chosen (p.b.u.h.), adopt monasticism in the early days of revelation? With a view to cleansing the soul (تزکیه نفس), purifying the heart (تصفیه قلب), brightening the spirit (تجلیه روح), and secluding the secret (تخلیه سر), did he not repeatedly retire to the mountain alone, and did not he retire for weeks together to the cave of Hira for the holy occupation of concentrating on His personal name, Allah? So it is highly incumbent and a great sunnat for every Muslim who is really and truly desirous of becoming a Muslim and faithful believer to completely dye his heart in God's color of His personal name, Allah, at least once in his lifetime and by way of "faith is written in their hearts," impress and write the figure of His personal name, Allah, on the tablet of his heart. After this, if he comes out into the world, divine assistance will help him everywhere and in every act. When every individual of the nation will appear with that dignity, the collective condition of the nation will also be changed then, and it will come to view with the quality of "Islam uplifts; it does not hurl down." Else, by assuming a Muslim name or being born in a Muslim family, one can never achieve salvation or worldly or religious progress. Through mere external Islamic appearance and customary practice, the nation cannot advance unless it cultivates live Islamic disposition, manner, and faith of the heart and pure intention. Tradition says, "Verily God does not look at your figures or actions but He looks into your hearts and intentions."

In short, when the insides of the Muslims become alight, their outsides will also become reformable and improvable. When the heart is reformed, the body is also improved consequently. As is laid down in the noble tradition:

اِنَّ فِیْ جَسَدِ بَنِیْ آدَمَ مُضْغَةً إِذَا صَلُحَتْ، صَلُحَ الْجَسَدُ كُلُّهُ آلَا وَهِیَ الْقَلْبُ۔

"In the body of mankind there is a piece of flesh; when it is reformed the entire body is reformed, beware! It is the heart."

In short, when the hearts and souls of the individuals of a nation are reformed and undergo a change, the external, worldly, political, economic, esoteric, religious, and spiritual conditions of the nation also change. Rulership of the world kissed the feet of the Muslims when they obeyed God the Most High and His Prophet and acted according to the Quran and tradition (i.e., they were God-fearing and pious). But when the Muslims relinquished obedience to God the Most High and His Prophet and fell in pursuit of passion and desire and gave up following the Quran and tradition, God the Most High imposed on them degradation and destitution as a chastisement of their disobedience and depriving them of their kingdoms and governments, handed these over to others. When the infidels among the Quraish tried their utmost to keep back His Holiness Muhammad the Prophet of Allah (p.b.u.h.) from spreading the faith and giving publicity to truth and were even determined to murder him and destroy the Islamic faith and compelled him to give up his native home, Makkah the Sacred, and migrate to Medina, he began to promulgate Islam and publicize the true religion there. When the wretched infidels came to know that he had begun his mission there also, and hewas proving more successful, the enemies of God did not allow him to remain peacefully there. They continued their efforts to wipe out his mission and began to attack him there. Then he also received permission from God the Most High to wage religious war against those antagonists and adversaries and to hoist the flag of the holy war. So that in accordance with "Until no disturbance remains and the religion of Allah alone remains," he and his majestic companions unsheathed the swords against all the adversaries, infidels, and polytheists merely for the sake of proclamation of the word of God and publicity of the true religion. The help of God the Most High accompanied him, and he attained full victory in his true crusade and rightful mission, and by showing obedience to the true faith, he and his successors and true followers were granted the kingdom and rulership of the world. The sun of unitarianism and true faith glittered wherever these faithful servants of God set their footsteps. The shadows of infidelity, polytheism, and disunion were dispelled, and the whole world was entirely changed. The hearts became clean, and the intentions were transformed. Everyone stopped short of evil out of fear of God and commenced virtuous deeds in hope of divine mercy, and thus the whole world began to lead a peaceful life under the safety of Islam, the protection of faith and security of gnosis. Justice and equality prevailed everywhere. Brotherhood and equality were established, and the darkness of tyranny, oppression, despotism, and capitalism were wiped off—and the world began to breathe the breath of relief and tranquility in the bright atmosphere of Islam.

Evil Consequences of Our Political Leaders about Religion

Unless a religious and spiritual sensation is created in our presentday leaders, neither can their intentions be pious nor their hearts be clean, nor can they ever succeed to show the path of worldly and religious salvation to the nation. But, alas, our present-day leaders have no faith in God the Most High and the next world. Whatever they do, they do for the present world. They are a sort of trader. If in order to serve their nation, they make a little temporary, personal, or corporeal sacrifice, they demand in return perpetual honor and worldly riches from the nation as a whole. Neither can an infidel and irreligious leader ever become the true leader and real liberator of the nation, nor can his intentions be good. Through a little personal capital, he wants to plunder the entire national wealth. He is a butcher who has concealed the knife of his intentions in his heart and donned the dress of a shepherd and protector. He alone can be the true leader and genuine liberator of his nation who has full faith in God the Most High, His prophets, and the day of resurrection, computation, retribution, and reward and every act of whose is for God the Most High. Such a person is the real well-wisher of the nation. He asks nobody for anything. He likes the people not for his own good but for theirs. His true bargain lies with God. He sells his goods to his Creator and seeks the price in the next world. He has no worldly objects or sensual dealings with the people. All the infidels and irreligious leaders are thieves, pickpockets, dacoits, and robbers. They can never establish peace in the world. That is why these "civilized" dacoits dub religious spiritualism as the cause of mutual strife, wish to wipe them (religion and spiritualism) out, and are bent on their eradication. These fools are being swept by the flow of infidelity and atheism. They think that if religion and spiritualism are out of the world, peace will come to it. But let it be remembered that if the Solomon (p.b.u.h.) of religion and spiritualism is no more in the world, the devil of atheism can never be expected to restore peace in the world. But one good is sure to come out of materialism and faithlessness, namely, that mankind will be relieved of God and his Prophet if not of human tyranny and despotism. The real progress of a nation consists in its external and internal, formal and real, worldly and religious, material and spiritual, political and theological—both sorts of—advancement. Else supposing the impossible, even if worldly progress is achieved by sacrificing faith and religion, it will be like getting the cap at the cost of the head and shoes through amputation of the feet and perpetual enslavement to the self and Satan for the sake of liberation from temporary bondage.

Except this worldly exchange and material bargain, what can he affect who denies God and the next world and whose ambitions are limited to this world?

بتوں سے تجھ کو امیدیں خدا سے نومیدی

مجھے بتا تو سہی اور کافری کیا ہے؟

(اقبالؒ)

"You are hopeful of the idols and hopeless of God. Tell me what else constitutes infidelity?" Those who lead an animal life in the world; whose hobby it is to eat, drink, and ease themselves; who came to the world and went away after eating and drinking like the animals for a few days; about whom God the Most High says:

وَلَقَدْ ذَرَأْنَا لِجَهَنَّمَ كَثِيرًا مِّنَ الْجِنِّ وَالْإِنْسِ ۖ لَهُمْ قُلُوبٌ لَّا يَفْقَهُونَ بِهَا ۖ وَلَهُمْ أَعْيُنٌ لَّا يُبْصِرُونَ بِهَا ۖ وَلَهُمْ آذَانٌ لَّا يَسْمَعُونَ بِهَا ۚ أُولَٰئِكَ كَالْأَنْعَامِ بَلْ هُمْ أَضَلُّ ۚ أُولَٰئِكَ هُمُ الْغَافِلُونَ ﴿١٧٩﴾

"I have prepared for the hell many of the jinn and men. They who have hearts but understand not; they have eyes but see not therewith, they have ears but hear not therewith; They are like animals; nay even worse, they are the negligent people."

Blind sensualists who are mere skeletons of flesh and bones and who think this world of elements (i.e., the material world) to be everything, who are deprived of esoteric senses and the light of faith, are excusable if they deny God the Most High and the next world, because their hearts are hidden in the cover of matter. What do these people know of the spirit and the spiritual world? The acts and effects of the spiritual world are present in this material world, but what can those who have neither esoteric eyes nor esoteric ears see and hear? The commemoration of God the Most High opens the esoteric senses. But they have neither come this way nor tried to do so. Now who is to blame? Turning away from commemoration of God the Most High and avoiding it is the cause of esoteric blindness. Says the Most High:

وَمَنْ أَعْرَضَ عَنْ ذِكْرِىْ فَاِنَّ لَهُ مَعِيْشَةً ضَنْكًا وَّنَحْشُرُهٗ يَوْمَ الْقِيٰمَةِ أَعْمٰى ﴿١٢٣﴾ (٢٠ طٰه:١٢٤)

"Ah! he who turned away from commemorating Me, for him there is scant of food and We will raise him blind on the Day of Resurrection."

وَالَّذِيْنَ جَاهَدُوْا فِيْنَا لَنَهْدِيَنَّهُمْ سُبُلَنَا ۗ (١٢٩ العنكبوت:٦٩)

Exertion is essential for observation: "And to those who strive We show them Our path." These people suffered from heart disease but never approached heart specialists for treatment. They had sore eyes and turned blind but never set in search of Solomon's collyrium.

Now by way of an illustration, we will proceed to mention the acts and effects of esoteric personalities and spiritual bodies in the material world. A study of these will convince the readers that besides this material world, there is an esoteric and spiritual world the effects of which appear in the material world now and then because the esoteric and spiritual world is so united to this material and elemental world as the spirit is linked to the elemental body.

The Acts and Effects of the Invisible Bodies In the Material World

In this material world, the invisible events of the spiritual world occasionally occur to man in dream only, and in dream alone, these invisible objects begin to appear. The effects of the other world partially reflect on the esoteric senses during sleep. As a sample of the whole, a man can occasionally feel in dream alone the effects of the invisible world and then guess the existence of another (an invisible one) world besides this material one because the external senses are closed at the time of sleep and all the material limbs are suspended of their actions. A sort of senselessness and death overtakes the man. It would be proper to designate sleep as minor death. Hence the saying, "sleep is the brother of death."

اے برادر من ثرا از زندگی دادم نشاں

خواب را مرگ سبک داں مرگ را خواب گراں

(اقبالؒ)

"O brother! I have given you a clue of life. Consider sleep a light death, and death a heavy sleep."

Death also stands for the suspension of the external senses, energies, and physical limbs. A partial sample of what will happen after death must appear in sleep. Manifestation of some of the post-death events during sleep is highly probable. The eyelet of dream alone has been provided for the common folk to peep toward the invisible world. From true dreams, a sound-minded person can draw very good results in proof of the next world. True dreams are therefore regarded as a part of prophethood. Dreams are twofold: when the imaginative power of the soul dominates a person during sleep, the comprehensions of the external senses are deposited in the treasure-house of imagination and reflected on the mirror of the heart. Then exactly the same habitual thoughts and imaginations personify and appear in dreams. "These are called confused ideas and are unreliable. But sometimes when, on account of the suspension of the five senses and external energies, the rational soul diverts from this perceptible world toward the imperceptible world or the universe of spirits, the incidents of the invisible world reflect on that clear essence just as the shapes of objects of a scene appear in a clear mirror. Afterward, they take place in waking in exactly the same way. To regard true incidents and to designate such dreams as distracted ideas is the excess of folly. But sometimes when the heart's mirror is purified from the customary ideas of the perceptible world and the reflection of the incidents of the invisible world cannot adequately fall on it, there is a conflict of true dreams and confused ideas in the heart. Then a third form is formed. Some parts of such dreams are true dreams while others are confused ideas. This is not a very reliable dream. But sometimes in dreams one enters an esoteric valley where the daily customary thoughts, sensual inclinations, and worldly ideas have no access, and in the dream, a person visualizes a clear and clean space free from the dust of doubt and misgiving like the true morn. The incidents of the invisible world are then reflected in the mirror of the heart exactly as the very same moving and talking figures appear on the film-screen. When a man sees such incidents in a dream, they invariably appear sooner or later either in the exact the same form or in the form of an interpretation or explanation. Such dreams unfailingly take place after a day or two, a week, a month, a year, and sometimes after many years. Such dreams are the prototypes of the true incidents of the heart.

In his lifetime, every man must have seen some true dream that must have come to pass, exactly as it was, sooner or later. If not, he must have tested the veracity of the dream of a near relative, friend, or companion. Because such incidents are very ordinary things. Small children, silly women, sinners—even infidels, polytheists, and hypocrites—can dream correct dreams of all sorts. This communal aperture is open for all. It has often been noticed that an incident dreamed at night appears exactly so in the day. Sometimes, information about a missing object is given in dream, and the thing is discovered accordingly. Or a medicine is suggested for a patient, and complete health is regained by acting on it. Or the news is given about the death of somebody orthe tidings were given of the birth of a male child, and it happens like that. Or the information is imparted about the successful ending of a litigation or the return of a relative or friend away on a journey, or a tragic or comic incident is seen in a dream, or a stranger or unseen house or a new city is seen in the dream—and later all of them happen exactly the same way in the waking state. Now this is an unpremeditated act and not the work of external senses and physical sensations. The heretical, materialistic blind put some sort of interpretation on such true facts and other esoteric sensations that their material intellects cannot weigh fully. But those who possess a bit of sound intellect and esoteric sense will surely infer from such incidents that besides this material world of ours, there certainly exists a spiritual world that can be occasionally discerned through the esoteric sense. Else the pious people daily see such true dreams and find them always true and never miss at all. Some live-hearted people visualize future events either in meditation or waking. The case of the prophets and saints is far above these. Their hearts are Jamshed's cups and Alexander's mirrors, which portray the incidents of the whole world. The human heart is a model of the Guarded Tablet of God (لوح محفوظ) the Most High, and according to his capacity, everyone can see in it the incidents of past, present, and future. Just as men have been endowed with external senses whereby they can feel the objects of the perceptible world whenever they like, similarly those endowed with esoteric senses by God the Most High can thereby observe the objects and incidents of the invisible world whenever they like.

ذٰلِكَ فَضْلُ اللّٰهِ يُؤْتِيهِ مَنْ يَشَاءُ ۚ وَاللّٰهُ ذُو الْفَضْلِ الْعَظِيمِ ۞ (الجمعة: ٦٢)

"That is the mercy of God which He bestows on whomever He likes, and God is the master of great mercy."

Correspondingly to the size of the lens of the telescope of one's heart is the measure of the manifestation of spiritual objects. Recently, the astrologers and scientists have invented a heavy and large telescope fixed in the observatory of California through which billions of planets and stars that were invisible previously came into view. In the future, the bigger and larger telescopes are expected to come into existence. When there is no control on this material vastness of vision, if God the Most High bestows power on the telescope of the heart of some prophet or saint in which he can view the whole world—what do you lose, O enviers?

يَعْلَمُونَ ظَاهِرًا مِّنَ الْحَيٰوةِ الدُّنْيَا ۖ وَهُمْ عَنِ الْاٰخِرَةِ هُمْ غٰفِلُونَ ۞ (الروم: ٣٠)

True: to know and feel the whole of the visible and invisible worlds at all times and at all moments individually and collectively, briefly and fully, externally and internally, perpetually possess the knowledge of the entire universe and every atom therein with the absence of defect and diminution in that knowledge for all times is the essence of God the Most High, Self-existent, Knower of the visible and invisible worlds. This is His special and distinctive attribute in which no other essence can participate or equal Him. The entire universe and its knowledge is a creation of Allah the Most High. If He bestows on someone the knowledge of the entire universe and gives the knowledge of the created to the created and that of the contingent to the contingent, it does not necessitate an atom of interference and partnership in the endless attribute of knowledge of that self-existent and uncreated Essence. Because at any cost, the Omnipresent and Omniscient knowledge of our entire world is created and stands no comparison with the Uncreated Creator. That essence is beyond the beyond and the beyond and above the knowledge and ignorance of the creation.

My friend, believe that with the eyes of esoteric sight and the vision of esoteric sight bestowed on the perfect man by God the Most High, he can see the visible and invisible objects of the universe. Every pot and utensil can accommodate a thing according to its capacity. Now understand! If the enviers and misers do not take it ill, we can safely say that since the religious law had made it lawful for the earthly men to see and face that omnipotent, peerless, and unparalleled Creator and to have unity and unison with Him either before or after death, what is the discriminative feature of the limited and created knowledge of the created that it should be unlawful unto him:

"Your manifestation is through me and my existence due to you. You don't manifest without me; I can't be without You." But we have been swept away by a lengthy and interminable discussion. Let us revert to our original topic (i.e., the effects of the invisible world). Some people have acquired great knowledge and sciences during sleep. For example, some people have been made to memorize lengthy Quranic verses during sleep, and on waking, they permanently remembered those verses. Moreover, some fortunate persons have been made to commit to memory the entire Quran in a single night, and on waking up in the morning, they had the whole Quran by heart. It has been related about some persons that they slept Ajamis at night and were endowed with the faculty of speaking Arabic in sleep, and on awaking in the morning, they were found to speak fluent Arabic and always spoke in that language. They have said, "I slept an Ajami and awoke an Arabi." Some people went to sleep ignorant and woke up scholars. It has often been noticed that a person received an injury in sleep the marks of which were clearly noticed on the body. The author saw a man who received a blow on his leg in a dream and got lame of the leg in the morning.

The following incident relates to the author: About thirty-five years ago, the month of Ramadan fell in the hot months of June and July. I fell ill and went in company of some other friends to a cool place in the western mount to keep the fasts. Due to some reasons, I could not stay there and was compelled to return to my home a day or two before the first of Ramadan. The night overtook me in a village a few miles away from our city. The moon was seen that night. Though I was sick, it was the month of fast the following day, and there was a good deal of foot journey ahead. I was mentally disturbed in the night whether to intend keeping the fast or not. Plucking up my courage, I however determined to keep the fast and set out for my house on foot in the day.

On the way, I was about to collapse on account of an excess of thirst. My mouth was dry. On arriving home, I took a bath and contrived many devices to allay the thirst but in vain. Lying down on a bed at noontime, I tried my utmost to fall asleep but could not do so on account of the thirst. At last, I fell asleep for a moment when I dreamed of searching for water to quench my thirst. In the same dream, somebody offered me a glass of syrup, which I drank. On waking up, I had not a sign of thirst left behind. It seemed as if I had drunk water in waking, so much so that I did not feel thirsty even at the time of breaking the fast.

The following narrative refers to the earlier career of the author. I was putting up in the court of my spiritual patron, Sultan Bahu Sahib (p.b.u.h.), in the earlier days of my life, having freshly deserted the college and assumed faqr. In the night, I was bitten on the leg by a snake, which was instantaneously killed by a fellow dervish of mine. On hearing of this, some other dervishes of the august court came to sympathize with me. Some of them thus questioned me about the symptoms of the influence of the poison: "Are you choking or feeling drowsy?" Though I was perfectly collected, their talk in this way made me concerned. I was lying down there and fell asleep. In a dream, I saw that blood was oozing from my mouth, nose, and ears, and my heart was palpitating.

Meanwhile, I saw somebody running toward me. On arriving, he gave me a tumbler of medicine to drink. There at, the blood stopped, and my heart became calm and quiet. I woke up and requested the people around me to leave me alone, as I was all right; I passed the night safely and peacefully and felt no ill-effects of the snake's venom. The dervishes of the noble court might still remember this incident.

This incident also relates to the author. I fell sick because of ear pain, and a white, foul-smelling puss began to flow from my ear. When the orifice of my ear used to fill up with the puss, I used to extract it with my finger. It so happened for a few days. Thereafter, either because of the discharge of the puss or through the repeated rubbing of my finger, a small abscess was formed in the ear near the orifice. The puss stopped, but the abscess swelled. There was a small hole in it. When I pressed it, the puss came out but was again collected after some time. I used to press it and empty it of the puss a few times a day, and there was no end to the puss. There was great pain and a burning sensation in the ear. I was highly disturbed and restless. It was incurable because no ointment or medicine could reach it. I was in a terrible state.

On account of the burning sensation, I could not sleep in the night. Tired of it, I had recourse to esoteric treatment and sought the help of a spiritual resident of a saint in the grave because it is said, if you are perplexed in your affairs, seek the help of the spiritual people. Consequently, I went to the grave of a saint at night and read the invocatory prayer of the Holy Quran and slept. In a dream, I saw a magnificent underground hospital in the same place. A comely and well-dressed doctor there was dispensing medicine among the patients. Showing the abscess in my ear, I requested him to treat it. On this, he brought out from an almirah a brilliant, long-necked vial like a test tube and bid me show him the ear. I turned my ear toward him. From the corner of my eye, it appeared to me as if my ear was on fire and emitting a red flame like that of a candle. Out of the vial, the spiritual doctor began sprinkling some white liquid on my ear. With the fall of the liquid on the ear, I could hear a simmering sound like the quenching fire. At last, the fire was put out, and my ear became cold like ice.

Simultaneously, I awoke from the sleep. Believe me, on examining my ear, there was no abscess or pain and no trace of either. I have related here only a few incidents of my life by way of an illustration merely for the sake of the satisfaction of hearts, pacification of the mind, and amplification of the faith of the readers. God is my witness that self-display and self-advertisement play no part in what I have said because these are very ordinary matters for faqirs and dervishes. Because things higher than these are outside the comprehension of the commonfolk and above their credulity, there is danger of verbosity and apprehension of self-aggrandizement; therefore I have confined myself to one or two items only. In the spiritual world, however, there is no dearth of such wonderful incidents.

Highly ignorant are those who deny the truthfulness of dreams and consider them the result of indigestion and mere customary thoughts. Only those dead-hearted sensualist people whose hearts are senseless and dead like stones are unaware of the importance of dreams. How can they know the reality of dreams who haven't dreamed a true dream all their lives? The practical scholars of the past have taught very wonderful and rare sciences to their pupils overnight. These sciences were transferred without an intermediary from breast to breast and in a moment. Whereas if taught in the ordinary way, their acquisition would have taken years and years. Similarly, after their death and from their graves through a single glance and attention, the perfect saints have made their pupils and followers traverse such difficult stages and esoteric places that if expressed in words would be unbelievable. There is a world of difference between the beastly commonfolk and the munificent saints. The dreams of the sensualist dead-hearted people are unreal, futile, void, senseless, meaningless, useless, and redundant. But the dreams of the selected slaves of God carry solid reality and are heavy, weighty, and resplendent with esoteric light and agreeable and acceptable to both the Creator and the created. These do not carry any tinge of Satanic naughtiness or admixture of sensual thoughts. The dream of a perfect man is a heap of solid realities compared to which the meaningless and futile wakening of the sensualist, dead-hearted people have no reality. Hence the dreams of the selected persons of God ought not to be conjectured after one's own manner.

Regarding the inauguration of his sermons, His Holiness Pir Mahbub-e-Subhani Sheikh Abdul Qadir Jilani (may Allah sanctify his precious secrets) says,

> Once I met my grandfather (His Holiness the munificent Prophet (p.b.u.h.)) in a dream. He ordered me, "Child! Deliver sermon." I submitted, "Sir, I am a man from Ajam, non-Arab, how can I open my lips before the eloquent and learned men of Iraq Arab?" He commanded, "Open your mouth." When I did so he blew puffs in my mouth seven times. Thereafter I met his Holiness Ali (may God glorify his face). He also said, "Child, why don't you preach?" I submitted the same thing to him. He also ordered me to open my mouth and puffed in six times. Thereupon, I submitted, "My lord, his Holiness the Refuge of Prophethood (p.b.u.h.) blew seven times, why did you confine yours to six times?" He replied, "I decreased one out of respect to his Holiness."

His Holiness Mahbub-e-Subhani says, "After this unbounded tides of unitarianism and gnosis began to surge in the sea of my heart and the flow of my nature, so to say, a surging river which began to bring the pearls of realities and gnosis to the shore of the tongue and sacrificed them among the audience." His sermons used to be a shoreless sea of divine conquests and revelations or a cloud of light.

When a tide appeared in this Godly ocean or lightning appeared in this divine cloud, the audience, which consisted of scholars and learned men of the dominions of Arabia and Persia and numbered about seventy thousand, experienced a very queer state. Some used to be overtaken by a state of ecstasy; some used to become agitated and uncontrolled and began to thunder and tear their clothes; some used to become absolutely unconscious and senseless and unable to bear the illuminations of the light of the essence of the Omnipotent; and some reckless lovers used to surrender their souls like the nation of Moses (p.b.u.h.). His son Sheikh Abu Abdullah relates that two to four men invariably used to expire in the assembly of his sermon. When the illumination of the electricity of his attention fell on some capable hearers, they flew from the meeting toward heaven. The breasts of some were opened through gnosis and secrets. Innumerable revelations and miracles involuntarily used to emanate from the generous person on the very chair of the sermon. It appeared as if the hearts of all the hearers were in his fingers, and he used to control them as he liked. Reading their minds, he used to address some and bestow the garb of saintliness on others. In short, his sermons used to be the shoreless ocean of the esoteric and exoteric munificence from which everyone used to carry his full share in accordance with the capacity of his utensil (heart). In his preaching assembly, thousands of heretics, Jews, Christians, and magicians used to embrace Islam, and innumerable sinners, immoderates, thieves, and dacoits repented and attained guidance. Jinn, angels, the spirits of the unseen, men, and even those of prophets and messengers used to attend his sermons. Many times, His Holiness the Great Prophet (p.b.u.h.) personally used to grace his sermons with his august presence. Once he came down the sermon dais during the course of a lecture and stood with a drooping head and folded hands for a long while. A number of well-informed perfect faqirs kept standing with him in the same manner. At the end of the sermon, he was asked, "Your Honor, what was the matter today?"

> He replied, "His Glorious Holiness, our great grandfather, the ruler of both the worlds (p.b.u.h.), had graced the assembly of the sermon with his

presence and ordered, 'Child! I had come to hear your sermon.'"

Coming down off the lecture chair, I submitted, "My lord, how can the slave open his mouth in the presence of your Essence which is the compendium of all perfection." Then his Holiness went away.

He used to say, "There is not a jinn, angel, saint, or prophet who has not come to the assembly of my sermon. The living with their exoteric forms and spirits with their esoteric persons have attended my sermons." Sometimes, when Khizr used to come to his sermons, he was thus addressed, "O Israelite! Stop and hear the speech of the Muhammadi." Briefly speaking, his sermons used to be an interminable chain of the wonders of the power of Allah the Most High, which used to emanate from his person.

Some Dreams of the Author

Let me narrate here an incident of my own life. Once during the course of spiritual travel, I felt a desire, for a few days, to learn the science of divining (علم جفر). In these days, I was staying at the luminous mausoleum of my spiritual patron, my lord Sultan Bahu Sahib. One night, I saw in a dream that a tall-statured elderly man wearing a long shirwani and dressed in the Indian fashion came to the holy mausoleum of his Holiness (p.b.u.h.). People pointed their fingers at him, saying that that was the greatest specialist in the science of divining (علم جفر) in the world that day. That elderly man came to me. When I saluted him and met him, he inquired of me if I had a mind to learn the science of divining. I replied, "Certainly I intend doing so."

He said, "Come along so that I may teach you the whole of it."

Then taking me by the hand, he led me to the spacious platform in front of the mausoleum of His Holiness the king of the gnostics and the mosque where there was a large almirah. When he opened the door of the almirah, it revealed a large tablet (i.e., a plank curiously printed). The alphabet was inscribed on it in different colors in bold letters. The names of the twelve signs of the Zodiac and the seven planets were also inscribed therein, in their proper places. Strings like that of a guitar were strung across it from end to end. In short, it was a very picturesque map of nature that was glittering in the Almirah. In his hand, the elderly man was holding a pointer with which he pointed to the tablet, saying, "This is the tablet of nature which contains the whole of the science of divining. Now, look, I will demonstrate to you an act in it. Later on, I will teach you the whole science."

At that time, I beheld a child of eight or ten years standing in front of us. He said, "Behold! I will vanish this boy through the science of divining." Then he struck the stick in his hand on the string across the tablet at the place where the word *Mercury* (which I very well remember) was written. It produced a strange noise, and I saw the boy vanish. Then taking hold of my hand, he said, "Let me now impart the whole science to you." Then he took me to the eastern side of the platform where a tank is situated now. Grasping my hand with one hand, he held his beard in the other, closed his eyes, and began to attend to me.

At that instant, I beheld His Holiness the king of gnostics with his bright face and red beard appear from his grave riding a horse. His Holiness beckoned me with his hand. I seemed to fly to him like a bird. Dismounting his horse and taking hold of my hand, His Holiness said, "Child, the science of divining entails worries of computation. Come, let me teach you the best and most perfect science."

I submitted, "That will be most kind of you."

Then his Holiness said, "Now behold. With a single look, I will reproduce the child who vanished through the science of divining."

When I cast a look at the blessed face of His Holiness (p.b.u.h.), I saw the two letters K (ک) and N (ن) written in bright solar colors and twinkling like two stars above his eyes in line with the eyebrows. A flame shot from the eyes of His Holiness (R.A) when he looked toward the place where the child had vanished, and the word *Kun* (کن) ("be") appeared written on the ground in bright letters. The ground seemed to shake, and veils upon veils had to be removed therefrom. Instantaneously, the boy reappeared. His Holiness said, "Isn't it superior to the science of divining?"

"It is the best of sciences, Your Holiness," I submitted.

Then holding my hand, His Holiness commanded, "Come, let me grant you this knowledge just now." So his Holiness led me by the hand into the mausoleum. I became unconscious. When I recovered, I found myself lying in the chamber where I was sleeping. At that moment, I saw my face. Above my eyes, in line with the eyebrows, I saw the letters K (ک) and N (ن) written in brilliant solar colors exactly like those of His Holiness (p.b.u.h.). At the moment, I recollected some important and difficult tasks of mine. The word "be" could be seen written on the place of execution of every task toward which I paid heed, and that task seemed being solved by the Grace of God and the kind look of my patron. Later on, at their proper times, all those tasks were executed very conveniently and appropriately. I feel that esoteric power in my mind and eyes forever, and whenever I pay some intention and heed to any task, it is solved by the grace of God, and that takes place sooner or later.

اے لقائے تو جواب ہر سوال

مشکل از تو حل شود بے قیل و قال

(رومی)

"Your visage answering every question. You solve difficulties without conversation." A thousand thanks are due to God the Most High and innumerable thanks to my bountiful and beneficent patron, more kind than the father and mother—the gratefulness and thanks which the tongue is unable to discharge:

گر برتنِ من زباں شود ہر موئے

یک شکر تو از ہزار نتوانم کرد

(خاقانی)

"If every hair on my person turns into a tongue, I cannot express one thank out of a thousand."

Listen to another incident. Once, in a dream, the author saw a large earthen mosque where his Holiness the King of the Universe (i.e., Prophet of Islam (p.b.u.h.) was acting as an imam. This poor soul (i.e., the author), along with a few prophets and chief companions, was standing behind him as followers and performing the prayers. So great was the relish derived from that prayer that standing there, we were moving like the branches of a tree, out of excessive love and joy. Contrary to our modern practice and without turning to the left or right but keeping his face toward the Qiblah as before, his Holiness (p.b.u.h.) raised his hands in supplication after he had finished performing the prayers. After His Holiness (p.b.u.h.) had finished praying, the author got up and submitted, "Your Holiness! There are some prophets and companions in this assembly. Will you kindly pray to God the Most High that his humble slave may have the honor of seeing and meeting all the prophets?"

Thereupon, His Holiness raised his hands in prayer a second time. I saw myself standing at the outer platform of the mosque, facing the Qiblah, and all the prophets coming toward me in a line, shaking this humble slave by the hand and then proceeding. Through the kindness of His Holiness (p.b.u.h.), I saw all prophets in a different pomp and show of nature in the various colors of their attributes and separate states of their virtuous actions.

There are also other ways to the effects and information of the heart besides dreams, which a man sometimes encounters in his life.

There is a fine aperture in the heart of a man through which he can sometimes peep toward the invisible world, which the external senses cannot feel. In his lifetime, a man comes across such cordial incidents and esoteric perceptibilities, but because of excessive material occupation, he cannot discern them. For example, a man sometimes feels in himself a causeless fear, sorrow, or dejection.

The result is that some terrible and sorrowful incident takes place after a few days. The more acute or lasting the "fright of the mind" preceding the incident, the more severe, hard, and prolonged is the incident that comes to pass. In contrast, to someone else, an unaccountable joy appears in the heart, and after a few days, some pleasant and happy incident takes place. The stronger the esoteric senses of a man, the sooner and clearer the sensation of these things. Those who do not feel these things in their hearts get predictions of the coming events on their external body in this manner. Sometimes, the left or right eye begins to wink, or some other part of the body begins to tremble. Sometimes, things fall from one's hand. Sometimes. one stumbles against objects. Sometimes, one is causelessly enraged. Sometimes, one cannot sleep. Sometimes, the children in the house get up from their sleep and cry without a cause. Sometimes, the dogs in the house begin to bark aimlessly and produce curious sounds. These things also are sometimes the precursors of bad and sorrowful coming events. Sometimes, when a joy is to take place in a house, the scenery of the house becomes more beautiful than before and an esoteric glamor and beauty drips from the four walls. It seems as if the house is full of joy and dancing. But an acute-sighted eye alone can feel these things. Sometimes, when a tragic incident is about to befall a house, its outlook appears distorted and ruined compared to that before. The four walls display sorrow and gloom. Similarly, if a general calamity is to befall a city or country, it wears that outlook for a certain time. If a happy or sad incident is to befall a man, the esoteric sighted person can feel its reflection on the man's countenance and body just as a scene is portrayed on the screen. The common folk, however, can see a fallen, dull, and wearied look alone.

Impending joys or sorrows are also discernible at the time of a new building or grave. The signs of felicity and inauspiciousness are also discernible in a coming marriage, some ceremony, or the coronation of a king. Sometimes, it so happens that while a person is engaged in some profession or deeply engrossed in some other idea, the thought of his friend, acquaintance, or close relative suddenly comes to his mind as an interruptive whim and breaks through the first chain of ideas. Later on, the same friend, acquaintance, or relative appears from somewhere or his letter or messenger arrives. The man with sharper and stronger esoteric senses also hears an esoteric sound along with that reminder saying, "So-and-so is coming or calling you." Sometimes, his form also appears before his eyes. Sometimes, a man intends to say something to another, but before he has uttered a syllable, the other one—if a bit sensitive esoterically—finds out the reflections of his talk in his own heart. In English, this science is called telepathy. The European nations are studying it. But so far, they have neither made much progress, nor can they correctly catch thoughts. But we see that songs, music, and speeches are heard through the radios from thousands of miles away, and voice and light are transmitted from one place to another through electricity. Recently, a man has invented an instrument that records thought waves. If one places it on the heart, it produces lines of various kinds. But experimentation is in progress. Different people, hundreds of miles away, produce thought waves in different places at a stipulated time, and every one puts into writing the waves received from a different place. Homogeneous thought waves were found to bear to homogeneity of form and character. So far, the experimentations have not succeeded in correctly interpreting and recording thoughts. But they have proved that thought waves can travel thousands of miles in their exact forms. In short, one heart has an excess to another, and reading the thoughts of another heart is a very ordinary thing for live-hearted and clear-minded people. Their hearts are powerful telepathic instruments that can clearly find out the thoughts of other people. But their tongues bear the seal of divine law. They conceal themselves and do not condescend to be self-advertising hypocritical shopkeepers. It is quite easy to find out, at home, the thoughts of a person by remembering him from a distance. But to find out the thoughts of any man at any time, irrespective of the distance intervening, by attending to his heart is a bit difficult and the sphere of a very perfect gnostic. This should not be wondered at because it is a science. The waves of the heart are borne by the air. That is why Jacob (A.S) discerned through cordial knowledge the fact of the brothers carrying the robes of Joseph (A.S) from Egypt to Canaan and uttered, "I smell of Joseph, if you do not ridicule me." Sometimes a man unreasonably dislikes another one without ever receiving any harm from him. The disliking, moreover, is not due to the ugly face and features of the man disliked. But the heart of the man dislikes him without any cause and reason. Now in such cases, it often happens that the man disliking invariably receives some harm or loss from the person hated. Contrarily, if a man is liked by another man without any reason, he certainly receives from him some benefit, sooner or later. This chain sometimes descends to the progeny. For example, if the father is disliked—though no injury may come from him—his descendants do harm to the person disliking or his offspring. Certainly goodness and beneficence should be similarly conjectured.

دل را بدل ربیست دریں گنبد سپهر

از کینه کینه خیزد و خیزد ز مهر مهر

(فردوسی)

"In this spherical dome, heart echoes toward heart. Hatred breeds hatred, and love breeds love."

One heart can smell enmity and friendship from another. Like the material mirror, which reflects things, the heart is a subtle esoteric mirror. On coming before the heart, all the subtle, esoteric objects are reflected and clearly seen, provided it is not covered with dust and the man who sees is endowed with esoteric sight. The human heart is a model and sample of the Guarded Tablet (لوح محفوظ) of God the Most High. Hence, the clear-minded can see the coming events in it. The material and elemental body of man is confined to space and time, which surround him completely. But the heart is a spaceless etheric personality—free from the restrictions of space and time. Hence, when a saint gains life and purification through commemoration of God the Most High, proximity, distance, time, and space are alike to him, so are things far away and close by. To him, the past and future are like the present. In short, the etheric personality of the heart gets out of the east, west, north, south, above and below—all the six directions of space and the past, present, and future states of time. His knowledge is much enlarged, and he can see very far off, as is related in the Tradition:

اِتَّقُوْا فِرَاسَةَ الْمُؤْمِنِ فِاِنَّهُ يَنْظُرُ بِنُوْرِ اللّٰهِ

"Beware of the sagacity of the Faithful because he sees through the light of Faith." Some people meet the jinn, angels, and spirits in graves. In dreams, some are graced with the spectacle of prophets, saints, Gauths, Qutbs, martyrs, chief companions, and even the Prophet of Allah (p.b.u.h.). It is incumbent on every follower to be favored with the glorious visitation of the great Master, His Holiness Muhammad (p.b.u.h.) at least once in his lifetime. Some selected persons, yearly, monthly, every Thursday, most perfectly every night, some holy personages accepted and liked by God and absolute devotees of the Prophet, every time and every moment they so desire, can reach the audience of his Holiness (p.b.u.h.) and are graced by seeing him and are favored by his company.

Sometimes, the appointed angels awaken in dreams some people to offer the prayer. Some people are awakened and informed before the occurrence of some danger or loss. For example, the appointed angels put some people on their guard by calling out to them or putting a whim in their hearts when, for example, a house catches fire or is about to fall or thieves break through or an enemy, animal, or beast is about to attack—or on various dangerous incidents of the type. One symptom of a true dream is that its effect on the heart is quite evident and very lasting. Generally, on seeing such a true dream, the eyes open up, one feels refreshed, and there are no traces of lassitude and slothfulness. Moreover, one cannot sleep for a long time after that. Sometimes, the same dream is repeatedly dreamed the same night. Some people do not dream all their lives. Some dream the whole night. Some dream very few but true dreams. Some have very upsetting and frightful dreams in the night. Some dream but cannot remember them on account of forgetfulness. Sometimes, a man sleeps in a dark house wearing a quilt and with his eyes closed. But when he thinks of the house, he can see all the objects inside the house as if the house is well-lit. This vision of some people grows bigger and bigger and reaches very far off. Some can see the moon and stars while sleeping in the night under a quilt. Sometimes, one can see very long dreams in a very short time. And though esoterically not a minute has passed, a long time seems to have escaped. Sometimes, contrarily, exoterically, the night comes to an end, but esoterically, he feels it as the time taken by a wink.

Some Dreams and Their Interpretations

If in a dream, a sick person sees himself or someone else taking a bath, it portends recovery. If a person dreams of a butcher carrying or sharpening knives in the house of an invalid, the invalid soon expires. The fall of a house indicates death. But if sometimes a man in the habit of offering prayers does not perform the early- or late-night prayer, goes to sleep, and dreams of the house falling, it signifies the demolition of the house of prayers. Death takes place in a house in which an inmate is seen to leave for an unknown destination or a marriage ceremony accompanied by merry-making is dreamed in a house without seeing the bride. If the bride is present and known, it foretells acquisition of wealth. A small child will die in a house where one dreams of a kite swooping or a cat attacking and carrying away a fowl chicken or a small bird.

If a case is on and the sound of a pipe or some other sonorous singing sound is heard in the courtroom or on the court's table, this is sign of victory and success. The killing of a harmful animal, like a snake or scorpion, in a dream, indicates the cessation of enmity and antagonism, and its escape means the continuation of the enmity. Attack by a dog or a beast during a dream means harm from a government official. If a departed friend or acquaintance gives something in a dream, it signifies profit and income; if the dead asks for something or receives something, it is an ill omen. The importation or seeing of a grain (e.g., wheat, millet, maize, and so on) is the harbinger of hardship and affliction; while a diet of roasted and cooked meat and baked loaves indicates wealth and bounty. Riding a horse, camel, elephant, or boat and reaching the destination or ascending a height or a high place is the sign of success in an adventure or task and of leadership and promotion in rank.

Storms, thunderstorms, or the report of a rifle in the dream foretells danger. A clouded sky, rainfall, and clean, flowing water is the sign of betterment. Green and white clothes in a dream are good. Yellow, red, and black clothes are bad. An earthquake means a revolution in the country. Fat and beautiful animals indicate prosperity in the land, and weak and lean animals indicate the contrary. Catching a bird in the dream is a sign of success.

I have recorded the aforementioned few indications and interpretations in haste and on the basis of my observation and experience. Through these, the reader may perhaps gain something in his life. Since this is not a book of interpretation of dreams, I have limited myself to the preceding.

A tradition has it that the preponderance of hope at the time of death (i.e., the satisfaction of the heart) is a sign of faithfulness. In life, too, a balance between fear and hope is the sign of wholesomeness of faith. As is said:

$$ اَلْإِيمَانُ بَيْنَ الْخَوْفِ وَالرَّجَآءِ $$

"The faith is between fear and hope." But the superabundant hope of divine favor and satisfaction and composure of the heart at the time of death is a sign of the safety of the faith. The reason hereof is that at the time of death, the spirit of a faithful senses the coming happiness, ease, and comfort in purgatory. More than that, some pious selected slaves of Allah receive tidings of paradise. Some also see paradise. Says the Most High:

تَتَنَزَّلُ عَلَيْهِمُ الْمَلَٰٓئِكَةُ أَلَّا تَخَافُوا۟ وَلَا تَحْزَنُوا۟ وَأَبْشِرُوا۟ بِالْجَنَّةِ الَّتِى كُنتُمْ تُوعَدُونَ ۝

(حٰمۤ السجدۃ:٣٠)

"The angels give them tidings not to fear and grieve but to make merry of receiving the Paradise promise."

Contrarily, at the time of death, the spirits of heretics, polytheists, and hypocrites see the impending affliction in purgatory. Therefore, their confusion and agitation at the time of death is certain.

The pious slaves of Allah draw an augury (i.e., read some supererogation and text to go to sleep) whenever they desire to know the good or evil end of a thing or future incident or state, and they receive a clear and true answer in the dream. Some practice bibliomany from the Quran or some other book. Sometimes, the augury comes out to be true and favorable. Some live-hearted gnostics attend to their minds during wakening and are informed in the twinkling of an eye.

It is said about such people, "Consult your heart." This pertains to the perfects. The common folk can do only this much. First of all, one should recite some supererogation and cleanse the heart by reciting, "Allah." Then he should purge the heart of all extraneous thoughts and through concentration on His personal name, "Allah" or the name of the Ruler of Universe (p.b.u.h.) attend to and supplicate the courtyard of God or the assembly of the Prophet and go into sleep. If he receives some indication or tiding during the trance or sleep so much the better. Else, if at the very termination of the trance or awakening from sleep, he finds his heart composed and inclined toward that thing, he should think that the work is beneficial and useful. But if he finds his heart distracted, fearful, and revolting against that thing, he should know that the work is harmful and dangerous. Because in sleep and trance, the heart can feel and sense the harmfulness or otherwise of a thing. The following are some of the symptoms of the revivification of the etheric personality of the heart of a seeker in the initial stages. First of all, he acquires consciousness during sleep (i.e., he acquires sense and understanding in the dream), and he understands that what he sees is in a state of dream. If this stage improves and he acquires sense and understanding in every dream, he has, so to say, acquired the state of meditation مراقبه. And when he can voluntarily go into sleep retaining his consciousness and senses and return voluntarily, he has, so to say, acquired the stage of trance. With the onstart of inspiration, some people can see the coming incidents in their houses, either in dream or in a trance, and they take place accordingly. When the sight grows larger, he comes to know of all the different states and incidents in his street, city, district, province, and even country. Some find out the facts of a week, month, year, or even the whole life. It behooves such a novice seeker to keep to himself such information of the unknown world. He should not seek fame by narrating them to everybody. Because as a result of such self-advertisement, he is deprived of this state, which he cannot regain. If such an inspired person conceals his secrets and remains steadfast, he is later on enlisted in the ranks of the people of Genesis Masters (Ghauth, Qutb, Autad, Abdal, Akhyar, and so on), and getting full inspiration and perpetual revelation, he is esoterically made office-bearer and spiritual servant (اہل تکوین متصرفین). Remember that among the followers of Muhammad (p.b.u.h.), there is a class of people of the Genesis Masters. They are all called the Unseen Men (رجال الغیب). Categorically, this class consists of Ghauth (غوث), Qutb (قطب), Autad (آوتاد), Abdal (ابدال) Nujaba' (نجبا), Nuqaba (نقبا), and Akhyar (اخیار). Ghauth or Qutb-al-aqtab is the chief of all. He is the esoteric successor or deputy and caliph of the Prophet (p.b.u.h.). There is always only one Ghauth in the world. He also officiates as the Teacher Qutb. These Qutbs work under him. Under him, there are seven Autads. Forty Abdals work under the Autads. The Nujaba', Nuqaba', and Akhyar work under them. This is an esoteric department consisting of 360 saints of Allah. They are in command of every inch of the world. The lowest master among them, called the Cultivator Master, is the vendetta and protector of people twelve miles around. He keeps even a sparrow's egg under his observation and control. In the territory under his control, he knows the amount of salt put by the women in the kettles and the amount of flour, and through divine knowledge bestowed by God the Most High, he is aware of all the small and big things and minor and major incidents in the area under his control. These are the people about whom God the Most High has said:

$$وَلَقَدْ كَتَبْنَا فِي الزَّبُورِ مِنْ بَعْدِ الذِّكْرِ أَنَّ الْأَرْضَ يَرِثُهَا عِبَادِىَ الصَّلِحُونَ ۝ إِنَّ فِي هَذَا$$
$$لَبَلَغًا لِّقَوْمٍ عَبِدِينَ ۝ (الانبيآء:١٠٥-١٠٦) (١٢١)$$

"Verily in the Psalms of David, after the account of commemoration, We have written down that the pious people will inherit Our land." "In this, there is a general message for the worshipful people."

"That is to say that there is a general proclamation for all my slaves for those who enter themselves among the pious (i.e., the virtuous and selected slaves of God the Most High through excess of commemoration and worship) are the real ones in power and heirs in the world. As it is said:

$$يَا أَيُّهَا الَّذِينَ آمَنُوا أَطِيعُوا اللّٰهَ وَأَطِيعُوا الرَّسُولَ وَأُولِي الْأَمْرِ مِنْكُمْ (النسآء:٥٩) (١٢)$$

'Obey God, His Prophet, and those in power amongst you.'"

"Those in power" does not at all mean the visible, heretical, tyrannical, infidel, and irreligious rulers of the world, who have taken illegal possession and unlawful control of the oppressed and helpless creation of God the Most High through treachery, deceit, tyranny, and oppression, the machinery of whose tyrannical and despotic governments oppresses and grinds the poor and destitute day and night and sucks the blood of the helpless, needy, and oppressed subjects. In fact, there is an esoteric, invisible government of the invisible world over and above this exoteric material government. The latter is like a shadow to the former. The exoteric material rulers have sway over the exoteric material bodies, whereas the esoteric, powerful, spiritual officials control the world of esoteric hearts and spirits. Since the exoteric body is in the bondage and control of the esoteric hearts and spirits, whatever the latter command, the former involuntarily obey. The body is in the grip of the heart like a pen in the hand of a writer, which writes whatever the master tells it to. Hence, the real rulers and men in command are those people who control the invisible world and rule the hearts and spirits. Real and true rulership belongs to the department of these Unseen Men, commandants, men of the genesis, and controllers, and in fact, they control the world. The exoteric and material rulers are subservient to them like the human body under the control and bondage of the heart and soul.

At the time of writing, a judgment of the heart of the exoteric ruler is in the fingers of the esoteric rulers like the pen in the finger of the exoteric ruler. Hence, they are the real people who deliver judgments and write orders, though ostensibly, the material people appear to us to rule and run the government. But externally, we can neither see them nor feel their actions. Isn't it that heart and spirit perform every act in the world, whereas their form and action are invisible to us? The blind, dead-hearted, slumbering, sensualist people know nothing about these spiritually enlightened people. The material world is like a spacious building with the earth for a floor and sky for its roof in which the dead-hearted, sensualist people are lying fast asleep under the material quilt of slothfulness and the spiritualist live-hearted people are awake and alert in this house. The sensualist sleepers are ignorant of themselves and others. But the live-hearted spiritualists have full knowledge of every inch of this world, all its objects, and all its sleeping and waking inhabitants. Like esoteric soldiers and watchmen, they patrol the material world and have knowledge of the territory under their control and care, and they protect it esoterically and exoterically. These people esoterically meet together, exchange ideas, and keep performing their esoteric duties. The exoteric sensualist people are utterly ignorant of their movements, actions, and conditions. These Unseen Men, commanders, and men of Genesis hold meetings and conferences in the invisible world. At first, they settle the affairs of the world in the unseen world, which are later on enjoined in the material world. They always number 360. Because of the rush of work, their number is sometimes increased above that, but it never goes down. When a Ghauth departs from the world, one of the three Qutbs is appointed in his stead. One of the Autads succeeds the Qutb, and the vacancy created by the Autad is filled up by one of the Abdals and so on and so forth. This department includes travelers (سالک) and attracted people (مجاذيب) of all sorts.

But when it is overwhelmed by the attracted insane people (مجاذيب), destitution, confusion, and riots take place in the world.

When the sensible (سالكين) predominate, peace and comfort prevail in the world. Generally, the Gauth stays in one place, while the other controllers travel about and are transferred.

Faqeer Jamshad Ahmed Sarwari Qadri (Shaheed)

Hazart Qabila Faqeer Haroon Ahmed Sarwari Qadri
Second Spiritual Successor

It was perhaps in 1909 or 1910 when on deserting the college and adopting faqiri, I intended to accompany my revered mother on a pilgrimage to Makkah. In those days, I was told in a dream that the Ghauth of the time resided in Jedda and that I should see him if I chanced to go that way. But I could not leave for the pilgrimage that year. It has been often observed that when a perfect gnostic faqir sets out on a journey, the controller of the area visits and meets him esoterically and presents him with the keys of that area, helps and assists him in every affair, and guards and protects him esoterically and exoterically. It is peculiar to these people that they assiduously guard the secrets and confide them to nobody. Display and fame is like poison to them. If any secret of theirs is divulged, they are immediately deposed from their office. They always remain anonymous. In the following, we will relate some traditions regarding the Unseen Men. Abu Na'im quotes Ibn Mas'ud that the Prophet of Allah (p.b.u.h.) has said,

> There are some special selected slaves of Allah the Most High through whose prayers and felicity God the Most High shows favours to people. Causes it to rain from the heaven and grows crops for them from the earth. They are sources of peace and tranquility in the world and they resemble as a soul in the body. The hearts of some of them resemble the heart of Adam (p.b.u.h.); Moses (p.b.u.h.); Abraham (p.b.u.h.); the other Israelite Prophets and the cherubim of other angels.

It is related from His Holiness Ans (God be pleased with him) in the book *Karamat-ul-Auliya* that the Prophet of Allah (p.b.u.h.) said, "The world is never void of such forty people through whose blessing rain falls down from the heaven and the earth produces vegetation. They are called Abdals of my followers."

Imam Ahmed quotes Abad son of Somit that the Prophet of Allah (p.b.u.h.) has said, "Up to the day of Resurrection there will always be forty men amongst my followers through whom the order and the discipline of the earth and the heaven will be maintained." His Holiness (p.b.u.h.) was asked, "What is their description?" He (p.b.u.h.) replied, "They are the people who forgive those who oppress them and reward evil with good."

Jalal-ud-din Sayuti (mercy be upon him) writes, "The information about the Abdals given in the Traditions is true. Moreover they are so continuous that they reach the degree of certainty."

Sakhawi writes,

> The most reliable account of the Abdals is the one quoted by Imam Ahmed from Sheikh son of Ubaid who says that his Holiness Ali (may God glorify his face) said, "Do not curse the people of Syria. Because forty Abdals live there. It rains through their blessings and they succour the faith."

Imam Sayuti has written that there are more than ten testimonials about the saying of His Holiness Ali (may God glorify his face), which Imam Ahmed has quoted.

Khatib quotes Tarikh-e-Baghdad Khitabi, saying,

> There are one hundred Nuqaba', seventy Nujaba', forty Abdals and seven Autads, three Qutbs and one Qutb-al-Aqtab or Gauth. He has also written that the Abdals are like the prophets, the Autads are like the messenger prophets, Nuqaba' and Nujaba' are like the Israelite prophets, the three Qutbs are like the four Caliphs and the Qutb-al-Aqtab or Ghauth is like his Holiness Muhammad the Chosen (p.b.u.h.), his shadow and his deputy and successor in the world.

The preceding testimonials establish that the existence of the Unseen Men (رجال الغيب) is proved from the unbroken and true traditions. It is not an invention of the moderns. This does not mean that there are only these 360 saints of Allah mentioned here. No! On the contrary, there are many saints superior to these. The aforementioned group is a special detachment of saints set up in the esoteric order and discipline of worldly affairs. They have nothing to do with the teaching and tutorship of the seekers. Only the Ghauth among them is a perfect guide and authorized teacher. The Qutb is half a guide. All the other men of Genesis controllers are the executives and workers of worldly affairs, order, and discipline. Their approval makes business brisk.

Difficulties are solved, matters upset or redressed, and desires fulfilled. Therefore, if one desires the support of these Unseen Men at the commencement of a task or the start of travel or adventure or beginning of something, he should read the blessings on the prophets in the beginning and salute them as follows and seek their help:

اَلسَّلَامُ عَلَيْكُمْ يَارِجَالَ الْغَيْبِ وَيَا اَرْوَاحَ الْمُقَدَّسَةِ اَغِيْثُوْنِيْ بِقُوَّةٍ اُنْظُرُوْنِيْ بِنَظْرَةٍ يَا نُقَبَاءُ يَا نُجَبَاءُ يَا اَبْدَالُ يَا اَوْتَادُ يَا اَقْطَابُ وَيَا غَوْثُ اَغِيْثُوْنِيْ بِحُرْمَةِ مُحَمَّدٍ صَلَّى اللهُ عَلَيْهِ وَعَلَى اٰلِهٖ وَاَصْحَابِهٖ وَاَهْلِ بَيْتِهٖ اَجْمَعِيْنَ وَبَارِكْ وَسَلَّمَ تَسْلِيْمًا كَثِيْرًا كَثِيْرًا ۔

"Peace be upon you, Unseen Men and Holy Spirits. Help me with power and see me with a sight. Nuqaba', Nujaba' Abdal, Autad, Aqtab, and Ghauth! Help me for the sake of Muhammad, peace be upon him, his descendants, companions, and Ahl-i- Bait—all. Peace and benedictions be upon them in plenty and in plenty."

It is much better if before and after this, he reads the benedictions, opening chapter, and the verses of Ikhlas three times and gifts it to these holy spirits. Some people have circulated strange stories about the forty Abdals. Some say that something flies over the head with great speed at nighttime. Most commonfolk take them for the forty Abdal. But this is incorrect. It is a sort of bird that comes out at night and flies past over the head. Some people have given in the books the chart of the forty Abdals, saying that they change their positions on particular lunar days and set for a certain direction on a certain date. But we doubt it. The Unseen Men, as the name indicates, tour the world and carry out business with an invisible esoteric personality. The common sensualist people cannot see them come and go. At the occasion of pilgrimage, all these people assemble in the House of Allah at a stipulated time. On the nights of Qadr and Raghaib or Barat and other blessed nights, these people also participate in the esoteric meetings of spiritualists. The perfect gnostic people invoke that in purely worldly affairs and seek their help. This is, so to say, a department of invisible police among the followers of Muhammad (p.b.u.h.) entrusted with the order and discipline of worldly affairs. For carrying out their functions, they have got the assistance and services of the esoteric appointed angels and use them for their affairs like peons and process-servers. With regard to the Unseen Men, we confine ourselves to this much only.

One who has neither experienced a true dream all his life long, nor experienced anything out of the aforementioned cordial incidents, he ought to get his heart treated by going to some (spiritual) cordialogist and try hard to incubate the egg of his worldly personality with the heat of commemoration of Allah; otherwise, misfortune and disappointment will embrace him.

THE LINK BETWEEN
THE PRECEPTOR AND DISCIPLE

A perfect guide is indispensable for a novice seeker. Just as a woman needs a husband for bearing a child, the esoteric child of the seeker's heart (i.e., the etheric personality of his heart) is quickened by the mere association and attention of the guide. It is like this: The perfect preceptor puts the semen of his luminous latifa (لطيفه) of His personal name, Allah, from his own animate, perfect, and mature heart in the womb of the heart of the disciple. By providence of Allah the Most High, that bright latifa assumes life and flourishes in the form of an esoteric embryo and fetus. That esoteric child is tied to the esoteric self (i.e., the heart of the preceptor) through an esoteric cord, just as a material child is tied to the mother's womb through the umbilical cord and receives nourishment through it. Similarly, the esoteric, invisible, luminous child of the disciple is tied to the esoteric womb of his patron through a bright cord and receives esoteric nourishment through the esoteric link and spiritual cord. In Sufistic terminology, it is called the Sheikh's Link (رابطه شيخ). Revival of the etheric personality of the heart without a patron sheikh is an impossibility. Cordial life cannot be attained through one's own efforts, mere recitations, performance of duties, and unguided quadragesimal seclusion (چله). These bring about some temporary purity through mere purification of the self.

Sometimes, there is also a bit of terrestrial revelation and inclination of the people. But the path to cordial life has another way:

وظيفوں، ورد چلّوں سے اگر حاصل خدا ہوتا

انگشتوں سے حمل ہوتا تو شوہر کب روا ہوتا

(ظفر علی خاں)

"God is unattainable through duties, recitations, and lent. Husbands would have been unallowable could fingers cause conception."

Just as innumerable lamps can be lighted from a live lamp, the perfect guide lights the cordial lamps of trillions of disciples from the esoteric lamp of his own heart. Just as in spite of the presence of oil, wick, and other paraphernalia in a lamp, another lighted one is needed to light it, an esoteric lighted lamp is highly essential for lighting the esoteric lamp of the heart. There is no other course besides this!

The semblance of the person of a perfect man on which the bright lamp of His name Allah is lighted is thus related in the munificent Quran by God the Most High:

> (The name) Allah is the light of the heaven and earth. The semblance of this light is like a nitch in which a lamp is placed in a globe like a brilliant star hanging on a blessed olive tree. It is from direction being neither eastern nor western. It may presently take fire, without the touch of material fire. It is light upon light. God guides towards His light whom He likes and relates examples for people. God is Omniscient. God permits His name to be raised and remembered in houses.

Here, the word *Allah* does not mean the essence of Allah at all. Because Allah is called the Light of heaven and earth and considered the illuminator of heaven and earth like a lamp, it necessitates—God forbid—the vassalship of His Essence like the sun, whereas God the Most High is the Creator of heaven and earth and all that is therein and all the creation besides that, as we have already stated. Therefore, the word *Allah* here means His personal name Allah. It means that God the Most High has placed as trust the lamp of His personal name Allah on the Day of Eternity in the body of the perfect man. The capability of taking directions and the bright ability is like oil.

The heart-like lotus flower and globe is hanging in the human body. In order to protect the lamp from the adverse wind, the breast of a perfect man is like a niche for holding the globe. The elemental body of a perfect man is like an olive tree on which this bright lamp hangs and which is steadfast like the tree on Sinai. Thus on the Day of Eternity, God the Most High has provided all the essentials of this bright lamp in man. Now if anything is needed, it is another lighted lamp from the flame of which it has to catch the light. In the following portion of the verse, God the Most High Himself says:

فِىْ بُيُوْتٍ اَذِنَ اللّٰهُ اَنْ تُرْفَعَ وَيُذْكَرَ فِيْهَا اسْمُهٗ (۱۲۴ النور:۳۶)

"God has bidden that His name be raised and commemorated in houses."

In other words, God the Most High says that like a powerhouse, He has placed His personal name Allah on the person of Muhammad (p.b.u.h.), which has illuminated the heaven and earth with its light, and God the Most High has ordered an electric post be pitched in every house, and every man should carry the wire of this light and electricity to the house of his heart, so that every house of the heart will be illuminated with the light of His personal name, Allah, and thus the whole world may shine with the universal light of His personal name, Allah:

اے خدا نور محمدؐ کو درخشاں کردے

نور عرفان سے دنیا میں چراغاں کردے

سینہ سینا ہو ہر اک آنکھ ہو بینا جس سے

خامہ مثل ید بیضا مرا تاباں کردے

"O God! illuminate Muhammad's light (نورمحمد)." Through thelight of Gnosis make the world bright. Let my pen shine like the shining hand of Moses; and make the breast Sinai and impart to the eyesight light."

In short, the disciple derives this esoteric electricity from his patron preceptor through the esoteric wire, namely, the link with the sheikh. That preceptor derives it from his own sheikh and patron and so on and so forth until this chain terminates in its real headquarters and true powerhouse, namely, the blessed being of His Holiness Muhammad the Prophet of Allah (p.b.u.h.). Thus are the wires of this esoteric electricity linked together one with the other. Esoterically, all Godly people are tied together through this bright cord and linked to this chain. The headquarters' highest center and powerhouse of all these chains and links (i.e., esoteric electric wires) is the blessed person of his Holiness, ruler of the two worlds, pride of all beings Muhammad the Chosen (p.b.u.h.). He is blessed essence and the compendium of all powers. All the chains, links, and esoteric electric wires emerge from there and terminate there. He is the beginning and end of all, and his blessed person is the cause of the creation of the universe and the manifestation of creation and invention. A net of these cords and links is to be seen spreading up in the esoteric world. All the esoteric lions of the time are tied to these chains.

همه شیران جهاں بستهٔ ایں سلسله اند

روبه از حیله چهاں بگسلد ایں سلسله را

"All lions of the world are tied to these chains. How can the fox snap this chain through cunnings?"

So that when this bright child gets fixed up and quickened in the seeker through the attention of the sheikh, the seeker first of all attains a sort of understanding and wakefulness during sleep. That is to say, while dreaming, he understands that what he sees is during sleep. This is the initial stage of trance. Later on, he progresses and intentionally comes and goes in the esoteric invisible world of dream and trance. In the initial stage, the seeker feels a sort of lively movement, bellowing, and heaviness in his breast. After some time in the heart, through His personal name, Allah, that child of light breaks the terrestrial egg and comes out like a divine bird by the command of the Omnipotent. This cordial etheric personality possesses the esoteric body of the invisible world and flies in the invisible world toward the atmosphere of the invisible world of sanctity like the phoenix of the Qaf. The first step that he takes reaches beyond the universe (i.e., the six directions). All the miracles of the prophets, the revelations of the saints, and the flight in all terrestrial and celestial places are the phenomena of this bright, invisible personality. Every moment fresh esoteric events and divine conquests descend on this bright personality. The heart of the traveler possessing this bright personality, so to say, overbrims with fresh esoteric sciences, mystical meanings, and virgin knowledge and secrets that are neither to be found in books nor to be circumscribed in writing or speech. A bright personality of this caliber is constantly occupied in prayers, recitation, and worship, and devotion during sleep, trance, and waking constitutes its food and energy through it.

This bright personality is ever present in the assemblies of the prophets and saints. At times, the novice seeker can see this personally, while at others, he loses sight of it. If the seeker intends to commit some sin, the bright personality keeps him back and takes him to hard task and rebukes him. If perchance he commits a sin, esoterically, that personality brings him to such regret, sorrow, and pain that the seeker burns the filth of that sin through repentance, lamentation, and crying.

In the stage of teaching, that bright personality appears in the form of the sheikh, and in the place of seeking, it appears in the form of the disciple, but its real form is a third one— an admixture of the forms of the sheikh and the seeker. It is seldom seen in its real form, just as a man can rarely see his own face while he can always see the forms of others. This is called the etheric personality of annihilation in the sheikh (لطیفه فنافی الشیخ). The more perfect the sheikh and the more capable the seeker, the more stout, powerful, beautiful, and perfect is this esoteric, invisible personality. In short, when this bright personality grows and attains maturity through the training and nourishment of the sheikh, it attains the rank of the teachership, and he attains the ability of reviving the hearts of other seekers. Then esoterically he receives orders and permission from the Court of God the Most High and the Prophet of Allah (p.b.u.h.) and his patron sheikh to teach, tutor, and benefit mankind, and by order of God the Most High, he enriches the hearts of mankind with esoteric favors, whether the people know it or not. Many times, slaves of God show esoteric favors to people without thrusting themselves in. Says the Most High:

$$قُلْ مَآ اَسْئَلُكُمْ عَلَيْهِ مِنْ اَجْرٍ (۱۲۵ الفرقان: ۵۷)$$

"Tell them: for this favor I do not ask you for a reward."

They do not resemble the modern, fake, shopkeeper, imperfect, sensualist preceptors who spread a net and make disciples of people with the sole object of accumulating gifts, offers, and money from them, who purchase properties and enjoy themselves day and night. The disciples cannot get oil to light a lamp while electric lights glitter and electric fans run in the house of the preceptor. The poor disciples walk on foot to the court of the preceptor, and thus economizing the earning of their honest labors, they place it before the preceptor. But the preceptor travels in magnificent cars and airplanes. He has radios in his house, eats with gold and silver utensils, and enjoys luxuries that nawabs and millionaires cannot afford. These contractors of paradise provide the paraphernalia of hell in their houses and are themselves about to become fuel for hell, but by extending false promises to their disciples, they give them great promises of accommodating them in paradise. Says the Most High:

يٰۤاَيُّهَا الَّذِيْنَ اٰمَنُوْۤا اِنَّ كَثِيْرًا مِّنَ الْاَحْبَارِ وَالرُّهْبَانِ لَيَأْكُلُوْنَ اَمْوَالَ النَّاسِ بِالْبَاطِلِ وَ يَصُدُّوْنَ عَنْ سَبِيْلِ اللّٰهِ ؕ وَالَّذِيْنَ يَكْنِزُوْنَ الذَّهَبَ وَالْفِضَّةَ وَلَا يُنْفِقُوْنَهَا فِيْ سَبِيْلِ اللّٰهِ ۙ فَبَشِّرْهُمْ بِعَذَابٍ اَلِيْمٍ ۝ يَّوْمَ يُحْمٰى عَلَيْهَا فِيْ نَارِ جَهَنَّمَ فَتُكْوٰى بِهَا جِبَاهُهُمْ وَ جُنُوْبُهُمْ وَ ظُهُوْرُهُمْ ؕ هٰذَا مَا كَنَزْتُمْ لِاَنْفُسِكُمْ فَذُوْقُوْا مَا كُنْتُمْ تَكْنِزُوْنَ ۝ (التوبة ۹: ۳۴-۳۵)

> O you believers, many of the false
> saints and bishops fraudulently devour
> the property of people and (entangling
> them in their snares) lead them astray
> from the path of Allah. They amass gold
> and silver and don't spend it in the way
> of Allah. Give them tidings of severe
> punishment when the gold and silver
> will be heated in the hell-fire and their
> flanks, backs and faces will be branded
> thereby and will be told: This is what
> you amassed for yourselves; now taste
> of your treasures!

The seeker should first of all test the preceptor and guide in worldly transactions. If he is greedy in worldly transactions and a miser amassing wealth, he should be quitted forthwith. Secondly, if he finds him to be a sensualist luxuriant, very fat and bulky, the disciple should forsake him straightaway. Because sages have said, "The physicians ought to be stout; the spiritual preceptor lean." That is, seek a stout and healthy physician and a thin and lean preceptor. If the physician is himself sick and weak, how will he treat you, and if the preceptor is himself a slave of passions and a fat sensualist like a tail-sheep, how can he guide you to the path of God? Thirdly, he should not be a formal and hereditary preceptor but should have traversed the esoteric stages in the service of a perfect man by undergoing the esoteric path and renunciation and should be aware of all the stages of the spiritual path. Moreover, a man can neither become a preceptor nor guide by merely studying books on mysticism, exoteric jurisprudence, or logic or being born in the house of saints or by formally purchasing bitumen from a shopkeeping preceptor, nor can one derive instruction or grace from such formal and customary preceptors. Empty and void themselves, what can they give to others? God protects us against the tumult created by the present-day imperfect, raw preceptors. May God guide these preceptors and bestow intellect and discrimination on the disciples!

The selected slaves of God the Most High instruct and teach the people by His command alone and for their good. The Prophet of Allah (p.b.u.h.) was ordered,

$$ خُذْ مِنْ اَمْوَالِهِمْ صَدَقَةً تُطَهِّرُهُمْ وَتُزَكِّيْهِمْ بِهَا (١٩التوبة:١٠٣) $$

"Take charities from their properties, they will be sanctified and purified thereby."

In short, the perfect guides purify the souls, cleanse the hearts, and polish the spirits of the seekers for the sake of Allah only. It is their aim and object that somehow the seeker should become a slave of Allah and unite with God the Most High by obtaining guidance.

Let it be remembered that everything can be reformed and trained, but it is highly difficult to do so in the case of a man. But if a seeker is decorated like a bride by a perfect bride-dresser in the form of really perfect and esoteric man (i.e., preceptor), the angels envy his decoration and pay him respect and homage.

$$ هر پا که بخدمت رسد سرگردد $$
$$ مقصود دو عالمش میسر گردد $$
$$ ما جمله مسیم تو کیمائی شاها $$
$$ هر مس که به کیمیا رسد زر گردد $$

"Every foot that reaches your court becomes a head and attains the object of the two worlds. We are all copper and you are alchemy, O King! The copper that reaches the alchemist becomes gold."

FALSE PRECEPTS OF SOME PEOPLE ABOUT TASAWWUF

Some people think that Tasawwuf (mysticism) is a mere compendium of whims and imagination and the Sufis (mystics) visualize their imagination and whims personified in their dreams and trances. But the real matter of Tasawwuf is distinct from dreams and fancy imagination, quite clear of doubt and misgiving, and quite free from whim and fancy. Like the true morn, it is a clear and solid world where the real sun is shining, which dispels the darkness of all whims, fancies, doubts, and false incidents. The man who esoterically dies in this sensualist material world, which is narrow and dark like the womb, is reborn in the form of a bright child in that real, spiritual, eternal, and bright world. After a long while, when that bright and esoteric personality of his grows and attains wisdom through the universal intellect and learns esoteric language from his esoteric mother, it gathers familiarity with the names and realities of the things there. After that, he hears and understands the talk of the spiritual and esoteric people there. He acquires esoteric sciences in the spiritual schools and colleges there, breast to breast and eye to eye without any mediator. Then his affairs surpass doubt and misgiving, and his degree of certainty is raised to visual certainty instead of academic certainty. The affair of such a seeker progresses from hearing (شنید) to seeing (دید) from seeing to reaching (رسید) and from reaching to finding (یافت). This is called true certainty (حق اليقين).

Those who have led an animal life throughout, who have had no other occupation or object of life except eating and drinking and, like the blind frog of the well, have spent all their lives in the material world, are unaware of the boundless and spacious spiritual world. O blessed seeker, if you crave eternal life and if you are destined to know, approach, observe, and have union with God the Most High, you must engage yourself with commemoration of Allah the Most High. Learn this essential and subtle knowledge from some perfect teacher so that you may attain the object of life in this world and reach your real goal, and attaining eternal life in the world of bounties, you may partake of such graces and esoteric relish which no eye has seen, no ear has heard, and no heart has ever thought about. Remember that without concentrating on His personal name,

Allah, the heart cannot be revived, the esoteric path cannot be opened, and God the Most High's proximity, union, and observation cannot be attained. Though a man may spend all his life in severe renunciation and ascetic exercises, he must keep watchful nights and fast in the day, because though external physical performances, devotion, and worship do purify the animal self, the heart remains dead and dark. Hence commemoration alone is the means of the slave's reaching the master. It is the creation's approach to the Creator. It is the only key to the knowledge, proximity, and union of God the Most High. Of all the commemorations, that of His personal name, Allah, is the most comprehensive and best. And of all the methods of commemoration, it is the best, sublimest, most perfect, easiest, and safest. I mean writing the figure of the noun Allah (الله) with the finger of meditation through imagination and concentration. Of the places of commemoration, the best is the eye, which opens the way to observation (مشاہدے). The observation of God the Most High is the aim and object of all worship, devotion, and asceticism; all orders and fundamentals of the religious law; and the path of truth and knowledge, as well as all the travel and Taswwuf. No bounty, rank, or degree is superior to that of observation. Therefore, the seeker should adopt the occupation of concentrating on His personal name, Allah. He should study from some esoteric teacher and a perfect guide the science of observation through concentration on His personal name, Allah. All the grades of the church and state and all the exoteric and esoteric treasures "are acquired through the science of observation."

$$مَنْ لَّهُ الْمَوْلٰى فَلَهُ الْكُلُّ$$

"He who has the Lord has everything." When the seeker begins practicing concentration on His personal name, Allah, Satan waylays him, and through multiple doubts and thoughts, he puts this thought in the heart of the seeker: "This concentration business is unaccomplishable; His personal name, Allah, cannot be impressed on the heart. It is a waste of time to carry on this business; it is better to engage in some prescribed supererogations and recitations instead. Because this will carry some reward at least."

When the seeker occupies himself with external actions, worship, and devotion and engages himself in outward worship, commemoration, recitation, and supererogations, observation of the breath and breath control in a room day and night, Satan takes possession of the room of his heart, which is the real and true seat of commemoration. So that while his tongue and other limbs are busy with commemoration and worship, the heart fumbles about with its sensual thoughts, worldly affairs, and Satanic passions, and Satan does not allow the commemoration to affect the heart.

Moreover, Satan makes the seeker famous and popular in the eyes of the people, giving out that so-and-so is very religious, pious, and keeps awake in the night. And fascinating him by public applause, Satan frustrates his labors and kills and destroys him with the dagger of pride and egotism. He thinks in his mind that he has rendered great worship, and going around and around like the ox of the flour mill, he conceives himself to have traversed a great distance. But on opening his eyes, he finds himself in the same place. When a man is engaged in external devotion, commemoration, meditation, and worship and the devil overpowers his heart, Satan laughs and exhilarates, standing beside him.

Hence, the seeker ought to continue the hobby of concentrating on His personal name, Allah, though His personal name, Allah, may not get fixed on the heart in the initial stage. Because the novice seeker is under the misconception that concentration on His personal name, Allah, means that the figure of His personal name, Allah, should be firmly fixed on the heart and the name Allah should remain ever illuminated so that whenever he turns and attends toward the heart, he should see His personal name, Allah, impressed and written there. In other words, he means that His personal name, Allah, should come into his control. But this is a tremendous blunder! For this very reason, the majority of seekers relinquish this blessed occupation. Remember that His personal name, Allah, is innate, while man and his thoughts and concentration are created. The innate thing cannot be controlled by the created. It is the other way around. That is to say that through concentration, the heart, mind, senses, and all the limbs of the seeker come under the bondage of His personal name, Allah.

When a man submerges his person in the concentration of the name, Allah, the body is lost in the name. All the impurities, alloys, slothfulness, pollution, darknesses, and invalidities of the person of the concentrator are repelled and removed through the light of His personal name, Allah. Thus, through constant concentration on His imaginary personal name, the seeker reaches the real and true gate of His personal name, Allah, which lies concealed, like a trust in the body of a man like the sun. At that moment, through His grace and mercy, God the Most High absorbs the seeker in the sea of light of His personal name, Allah. If a perfect teacher, companion, and guide is his partner, he unites the mature, personed, capable seeker with God the Most High through a single attention or enters him in constant attendance in the court of his Holiness the Holy Prophet (p.b.u.h.). But in the beginning, the seeker should not crave to bring His personal name, Allah, under his control and see it speedily impressed on the page of his heart.

Unless the spirit and sensuality of the seeker is annihilated through concentration on this name, Allah, and through the heat in His personal name, Allah, and the attention of the perfect guide, the innate, boundless bird of the etheric personality of the heart emerges headfirst from inside the terrestrial egg, he should never think of seeing His personal name, Allah, impressed, established, and illuminated on his heart but should vigorously continue his work day and night. Moreover, like a child, he should not hanker after trances, revelations, flights, celestial travel, miracles, or other spiritual spectacles and esoteric feats. But he should always try perseveringly to establish the print of His personal name, Allah, in his heart and brain so as to banish from his person sensualist slothfulness, satanic darkness, and the dirt of the distracted worldly thoughts through the heat and light of the sun of His personal name, Allah.

The Seeker Must Not Renounce the World and His Family

When the concentration of His personal name, Allah, begins to influence the person of the meditator, first of all, a sort of heat appears inside the seeker, and he feels something like the heat of fever in himself. He cannot sleep at night, and he especially feels pain when he sleeps on his left side. If it occurs so, the seeker should not become frightened. These are the signs of eternal perfect health. Thoughts of renunciation and reliance on God creep up in the heart of the seeker at the time. He abhors people. He thinks of leaving behind his house, divorcing his wife, taking to the jungle, wearing the patched garment, and becoming a faqir. But beware! Let him never do so unless he receives explicit permission or orders for such things either esoterically or from a perfect guide. The practice of the faqir of Muhammad (p.b.u.h.) is to remain gregarious with the people. He is to guard his own secrets, make a point of remaining oblivious, and never allow himself to be detected and pointed at. Because sometimes, temporarily, imitatively, an idea of renunciation, resignation, and relinquishing the house overtakes the seeker for a short while. After divorcing his wife and deserting his children, he starts for the jungle, and donning a patched garment, he becomes a recluse faqir. Such a foolish, hasty, imitative, formal, and new seeker has no access to the esoteric path. He suffers great hardships by way of trials. When he encounters hunger, thirst, and diverse hardships in this path, the intoxication of his temporary imitative renunciation and resignation melts away after a short time. Then he feels sorry in his heart. But as he becomes famous among the people as a recluse faqir, he is ashamed of remingling with the people and resuming worldly affairs. Hence, he is entangled in severe distress and perplexity. He is between the devil and the deep sea. God protect us against such a state of affliction and remorse! Therefore, pursuant to his false thoughts, the novice seeker ought never to desert his wife and children and take to the jungle. How well has someone said:

اک شخص چلا گھر سے نکل کر سوئے صحرا   مولا کی طلب میں زن و فرزند کو چھوڑا

سمجھا زن و فرزند ہی ہیں مانعِ دیدار   ہے منزلِ مقصود میں حائل یہی دیوار

صحرا میں سمندر میں اسے ڈھونڈ رہا تھا   ہر بحر ہر بر میں اسے ڈھونڈ رہا تھا

کھویا گیا خود آپ مگر اس کو نہ پایا   سب کھو کے بھی بیچارے کو کچھ ہاتھ نہ آیا

مایوسی سے دل ٹوٹ گیا پاؤں کی ماند   ڈھلتی رہی عمر اس کی یونہی چھاؤں کی ماند

بیچارے پے جس وقت گھٹا موت کی چھائی   اس وقت کسی کی یہ صدا کانوں میں آئی

اے طالبِ حق، حق تو تیرے گھر میں مکیں تھا   جس جا سے تو نکلا تھا ارے میں تو وہیں تھا

(میر حسن)

"A man left his home for the desert, in search of the Lord, deserting his wife and children. He thought that the wife and children were hindrances in the way of God. This was the wall that intervened between the destination. He searched for Him in every desert, in every ocean, and every land. He lost himself but found Him not. He lost everything but acquired naught. In despair, his heart and legs broke alike. Like the shadow, he decreased his life. When the clouds of death surrounded the wretch, his ears did someone's calling catch: 'O seeker of God, God dwelt with you in your house. He was there whence you went.'"

Hence, the seeker should never change his condition according to his whim and imagination. He should rather wait until God the Most High makes the conditions and circumstances amiable to him and changes them.

Thence, at the appearance of such a condition, because of the heat of His personal name, Allah, and the horrible thoughts of renunciation and resignation, he should cool down or extinguish this terribleness or heat either by concentrating on the name of Muhammad (p.b.u.h.) or through excessive repetition of blessings (درود شریف) on him because the name *Muhammad* (p.b.u.h.) has anesoterical cool nature. Its coolness and lovability (جمال) create forbearance, toleration, and immense patience in the person of the seeker, and he successfully bears up the heavy weight of the terribleness (جلال) of His personal name, Allah, and does not get impatient, intolerant, and restless.

Sometimes, the excessive heat of concentrating on His personal name, Allah, causes slackness in outward worship, and idleness takes place in external supererogations, verbal commemoration, and virtuous physical actions. They lose their importance and value in the eyes of the seeker to such an extent that he relinquishes even the obligatory prayers. It is incumbent on the seeker to avoid such a state and on no account to dispense with the obligatory prayers and observations of the external religious law. This is also a great trick and deception of Satan. So much so that in the beginning of concentration, Satan shows some people excellent shows and esoteric scenes during sleep and trances, and when he reverts to external worship and the obligatory prayers, a diminution occurs in these esoteric satanic scenes and entertainments.

Consequently, the foolish seeker falls prey in the snare of Satan and gives up the obligatory prayers and observation of the religious law. Thus, he becomes eternally condemned and an apostate in the path. Thousands of seekers have been observed to be ensnared in such apostasy and returns. He who once gets drowned in these whirlpools of the path can never see the coast of salvation again.

دریں ورطه کشتی فروشد هزار   که پیدا نه شد تختهٔ برکنا

(سعدی)

"Thousands of boats went down this whirlpool of which not a plank appeared on the shore." Sometimes, it so happens that when the seeker practices concentrating on His personal name, Allah, he feels as if all his limbs are being pressed in a press or oil machine. After the exercise, he feels very tired and exhausted. The body becomes injured and broken. In such a case, the seeker should revert to external worship. Thus, exoterically and esoterically, the seeker should never disengage himself from commemorating Allah because commemoration of God consists in opposing the self.

Sometimes, thoughts and whims like the following induce the novice seeker toward renunciation, resignation, and Faqr. When I take up faqiri, I will have no worries about external worldly riches, because the moment that I take a step in that direction, I will become an associate and friend of God. I will receive livelihood from the Invisible. Jinns and angels shall obey me and bring me whatever I command them to do. A daily income will be fixed for me. Or I will have an invisible income from them or will be able to see the treasures and buried wealth underground. Or I will be taught the prescriptions of alchemy and elixirs. Or I will get the philosopher's stone. In short, thousands of such silly whims and thoughts take root in the mind of the seeker. Showing him such an imaginary Utopia, Satan seduces the seeker to give up his external livelihood and business and become a faqir. Some foolish seekers resign from services. Some sell and squander away their properties. Since such seekers are not sincere at heart, when they get nothing after wandering about for a while, they make an ignominious retreat, and all their life, they regret in sorrow and shame. When such foolish seekers fall into the clutches of imperfect shopkeepers and false guides, they are shown similar green gardens and extended false promises, plundered, kept in service, and made to waste away their valuable lives by being given false promises from day to day. When some seekers repeatedly worry the shopkeeper, cunning guides for the fulfillment of those promises, the false guides employ those seekers in (چلوں، خلوتوں) retirement and asceticism. Now some of the seekers turn mad during these seclusions. Some fall sick while others set off for unknown directions after futile endeavors, and thus the guide gets rid of them. Hence the seeker should avoid such foolery and melancholia.

Concentration on His personal name, Allah, is the best, sublimest, easiest, and safest of all the methods of commemoration. The tongue of a man gets patched at the time of death, and all the other limbs and senses fail to function. Then, for commemoration, man is left with only the instrument of concentration and meditation. If in his lifetime the seeker has practiced His personal name, Allah, through concentration and meditation and established His personal name, Allah, in himself, submerged his person in it, and revived his heart thereby, he will come to know the value and price of his aforementioned blessed occupation at the last critical time of death when through the esoteric flash of concentration on His personal name, all his esoteric etheric personalities, flesh, skin, limbs, and hairs will begin to commemorate Allah and vigorously and fervently shout out, "Allah! Allah!" and all the body will play the commemoration of Allah like an instrument. Like the strings of the playing instrument, the esoteric tunes of the commemoration of Allah will be heard from every vein and tissue of the body.

Blessed is the end of such a person because Satan cannot approach such a man at the time of death. When one who has practiced concentration on His personal name, Allah, is awakened in the grave by Munkir and Nakir (منکرنکیر) to answer their questions, he gets up in the grave while His personal name, Allah, is written on his forehead, breast, and both the palms in resplendent:

> words bright and shines like the sun. At the sight thereof the recording angels are put to astonishment, they respect-fully stand up with folded hands and say, "O slave of Allah! sleep as the bride sleeps: May Allah reward you

well in both the worlds! You need not answer questioning; your blessed person is evidence of itself. Bravo! your magnanimity and well done your earning. Your hands, feet, and other limbs are colored in the color of Allah, namely, His personal name, Allah. We are ashamed of putting questions to you. Now you can sleep like a bride in expectation of the observation and union of your master, God the Most High."

The elemental body of a person is like a hole in which the soul (نفس) and Satan have entered like a snake. Worship, commemoration, and meditation with the external body and physical limbs and organs is shaking at the hole of the snake with sticks. The soul and Satan inside the hole are not at all injured thereby and do not even know of it. But concentration on His personal name, Allah, is like pouring boiling water or a stream of boiling oil inside the hole, which burns down the soul and Satan to dust. It should be regarded a very cheap and easy bargain even if it is acquired after spending life and wealth and lengthy years of labor and endeavor for it.

To deter a man from this blessed and precious business, Satan exercises billions and trillions of devices, treacheries, and tricks. Sometimes he says that His personal name, Allah, cannot be fixed up without the attention of a perfect guide; therefore, one should take up some external physical worship. But remember that the perfect guide attends to the seeker, the pot of whose person is clean, strong, and large in capacity. Now these things cannot be acquired without concentrating on His personal name, Allah. Therefore, concentration on His personal name, Allah, entitles a person to the mercy of God the Most High and the favors of the guide. Through concentration on His personal name, Allah, the seeker reaches the esoteric door of the guide and makes the guide kind toward him. But the evil self and Satan keep the seeker from this blessed hobby through all sorts of pretentions because concentration on His personal name, Allah, is like a deadly venom to

Satan. The evil self soon perishes thereby. When the concentrator on His personal name, Allah, gets himself busy with concentration, it sets the house of Satan on fire—so to say, a commotion and agitation is set up among the human and jinn; Satan and the forces of Iblis are sent in battalions to combat him, and somehow or other, they keep him off from this hobby at any cost. So much so that when after traversing stage after stage, the concentrator is about to enter the proximity of God the Most High, the Iblis, with his accursed person himself, comes forward to oppose him. Therefore, O fortunate seekers, pluck courage and devote all your life to this blessed hobby. Never relinquish this holy business even for a moment. God willing, you will very soon obtain the key to the treasures of the two worlds.

Methods of Concentrating on His Personal Name, Allah

At the time of physical exercise, the novice concentrator is highly perplexed as to how to practice concentration on the name Allah in the heart, brain, and other parts of the body and how to impress the figure of His personal name, Allah, within himself whether he should make himself stand before Him in the form of a separate individual and write the figure of His personal name, Allah, on his heart, brain, breast, and other limbs through imagination and meditation or imagine another person writing on his limbs or how and whence himself to write and impress the name, Allah, on his own body. Since these things are highly essential and are not to be found in books, we will therefore narrate some important and easy methods based on our experience and observations. If the operator and concentrator practices these instructions, he will greatly be helped in impressing and writing His personal name, Allah, and he will very quickly succeed in this blessed mission. These are highly true, useful, and valuable information for concentrating on His personal name, Allah, which we present to the readers and which have been accumulated after a long time and years of self-practice and exercise.

The concentrator on His personal name, Allah, ought to perform the ablutions, wear clean clothes, and sit cross-legged in a clean place. He should empty and distract his heart from all extraneous thoughts, worldly worries, and sensual fancies.

To stop the passage of external satanic thoughts and sensual fancies, he should form the following safeguard around himself. He should read the following prayers three times each and blow on the chest, and after blowing on the palms of both hands, he should rub them over the entire body.

بِسْمِ اللهِ الرَّحْمٰنِ الرَّحِيْمِ

اَلْحَمْدُ لِلّٰهِ رَبِّ الْعٰلَمِيْنَۙ ۞ الرَّحْمٰنِ الرَّحِيْمِۙ ۞ مٰلِكِ يَوْمِ الدِّيْنِ ۞

اِيَّاكَ نَعْبُدُ وَاِيَّاكَ نَسْتَعِيْنُ ۞ اِهْدِنَا الصِّرَاطَ الْمُسْتَقِيْمَۙ ۞

صِرَاطَ الَّذِيْنَ اَنْعَمْتَ عَلَيْهِمْ ۙ غَيْرِ الْمَغْضُوْبِ عَلَيْهِمْ وَلَا الضَّآلِّيْنَ ۞

بِسْمِ اللهِ الرَّحْمٰنِ الرَّحِيْمِ

اَللهُ لَاۤ اِلٰهَ اِلَّا هُوَ الْحَيُّ الْقَيُّوْمُ ۚ لَا تَأْخُذُهٗ سِنَةٌ وَّلَا نَوْمٌ ۚ لَهٗ مَا فِي السَّمٰوٰتِ وَمَا فِي الْاَرْضِ ۗ مَنْ

ذَا الَّذِيْ يَشْفَعُ عِنْدَهٗۤ اِلَّا بِاِذْنِهٖ ۚ يَعْلَمُ مَا بَيْنَ اَيْدِيْهِمْ وَمَا خَلْفَهُمْ ۚ وَلَا يُحِيْطُوْنَ بِشَيْءٍ

مِّنْ عِلْمِهٖۤ اِلَّا بِمَا شَآءَ ۚ وَسِعَ كُرْسِيُّهُ السَّمٰوٰتِ وَالْاَرْضَ ۚ وَلَا يَـُٔوْدُهٗ حِفْظُهُمَا ۚ وَهُوَ الْعَلِيُّ

الْعَظِيْمُ ۞ ٢٥٥

بِسْمِ اللهِ الرَّحْمٰنِ الرَّحِيْمِ

قُلْ يٰۤاَيُّهَا الْكٰفِرُوْنَۙ ۞ لَاۤ اَعْبُدُ مَا تَعْبُدُوْنَۙ ۞ وَلَاۤ اَنْتُمْ عٰبِدُوْنَ مَاۤ اَعْبُدُۚ ۞

وَلَاۤ اَنَا عَابِدٌ مَّا عَبَدْتُّمْۙ ۞ وَلَاۤ اَنْتُمْ عٰبِدُوْنَ مَاۤ اَعْبُدُۗ ۞ لَكُمْ دِيْنُكُمْ وَلِيَ دِيْنِ ۞

بِسْمِ اللهِ الرَّحْمٰنِ الرَّحِيْمِ

قُلْ هُوَ اللهُ اَحَدٌۚ ۞ اَللهُ الصَّمَدُۚ ۞ لَمْ يَلِدْ ۙ وَلَمْ يُوْلَدْ ۙ ۞ وَلَمْ يَكُنْ لَّهٗ كُفُوًا اَحَدٌ ۞

بِسْمِ اللهِ الرَّحْمٰنِ الرَّحِيْمِ

قُلْ اَعُوْذُ بِرَبِّ الْفَلَقِ ۞ مِنْ شَرِّ مَا خَلَقَ ۞ وَمِنْ شَرِّ غَاسِقٍ اِذَا وَقَبَ ۞

وَمِنْ شَرِّ النَّفّٰثٰتِ فِى الْعُقَدِ ۞ وَمِنْ شَرِّ حَاسِدٍ اِذَا حَسَدَ ۞

بِسْمِ اللهِ الرَّحْمٰنِ الرَّحِيْمِ

قُلْ اَعُوْذُ بِرَبِّ النَّاسِ ۞ مَلِكِ النَّاسِ ۞ اِلٰهِ النَّاسِ ۞

مِنْ شَرِّ الْوَسْوَاسِ ۙ الْخَنَّاسِ ۞ الَّذِىْ يُوَسْوِسُ فِىْ صُدُوْرِ النَّاسِ ۞

مِنَ الْجِنَّةِ وَالنَّاسِ ۞

بِسْمِ اللهِ الرَّحْمٰنِ الرَّحِيْمِ

اللّٰهُمَّ صَلِّ عَلٰى سَيِّدِنَا مُحَمَّدٍ وَّ عَلٰى آلِ مُحَمَّدٍ وَبَارِكْ وَسَلِّمْ۔

اَسْتَغْفِرُ اللهَ رَبِّىْ مِنْ كُلِّ ذَمْبٍ وَّ اَتُوْبُ اِلَيْهِ

سَلٰمٌ قَوْلًا مِّنْ رَّبٍّ رَّحِيْمٍ ۞

وَاللهُ الْمُسْتَعَانُ عَلٰى مَا تَصِفُوْنَ۔

سُبْحَانَ اللهِ وَالْحَمْدُ لِلّٰهِ وَلَا اِلٰهَ اِلَّا اللهُ وَاللهُ اَكْبَرُ وَلَا حَوْلَ وَلَا قُوَّةَ اِلَّا بِاللهِ الْعَلِىِّ الْعَظِيْمِ

لَا اِلٰهَ اِلَّا اللهُ وَحْدَهُ لَاشَرِيْكَ لَهُ لَهُ الْمُلْكُ وَلَهُ الْحَمْدُ يُحْى وَيُمِيْتُ وَهُوَ حَىٌّ لَّا يَمُوْتُ اَبَدًا

اَبَدًا ذُوالْجَلَالِ وَالْاِكْرَامِ بِيَدِهِ الْخَيْرُ وَهُوَ عَلٰى كُلِّ شَيْئٍ قَدِيْرٌ۔

اَشْهَدُ اَنْ لَّا اِلٰهَ اِلَّا اللهُ وَحْدَهُ لَا شَرِيْكَ لَهُ وَاَشْهَدُ اَنَّ مُحَمَّدًا عَبْدُهُ وَرَسُوْلُهُ۔

لَا اِلٰهَ اِلَّا اللهُ مُحَمَّدٌ رَّسُوْلُ اللهِ صَلَّى اللهُ عَلَيْهِ وَ آلِهِ وَسَلَّمَ۔

Here, we give the preceding Quranic chapters and verses in Roman characters for the facility of those readers who cannot read Arabic script.

1. *Tasmia:* Bismillah-irrahman-irrahim.
2. *Surah Fatiha:* Alhamdu lillahi rabbil alamfn arrahman irrahim, maliki yaumiddfn, iyyaka n'abudu wa iyyaka nastain, ihdinassirat al mustaqfma siratallazina an'amta 'alaihim, ghair il-maghdub 'alaihim waladdalfn. Amin.
3. *Ayat-Alkursi:* Allaho lailahaillahowal hayyul-qayyum, la takhuzahu sinatun wa la naum, Ihu ma fissamawat-i-wama filard, man zallazi yashfa'o 'indahu ilia bi iznih, y'alamo ma baina aidihim wa-ma khalfahum wala yuhftuna bishai-in rnin ilmihi ilia bimashaa wasia'kursiyyu-hussamawati walard, wala yaudohu hifzohoma wa howal 'alyyulazim.
4. *Surah Kafiroon:* Qul ya ayyohal kafi-runa la 'abudo ma ta'abuduna a la antum 'abuduna ma 'abud, wa la ana'abedum ma 'abadtum, wala untum abediin ma'abud; lakum dinokum waliyadin.
5. *Surah Ikhlas:* Qul howallaho ahad, allahus Samad, lamyalid, wa lamyulad, wa lam ya-kullahu kofowan ahad.
6. *Surah Falaq:* Qul a'uzubi rabbil falaqi min sharri ma khalaqa wa min sharri ghasiqin eza waqaba wa min sharrinaffasati fil'uqadi wa min sharri hasidin eza hasad.
7. *Surah Wannas:* Qul a'uzo birabbinnisi malikinnasi ilahinnasi min sharril waswasil khannas-illazf yowaswiso fi'sudiirinnasi minal-jinnati wannas.
8. *Astaghfar:* Astaghfirullaha rabbi min kulli zambin wa atiibu 'ilahi.
9. *Verse:* Salamun qaulan min Rabbir-Rahim.
10. *Verse:* Wallahul mustan alamatasifun.
11. *Kalma-i-Tamjid:* Subhanallahi wal-hamdu lillahi wa la ilaha illallaho wallaho akbar wa la haul wa la quwwata ilia billa hil 'alyyil azfm.
12. *Kalma-i-Tauhid*: La ilaha illallaho wahdula sharikalahu lahulmulko walahul hamdo yuhyi wa yumlto wa howa 'ala kulli shai'n qadir.
13. *Kalma-i-Shahadat:* Ashhado alia ilah illallaho wa ashhado anna Muhammad 'abduhu wa rasuluhu.
14. Lailah illallaho Muhammad-ar-rasul-allah.

Then closing his eyes, he should contemplate observation of God the Most High, the assembly of his Holiness the Prophet (p.b.u.h.), and the assemblies of the prophets and saints and recollect death, the resurrection, the grave, the revival, and similar thoughts. He should try over and over again to inscribe His personal name, Allah, on his forehead and his heart and the name of Muhammad (p.b.u.h.), with the forefinger of imagination. If one is straggling and does not relinquish sinning, one should imagine writing His personal name, Allah, on the seat of the navel. The concentrator should imagine his forefinger to be a pen and the sun as an inkpot in front of him. Dipping his finger into the inkpot of the sun, he should write His personal name, Allah, on his forehead by imagining his head to be a large lantern and sitting therein should inscribe His personal name, Allah, on the glass in front of him. This will generate terrible attraction (جذب جلالی), and he should write the prolongated name Muhammad (p.b.u.h.) on his chest so that both the M's should come on the nipples and the letterd should come on the heart. This will generate cold attraction (جذب جلالی). He should write the name *Muhammad* (p.b.u.h.) with a white lunar color. But if he experiences difficulty in writing afresh His personal name, Allah, and the name Muhammad the Prophet on the aforementioned places, namely the forehead and breast, he should imagine His personal name, Allah, written in a large, beautiful script as large as the size of the breadth of the forefinger in a red solar color on his breast or head and trace it with his forefinger—in his imagination and concentration, he should rub the finger on it like a pen. Similarly, he should imagine the name *Muhammad* (p.b.u.h.) written on his chest in a white lunar color and try to rub the forefinger on it. Some find this second method easier. Alongside this, he should carry on observation of breathing in the heart; when he inhales, he should utter the word, Allah (الله), in his mind, and when he exhales, he should mentally pronounce the word (هو) "Hu." When he practices the name *Muhammad* (p.b.u.h.), he should utter "Muhammad the Prophet of Allah" مُحَمَّدُ رَّسُولَ اللّٰهُ at the time of inhalation and mentally pronounceصَلَّى الله عَلَيْهِ وَ آلِهِ وَسَلَّمُ "Benediction of Allah be upon him and peace" in his mind. Thus through repeated practice, His personal name, Allah, and the name of Muhammad the Prophet (p.b.u.h.) will shine inside the seeker. If the seeker has a perfect guide, he should imagine the guide sitting inside his head, chest, and heart and writing His personal name, Allah, and the name of His Holiness (p.b.u.h.). This makes it still easier. Simultaneously, he should observe his breathing. In this way, the seeker succeeds very soon. When the concentration and meditation of the seeker, the attention and power of the perfect guide, the labors of the seeker, and the attraction of the guide centralize and unite on His personal name, Allah, or the name of his Holiness the Prophet (p.b.u.h.), it sometimes generates the light and electricity of awe (برقِ جلال) and drowns and stupefies the seeker esoterically. Then he does not remember the esoteric incidents. But if he has been pulled by the electricity of lovable attraction (نورِ جمال), He remembers the esoteric incidents in dreams or meditation. The assemblies of the prophets and saints and commemoration then appear to him, and the seeker attends the assembly of Muhammad (p.b.u.h.), the assemblies of prophets and saints, (ذکر نفسی، قلبی، روحی، سری) the commemoration of the soul or heart or spirit, or secret commencement. Or the personal, attributive, or actional illuminations of God the Most High occur to the seeker. Or the seeker acquires flight and travels in celestial or terrestrial stages. If, because of the excess of satanic whims and sensual darknesses, the impression of His personal name, Allah, and the name of His Holiness Prophet Muhammad (p.b.u.h.) cannot settle in the heart, the seeker ought to commence physical practice—to impress His personal name on all the parts of the body. So that being decorated with His personal name, Allah, the whole person should be purified and cleansed and rendered fit for attending the court of the Prophet (p.b.u.h.) and observing the True Essence.

$$ اِسْمُ اللّٰهِ شَیْءٌ طَاهِرٌ لَا یَسْتَقِرُّ اِلَّا بِمَکَانٍ طَاهِرٍ $$

"The name Allah is a thing pure and does not rest except, in a pure place." No time is prescribed for the hobby of concentrating on His personal name, Allah. It can be practiced at all times. But the best time is from dawn to sunrise or an hour or two later.

Sketch is given in the start of book.

When His personal name, Allah, gets written on the heart, the etheric personality of the heart blossoms like a rose, whereby seven bright etheric personalities like seven petals, red in color, scented and odiferous, appear around the heart. Every etheric personality glows with the lights of the seven personal attributes of the light of His personal name, Allah. The map of the name written on the circle of the heart that opens like the rose, with the seven etheric personalities inscribed with the name Allah around it, is given here:

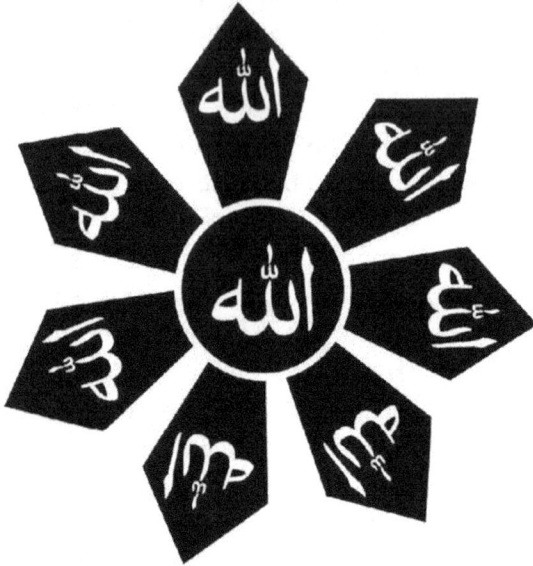

When His personal name, Allah, gets inscribed on any limb, a flash of light appears from it. The place with that etheric personality begins to recite the commemoration of Allah or the holy formula, and that limb traverses the light of his personal name, Allah, and is revived therein with the etheric personality of the commemoration of Allah.

The seeker should also inscribe the name Allah on the two palms of the hands and the two flanks and the seat of the navel. The seeker should imagine his elemental body to be a garment that the spirit and soul is wearing from top to toe and as if His personal name, Allah, is printed on the inner side of that garment at the places to be concentrated upon. The seeker should think himself sitting inside that garment and practice drawing from within his *index* finger on His personal name, Allah, printed on the places of concentration. God the Most High says, "Remember Me: I'll remember thee." We have already amply elucidated this verse, stating that with whatever attribute and organ we remember God the Most High, He causes the illumination of that very name to reach that organ, which is revived and illuminated with the light of God the Most High. It is related in a tradition to Sahih Bukhari: God says, "Through excessive commemoration and supererogation, a man gets so close to Me that

I become his eyes and he sees through me; I become his ears, and he hears through Me; I become his hands and feet, and he grasps and walks through Me." God the Most High becomes the limbs and organs of His pious slave, which means that the name of God the Most High gets written in luminous letters on all the limbs of the gnostic traveler, and all his limbs and brain get revived and illuminated through the light of His personal name, Allah.

It is difficult to inscribe the figure of His personal name, Allah, on every limb of the body. The place on which it can be easily written and the name that can be successfully and easily written should be practiced first of all. Closing his eyes, one should meditate on the written form of His personal name, Allah, wherever it is possible to do so. When His personal name, Allah, is written down in luminous letters inside the concentrator, it involuntarily takes hold of its particular part of the body. Also remember that if a seeker is dull-minded and block-headed and unable to concentrate on His personal name, Allah, he should place before him a copy of His personal name, Allah, beautifully written and *glazed* on a glass pane or paper, for the sake of comparison. At the time of concentration, he should try to fix that in himself. By his repeatedly doing so, the picture of the name of Allah gets established. If greater ease is sought after, he should repeatedly write the name of Allah on a slate with a thick pencil or chalk at leisure time during the day or night. He should write it at least sixty-six times a day. Thus also His personal name, Allah, soon comes into concentration. Before going to sleep in the day or night, one must practice concentrating on His personal name, Allah. Or he should place before him a copy of His personal name, Allah, beautifully written on a piece of paper or glass and look at it while going to sleep. He should repeatedly try to get it impressed within himself and go to sleep in that condition. By doing so, he ensures the name Allah gets illuminated in sleep also.

For concentration, there are seven names that are like keys for the seven esoteric treasures. There are separate names for the seven etheric personalities. The following are the names:

(١)اللّٰه،(٢)بِللّٰهِ،(٣)لَهُ،(٤)هُوَ،(٥)محمد صَلَّ اللّٰهُ عَلَيْهِ وَآلِهِ وَسَلَّمَ،(٦)فقر،

(٧)لَآ اِلٰهَ اِلَّا اللّٰهُ مُحَمَّدٌ رَّسُوْلُ اللّٰه صَلَّ اللّٰهُ عَلَيْهِ وَآلِهِ وَسَلَّمَ۔

Allah, Lilla, Lahu, Hu, Muhammad, Faqr La Illaha Ilia Allah Muhammad Rasul Allah (p.b.u.h.). The ninety-nine names of God the most High and the thirty letters of the alphabet are also concentrated upon. Besides these, there are various physical drawings. Their mention will result in prolixity. Their concentration brings about unaccountable esoteric benefits. If the seeker desires details of these esoteric treasures, he should order and study the book *Nurul Huda* or *Aql-i-Baidar*, composed by His Holiness, the king of the gnostics, his eminence Sultan Bahu (p.b.u.h.).

The sign of His personal name, Allah, being properly impressed through concentration is this: that on being written down, it shines like the sun, the concentrator immediately gets absorbed and obliterated in God, and the etheric personality of the heart, soul, or secret utters the commemoration of Allah or recites the holy formula, and the seeker acquires some sort of observation or revelation during a state of absorption.

O blessed seeker! We have narrated the few aforementioned, most useful, easy, safe, correct, and true methods of concentrating on His personal name, Allah, which we came to know after spilling our life blood protractedly. If you realize the worth and act on them, you will certainly very soon reach the highest heaven of esoteric travel and spiritualism, attain union with your True Beloved, and enter the assemblies of prophets and saints. You will enjoy such esoteric relishes and spiritual joys as no eye has ever seen, no ear ever heard, and no heart ever thought of.

These are the advantages of concentration. It is a highly secret, unhypocritical, safe, and quick-acting method of commemoration. Neither does it necessitate any particular time or spot nor require any restriction of ablution or cleanliness of clothes or place. There is no need for a stipulated number or enumeration of commemoration. Without it, the opening of esoteric etheric personalities is difficult and impossible. The seeker can never traverse any spiritual stage or station without concentration. If you contemplate the principles of the esoteric stages and degrees of Islam اسلام, faith ایمان, certainty ایقان, gnosis عرفان, proximity قرب, observation of God مشاہدہ, union, annihilation, and immortality in God, it transpires that their object and motive is to fix human attention, concentration, meditation, and possession on one point.

This is called concentration in religion. For example, behold that unitarianism is the real thing in Islam, whereupon all Islamic actions and performances depend. That is to say that diverting his attention from the worship of multiple deities, one inclines to a single deity. Says the Most High, "Are numerous and different Lords and gods better or the single Omnipotent Essence of one Allah?" Hence for diverting human attention toward a single true deity, Islam has made commemoration incumbent on every action and performance, as we have already narrated in the earlier portions of this book. All the commemorations have been gathered in the commemoration of His personal name, Allah, and of all the methods of focusing human attention on a single center, that of concentration is the best of its adoption. In short, if carefully viewed, the method of concentration on His personal name, Allah, is the original, last, and comprehensive key for the acquisition of Islam, faith, gnosis, certainty, proximity, observation, union, and the degrees and stages of annihilation and eternity. In other words, one object of concentration of His personal name, Allah, is to bring the seeker from the world of plurality toward the chamber of unity only. Its second object is to take the seeker from the darkness of opacity toward the light of subtlety. As Allah the Most High says:

اَللّٰهُ وَلِيُّ الَّذِيْنَ اٰمَنُوْا يُخْرِجُهُمْ مِّنَ الظُّلُمٰتِ اِلَى النُّوْرِ (البقرة ٢: ٢٥٧)

"Allah is the friend of those who have brought faithful. He extracts them from the world of darkness and takes them towards the world of Light."

Hence the traveler needs the following two unavoidable wings for flying over the two high places of unity of presence and subtlety of light:

(1) Concentration on His personal name, Allah

(2) Invocations

As God the Most High says, "Didn't We provide man with two eyes, one tongue, and two lips and showed him two paths?" Now the path of the eyes is the path of concentration on His personal name, Allah, and the path of the tongue and two lips is the path of incessant labor and religious duty, that is, invocation whereby the traveler comes out of the darkness of the opaque world and enters the luminous invisible world, and mixing with the bright, invisible creation of the invisible world, he derives benefits from them. Hence, just as the eyes and light are correlative (i.e., light is useless if the eyes are wanting, and the world appears dark to the eyes if there be no light), similarly, the two paths and methods of concentration on His personal name, Allah, and invocation are correlative. For the gnostic, they are like wings and feathers. We have already explained the method of concentration on His personal name, Allah. We will narrate for the readers and seekers the second important path of invocation of spirits in the second part of *Irfan*.

The End

Thanks to Allah SWT that Irfan has been published in the USA for the 3rd time. This amazingly great book had been published in Urdu for the first time by Faqeer Noor Muhammad Sarwari Qadri (May Allah Has mercy on him) in late 1930s. It has been published several times ever since. Now under the patronage of Faqeer Haroon Ahmed Sarwari Qadri, (second spiritual successor of the Author), Irfan has been translated into Sindhi, Pashto (Pakistani regional languages) and Gurmokhi (Indian Punjabi).

Many other projects, like prestigious built of Bab-e- Fareedoon has been completed. Expansion of Nori Darbar's front yard for which land, equal to a soccer field, has been bought, and quite a few projects are in the pipeline.

Following are the projects which need your
generous financial and moral support soon.

Projects in the USA

- Translation of Irfan into different world languages like, Spanish, Arabic, Chinese, French, Russian, German, Turkish, Persian etc.
- Building a Sufi Islamic center and Mosque in Maryland.
- A rehabilitation center for psychological patients and drug addicts.
- An orphanage for the children from war torn countries.

Projects in Pakistan

- Phase II expansion of Noori Darbar's front yard
- All year long running kitchen (Lunger) for visitors from all over the world.
- Support for already running Quran teachings for poor and destitute kids of the area.
- Establishing a school for spiritual Islamic studies and modern education.

As directed by Faqeer Haroon Ahmed Sarwari Qadri, we have launched an entity, **Noor (The light)**, in the state of Maryland, USA. It is registered as a tax-exempt non-profit organization, under Internal Revenue Code Section 501(c)(3).

Please donate to bring into existence the above-mentioned goals and to amplify the spread of true Islamic Sufism, A religion for humanity.

Bank of America
Account # 446051808323

CITI Bank
Account # 9109681752
Routing # 254070116
Swift code: CITI US 33.

For contact in Pakistan
Faqeer Haroon Ahmed Sarwari Qadri
Second spiritual Successor Noori Darbar,
Patron in chief, NOOR (The Light)
Ph# 92-302 5797919
For contact in USA
Faqeer Muhammad Zahid Iqbal Sarwari Qadri
Authorized Khalifa Sarwari Qadri Order
Ph: 443-449-1513
334-Carronade Way Arnold MD, 21012 USA. Email: mohamadzahid@ yahoo.com

Hazart Qabila Faqeer Haroon Ahmed Sarwari Qadri

www.ingramcontent.com/pod-product-compliance
Lightning Source LLC
Chambersburg PA
CBHW022044020426
42335CB00012B/534